BLUES
LEGACIES
AND
BLACK
FEMINISM

Also by

ANGELA Y. DAVIS

ANGELA DAVIS:
AN AUTOBIOGRAPHY

IF THEY COME IN THE MORNING:
VOICES OF RESISTANCE

WOMEN, CULTURE, AND POLITICS

WOMEN, RACE, AND CLASS

BLUES
LEGACIES
AND
BLACK
FEMINISM

Gertrude "Ma" Rainey,
Bessie Smith,
and Billie Holiday

ANGELA Y. DAVIS

PANTHEON BOOKS
NEW YORK

Permissions acknowledgments are on pages 423–27.

Library of Congress Cataloging-in-Publication Data

Davis, Angela Yvonne, 1944–
Blues legacies and black feminism : Gertrude "Ma" Rainey, Bessie
Smith, and Billie Holiday / Angela Y. Davis.
p.   cm.
Includes bibliographical references and index.
ISBN 0-679-45005-X
1. Blues (Music) — History and criticism.   2. Blues (Music) — Texts.
3. Feminism and music — United States.   4. Women blues musicians —
United States.   5. Afro-American women.   6. Rainey, Ma, 1886–1939.
7. Smith, Bessie, 1898?–1937.   8. Holiday, Billie, 1915–1959.
I. Title.
ML3521.D355   1998
782.421643'082 — dc21   97-33021
                                                              CIP
                                                              MN

Random House Web Address: http://www.randomhouse.com

Book design by Deborah Kerner

Printed in the United States of America

4   6   8   9   7   5

IN LOVING MEMORY

OF KENDRA AND FRANKLIN ALEXANDER

CONTENTS

ACKNOWLEDGMENTS   *ix*

INTRODUCTION   *xi*

I USED TO BE YOUR SWEET MAMA
IDEOLOGY, SEXUALITY, AND DOMESTICITY   *3*

MAMA'S GOT THE BLUES
RIVALS, GIRLFRIENDS, AND ADVISORS   *42*

HERE COME MY TRAIN
TRAVELING THEMES AND WOMEN'S BLUES   *66*

BLAME IT ON THE BLUES
BESSIE SMITH, GERTRUDE "MA" RAINEY,
AND THE POLITICS OF BLUES PROTEST   *91*

PREACHING THE BLUES
SPIRITUALITY AND SELF-CONSCIOUSNESS   *120*

UP IN HARLEM EVERY SATURDAY NIGHT
BLUES AND THE BLACK AESTHETIC   *138*

WHEN A WOMAN LOVES A MAN
SOCIAL IMPLICATIONS OF BILLIE HOLIDAY'S
LOVE SONGS   *161*

"STRANGE FRUIT"
MUSIC AND SOCIAL CONSCIOUSNESS   *181*

Lyrics to Songs Recorded by
GERTRUDE "MA" RAINEY   *199*

Lyrics to Songs Recorded by
BESSIE SMITH   *257*

Notes   *359*

Works Consulted   *393*

Index   *407*

Permissions Acknowledgments   *423*

ACKNOWLEDGMENTS

It is both a rewarding and a daunting task to reflect at the end of a project such as this one upon the many people who have lent their time, energy, and spirits to assist in its completion. As thankful as I am to the following individuals and institutions for their invaluable contributions, it is not really possible for me to convey here the full impact each has had upon this work as a whole. I therefore trust all those I name here to know that my gratitude extends far beyond these few paragraphs of thanks, and I ask forgiveness of anyone I may have overlooked.

First, I want to thank my mother, Sallye Davis, and my nephew Ben Davis for enabling me to live and work under one roof.

At the earliest stages of this project, Kipp Harvey assisted me with the challenging and thrilling process of transcribing women's blues lyrics. At different stages, Roberta Goodman and Vicki Smith served as my research assistants. Vicki reconstructed the footnotes after a computer crash wiped them out, handling a latter-twentieth-century crisis with skill and grace.

I have benefited greatly from the insights of my close friends Terri Lynne Carrington, Faith Nolan, and Dianne Reeves on music and performance history. My exchanges with Edward Guerrero, whom I interviewed about the blues on my radio program on KPFA some years ago, helped to shape my analysis of the blues aesthetic. My long-time friend and comrade Charlene Mitchell, who has a great love for Bessie Smith, provided important inspiration and vital resources from her record collection.

Linda Tillery and Teresa Trull—both of whom addressed my class on women's music at San Francisco State University—provided a contemporary link with the blues women whose legacies are at the heart of this book. All of the students in the classes I have taught on women's music at a number of Bay Area institutions have helped to keep my perspective fresh as I delved into this blues history.

At different phases, Nikky Finney and Joy James read portions of the manuscript and provided thoughtful feedback that I hope they find justly incorporated into this final version.

My sister, Fania Davis, lent her support as always, but I am especially thankful to her for the legal expertise she devoted to the protracted and often tedious process of obtaining permissions to reprint the Rainey and Smith lyrics. Robert and Michael Meeropol helped me to secure permission to use "Strange Fruit." Patsy Moore provided eleventh-hour clarification of some of the more inaudible lyrics.

Over the years, my work on this project and others that have complemented it has been aided by my associations with the following: the Women Studies and Ethnic Studies programs at San Francisco State University; the Women of Color Resource Center in Berkeley; Cedric Robinson and the Black Studies program at the University of California, Santa Barbara, which I think of as my academic home away from home; the faculty, staff, and students of the History of Consciousness Department at the University of California, Santa Cruz, which is my academic base; and the members of the Research Cluster for the Study of Women of Color in Collaboration and Conflict.

I have been blessed with a tremendous amount of practical assistance and moral support from my editor, Peter Dimock, whose skills and humanity defy description. Peter handled this project with an intelligence and a tenderness that went beyond the call of duty, and I am grateful that his mark is upon this work.

Last, but not least, I wish to thank my friend, business manager, and intellectual comrade, Stefanie Kelly, whose thoroughgoing participation facilitated the long-term production of this book. She invested countless days and (late) nights working with me at every stage, performing tasks I would have entrusted to no one else. I thank her for the remarkable skills and boundless support she brought to this project, and I especially thank her for her patience and constancy.

INTRODUCTION

Blues Legacies and Black Feminism is an examination of the work of three women artists who played decisive roles in shaping the history of popular music culture in the United States. It is an inquiry into the ways their recorded performances divulge unacknowledged traditions of feminist consciousness in working-class black communities. The connection I attempt to make between blues legacies and black feminism is not without its contradictions and discontinuities; to attempt to impute a feminist consciousness as we define it today to Gertrude "Ma" Rainey, Bessie Smith, and Billie Holiday would be preposterous, and not very interesting at that. What *is* most interesting—and provocative—about the bodies of work each of these women left behind is the ways in which hints of feminist attitudes emerge from their music through fissures of patriarchal discourses. While I try to situate their recorded performances, the primary material with which I work, in relation to historical developments of the 1920s, 1930s, and 1940s, I am most concerned with how these women's performances appear through the prism of the present, and with what these interpretations can tell us about past and present forms of social consciousness.

Given the long histories of slavery and segregation in the United States, it is understandable that black social consciousness has been overdetermined by race. This one-dimensionality is also often reflected in works that attempt to recapitulate those histories. While an impressive body of literature establishing historical antecedents for contemporary black feminism has been produced during the last two decades, there remains a paucity of research on the class-inflected character of historical black feminism. As the works of nineteenth- and early twentieth-century black women writers have been made increasingly available through projects such as the Schomburg Library Nineteenth-Century Black Women Writers series, efforts to reconstruct black feminist historical traditions tend to focus on texts such as these.[1] To a large extent, therefore, what are constituted as black feminist traditions tend to exclude ideas produced by and within poor and working-class communities, where women historically have not had the means or access to publish written texts. But some poor black women did have access to publishers of *oral* texts. In fact, in the 1920s, many black women were sought after—and often exploited by—burgeoning recording companies.

Black women were the first to record the blues. In 1920, Mamie Smith's version of Perry Bradford's "Crazy Blues," her second recording on Columbia's Okeh label, was so popular that 75,000 copies of the record were sold within the first month of its release. One dollar, the cost of each record, was a small fortune then for the mostly poor black people who bought "Crazy Blues." The song's runaway sales marked the successful debut of a black woman blues singer, which in turn opened the door for scores of other black women artists, who were sought after by representatives of the recording industry as entrees into a previously ignored and untapped black market. Women like Alberta Hunter, Ida Cox, Ethel Waters, Lucille Hegamin, Edith Wilson, Victoria Spivey, Rosa Henderson, Clara Smith, Trixie Smith, Sippie Wallace, and many other less-known artists could be heard during the 1920s not only in theaters and clubs but also on labels such as Paramount and Columbia—both of which launched "race records" campaigns—and Black Swan, the only black-owned recording company of the period. At the peak of the classic blues era, which loosely spanned the decade of the twenties, hundreds of women had the opportunity to record their work.

That women were given priority over men as recording artists attests to the reductive marketing strategies of the then-embryonic recording industry, strategies we still see reflected today in the industry's efforts to categorize—or, in effect, to segregate culturally—different genres of music that in fact claim an increasingly diverse listening public. The companies' attempts to construct and tap a new black market were elaborated around the assumption that because the initial successes were with women's blues, only women could be successful recording artists. Between 1923 and 1926—when Bessie Smith and Gertrude "Ma" Rainey respectively recorded their first songs—few men, aside from Papa Charlie Jackson (who also did duets with Rainey), were signed up by Paramount and Columbia, the two major companies of that period.[2] However, when male country blues caught on in 1926, their growing popularity initiated a pattern that eventually marginalized women blues singers after the classic blues era began to decline with the stock market crash of 1929. The 1930s became an era of widespread exploitation of black men blues singers, who were sought out aggressively by profit-hungry recording companies that paid them paltry sums for their recorded performances, some of which continue to be published on compact discs today. The story of Robert Johnson is only the most dramatic example of this phenomenon. At the same time, many once highly commodified black women blues singers—including Bessie Smith, the "Empress of the Blues"—were struggling to find work in other genres such as theater and the emergent motion picture industry.

Even though the period of ascendancy of black women blues singers was relatively short, these women nonetheless managed to produce a vast body of musical texts and a rich cultural legacy. One might expect that because the classic blues era coincided with the Harlem Renaissance, this musical articulation of African-American culture would have been treated extensively by the writers and intellectuals of the day. However, because women like Bessie Smith and Ida Cox presented and embodied sexualities associated with working-class black life—which, fatally, was seen by some Renaissance strategists as antithetical to the aims of their cultural movement—their music was designated as "low" culture, in contrast, for example, to endeavors such as sculpture, painting, literature, and classical music (through which the spirituals could be reformed). Consequently, few writers—with the notable exception of Langston Hughes, who often found himself at odds with his contemporaries—were willing to consider seriously the contributions blues performers made to black cultural politics. In her examination of Hughes's 1930 novel, *Not Without Laughter*, Cheryl Wall argues that Hughes was not only "the first writer to represent the figure of the blues woman in literature, [but] no comparable representation would appear in the fiction of black women for decades to come."[3] Indeed, in the early works of first-generation contemporary black women writers, fictionalized portraits of blues women were created by Toni Cade Bambara, Gayl Jones, Sherley Anne Williams, and Alice Walker. Mary

Helen Washington entitled her second collection of black women's short stories *Any Woman's Blues*, and Toni Morrison's Sula, "an artist without an art form," might well have been a blues woman had she only found her voice. Alexis De Veaux wrote a poetic biography of Billie Holiday, and Jessica Hagedorn wrote an extended poem, "Sometimes You Look Like Lady Day."

These were some of the women of color writers who helped to shape my gender consciousness, whose works piqued my curiosity about the figures that had inspired such marvelously irreverent characters and moving portraits. I wondered how these "foremothers" might differ from the black women we were beginning to claim as ancestors in the gender struggles we encountered as we mounted our radical opposition to racism. What can we learn from women like Gertrude "Ma" Rainey, Bessie Smith, and Billie Holiday that we may not be able to learn from Ida B. Wells, Anna Julia Cooper, and Mary Church Terrell? If we were beginning to appreciate the blasphemies[4] of fictionalized blues women—especially their outrageous politics of sexuality—and the knowledge that might be gleaned from their lives about the possibilities of transforming gender relations within black communities, perhaps we also could benefit from a look at the artistic contributions of the original blues women.

When I first began researching the literature on blues and jazz women I discovered that, with some significant exceptions, the vast majority comprised either biographies or technical studies within the disciplines of music and musicology. I am not suggesting that investigations of these artists' lives and music are not interesting. However, what I wanted to know more about was the way their work addressed urgent social issues and helped to shape collective modes of black consciousness. Because most studies of the blues have tended to be gendered implicitly as male, those that have engaged with the social implications of this music have overlooked or marginalized women.

When I decided to look closely at the music produced by Ma Rainey, Bessie Smith, and Billie Holiday, what I expected to find was a strong consciousness of race against a backdrop of prevailing patriarchal constructions of gender. This is certainly the impression one gets from the biographical material on the three singers. In fact, the original title of my study was *Gertrude "Ma" Rainey, Bessie Smith, and Billie Holiday: Black Women's Music and Social Consciousness*. However, the more I listened to their recorded performances—of songs composed both by the artists themselves and by others—the more I realized that their music could serve as a rich terrain for examining a historical feminist consciousness that reflected the lives of working-class black communities. That their aesthetic representations of the politics of gender and sexuality are informed by and interwoven with their representations of race and class makes their work all the more provocative.

What gives the blues such fascinating possibilities of sustaining emergent feminist consciousness is the way they often construct seemingly antagonistic relationships as noncontradictory oppositions. A female narrator in a women's blues song who represents herself as entirely subservient to male desire might simultaneously express autonomous desire and a refusal to allow her mistreating lover to drive her to psychic despair. Ma Rainey and Bessie Smith both recorded versions of Herbert and Russell's "Oh Papa Blues."[5] These are the lyrics Rainey sings:

Just like a rainbow I am faded away
My daddy leaves me 'most every day
But he don't mean me no good, why?
Because I only wish he would
I've almost gone insane
I'm forever tryin' to call his name

. . . .
Oh, papa, think when you away from home
You just don't want me now, wait and see
You'll find some other man makin' love to me, now
Papa, papa, you ain't got no mama now.[6]

Bessie Smith's recording is entitled "Oh Daddy Blues" and these are her first and last stanzas:

Just like a flower I'm fading away
The doctor calls to see me most every day
But he don't do me no good
Why? Because I'm lonesome for you
And if you care for me, then you will listen to my plea
. . . .
Oh, daddy, think when you all alone
You know that you are getting old
You'll miss the way I baked your jelly roll
Then, daddy, daddy, you won't have no mama at all.[7]

I should point out here that these transcriptions are my own. A large part of the project of producing this study has been the transcription of the entire bodies of Rainey's and Smith's available recordings, 252 songs in all, some of which are very difficult to hear. When I began this aspect of my research, compact discs had not yet begun to be mass-marketed, and I was working strictly from vinyl reproductions. When their work was reissued on CD,[8] the transcription work became considerably easier, yet many of the original recordings that are reproduced on CD have deteriorated so much as to render them nearly inaudible in places. The second section of this study, following my critical examination of Rainey's, Smith's, and Holiday's work, contains my transcriptions of all of Rainey's and Smith's extant recordings. The transcriptions are included here because both blues women frequently improvised even as they sang precomposed lyrics that were not always their own. This process of revision obviously had a significant impact on the recordings to which we have access today, and it is on the basis of these recordings—these often revised renditions of the lyrics that appeared on the lead sheets from which Rainey and Smith worked— that I have worked out my own analyses of the songs as they were performed. Thus, while other transcriptions exist in numerous studies of the music and of the artists themselves, my own listenings have revealed numerous inaccuracies in those transcriptions. For this reason, I have chosen to work with firsthand transcriptions, which no doubt contain their own inaccuracies, and for which I take complete responsibility. As the complete lyrics of Rainey's and Smith's songs are not available elsewhere, I have included them in this book in order to facilitate further research on this material. I have not included transcriptions of Billie Holiday's recordings because the popular material that constitutes her body of work remains readily available in print today. Moreover, her originality consists not so much in what she sang, but rather in how she sang the popular songs of her era.

In the contemporary period, which is marked by a popular recognition of the politicalization of sexuality, the blues constitute an exceptionally rich site for feminist investigation. The overarching sexual themes that define the content of the blues form point the way toward a consideration of the historical politics of black sexuality. Considering the stringent taboos on representations of sexuality that characterized most dominant discourses of the time, the blues constitute a privileged discursive site.

In this book, I attempt to explore the feminist implications of the recorded performances of three women: one who stands at the beginning of the classic blues tradition, another who pushes the blues form to its very limits and begins to use popular song as a blues vehicle, and yet another who, in moving away from the blues and establishing jazz vocals with a genius and originality that has yet to be surpassed, remains solidly anchored in the blues tradition. All of their performances illuminate the politics of gender and sexuality in working-class black communities.

Whether we listen to these musicians today primarily for pleasure or for purposes of research—which is not to suggest that pleasure is without its critical dimensions or that research is without its pleasures—there is a great deal to be learned from their bodies of work about quotidian expressions of feminist consciousness. These quotidian expressions of feminist consciousness are what I attempt to accentuate in this book. In this sense, my study is far less ambitious than a work like Daphne Duval Harrison's *Black Pearls*. Whereas Harrison's fine investigation comprehensively takes up the classic blues tradition, mine is confined to three artists, two of whom—Ma Rainey and Bessie Smith—decisively defined the classic blues era, and one of whom—Billie Holiday—ushered in the period of modern jazz, recording her first song shortly after Bessie Smith recorded her last. Harrison's work examines the blues women of the 1920s

> as pivotal figures in the assertion of black women's ideas and ideals from the standpoint of the working class and the poor. It reveals their dynamic role as spokespersons and interpreters of the dreams, harsh realities, and tragicomedies of the black experience in the first three decades of this century; their role in the continuation and development of black music in America; their contributions to blues poetry and performance. Further, it expands the base of knowledge about the role of black women in the creation and development of American popular culture; illustrates their modes and means for coping successfully with gender-related discrimination and exploitation; and demonstrates an emerging model for the working woman—one who is sexually independent, self-sufficient, creative, and trend-setting.[9]

I hope my study will complement Harrison's in the sense that it attempts to accentuate the feminist contributions of two pivotal women of the classic blues era, as well as those of the most significant jazz woman, the story of whose troubled life has persistently overshadowed the important contributions she made as an artist.

Contemporary blues and jazz women come from diverse ethnic and racial backgrounds, and certainly the audience for this music resides not only within but far beyond the borders of black culture. With the globalization of music distribution—indeed, with such developments as unauthorized CD production in some countries—the scope of black music and its historically broad cultural implications can no longer be confined to African-American communities. In this context, feminist interpretations of blues and jazz women's legacies can contribute to an understanding of feminist consciousness that crosses racial and class borders.[10] I hope that readers of this book will also read, for example, María Herrera-Sobek's feminist interpretations of *corridos*, Mexican folk ballads.[11] Moreover, beyond the realm of musical culture, many feminists of color are rethinking mainstream feminist historiographies, not simply to carve out a place for women of color, but rather to contest the very validity of the discourses employed in those works.[12] At the same time that I see my own work as connected with these various projects, I hope the arguments I propose in this book will make a specific intervention into current popular debates regarding the legitimacy of women of color feminisms, and of black feminisms in particular.

Twenty-five years after the second-wave debates on what counts as feminism, popular assumptions that the historical origins of feminism are white stubbornly persist in many black communities, despite significant feminist (and womanist) activism and research. The tendency to construct women like Anita Hill as race traitors is a dramatic by-product of the recalcitrant idea that black women who speak out against black men are following in the footsteps of white feminists. The fact that a productive debate about the problematic gender politics (and indeed the overarching conservatism) of the Million Man March failed to emerge—and that feminists like Kimberlé Crenshaw, Luke Harris, Marcia Gillespie, Paula Giddings, Jewel Jackson McCabe, Gina Dent, and I were harshly criticized for even desiring to initiate such a debate—are yet further examples of widespread views in black communities that race must always take precedence, and that race is implicitly gendered as male.

A book like *Blues Legacies and Black Feminism* will not popularize feminism in black communities. However, I do hope it will demonstrate that there are multiple African-American feminist traditions. I hope it will demonstrate that feminist traditions are not only written, they are oral, and that these oralities reveal not only rewrought African cultural traces, but also the genius with which former slaves forged new traditions that simultaneously contested the slave past and preserved some of the rich cultural products of slavery. According to cultural critic Stuart Hall, black popular culture

[i]n its expressivity, its musicality, its orality, in its rich, deep, and varied attention to speech, in its inflections toward the vernacular and the local, in its rich production of counternarratives, and above all, in its metaphorical use of the musical vocabulary . . . has

enabled the surfacing, inside the mixed and contradictory modes even of some mainstream popular culture, of elements of a discourse that is different—other forms of life, other traditions of representation.[13]

I hope, therefore, that the analyses I present here will persuade readers that it is possible to interpret the work of these three prominent performing artists of the African-American past as helping to forge other legacies—blues legacies, black working-class legacies—of feminism. Finally, I hope this study will inspire readers to listen to the recordings of Ma Rainey, Bessie Smith, and Billie Holiday both for pleasure *and* for purposes of research, and that it will occasion further interdisciplinary studies of the artistic and social contributions of blues and jazz women.

BLUES

LEGACIES

AND

BLACK

FEMINISM

I USED TO BE
YOUR SWEET MAMA

IDEOLOGY, SEXUALITY, AND DOMESTICITY

You've had your chance and proved unfaithful
So now I'm gonna be real mean and hateful
I used to be your sweet mama, sweet papa
But now I'm just as sour as can be.

— "I USED TO BE YOUR SWEET MAMA"[1]

Like most forms of popular music, African-American blues lyrics talk about love. What is distinctive about the blues, however, particularly in relation to other American popular musical forms of the 1920s and 1930s, is their intellectual independence and representational freedom. One of the most obvious ways in which blues lyrics deviated from that era's established popular musical culture was their provocative and pervasive sexual—including homosexual—imagery.[2]

By contrast, the popular song formulas of the period demanded saccharine and idealized nonsexual depictions of heterosexual love relationships.[3] Those aspects of lived love relationships that were not compatible with the dominant, etherealized ideology of love—such as extramarital relationships, domestic violence, and the ephemerality of many sexual partnerships—were largely banished from the established popular musical culture. Yet these very themes pervade the blues. What is even more striking is the fact that initially the professional performers of this music—the most widely heard individual purveyors of the blues—were women. Bessie Smith earned the title "Empress of the Blues" not least through the sale of three-quarters of a million copies of her first record.[4]

The historical context within which the blues developed a tradition of openly addressing both female and male sexuality reveals an ideological framework that was specifically African-American.[5] Emerging during the decades following the abolition of slavery, the blues gave musical expression to the new social and sexual realities encountered by African Americans as free women and men. The former slaves' economic status had not undergone a radical transformation—they were no less impoverished than they had been during slavery.[6] It was the status of their personal relationships that was revolutionized. For the first time in the history of the African presence in North America, masses of black women and men were in a position to make autonomous decisions regarding the sexual partnerships into which they entered.[7] Sexuality thus was one of the most tangible domains in which emancipation was acted upon and through which its meanings were expressed. Sovereignty in sexual matters marked an important divide between life during slavery and life after emancipation.

Themes of individual sexual love rarely appear in the musical forms produced during slavery. Whatever the reasons for this—and it may have been due to the slave system's economic management of procreation, which did not tolerate and often severely punished the public exhibition of self-initiated sexual relationships—I am interested here in the disparity between the individualistic, "private" nature of sexuality and the collective forms and nature of the music that was produced and performed during slavery. Sexuality after emancipation could not be adequately expressed or addressed through the musical forms existing under slavery. The spirituals and the work songs confirm that the individual concerns of black people expressed through music during slavery centered on a collective desire for an end to the system that enslaved them. This does not mean there was an absence of sexual meanings in the music produced by African-American slaves.[8] It means that slave music—both religious and secular—was quintessentially collective music. It was collectively performed and it gave expression to the community's yearning for freedom.[9]

The blues, on the other hand, the predominant postslavery African-American musical form, articulated a new valuation of individual emotional needs and desires. The birth of the blues was aesthetic evidence of new psychosocial realities within the black population. This music was presented by individuals singing alone, accompanying themselves on such instruments as the banjo or guitar. The blues therefore marked the advent of a popular culture of performance, with the borders of performer and audience becoming increasingly differentiated.[10] Through the emergence of the professional blues singer—a predominantly female figure accompanied by small and large instrumental ensembles—as part of the rise of the black entertainment industry, this individualized mode of presenting popular music crystallized into a performance culture that has had an enduring influence on African-American music.

The spirituals, as they survived and were transformed during the postslavery era, were both intensely religious and the aesthetic bearers of the slaves' collective aspirations for worldly freedom.[11] Under changed historical circumstances in which former slaves had closer contact with the religious practices and ideologies of the dominant culture, sacred music began to be increasingly enclosed within institutionalized religious spaces. Slave religious practices were inseparable from other aspects of everyday life—work, family, sabotage, escape. Postslavery religion gradually lost some of this fluidity and came to be dependent on the church. As sacred music evolved from spirituals to gospel, it increasingly concentrated on the hereafter. Historian Lawrence Levine characterizes the nature of this development succinctly. "The overriding thrust of the gospel songs," he writes,

> was otherworldly. Emphasis was almost wholly upon God with whom Man's relationship was one of total dependence. . . . Jesus rather than the Hebrew children dominated the gospel songs. And it was not the warrior Jesus of the spirituals but a benevolent spirit who promised His children rest and peace and justice in the hereafter.[12]

The blues rose to become the most prominent secular genre in early twentieth-century black American music. As it came to displace sacred music in the everyday lives of black people, it both reflected and helped to construct a new black consciousness. This consciousness interpreted God as the opposite of the Devil, religion as the not-secular, and the secular as largely sexual. With the blues came the designations "God's music" and "the Devil's music." The former was performed in church—although it could also accompany work[13]—while the latter was performed in jook joints, circuses, and traveling shows.[14] Despite the new salience of this binary opposition in the everyday lives of black people, it is important to underscore the close relationship between the old music and the new. The new music had old roots, and the old music reflected a new ideological grounding of black religion. Both were deeply rooted in a shared history and culture.

God and the Devil had cohabited the same universe during slavery, not as polar opposites but rather as complex characters who had different powers and who both entered into relationships with human beings. They also sometimes engaged with each other on fairly equal terms. As Henry Louis Gates, Jr., and others have argued, the Devil was often associated with the trickster orisha Legba, or Elegua, in Yoruba religions.[15] Some of the folktales Zora Neale Hurston presents in *Mules and Men* portray the Devil not as evil incarnate but as a character with whom it was possible to identify in humorous situations.[16]

In describing the religious household in which she was reared, veteran blues woman Ida Goodson emphasizes that the blues were banned from her childhood home. Nevertheless, she and her playmates often played and sang the blues when her parents were away. On those occasions when her parents showed up unexpectedly, they easily made the transition to gospel music without missing a beat:

> My mother and father were religious persons. And they liked music, but they liked church music. They didn't like jazz like we do. And of course we could not even play jazz in our home while they were there. But just the moment they would turn their back, go to their society or church somewhere or another, we'd get our neighborhood children to come in there and we'd get to playing the blues and having a good time. But still we'd have one girl on the door

watching to see when Mr. Goodson's coming back home or Mrs. Goodson. Because I knew if they came and caught us what we would get. . . . Whenever we'd see my father or my mother coming back home, the girl be saying, "There come Mr. Goodson 'nem." And they'd be so close up on us, we'd change the blues, singing "Jesus keep me near the cross." After that my mother and father would join us and we'd all get to singing church songs.[17]

As if reconciling the two positions—that of herself as a young musician and that of her religious parents—Goodson later explains that "the Devil got his work and God got his work."

During slavery, the sacred universe was virtually all-embracing. Spirituals helped to construct community among the slaves and infused this imagined community with hope for a better life. They retold Old Testament narratives about the Hebrew people's struggle against Pharaoh's oppression, and thereby established a community narrative of African people enslaved in North America that simultaneously transcended the slave system and encouraged its abolition. Under the conditions of U.S. slavery, the sacred—and especially sacred music—was an important means of preserving African cultural memory. Karl Marx's comments on religion as the "opium of the people"[18] notwithstanding, the spirituals attest to the fact that religious consciousness can itself play a transformative role. As Sojourner Truth and other abolitionists demonstrated—as well as insurrectionary leaders Nat Turner, Denmark Vesey, and the Underground Railroad conductor Harriet Tubman—religion was far more than Marx's "illusory sun." Spirituals were embedded in and gave expression to a powerful yearning for freedom.[19] Religion was indeed, in Marx's words, the "soul" of "soulless conditions."[20]

The spirituals articulated the hopes of black slaves in religious terms. In the vast disappointment that followed emancipation—when economic and political liberation must have seemed more unattainable than ever—blues created a discourse[21] that represented freedom in more immediate and accessible terms. While the material conditions for the freedom about which the slaves had sung in their spirituals seemed no closer after slavery than they had seemed before, there were nevertheless distinct differences between the slaves' personal status under slavery and during the post–Civil War period. In three major respects, emancipation radically transformed their personal lives: (1) there was no longer a proscription on free individual travel; (2) education was now a realizable goal for individual men and women; (3) sexuality could be explored freely by individuals who now could enter into autonomously chosen personal relationships. The new blues consciousness was shaped by and gave expression to at least two of these three transformations: travel and sexuality. In both male and female blues, travel and sexuality are ubiquitous themes, handled both separately and together. But what finally is most striking is the way the blues registered sexuality as a tangible expression of freedom; it was this dimension that most profoundly marked and defined the secularity of the blues.

Theologian James Cone offers the following definition of the blues, agreeing with C. Eric Lincoln's succinct characterization of them as "secular spirituals." Cone writes:

> They are secular in the same sense that they confine their attention solely to the immediate and affirm the bodily expression of black soul, including its sexual manifestations. They are spirituals because they are impelled by the same search for the truth of black experience.[22]

It is not necessary to accede to Cone's essentialist invocation of a single metaphysical "truth" of black experience to gain from his description a key insight into why the blues were condemned as the Devil's music: it was because they drew upon and incorporated sacred consciousness and thereby posed a serious threat to religious attitudes.

Levine emphasizes the blurring of the sacred and the secular in both gospel music and the blues. It may not have been the secularity of the blues that produced such castigation by the church, he argues, but rather precisely their sacred nature. He writes:

> The blues was threatening not primarily because it was secular; other forms of secular music were objected to less strenuously and often not at all. Blues was threatening because its spokesmen and its

ritual too frequently provided the expressive communal channels of relief that had been largely the province of religion in the past.[23]

Although both Cone and Levine make references to Mamie Smith, Ma Rainey, Bessie Smith, and other women who composed and performed blues songs, they, like most scholars, tend to view women as marginal to the production of the blues. Note that in the passage quoted above, Levine refers quite explicitly to the "spokesmen" of the blues. With the simple substitution of "spokeswomen," his argument would become more compelling and more revealing of the new religious consciousness about which he writes.

Blues practices, as Levine asserts, did tend to appropriate previously religious channels of expression, and this appropriation was associated with women's voices. Women summoned sacred responses to their messages about sexuality.[24] During this period, religious consciousness came increasingly under the control of institutionalized churches, and male dominance over the religious process came to be taken for granted. At the same time that male ministers were becoming a professional caste, women blues singers were performing as professional artists and attracting large audiences at revival-like gatherings. Gertrude "Ma" Rainey and Bessie Smith were the most widely known of these women. They preached about sexual love, and in so doing they articulated a collective experience of freedom, giving voice to the most powerful evidence there was for many black people that slavery no longer existed.

The expression of socially unfulfilled dreams in the language and imagery of individual sexual love is, of course, not peculiar to the African-American experience. As part of the capitalist schism between the public and private realms within European-derived American popular culture, however, themes of romantic love had quite different ideological implications from themes of sexuality within postslavery African-American cultural expression. In the context of the consolidation of industrial capitalism, the sphere of personal love and domestic life in mainstream American culture came to be increasingly idealized as the arena in which happiness was to be sought.[25] This held a special significance for women, since love and domesticity were supposed to constitute the outermost limits of their lives. Full membership in the public community was the exclusive domain of men. Therefore, European-American popular songs have to be interpreted within this context and as contributing to patriarchal hegemony.

The blues did not entirely escape the influences that shaped the role of romantic love in the popular songs of the dominant culture. Nevertheless, the incorporation of personal relationships into the blues has its own historical meanings and social and political resonances. Love was not represented as an idealized realm to which unfulfilled dreams of happiness were relegated. The historical African-American vision of individual sexual love linked it inextricably with possibilities of social freedom in the economic and political realms. Unfreedom during slavery involved, among other things, a prohibition of freely chosen, enduring family relationships. Because slaves were legally defined as commodities, women of childbearing age were valued in accordance with their breeding potential and were often forced to copulate with men—viewed as "bucks"—chosen by their owners for the sole purpose of producing valuable progeny.[26] Moreover, direct sexual exploitation of African women by their white masters was a constant feature of slavery.[27] What tenuous permanence in familial relationships the slaves did manage to construct was always subject to the whim of their masters and the potential profits to be reaped from sale. The suffering caused by forced ruptures of slave families has been abundantly documented.[28]

Given this context, it is understandable that the personal and sexual dimensions of freedom acquired an expansive importance, especially since the economic and political components of freedom were largely denied to black people in the aftermath of slavery. The focus on sexual love in blues music was thus quite different in meaning from the prevailing idealization of romantic love in mainstream popular music. For recently emancipated slaves, freely chosen sexual love became a mediator between historical disappointment and the new social realities of an evolving African-American community. Ralph Ellison alludes to this dimension of the blues, I think, when he notes "their mysteriousness . . . their ability to imply far more than they state outright and their capacity to make the details of sex convey meanings which touch on the metaphysical."[29]

Sexuality was central in both men's and women's blues. During the earliest phases of their history, blues were essentially a male phenomenon. The archetypal blues singer was a solitary wandering man accompanied by his banjo or guitar, and, in the words of blues scholar Giles Oakley, his principal theme "is the sexual relationship. Almost all other themes, leaving town, train rides, work trouble, general dissatisfaction, sooner or later revert to the central concern."[30] In women's blues, which became a crucial element of the rising black entertainment industry, there was an even more pronounced emphasis on love and sexuality.

The representations of love and sexuality in women's blues often blatantly contradicted mainstream ideological assumptions regarding women and being in love. They also challenged the notion that women's "place" was in the domestic sphere. Such notions were based on the social realities of middle-class white women's lives, but were incongruously applied to all women, regardless of race or class.[31] This led to inevitable contradictions between prevailing social expectations and black women's social realities. Women of that era were expected to seek fulfillment within the confines of marriage, with their husbands functioning as providers and their children as evidence of their worth as human beings. The sparsity of allusions to marriage and domesticity in women's blues therefore becomes highly significant.

In Bessie Smith's rendition of "Sam Jones Blues," which contains one of the few commentaries on marriage to be found in her body of work, the subject is acknowledged only in relation to its dissolution. Her performance of this song satirically accentuates the contrast between the dominant cultural construction of marriage and the stance of economic independence black women were compelled to assume for their sheer survival:

Sam Jones left his lovely wife just to step around
Came back home 'bout a year, lookin' for his high brown

Went to his accustomed door and he knocked his knuckles sore
His wife she came, but to his shame, she knew his face no more

Sam said, "I'm your husband, dear."
But she said, "Dear, that's strange to hear
You ain't talking to Mrs. Jones, you speakin' to Miss Wilson now

"I used to be your lofty mate
But the judge done changed my fate

"Was a time you could have walked right in and called this place your
    home sweet home
But now it's all mine for all time, I'm free and livin' all alone

. . . .

"Say, hand me the key that unlocks my front door
Because that bell don't read 'Sam Jones' no more, no
You ain't talkin' to Mrs. Jones, you speakin' to Miss Wilson now."[32]

Although the written lyrics reveal a conversation between "proper"
English and black working-class English, only by listening to the song do
we experience the full impact of Smith's manipulation of language in her
recording. References to marriage as perceived by the dominant white culture are couched in irony. She mocks the notion of eternal matrimony—"I
used to be your lofty mate"—singing genteel words with a teasing intona-
tion to evoke white cultural conceptions. On the other hand, when she
indicates the perspective of the black woman, Miss Wilson—who "used
to be Mrs. Jones"—she sings in a comfortable, bluesy black English. This
song is remarkable for the way Smith translates into musical contrast and
contention the clash between two cultures' perceptions of marriage, and
particularly women's place within the institution. It is easy to imagine the
testifying responses Smith no doubt evoked in her female audiences,
responses that affirmed working-class black women's sense of themselves as
relatively emancipated, if not from marriage itself, then at least from some
of its most confining ideological constraints.

The protagonists in women's blues are seldom wives and almost never
mothers. One explanation for the absence of direct allusions to marriage

may be the different words mainstream and African-American cultures use to signify "male spouse." African-American working-class argot refers to both husbands and male lovers—and even in some cases female lovers—as "my man" or "my daddy." But these different linguistic practices cannot be considered in isolation from the social realities they represent, for they point to divergent perspectives regarding the institution of marriage.

During Bessie Smith's era, most black heterosexual couples—married or not—had children. However, blues women rarely sang about mothers, fathers, and children. In the subject index to her book *Black Pearls*, black studies scholar Daphne Duval Harrison lists the following themes: advice to other women; alcohol; betrayal or abandonment; broken or failed love affairs; death; departure; dilemma of staying with man or returning to family; disease and afflictions; erotica; hell; homosexuality; infidelity; injustice; jail and serving time; loss of lover; love; men; mistreatment; murder; other woman; poverty; promiscuity; sadness; sex; suicide; supernatural; trains; traveling; unfaithfulness; vengeance; weariness, depression, and disillusionment; weight loss.[33] It is revealing that she does not include children, domestic life, husband, and marriage.

The absence of the mother figure in the blues does not imply a rejection of motherhood as such, but rather suggests that blues women found the mainstream cult of motherhood irrelevant to the realities of their lives.[34] The female figures evoked in women's blues are independent women free of the domestic orthodoxy of the prevailing representations of womanhood through which female subjects of the era were constructed.

In 252 songs recorded by Bessie Smith and Ma Rainey, there are only four—all by Bessie Smith—that refer to marriage within a relatively neutral context or in a way that takes the marital relationship for granted. In "Poor Man's Blues," mention is made of the gross disparities between the economic conditions of the working man's wife and the rich man's wife: "Poor working man's wife is starvin', your wife's livin' like a queen."[35] In "Pinchback Blues," advice is offered to women with respect to the foremost quality they should seek in a husband—namely, that he be a working man. Bessie Smith sings the following phrases in a way that demands she be taken seriously:

. . . girls, take this tip from me
Get a workin' man when you marry, and let all these sweet men be
. . . .
There's one thing about this married life that these young girls have got to
know
If a sweet man enter your front gate, turn out your lights and lock your
door.[36]

Even though this song assumes that most women listeners will get married,
it does not evoke the romantic expectations usually associated with marriage. Instead, it warns women not to enter into marriages in which they
will end up supporting an exploitative man—a "sweet man" or a "pinchback."

"Take Me for a Buggy Ride," a popular song filled with sexual innu-
endo and recorded in 1933 during the very last session of Bessie Smith's
career, contains a passing uncritical reference to marriage:

Daddy, you as sweet as you can be when you take me for a buggy ride
When you set me down upon your knee and ask me to be your bride.[37]

Even these explicit references to marriage may be attributed to the fact
that Smith was seeking ways to cross over into mainstream musical culture.
She herself decided to record no blues during what would be her final
recording session. She wanted to sing only popular songs, all of which were
composed by the husband-and-wife team of Leola B. Wilson and Wesley
"Socks" Wilson.[38] Her producer, John Hammond, may also have had
something to do with this decision to exclude blues songs. After a hiatus in
her recording career—occasioned both by the anticipated obsolescence of
the blues and the 1929 stock market crash that left the recording industry
in shambles—there were obvious economic reasons for wanting to appeal
to as broad an audience as possible.

The sexual allusions in these songs, along with songs recorded earlier
in the thirties, have caused them to be labeled quasi-pornographic. While
sexual metaphors abound in these songs, the female characters are clearly
in control of their sexuality in ways that exploit neither their partners nor

themselves. It is misleading, I think, to refer to songs such as "Need a Little Sugar in My Bowl" as pornographic. Nevertheless, Hammond is probably correct in his contention that, given their superficial approach to sexuality, "they do not compare with Bessie's own material of the twenties."[39] The reference to marriage in "Take Me for a Buggy Ride" may very well be a result of Bessie Smith's attempt to cross over into a cultural space that required her to position herself in greater ideological proximity to white audiences, while maintaining her connection with black fans. Having put together a swing accompaniment for this last session consisting of black and white musicians—Buck Washington, Jack Teagarden, Chu Berry, Frankie Newton, Billy Taylor, and Bobby Johnson, with Benny Goodman playing on one number—John Hammond certainly was expecting to see these records distributed outside the "race records" market.

Gertrude "Ma" Rainey, a pioneer on the black entertainment circuit and the person responsible for shaping women's blues for many generations of blues women, received her title "Mother of the Blues" before she made her first recording. In the songs she recorded, the institution of monogamous marriage often was cavalierly repudiated with the kind of attitude that is usually gendered as male. "Blame It on the Blues," for example, implicitly rejects the sexual exclusivity of marriage. Reflecting on the source of her distress, the protagonist finds that she can blame it neither on her "husband," her "man," nor her "lover." The lyrics of this song—and the tragicomic way Rainey sings them—refuse to privilege marriage over non- or extramarital sexual partnerships:

Can't blame my mother, can't blame my dad
Can't blame my brother for the trouble I've had
Can't blame my lover that held my hand
Can't blame my husband, can't blame my man.[40]

In "Shave 'Em Dry," a song rich in provocative sexual metaphors, Rainey sings about a woman involved with a married man.[41] "When your wife comes," she sings with unflappable seriousness, "tell her I don't mean no harm." And in the spoken introduction to "Gone Daddy Blues," the woman who has left her husband for another man seems to play with the notion of convincing him to take her back:

Unknown man: Who's that knocking on that door?
Rainey: It's me, baby.
Man: Me who?
Rainey: Don't you know I'm your wife?
Man: What?! Wife?!
Rainey: Yeah!
Man: Ain't that awful? I don't let no woman quit me but one time.
Rainey: But I just quit one li'l old time, just one time!
Man: You left here with that other man, why didn't you stay?[42]

"Misery Blues" is the only one of Rainey's songs in which the woman appears truly oppressed by the expectations associated with the institution of marriage. She is singing the "misery blues" because she has allowed herself to be deceived by a man who promised to marry her, that is, to support her in the traditional patriarchal way. She expected marriage to free her from her daily toil. The husband-to-be in this song not only reneges on his promise of marriage, but absconds with all her money:

I love my brownskin, indeed I do
Folks I know used to me being a fool
I'm going to tell you what I went and done
I give him all my money just to have some fun

He told me that he loved me, loved me so
If I would marry him, I needn't to work no mo'
Now I'm grievin', almost dyin'
Just because I didn't know that he was lyin'.[43]

While Rainey's performance mournfully emphasizes the woman's grief, "Misery Blues" can be construed as an "advice" song that cautions women who might similarly be deceived by the romantic expectations associated with the bourgeois, patriarchal institution of marriage.

Bessie Smith's work poses more explicit challenges to the male dominance that ideologically inheres in this institution. In "Money Blues," for example, the wife makes life unbearable for her husband with her incessant demands for money and high living.[44] The husband, Samuel Brown, has "beer money," but his wife demands champagne. (As is often the case, the "blues" in the title notwithstanding, this is a popular song, not a twelve-bar blues.) In "Young Woman's Blues," one of Smith's own compositions, the protagonist is simply not interested in marriage. Smith's performance of the following verse exudes a self-confident sense of female independence and unabashed embrace of sexual pleasure:

No time to marry, no time to settle down
I'm a young woman and ain't done runnin' 'round.

The same sentiment is definitively restated in the closing lines of the song:

I ain't no high yella, I'm a deep killer brown
I ain't gonna marry, ain't gon' settle down
I'm gon' drink good moonshine and run these browns down
See that long lonesome road, Lord, you know it's gotta end
And I'm a good woman and I can get plenty men.[45]

In what is undoubtedly the most disturbing reference to marriage in Bessie Smith's work, the narrator of "Hateful Blues" threatens to use the butcher knife she received as a wedding present to carve up her fickle husband.[46]

Early women's blues contain few uninflected references to marriage. Evocations of traditional female domesticity, whether associated with marriage or not, are equally rare. When women are portrayed as having fulfilled the domestic requirements socially expected of women in relationships with men, it is often to make the point that the women have been abused or abandoned. In Bessie Smith's "Weeping Willow Blues," the narrator proclaims:

Folks, I love my man, I kiss him mornin', noon, and night
I wash his clothes and keep him clean and try to treat him right
Now he's gone and left me after all I've tried to do.[47]

Smith sings these lines with convincing sincerity, thus debunking the notion that the fulfillment of conventional female domestic responsibilities is the basis for happiness in marriage. On the other hand, "Yes, Indeed He Do" is full of irony in its references to domesticity, implicitly criticizing the stultifying household work women are compelled to do for their men:

I don't have to do no work except to wash his clothes
And darn his socks and press his pants and scrub the kitchen floor.[48]

The sardonic "Safety Mama," another Smith composition, humorously critiques the sexual division of labor that confines women to the household. The song contains an inverted image of domesticity, in which the man is compelled by the woman to take on what are assumed to be female household chores as punishment for his sexist behavior in the relationship:

So wait awhile, I'll show you, child, just how to treat a no-good man
Make him stay at home, wash and iron
Tell all the neighbors he done lost his mind.[49]

The manner in which Bessie Smith creates this musical caricature of domesticity reveals the beginnings of an oppositional attitude toward patriarchal ideology.

There are important historical reasons that romanticized images of marriage—and the permanency in personal relationships implied by this social institution—are absent from women's blues. Normative representations of marriage as the defining goal of women's lives blatantly contradicted black social realities during the half-century following emancipation. A poor black woman of the era who found herself deserted or rejected by a male lover was not merely experiencing private troubles; she also was caught in a complex web of historical circumstances. However smoothly a personal relationship may have been progressing, a recently emancipated black man was compelled to find work, and even if he found a job near the neighborhood where he and his partner had settled, he nevertheless might be seduced by new possibilities of travel. In search of work—and also in search of the perpetually elusive guarantees of security and happiness—men jumped freight trains and wandered from town to town, from state to state, from region to region. There were imperative economic reasons for undertaking journeys away from home, yet even when jobs were not to be found and available employment was backbreaking and poorly compensated, the very process of traveling must have generated a feeling of exhilaration and freedom in individuals whose ancestors had been chained for centuries to geographical sites dictated by slave masters.[50] This impulse to travel would infect great numbers of black men as a sociohistorically initiated compulsion, and would later be rendered in song in Robert Johnson's "Hellhound on My Trail":

I got to keep moving, I got to keep moving
Blues falling down like hail, blues falling down like hail
I can't keep no money, hellhound on my trail
Hellhound on my trail, hellhound on my trail.[51]

Many of the absconding and unfaithful lovers memorialized by blues women were in pursuit of that fleeting glimpse of freedom offered by the new historical possibility of self-initiated travel. Most women, on the other hand, were denied the option of taking to the road. In his "C. & A. Blues," Peetie Wheatstraw offered one of the many blues versions of this disparity between the male and female conditions. He portrayed the man assuaging his pain through travel and the woman assuaging hers with tears:

When a woman gets the blues, she hangs her head and cries
When a man gets the blues, he flags a freight train and rides.[52]

A few songs recorded by Bessie Smith—"Chicago Bound Blues" is one[53]—support the masculinist view of men's and women's divergent responses to new forms of emotional pain in the postslavery era. In general, however, blues women did not acquiesce to the idea—which appears in various forms in male country blues—that men take to the road and women resort to tears. The women who sang the blues did not typically affirm female resignation and powerlessness, nor did they accept the relegation of women to private and interior spaces.

Although women generally were not socially entitled to travel on as wide a scale as men, significantly, blues women overcame this restriction.[54] Likewise, in their music, they found ways to express themselves that were at variance with the prevailing standards of femininity. Even as they may have shed tears, they found the courage to lift their heads and fight back, asserting their right to be respected not as appendages or victims of men but as truly independent human beings with vividly articulated sexual desires. Blues women provided emphatic examples of black female independence.

A significant number of songs in Gertrude "Ma" Rainey's recorded legacy suggest ways in which the structures of gender politics in black communities deviated from those of the dominant culture. In the call-and-response tradition, many of her love- and sex-oriented songs mirror or furnish responses to songs associated with the male country blues tradition. Male blues deal with a wider range of experiences, many accumulated on the job or on the road. But those that revolve around sexuality or include observations on love relationships are not radically different from their female counterparts in the behavior they describe and the images they evoke. Contrary to prevailing assumptions, as Sandra Lieb, author of *Mother of the Blues: A Study of Ma Rainey*, has observed, relatively few of Rainey's songs evoke women so incapacitated by their lover's infidelity, desertion, or mistreatment that they are bereft of agency or driven to the brink of self-destruction. "Only thirteen of her [ninety-two recorded] songs describe a woman in abject sorrow, lying in bed and weeping for her absent man."[55] Far more typical are songs in which women explicitly celebrate their right to conduct themselves as expansively and even as undesirably as men. The protagonists in Ma Rainey's blues often abandon their men and routinely and cavalierly threaten them, even to the point of violence.

While the overwhelming majority of Bessie Smith's 160[56] available recorded songs allude to rejection, abuse, desertion, and unfaithful lovers, the preponderant emotional stance of the singer-protagonist—also true of Ma Rainey—is far from resignation and despair. On the contrary, the most frequent stance assumed by the women in these songs is independence and assertiveness—indeed defiance—bordering on and sometimes erupting into violence. The first song Bessie Smith recorded, a cover of Alberta Hunter's popular "Down Hearted Blues," portrays a heartbroken woman whose love for a man was answered with mistreatment and rejection. But her bout with the blues does not result in her dejectedly "hanging her head and crying." Smith represents this woman as proud and even contemptuous of the man who has mistreated her, accentuating, in the following lines, the woman's self-respect:

It may be a week, it may be a month or two
It may be a week, it may be a month or two
But the day you quit me, honey, it's comin' home to you.[57]

It may be true, as Paul Garon has observed, that "[t]he blues is . . . a self-centered music, highly personalized, wherein the effects of everyday life are recounted in terms of the singers' reactions."[58] At the same time, however, the blues give expression to larger considerations reflecting worldviews specific to black working-class communities. Thus, "Down Hearted Blues" does not conclude with the implicit threat made against the man who has mistreated and deserted the female protagonist. Instead, it ends with an address to men in general—a bold, perhaps implicitly feminist contestation of patriarchal rule:

I got the world in a jug, the stopper's in my hand
I got the world in a jug, the stopper's in my hand
I'm gonna hold it until you men come under my command.[59]

An equally bold challenge can be found in Ma Rainey's wonderfully humorous "Barrel House Blues," which celebrates women's desires for alcohol and good times and their prerogative as the equals of men to engage in acts of infidelity:

Papa likes his sherry, mama likes her port
Papa likes to shimmy, mama likes to sport
Papa likes his bourbon, mama likes her gin
Papa likes his outside women, mama like her outside men.[60]

This signifying blues, in drawing parallels between male and female desire, between their similar inclinations toward intoxication, dance, and sex, launches a brazen challenge to dominant notions of women's subordination. "Barrel House Blues" sketches a portrait of a good-time "mama" no less at ease with her body and her sexuality than her "papa." Such glimpses of women who assert their sexual equality with men recur again and again in the work of the classic blues singers.[61] Indeed, some of these fictional portraits probably reflect actual experiences of black women who traveled the professional entertainment circuits. Ma Rainey was notorious for being able to outshine any man with her amazing sexual voracity—and Bessie Smith was known for being able to trounce any man who challenged her to a drinking duel.

In Gertrude "Ma" Rainey's and Bessie Smith's times, women's blues bore witness to the contradictory historical demands made of black American women. On the one hand, by virtue of their femaleness, they faced ideological expectations of domesticity and subordination emanating from the dominant culture. On the other hand, given the political, economic, and emotional transformations occasioned by the disestablishment of slavery, their lived experiences rendered such ideological assumptions flagrantly incongruous. In the blues, therefore, gender relationships are stretched to their limits and beyond. A typical example is one of Bessie Smith's early songs, "Mistreatin' Daddy," which opens with an address to an abusive and insensitive lover:

> Daddy, mama's got the blues, the kind of blues that's hard to lose.
> 'Cause you mistreated me and drove me from your door.

Smith sings these lines as if to convince us that this woman has attempted to make the relationship work, and is utterly despondent about having been abused by a man she may have loved. Before long, however, she menacingly informs him,

> If you see me setting on another daddy's knee
> Don't bother me, I'm as mean as can be
> I'm like the butcher right down the street
> I can cut you all to pieces like I would a piece of meat.[62]

Fearless, unadorned realism is a distinctive feature of the blues. Their representations of sexual relationships are not constructed in accordance with the sentimentality of the American popular song tradition. Romantic love is seldom romanticized in the blues. No authentic blues woman could, in good faith, sing with conviction about a dashing prince whisking her into the "happily-ever-after." Only a few songs among Bessie Smith's recorded performances—and none in Rainey's—situate love relationships and sexual desire within a strictly masculinist discursive framework. The classic blues women sang of female aspirations for happiness and frequently associated these aspirations with sexual desire, but they rarely ignored the attendant ambiguities and contradictions. In "Honey, Where You Been So Long?" for example, Ma Rainey evokes a woman who is overjoyed that her man is returning:

> He'll soon be returning and glad tidings he will bring
> Then I'll throw my arms around him, then begin to sing.

But she does not attempt to pretend that this man is a paragon of perfection:

> Honey, where you been so long?
> Never thought you would treat me wrong
> Look how you have dragged me down.[63]

Note a language that mocks the dominant white culture with down-home black English. Bessie Smith's "Sam Jones Blues" uses the same technique to highlight cultural contradictions black women experienced when comparing their own attitudes toward love and sex with the idealizations of the dominant culture.

The woman in Ma Rainey's "Lawd, Send Me a Man Blues" harbors no illusions about the relationship she desires with a man. She is lonely and wonders "who gonna pay my board bill now." Appealing for any man she can get, she pleads with a bluesy zeal:

> Send me a Zulu, a voodoo, any old man
> I'm not particular, boys, I'll take what I can.[64]

Bessie Smith's "Baby Doll" conveys a similar message:

> I wanna be somebody's baby doll so I can get my lovin' all the time
> I wanna be somebody's baby doll to ease my mind
> He can be ugly, he can be black, so long as he can eagle rock and ball the
>   jack.[65]

These blues women had no qualms about announcing female desire. Their songs express women's intention to "get their loving." Such affirmations of sexual autonomy and open expressions of female sexual desire give historical voice to possibilities of equality not articulated elsewhere. Women's blues and the cultural politics lived out in the careers of the blues queens put these new possibilities on the historical agenda.

The realism of the blues does not confine us to literal interpretations. On the contrary, blues contain many layers of meanings and are often astounding in their complexity and profundity. Precisely because the blues confront raw emotional and sexual matters associated with a very specific historical reality, they make complex statements that transcend the particularities of their origins. There is a core of meaning in the texts of the classic blues women that, although prefeminist in a historical sense, reveals that black women of that era were acknowledging and addressing issues central to contemporary feminist discourse.

By focusing on the issue of misogynist violence, the first activist moments of the second-wave twentieth-century women's movement exposed the centrality of the ideological separation of the public and private spheres to the structure of male domination. In the early 1970s, women began to speak publicly about their experiences of rape, battery, and the violation of their reproductive rights. Obscured by a shroud of silence, these assaults against women traditionally had been regarded as a fact of private life to be shielded at all costs from scrutiny in the public sphere. That this cover-up would no longer be tolerated was the explosive meaning behind feminists' defiant notion that "the personal is political."[66]

The performances of the classic blues women—especially Bessie Smith—were one of the few cultural spaces in which a tradition of public discourse on male violence had been previously established. One explanation for the fact that the blues women of the 1920s—and the texts they present—fail to respect the taboo on speaking publicly about domestic violence is that the blues as a genre never acknowledges the discursive and ideological boundaries separating the private sphere from the public. Historically, there has been no great body of literature on battering because well-to-do white women who were in a position to write about their experiences in abusive relationships only recently have been convinced that such privately executed violence is a suitable subject of public discourse.

There is, however, a body of preserved oral culture—or "orature," to use a term employed by some scholars[67]—about domestic abuse in the songs of blues women like Gertrude Rainey and Bessie Smith. Violence against women was always an appropriate topic of women's blues. The contemporary urge to break the silence surrounding misogynist violence and the organized political movement challenging violence against women has an aesthetic precursor in the work of the classic blues singers.

Women's blues have been accused of promoting acquiescent and therefore antifeminist responses to misogynist abuse. It is true that some of the songs recorded by Rainey and Smith seem to exemplify acceptance of male violence—and sometimes even masochistic delight in being the target of lovers' beatings. Such claims do not take into account the extent to which blues meaning is manipulated and transformed—sometimes even into its opposite—in blues performance. Blues make abundant use of humor, satire, and irony, revealing their historic roots in slave music, wherein indirect methods of expression were the only means by which the oppression of slavery could be denounced. In this sense, the blues genre is a direct descendant of work songs, which often relied on indirection and irony to highlight the inhumanity of slave owners so that their targets were sure to misunderstand the intended meaning.[68]

Bessie Smith sings a number of songs whose lyrics may be interpreted as accepting emotional and physical abuse as attendant hazards for women involved in sexual partnerships. But close attention to her musical presentation of these songs persuades the listener that they contain implicit critiques of male abuse. In "Yes, Indeed He Do," Smith's sarcastic presentation of the lyrics transforms observations on an unfaithful, abusive, and exploitative lover into a scathing critique of male violence:

> Is he true as stars above me? What kind of fool is you?
> He don't stay from home all night more than six times a week
> No, I know that I'm his Sheba, and I know that he's my sheik
> And when I ask him where he's been, he grabs a rocking chair
> Then he knocks me down and says, "It's just a little love lick, dear."
> . . . .
> If he beats me or mistreats me, what is that to you?
> I don't have to do no work except to wash his clothes
> And darn his socks and press his pants and scrub the kitchen floor
> I wouldn't take a million for my sweet, sweet daddy Jim
> And I wouldn't give a quarter for another man like him
>
> Gee, ain't it great to have a man that's crazy over you?
> Oh, do my sweet, sweet daddy love me? Yes, indeed he do.[69]

Edward Brooks, in *The Bessie Smith Companion*, makes the following comment about this song:

> Bessie delivers the song with growling gusto, as if it were really a panegyric to an exemplary lover; she relates his wrongs with the

approval of virtues and it comes as a jolt when the exultation in her voice is compared with her actual words.[70]

Brooks's analysis assumes that Smith was unselfconscious in her performance of this song. He therefore misses its intentional ambiguity and complexity. Smith was an accomplished performer, actor, and comedian and was therefore well acquainted with the uses of humor and irony. It is much more plausible to characterize her decision to sing "Yes, Indeed He Do" with mock praise and elation as a conscious effort to highlight, in the most effective way possible, the inhumanity and misogyny of male batterers.

"Yes, Indeed He Do" was recorded in 1928, five years after Smith began her career as a recording artist. In 1923, she recorded "Outside of That," a song about a man who was regularly abusive, but also a superb lover. The sarcasm in "Yes, Indeed He Do" is far more conspicuous than in the earlier song, but "Outside of That" also deserves a close examination. The protagonist enthusiastically proclaims her love for a man who batters her, and who becomes especially violent in response to her announcement—in jest, claims the narrator—that she no longer loves him:

I love him as true as stars above
He beats me up but how he can love
I never loved like that since the day I was born.

I said for fun I don't want you no more
And when I said that I made sweet papa sore
He blacked my eye, I couldn't see
Then he pawned the things he gave to me
But outside of that, he's all right with me.

I said for fun I don't want you no more
And when I said that I made sweet papa sore
When he pawned my things, I said you dirty old thief
Child, then he turned around and knocked out both of my teeth
Outside of that, he's all right with me.[71]

At first glance, this song appears to embrace—and even glorify—male violence. It is often interpreted as overtly condoning sadomasochistic relationships. But when one considers the lyrics carefully—even apart from Smith's interpretation—there is no convincing evidence that the woman derives pleasure from the beatings she receives. On the contrary, she lauds her lover for his sexual expertise and proclaims that she loves him despite the brutality he inflicts upon her. Smith's presentation of "Outside of That" is somewhat more subtle than in "Yes, Indeed He Do," but a close listening does confirm that she uses her voice to ironize and criticize the woman—even if she herself happens to be that woman—who would embrace with such enthusiasm a partnership so injurious to her physical and emotional well-being.

The historically omnipresent secrecy and silence regarding male violence is linked to its social construction as a private problem sequestered behind impermeable domestic walls, rather than a social problem deserving political attention. Until very recently, it was so effectively confined to the private sphere that habitually police officers would intervene in "domestic disputes" only in "life and death" situations. Even in the 1990s, police intervention, when it does occur, is still accompanied by a serious reluctance to insert the public force of the state into the private affairs of individuals.[72] "Outside of That" effectively presents violence against women as a problem to be reckoned with publicly. The song names the problem in the voice of the woman who is the target of the battering: "He beats me up . . . He blacked my eye, I couldn't see . . . he turned around and knocked out both of my teeth." It names domestic violence in the collective context of blues performance and therefore defines it as a problem worthy of public discourse. Hearing this song, women who were victims of such abuse consequently could perceive it as a shared and thus social condition.

Whether individual women in Bessie Smith's audience were able to use her performance as a basis for developing more critical attitudes toward the violence they suffered is a matter for speculation. Certainly, the organized campaign to eradicate domestic violence did not emerge in the United States until the 1970s. Women involved in these early efforts borrowed a "consciousness-raising" strategy from the Chinese women's movement referred to as "speak bitterness," or "speak pains to recall pains."[73] This strategy resonates strikingly with blues practices. Among black working-class women, the blues made oppositional stances to male violence culturally possible, at least at the level of individual experience. The lyrics indicate resistance by the victim: "I said for fun I don't want you no more . . . When he pawned my things, I said you dirty old thief." Though these comments are offered in a humorous vein, they nevertheless imply that the victim does not cower before the batterer but rather challenges his right to assault her with impunity. In Bessie Smith's rendering of this song, the recurring phrase "outside of that, he's all right with me" is sung with a satirical edge, implying that its significance may be precisely the opposite of its literal meaning.

Ma Rainey's "Black Eye Blues," a comic presentation of the issue of domestic violence, describes a woman named Miss Nancy who assumes a posture of defiance toward her abusive partner:

I went down the alley, other night
Nancy and her man had just had a fight
He beat Miss Nancy 'cross the head
When she rose to her feet, she said

"You low down alligator, just watch me
Sooner or later gonna catch you with your britches down
You 'buse me and you cheat me, you dog around and beat me
Still I'm gonna hang around

"Take all my money, blacken both of my eyes
Give it to another woman, come home and tell me lies
You low down alligator, just watch me
Sooner or later gonna catch you with your britches down
I mean, gonna catch you with your britches down."[74]

Women's blues suggest emergent feminist insurgency in that they unabashedly name the problem of male violence and so usher it out of the shadows of domestic life where society had kept it hidden and beyond public or political scrutiny. Even when she does not offer a critical perspective, Bessie Smith names the problem and the ambivalence it occasions. In "Please Help Me Get Him off My Mind," for example, the protagonist consults a Gypsy about her emotional entanglement with a violent man, whose influence she wishes to exorcise.[75]

Other explicit references to physical abuse in Smith's work can be found in "It Won't Be You,"[76] "Slow and Easy Man,"[77] "Eavesdropper's Blues,"[78] "Love Me Daddy Blues,"[79] "Hard Driving Papa,"[80] and "'Tain't Nobody's Bizness If I Do."[81] In the first song, the protagonist sardonically celebrates her decision to leave her man by informing him that if in fact her next partner "beats me and breaks my heart," at least "it won't be you." "Slow and Easy Man" presents a woman who presumably delights in the sexual pleasures offered her by a partner, but there is a casual reference to the fact that this man "curses and fights."

We can assume that the woman in "Eavesdropper's Blues" is the target of verbal and physical abuse since the man turns her "eyes all blue" if she has no money to offer him. In "Love Me Daddy Blues," as in "Please Help Get Him off My Mind," the woman experiences the dilemma typical of battered wives who continue to love their abusers.

Edward Brooks describes the last lines of "Hard Driving Papa" as "a celebration of masochism."[82] But when Bessie Smith sings "Because I love him, 'cause there's no one can beat me like he do," it is clear from her performance that far from relishing the beatings she has received, she is expressing utter desperation about her predicament. The penultimate line, "I'm going to the river feelin' so sad and blue" is delivered with such melancholy that we are all but certain the protagonist is intent upon suicide. This is a rare moment of unmitigated despair in Smith's work. To interpret the reference to battering as a celebration of masochism ignores the larger truth-telling and complexity in the song.

Bessie Smith's recorded performance of Porter Grainger's "'Tain't Nobody's Bizness If I Do"—a song also associated with Billie Holiday—is one of Smith's most widely known recordings. Like "Outside of That," it has been interpreted as sanctioning female masochism. It is indeed extremely painful to hear Smith and Holiday sing the following verse so convincingly:

> Well, I'd rather my man would hit me than to jump right up and quit me
> 'Taint nobody's bizness if I do, do, do, do
> I swear I won't call no copper if I'm beat up by my papa
> 'Tain't nobody's bizness if I do, if I do.[83]

The lyrics of this song touched a chord in black women's lives that cannot be ignored. While it contradicts the prevailing stance in most of Bessie Smith's work, which emphasizes women's strength and equality, it certainly does not annul the latter's sincerity and authenticity. Moreover, the song's seeming acquiescence to battering occurs within a larger affirmation of women's right as individuals to conduct themselves however they wish—however idiosyncratic their behavior might seem and regardless of the possible consequences. The song begins:

> There ain't nothin' I can do or nothin' I can say
> That folks don't criticize me
> But I'm going to do just as I want to anyway
> And don't care if they all despise me.[84]

Violence against women remains pandemic. Almost equally pandemic—although fortunately less so today than during previous eras—is women's inability to extricate themselves from this web of violence. The conduct defended by the woman in this male-authored song is not so unconventional after all. " 'Tain't Nobody's Bizness If I Do" may well have been a catalyst for introspective criticism on the part of many women in Bessie Smith's listening audience who found themselves entrapped in similar situations. To name that situation so directly and openly may itself have made misogynist violence available for criticism.

Gertrude Rainey's "Sweet Rough Man"[85] has been described as a "classic expression of the 'hit me, I love you' tradition of masochistic women's songs." In her analysis, Sandra Lieb argues that this song is an exception within the body of Rainey's work for its presentation of "a cruel, virile man abusing a helpless, passive woman."[86] Feminist literary critic Hazel Carby calls it "the most explicit description of sexual brutality in [Rainey's] repertoire," emphasizing that it was composed by a man and reiterating Lieb's argument that there are differing responses to male violence in female- and male-authored blues.[87] The lyrics to "Sweet Rough Man" include the following lines:

> I woke up this mornin', my head was sore as a boil
> I woke up this mornin', my head was sore as a boil
> My man beat me last night with five feet of copper coil
>
> He keeps my lips split, my eyes as black as jet
> He keeps my lips split, my eyes as black as jet
> But the way he love me makes me soon forget
>
> Every night for five years, I've got a beatin' from my man
> Every night for five years, I've got a beatin' from my man
> People says I'm crazy, I'll explain and you'll understand
> . . . .
> Lord, it ain't no maybe 'bout my man bein' rough
> Lord, it ain't no maybe 'bout my man bein' rough
> But when it comes to lovin', he sure can strut his stuff.[88]

Of all the songs recorded by Bessie Smith and Gertrude Rainey, this one is the most graphic in its evocation of domestic violence and goes farthest in revealing women's contradictory attitudes toward violent relationships. Though it was composed by a man, Rainey chose to sing it enthusiastically. We should recognize that to sing the song at all was to rescue the issue of men's violence toward women from the silent realm of the private sphere and reconstruct it as a public problem. The woman in the song assumes a stance which is at once "normal" and pathological. It is pathological to desire to continue a relationship in which one is being systematically abused, but given the prevailing presumptions of female acquiescence to male superiority, it is "normal" for women to harbor self-deprecatory ideas. Rainey's rendering of "Sweet Rough Man" does not challenge sexist conduct in any obvious way, but it does present the issue as a problem women confront. The female character acknowledges that "people says I'm crazy" for loving such a brutal man, and the song very clearly states the dilemma facing women who tolerate violence for the sake of feeling loved.

Naming issues that pose a threat to the physical or psychological well-being of the individual is a central function of the blues. Indeed, the musical genre is called the "blues" not only because it employs a musical scale containing "blue notes" but also because it names, in myriad ways, the social and psychic afflictions and aspirations of African Americans. The blues preserve and transform the West African philosophical centrality of the naming process. In the Dogon, Yoruba, and other West African cultural traditions, the process of nommo—naming things, forces, and modes—is a means of establishing magical (or, in the case of the blues, aesthetic) control over the object of the naming process.[89] Through the blues, menacing problems are ferreted out from the isolated individual experience and restructured as problems shared by the community. As shared problems, threats can be met and addressed within a public and collective context.

In Ma Rainey's and especially in Bessie Smith's blues, the problem of male violence is named, and varied patterns of implied or explicit criticism and resistance are woven into the artists' performance of them. Lacking, however, is a naming or analysis of the social forces responsible for black men's propensity (and indeed the male propensity in general) to inflict violence on their female partners. The blues accomplish what they can within the confines of their form. The political analysis must be developed elsewhere.

There are no references to sexual assault in either Rainey's or Smith's music. Certainly, black women of that era suffered sexual abuse—both by strangers and acquaintances. It is tempting to speculate why the blues do not name this particular problem. One possibility, of course, is that "rape" was still an unacknowledged and unarticulated dimension of domestic violence, and that black public discourse on rape was firmly linked to the campaign against racist violence. The birth of the blues coincided with a period of militant activism by middle-class black women directed at white racists for whom rape was a weapon of terror, and at white employers who routinely used sexual violence as a racialized means of asserting power over their female domestic help. Leaders like Mary Church Terrell and Ida B. Wells, who were instrumental in the creation of the black women's club movement,[90] linked the rape of black women by white men to the manipulative use of false rape charges against black men as a justification for the widespread lynchings of the period.[91] Black men were habitually represented as savage, sex-crazed rapists, bent on violating the physical and spiritual purity of white womanhood.[92] It may well be that the discourse on rape was so thoroughly influenced by the prevailing racism that intraracial rape could not be named. The difficult and delayed emergence of the beginnings of a collective consciousness around sexual harassment, rape, and incest within the black community is indicative of how hard it has been to acknowledge abuse perpetrated by the abused.[93]

Another explanation for the absence of allusions to rape within women's blues may be the very nature of female blues discourse. Even in their most despairing moods, the female characters memorialized in women's blues songs do not fit the mold of the typical victim of abuse. The independent women of blues lore do not think twice about wielding weapons against men who they feel have mistreated them. They frequently brandish their razors and guns, and dare men to cross the lines they draw. While acknowledging the physical mistreatment they have received at the hands of their male lovers, they do not perceive or define themselves as powerless in face of such violence. Indeed, they fight back passionately. In many songs Ma Rainey and Bessie Smith pay tribute to fearless women who attempt to avenge themselves when their lovers have been unfaithful. In "Black Mountain Blues," Bessie Smith sings:

> Had a man in Black Mountain, sweetest man in town
> Had a man in Black Mountain, the sweetest man in town
> He met a city gal, and he throwed me down
>
> I'm bound for Black Mountain, me and my razor and my gun
> Lord, I'm bound for Black Mountain, me and my razor and my gun
> I'm gonna shoot him if he stands still, and cut him if he run.[94]

In Smith's "Sinful Blues," a woman's rage also turns into violence:

> I got my opinion and my man won't act right
> So I'm gonna get hard on him right from this very night
> Gonna get me a gun long as my right arm
> Shoot that man because he done me wrong.
> Lord, now I've got them sinful blues.[95]

In Ma Rainey's "See See Rider Blues," the protagonist who has discovered that her man has another woman friend announces her intention to buy herself a pistol and to "kill my man and catch the Cannonball."[96] Her concluding resolution is: "If he don't have me, he won't have no gal at all." In Rainey's "Rough and Tumble Blues," the woman attacks not the man, but the women who have attempted to seduce him:

> I got rough and killed three women 'fore the police got the news
> 'Cause mama's on the warpath with those rough and tumble blues.[97]

In Rainey's "Sleep Talking Blues," the woman threatens to kill her man if he mentions another woman's name in his sleep. The woman in Smith's "Them's Graveyard Words" responds to her lover's confession that he has acquired a new woman friend with the murderous threat "them's graveyard words":

> I done polished up my pistol, my razor's sharpened too
> He'll think the world done fell on him when my dirty work is through.[98]

In some songs, the woman actually does kill her partner and is condemned to prison—or to death. Frequently, she kills out of jealousy, but sometimes, as in Rainey's "Cell Bound Blues," she kills in self-defense, protecting herself from her man's violent blows.[99] In two of Bessie Smith's songs—"Sing Sing Prison Blues" and "Send Me to the 'Lectric Chair"— when she comes before the criminal justice system, the woman is ready and willing to pay the consequences for having killed her man. In the former, directing her words to the judge, the woman says:

> You can send me up the river or send me to that mean old jail
> You can send me up the river or send me to that mean old jail
> I killed my man and I don't need no bail.[100]

In "Send Me to the 'Lectric Chair," the woman pleads with the judge to give her the death penalty. She is not prepared to spend the rest of her life in prison and she is willing to accept the punishment she deserves for having "cut her good man's throat." The striking postures assumed by these women offer not even a hint of repentance for having taken their lovers' lives. In "Send Me to the 'Lectric Chair," the woman sardonically describes the details of her crime:

> I cut him with my barlow, I kicked him in the side
> I stood there laughing over him while he wallowed 'round and died.[101]

These rowdy and hardened women are not simply female incarnations of stereotypical male aggressiveness. Women's blues cannot be understood apart from their role in the molding of an emotional community based on the affirmation of black people's—and in particular black women's—absolute and irreducible humanity. The blues woman challenges in her own way the imposition of gender-based inferiority. When she paints blues portraits of tough women, she offers psychic defenses and interrupts and discredits the routine internalization of male dominance. In Bessie Smith's "Hateful Blues" the woman is responding to a male partner who has skipped out on her. She is feeling "low down," but she does not hesitate to inform us that "nothin' ever worries me long." Although she has cried and cried, she persuades herself to stop: "I ain't gonna cry no more." And, with increased determination, she announces that "if he can stand to leave me, I can stand to see him go." Finally, she entertains thoughts of violent revenge:

> If I see him I'm gon' beat him, gon' kick and bite him, too
> Gonna take my weddin' butcher, gonna cut him two in two.[102]

This rough-and-tumble, sexually aware woman is capable of issuing intimidating threats to men who have mistreated her, and she is more than willing to follow through on them; she is a spiritual descendant of Harriet Tubman, who, it is said, always warned her passengers on the Underground Railroad that no one would be permitted to turn back, that they would all forge onward or die at her hands. This was the only way to guarantee confidentiality regarding their route of escape. The female portraits created by the early blues women served as reminders of African-American women's tradition of womanhood, a tradition that directly challenged prevailing notions of femininity.

The lives of many of the blues women of the twenties resembled those of the fearless women memorialized in their songs. We know that at times Bessie Smith was a victim of male violence and also that she would not hesitate to hurl violent threats—which she sometimes carried out—at the men who betrayed her. Nor was she afraid to confront the most feared embodiments of white racist terror. One evening in July of 1927, robed and hooded Ku Klux Klansmen attempted to disrupt her tent performance by pulling up the tent stakes and collapsing the entire structure. When Smith was informed of the trouble, she immediately left the tent and, according to her biographer,

> ran toward the intruders, stopped within ten feet of them, placed one hand on her hip, and shook a clenched fist at the Klansmen. "What the fuck you think you're doin'," she shouted above the sound of the band. "I'll get the whole damn tent out here if I have to. You just pick up them sheets and run!"
>
> The Klansmen, apparently too surprised to move, just stood there and gawked. Bessie hurled obscenities at them until they finally turned and disappeared quietly into the darkness. . . .
>
> Then she went back into the tent as if she had just settled a routine matter.[103]

Daphne Duval Harrison has noted that women's blues in the 1920s "introduced a new, different model of black women—more assertive, sexy, sexually aware, independent, realistic, complex, alive." Her explication of the blues' importance for redefining black women's self-understanding deserves extensive quotation:

> The blues women of Ida Cox's era brought to their lyrics and performances new meaning as they interpreted and reformulated the black experience from their unique perspective in American society as black females. They saw a world that did not protect the sanctity of black womanhood, as espoused in the bourgeois ideology; only white middle- or upper-class women were protected by it. They saw and experienced injustice as jobs they held were snatched away when white women refused to work with them or white men returned from war to reclaim them. They pointed out the pain of sexual and physical abuse and abandonment.[104]

Blues women were expected to deviate from the norms defining orthodox female behavior, which is why they were revered by both men and women in black working-class communities. Ida Cox's "Wild Women Don't Have the Blues" became the most famous portrait of the nonconforming, independent woman, and her "wild woman" has become virtually synonymous with the blues queen herself:

> I've got a disposition and a way of my own
> When my man starts kicking, I let him find another home
> I get full of good liquor and walk the street all night
> Go home and put my man out if he don't treat me right
> Wild women don't worry, wild women don't have the blues
>
> You never get nothing by being an angel child
> You'd better change your ways and get real wild
> I want to tell you something, I wouldn't tell you no lie
> Wild women are the only kind that really get by
> 'Cause wild women don't worry, wild women don't have the blues.[105]

In "Easy Come, Easy Go Blues," Bessie Smith also explored the theme of the "wild woman"—the woman who consciously rejects mainstream values, especially those prescribing passivity in relations with men. This song is about a woman who refuses to allow the mistreatment she has suffered at the hands of a man to plunge her into depression. She refuses to take love so seriously that its loss threatens her very essence:

> If my sweet man trifles, or if he don't
> I'll get someone to love me anytime he won't.

She concludes with a summary statement of her bold position:

> This world owe me a plenty lovin', hear what I say
> Believe me, I go out collectin' 'most every day
> I'm overflowing with those easy come, easy go blues.[106]

"Prove It on Me Blues," composed by Gertrude Rainey, portrays just such a "wild woman," who affirms her independence from the orthodox norms of womanhood by boldly flaunting her lesbianism. Rainey's sexual involvement with women was no secret among her colleagues and her audiences. The advertisement for the release of "Prove It on Me Blues" showed the blues woman sporting a man's hat, jacket, and tie and, while a policeman looked on, obviously attempting to seduce two women on a street corner. The song's lyrics include the following:

> They said I do it, ain't nobody caught me
> Sure got to prove it on me
> Went out last night with a crowd of my friends
> They must've been women, 'cause I don't like no men
>
> It's true I wear a collar and a tie
> Make the wind blow all the while
> 'Cause they say I do it, ain't nobody caught me
> They sure got to prove it on me
> . . . .
> Wear my clothes just like a fan
> Talk to the gals just like any old man

'Cause they say I do it, ain't nobody caught me
Sure got to prove it on me.[107]

Sandra Lieb has described this song as a "powerful statement of lesbian defiance and self-worth."[108] "Prove It on Me Blues" is a cultural precursor to the lesbian cultural movement of the 1970s, which began to crystallize around the performance and recording of lesbian-affirming songs. In fact, in 1977 Teresa Trull recorded a cover of Ma Rainey's song for an album entitled *Lesbian Concentrate*.[109]

Hazel Carby has insightfully observed that "Prove It on Me Blues"

> vacillates between the subversive hidden activity of women loving women [and] a public declaration of lesbianism. The words express a contempt for a society that rejected lesbians. . . . But at the same time the song is a reclamation of lesbianism as long as the woman publicly names her sexual preference for herself. . . .

Carby argues that this song "engag[es] directly in defining issues of sexual preference as a contradictory struggle of social relations."[110]

"Prove It on Me Blues" suggests how the iconoclastic blues women of the twenties were pioneers for later historical developments. The response to this song also suggests that homophobia within the black community did not prevent blues women from challenging stereotypical conceptions of women's lives. They did not allow themselves to be enshrined by the silence imposed by mainstream society.

Memphis Willie B. (Borum)'s song "Bad Girl Blues" is one example of how lesbianism was addressed by blues men. The lyrics lack any hint of moral condemnation:

> Women loving each other, man, they don't think about no man
> Women loving each other and they don't think about no man
> They ain't playing no secret no more, these women playing it a wide open
>   hand.[111]

Ma Rainey's "Sissy Blues" similarly recognizes the existence of male homosexuality in the black community without betraying any moral disapprobation. As is generally the case with the blues, the issue is simply named:

I dreamed last night I was far from harm
Woke up and found my man in a sissy's arms

. . . .

My man's got a sissy, his name is Miss Kate
He shook that thing like jelly on a plate

. . . .

Now all the people ask me why I'm all alone
A sissy shook that thing and took my man from home.[112]

The blues songs recorded by Gertrude Rainey and Bessie Smith offer us a privileged glimpse of the prevailing perceptions of love and sexuality in postslavery black communities in the United States. Both women were role models for untold thousands of their sisters to whom they delivered messages that defied the male dominance encouraged by mainstream culture. The blues women openly challenged the gender politics implicit in traditional cultural representations of marriage and heterosexual love relationships. Refusing, in the blues tradition of raw realism, to romanticize romantic relationships, they instead exposed the stereotypes and explored the contradictions of those relationships. By so doing, they redefined women's "place." They forged and memorialized images of tough, resilient, and independent women who were afraid neither of their own vulnerability nor of defending their right to be respected as autonomous human beings.

MAMA'S GOT THE BLUES

RIVALS, GIRLFRIENDS, AND ADVISORS

Trust no man, trust no man, no further than your eyes can see
I said, trust no man, no further than your eyes can see
He'll tell you that he loves you and swear it is true
The very next minute he'll turn his back on you
Ah, trust no man, no further than your eyes can see.

— "TRUST NO MAN"[1]

Classic blues comprised an important elaboration of black working-class social consciousness. Gertrude Rainey's and Bessie Smith's songs constituted historical preparation for social protest. They also foreshadowed a brand of protest that refused to privilege racism over sexism, or the conventional public realm over the private as the preeminent domain of power. Because women's blues were not ideologically structured by the assumptions that defined the prominent black women's organizations of the era as middle-class, they could issue more direct and audacious challenges to male dominance. It is important, I think, to understand women's blues as a working-class form that anticipates the politicalization of the "personal" through the dynamic of "consciousness-raising," a phenomenon associated with the women's movement of the last three decades.

Studies of feminist dimensions in African-American women's historical activism tend to focus on individuals and organizations solidly anchored in the developing black middle class. Paula Giddings points out that while the mission of the black women's club movement was fundamentally antiracist, it shared certain class assumptions with the white women's movement it criticized:

> The Black women's club movement did have a number of things in common with the White club movement. . . . [T]he membership of both organizations consisted mostly of middle-class educated women who were steeped in the Protestant ethic. Neither group questioned the superiority of middle-class values or way of life, or had any romantic notions of the inherent nobility of the poor, uneducated masses; education and material progress were values that Black and White women shared. Both also believed in the importance of the home and the woman's moral influence within it. Black and White women saw the family as a microcosm and cornerstone of society.[2]

When the National Association of Colored Women was founded in 1896, it chose for its motto "Lifting as We Climb." This motto called upon the most educated, most moral, and most affluent African-American women to recognize the extent to which the dominant culture's racist perceptions linked them with the least educated, most immoral, and most impoverished black women. Mary Church Terrell described this cross-class relationship as a determination "to come into the closest possible touch with the masses of our women, through whom the womanhood of our people is always judged." More explicitly, "[s]elf-preservation demands that [educated black women] go among the lowly, illiterate and even the vicious, to whom they are bound by ties of race and sex . . . to reclaim them."[3] While this posture was certainly admirable and helped to produce a distinguished tradition of progressive activism among black middle-class women from the NACW to the National Council of Negro Women and similar organizations today, what was and remains problematic is the premise that middle-class women embody a standard their poorer sisters should be encouraged to emulate.

The black women's club movement was especially concerned with the notion of "defending our name" against pervasive charges of immorality and sexual promiscuity.[4] Given the extent to which representations of black inferiority emanating from the dominant culture were bound up with notions of racial hypersexualization—the deployment of the myth of the black rapist to justify lynching is the most obvious example—it is hard to imagine that women like Fannie Barrier Williams, Ida B. Wells, and Mary Church Terrell could have been as effective as they were without defending the sexual purity of their sisters. Yet, in the process of defending black women's moral integrity and sexual purity, they almost entirely denied sexual agency. As I emphasized in the first chapter, sexuality was one of the few realms in which masses of African-American women could exercise autonomy—and thus tangibly distinguish their contemporary status from the history of enslavement. Denial of sexual agency was in an important respect the denial of freedom for working-class black women.

The women about whom Gertrude Rainey and Bessie Smith sing are precisely those who were perceived by the club women as in need of salvation. Yet, middle-class women were not the only black women who engaged in community-building. I want to suggest that women's blues provided a cultural space for community-building among working-class black women, and that it was a space in which the coercions of bourgeois notions of sexual purity and "true womanhood" were absent.

During the period following World War I, large numbers of black people left the South or moved from rural areas into southern cities and thus into new job markets. At the same time, a distinctly postslavery music culture was widely disseminated, thus accelerating and complicating the development of a postslavery working-class consciousness. Yet, blues scholars working within the discipline of musicology are rarely concerned with the ideological implications of the blues, and historians studying the African-American past rarely turn to blues history. In the few works that attempt to probe blues history for insights about the development of black cultural consciousness, masculinist bias almost inevitably leads to a failure to take seriously the efforts of women blues musicians and the female reception of their work. As a consequence, the central part played by women both in the blues and in the history of African-American cultural consciousness is often ignored.

Perhaps women's blues history has been so readily marginalized because the most frequently recurring themes of women's blues music revolve around male lovers and the plethora of problems posed by heterosexual relationships complicated by expressions of autonomous female sexuality. As I have attempted to point out, these love themes have complex social implications. Moreover, it is usually left unremarked that these songs provide a rich and complex backdrop for working-class women's lives, reflecting how they dealt with and experienced each other. Blues lyrics often construct these intragender relationships as antagonistic, as negotiations of encounters between competitors and rivals. At the same time, there are songs that highlight friendship, sisterhood, love, and solidarity between women. These range from Gertrude Rainey's "Prove It on Me Blues"[5]—and other songs recorded by women of that era celebrating sexual love between women—to songs such as Bessie Smith's "A Good Man Is Hard to Find," presenting advice to women on how to conduct themselves within their heterosexual relationships.[6]

As I argued in the first chapter, the abundance of themes revolving around love and sexuality in women's blues indicate the extent to which, for African Americans during the decades following emancipation, sexual love was experienced as physical and spiritual evidence—and the blues as aesthetic evidence—of freedom. From this historical vantage point, competition and rivalry in love may be seen as evidence of the historical construction of black working-class individuality. Although sexual rivalries no doubt existed among the emergent black middle class, ideological prohibitions required women either to be silent or to engage in a "proper" way of speaking about such matters.

As slave music suggests, the conditions for physical and spiritual survival during slavery (as well as the survival of transmuted African ancestral cultures) defined the value of the individual as subordinate to the community. The abolition of slavery, while it did not bring economic and political freedom, created a backdrop for new kinds of relationships between black individuals and thus for a different valuation of the individual in general. The new African Americans—women and men alike—came to perceive their individual selves not only as welded together within the community, but as different from and in opposition to one another as well. For working-class women and men, the blues both allowed and furnished cultural representations of this new individuality.

Blues portraits of women in competition with each other for sexual partners—as "vicious" as they may have appeared to women like Mary Church Terrell—revealed working-class women as capable of exercising some measure of agency in choosing their partners. This is not to deny the problematic aspects of blues constructions of female jealously and rivalry, sometimes to the point of violence. On the contrary, while representations of female sexual agency no doubt played a progressive role by encouraging assertiveness and independence among black women, these representations simultaneously legitimized a tradition of real and often murderous violence between women. As African-American women forged a continuum of independent womanhood—in contradiction to the prevailing ideology of women's place—they also affirmed, in frequently exaggerated forms, sexist models of women's conduct. While this contradictory character of the emergence of black female working-class individuality is far from inconsequential—and I will later identify some of the ways these contradictions are manifested in blues performances—I want to emphasize, for the moment, the importance of women's blues as a site for the independent elaboration and affirmation of subjectivity and community for women of the black working class. Through the blues, black women were able to autonomously work out—as audiences and performers—a working-class model of womanhood. This model of womanhood was based in part on a collective historical memory of what had been previously required of women to cope with slavery. But more important, it revealed that black women and men, the blues audience, could respond to the vastly different circumstances of the postslavery era with notions of gender and sexuality that were, to a certain extent, ideologically independent of the middle-class cult of "true womanhood." In this sense, as Hazel Carby has pointed out, the blues was a privileged site in which women were free to assert themselves publicly as sexual beings.

Beginning with W. E. B. Du Bois's essay in *Darkwater*, many studies have emphasized the extent to which black working-class women's relative economic independence summoned various modes of female consciousness that emphasized strength, resilience, and autonomy.[7] However, such arguments often assume a strictly causal relationship between the economic conditions of slavery—which inflicted responsibilities for production on women that were equal to those placed on men—and the gendered consciousness among working-class black women that privileged independence.[8] I want to emphasize women's blues as an important cultural mediator for this gendered consciousness that transformed collective memories of slavery as it worked with a new social construction of love and sexuality. The blues provided a space where women could express themselves in new ways, a space in which they sometimes affirmed the dominant middle-class ideology but also could deviate from it.

I begin with the most complicated expressions of women's independence and assertiveness, in which an independent sense of women's strength was interwoven with themes of female rivalry over a male lover. "Rough and Tumble Blues," composed and recorded by Gertrude "Ma" Rainey, presents a powerful, fighting, rough-and-tumble woman, who boasts about her assertiveness and power. Her boasts, however, are directed at the women—Mama Tree Top Tall and Miss Shorty Toad—who have their eyes on her man. Her power is established partly by virtue of her ability to support the man financially—evidenced by the fact that she has bought him a "struttin' suit." The final verse of this song proclaims:

> I got rough and killed three women 'fore the police got the news
> I got rough and killed three women 'fore police got the news
> 'Cause mama's on the warpath with those rough and tumble blues.[9]

A similar song, "Wringing and Twisting Blues," composed by Paul Carter and also recorded by Rainey, announces the protagonist's desire to poison the woman for whom her lover left her:

> But if I know that woman that caused my heart to moan
> I'd cook a special dinner, invite her to my home
> . . . .
> If she eats what's on my table, she will be graveyard bound

I'll be right there to tell her, when they put her in the ground
"You're the cause of me having those wringin' and a-twistin' blues."[10]

There are comparable images of female violence directed against other women in Bessie Smith's songs:

But if I find that gal
That tried to steal my pal
I'll get her told, just you wait and see.[11]

Or, in more aggressive terms:

St. Louis gal, I'm gonna handle you, I said manhandle you
. . . .
Your life won't be worth a dime
You stole my pal, St. Louis gal

I'm goin' a-huntin', root-dooti-doot
You know just what I'm gonna shoot
You stole my pal, St. Louis gal.[12]

Such representations of jealousy and violence need not be taken literally. However, we should keep in mind the current discourse on racialized violence that merges real violence and representations of violence. Critiques of gangsta rap, for example, argue for a rather simple and mechanical relation between cultural images and material reality. Of course, the murders of rappers Tupac Shakur and Biggie Smalls within six months of one another in late 1996 and early 1997 tended to affirm this. But, with respect to the role of violence in Rainey's and Smith's work, I am arguing that these performed lyrics provide a glimpse of a kind of working-class women's community-building that, rather than advocating violence, proclaims women's complexity by refusing to deny or downplay female antagonism. The jealousy and competitiveness that was so openly expressed in the blues surely also characterized middle-class women's relations with each other. Remaining unnamed and unacknowledged, these antagonisms must have had vast political consequences about which we could not even begin to speculate today.

Jealousy and rivalry, as they defined female blues subjects' attitudes toward other women, do not always erupt into actual or imagined violence as in the songs cited above. Often, there is simply suspicion, as in Bessie Smith's "Empty Bed Blues":

> Lord, he's got that sweet somethin', and I told my gal friend Lou
> He's got that sweet somethin', and I told my gal friend Lou
> From the way she's ravin', she must have gone and tried it too.

"Empty Bed Blues, Part II" concludes with a word of advice offered to other women:

> When you get good lovin', never go and spread the news
> Yeah, it will double cross you and leave you with them empty bed blues.[13]

In a similar vein, "He's Got Me Goin'"—a song replete with erotic imagery—reveals a subject so utterly captivated by her lover that she fears other women may hear about him and try to attract his attentions:

> 'Fraid to advertise my man, simply scared to death
> These gals'll hear about him and try him for they self.[14]

Unmitigated jealousy, however, is not always the posture assumed by jealous blues subjects. The blues never remain fixed on one perspective, but rather different songs—sometimes the same song—explore experiences from various vantage points. This feature of the blues, the aesthetic incorporation of several perspectives and dimensions, may be interpreted as reflective of West African philosophical outlooks and representational strategies. Beneath the apparent simplicity and straightforwardness of the blues, complex visions—reflecting the complexity with which reality is perceived—can always be uncovered. This is another way in which the blues are located on an African cultural continuum.[15]

Some songs describe the woman succumbing to feelings of jealousy. In other songs, jealousy is named and acknowledged—even celebrated as an important subject and a powerful blues theme. Still other songs reveal a critical attitude toward jealousy, pointing to its potential destructiveness. Within the body of Gertrude Rainey's work, all three of these attitudes are evident. In "Sleep Talking Blues," the protagonist warns her man of the disastrous consequences of calling another woman's name in his sleep:

> When you talk in your sleep, be sure your mama's not awake
> When you talk in your sleep, be sure your mama's not awake
> You call another woman's name, you'll think you wake up in a earthquake.[16]

In "Jealous Hearted Blues"—one of Lovie Austin's compositions—jealousy is repeatedly named, as the jealous woman acknowledges the extent to which she has been overcome by this emotion. The following chorus is repeated four times:

> Yes I'm jealous, jealous, jealous hearted me
> Lord, I'm just jealous, jealous as I can be.

Indeed, the protagonist is so utterly driven by her jealousy that she announces this measure:

> Gonna buy me a bulldog to watch him while I sleep
> To keep my man from making his midnight creep.[17]

Finally, in "Jealousy Blues," an analytical and implicitly critical posture is assumed. This song focuses on the catastrophic potential of jealousy for relationships and for one's psychological well-being, as well as on its violence and its material consequences:

> If all the world is evil, all the world is evil, oh jealousy is the worst of all
> It'll make you mad and lonely, your sweet love will feel so pale
> It'll steal your loving daddy, have many folks in jail.[18]

The most complicated evocation of jealousy can be found in "My Man Blues," a song written by Bessie Smith and performed as a duet with Clara Smith, who was known during the period as the Empress's most serious musical rival. The piece is about competition for the attentions of a man who each woman insists belongs to her. There are powerful resonances in this song: the actual competitive relationship between the two Smiths as entertainers; the rivalry in general between women; and a troubled but unmistakable reconciliation:

Bessie: Clara, who was that man I saw you with the other day?
Clara: Bessie, that was my smooth black daddy that we call Charlie Gray.
Bessie: Don't you know that's my man? Yes, that's a fact.
Clara: I ain't seen your name printed up and down his back.
Bessie: You better let him be.
Clara: What, old gal? Because you ain't talkin' to me.
Bessie: That's my man, I want him for my own.
Clara: [Spoken] No! No! [Sung] He's my sweet daddy.
            You'd better leave that man alone.
Bessie: See that suit he got on? I bought it last week.
Clara: I been buyin' his clothes for five years, for that is my black sheik.

[CHARLIE WHISTLES]

[SPOKEN]
Bessie: Is that you, honey?
Charlie: 'Tain't nobody but—who's back there?
Clara: It sounds like Charlie.
Bessie: It 'tis my man, sweet papa Charlie Gray.
Clara: Your man? How do you git that way?
Bessie: Now, look here, honey. I been had that man for sumpteen years.
Clara: Child, don't you know I'll turn your damper down?
Bessie: Yes, Clara, and I'll cut you every way but loose!
Clara: Well, you might as well be get it fixed.
Bessie: Well, then.

[*SUNG*]

Bessie: I guess we got to have him on cooperation plan.
          I guess we got to have him on cooperation plan.

[*SPOKEN*]

Clara: Bessie!
Bessie: Clara!

[*SUNG*]

Both: Ain't nothin' different 'bout all those other two-time men.

[*SPOKEN*]

Bessie: How 'bout it?
Clara: Suits me.
Bessie: Suits me too.
Clara: Well, then.[19]

Edward Brooks has called this humorous song "a fascinating document
. . . which completely dispels the doubts of some commentators about
Bessie Smith's supremacy over her nearest rival."[20] With respect to the content of the song, the women apparently are equal competitors for the love
of the same man. That this rivalry is presented in broadly comic terms
encourages in the audience a critical attitude toward such conduct on the
part of women. What is most striking about this song is its resolution: the
two women agree to share the man over whom they have been engaging in
a verbal duel. Bessie proposes to Clara, "I guess we got to have him on
cooperation plan." Her suggestion seems to imply how futile it is for them
to be so consumed by jealousy that they constantly are at loggerheads with
one another. At this point in the song, their focus on the male lover is dis-
placed by their mutual acknowledgment of each other: each calls the
other's name. And, in the final moments of the song, they sing together for
the first time, agreeing that, since most other men would be as unfaithful
as the one over whom they have been battling, they may as well act on
Bessie's suggestion. The reconciliation with which the piece concludes, as

comically as it may be formulated, alludes to a possibility of sisterhood and solidarity that is forged in and through struggles around sexuality.

The concluding posture of "My Man Blues" is especially interesting for the way it provides an imagined alternative to the notions of women's community-building on which middle-class black club women relied. From their vantage point, women could only come together in defense of sexual purity. In other words, sexuality could only play a role in community-building as an object of ideological protest and cleansing. Of course, the kind of political work the club women set out to do would have been impossible had they not denied the sexually motivated antagonisms so central in blues discourse. In light of the emergence of sexuality in recent decades as an important arena of political struggle, it is important, nevertheless, to understand the blues as a form that did allow explicit artic-ulations and explorations of sexual politics.

There are far more songs of advice among women's blues recordings than there are songs of female competition. One of the principal modes of community-building in women's blues is that of sharing experiences for the purpose of instructing women how to conduct their lives. Many of the songs that describe the difficulties of romantic partnerships are peda-gogical in character. In some instances, the instruction warns women to beware of the powers of seduction some men possess, as in the following stanza from Bessie Smith's "Lookin' for My Man Blues":

> He's a red hot papa, melt hearts as cold as ice
> He's a red hot papa, melt hearts as cold as ice
> Girls, if he ever love you once, you bound to love him twice.[21]

Or, as in Ma Rainey's "Trust No Man," women are instructed to "[t]rust no man, no further than your eyes can see."[22]

There are also songs that advise women how to avoid triangular entan-glements—and how to keep other women from eyeing their men. In Bessie Smith's "Keep It to Yourself," there is an underlying perception of other women as competitors and rivals. However, the instruction seeks to avoid active rivalry over men:

If your man is nice and sweet, servin' you lots of young pigmeat
Oh, yeah, keep it to yourself

. . . .

If your man is full of action, givin' you a lots of satisfaction
Oh, yeah, keep it to yourself

. . . .

If he tries to treat you right, give you lovin' every night
Oh, yeah, keep it to yourself

He don't fall for no one, he don't call for no one
He don't give nobody his L-O-V-E, 'cause it's yours
With your man you've got the best go, don't broadcast it on nobody's radio
Oh, yeah, keep it to yourself.[23]

There is an interesting dialectic here between the individual woman and the larger female community. While women are clearly perceived as antagonists—as potential intruders into others' relationships—they are also viewed as possessing common fears and common interests. They are located both outside and inside a community of women. This aesthetic community of women emerges in its most developed form when blues women share stories about abusive partners or advise their sisters how to conduct themselves in relation to such men. Daphne Duval Harrison points out in her pioneering study of the classic blues singers that "[a]dvice to other women is a staple among women's blues themes, especially on how to handle your men."[24] Much of this advice seems to accept male supremacy without overtly challenging it, but it also displays unmistakable oppositional attitudes in its rejection of sexual passivity as a defining characteristic of womanhood.

A process similar to the consciousness-raising strategies associated with the 1960s women's liberation movement unfolds in these songs, which are conversations among women about male behavior in which the traditional call-and-response structure of West African–based music takes on a new feminist meaning. Consciousness-raising groups affirmed the most dramatic insight of the early women's liberation movement: the personal is political. Individual women shared personal experiences with the aim of rendering explicit the underlying politics shaping women's lives. Because of the complicated racial politics of the 1960s, which defined the women's movement as white, and because of its emphasis on personal micropolitics (often seen as a retreat from the macropolitics of race), black women generally found it difficult to identify with the strategy of consciousness-raising. In retrospect, however, it is possible to detect ways in which the sharing of personal relationships in blues culture prefigured consciousness-raising and its insights about the social construction of individual experience. Seen in this light, the blues women can be understood as being responsible for the dissemination of attitudes toward male supremacy that had decidedly feminist implications.

That the blues is a highly "personal" aesthetic form in no way diminishes its important social and political dimensions. Lawrence Levine has pointed out that

[t]he blues was the most highly personalized, indeed, the first almost completely personalized music that Afro-Americans developed. It was the first important form of Afro-American music in the United States to lack the kind of antiphony that had marked other black musical forms. The call and response form remained, but in blues it was the singer who responded to himself or herself either verbally or on an accompanying instrument. In all these respects blues was the most typically American music Afro-Americans had yet created and represented a major degree of acculturation to the individualized ethos of the larger society. . . .[25]

Levine is certainly accurate in his emphasis on the personal and personalizing dimensions of the blues, but he fails to recognize a more complicated persistence of the call-and-response form. The blues in performance creates space for spontaneous audience response in a manner that is similar to religious testifying. Just as the sermon lacks vitality when no response is forthcoming from the congregation, so the blues performance falls flat without the anticipated affirmations of the audience. It was this invitation to respond that rendered women's blues such a powerful site for the construction of working-class consciousness and one of the only arenas in which working-class black women could become aware of the deeply social character of their personal experiences.

The contemporary blues woman Koko Taylor has pointed out that the songs she writes and performs do not always reflect her own individual experiences. Yet, as she insists, she knows that among the women in her audiences, some will certainly identify with the situation she constructs:

> Now when I write a song, I'm thinking about people in general, everyday living. Just look around, you know. Say, for instance, like when I wrote this tune "Baby Please Don't Dog Me." You know what I'm saying. I'm thinking about, O.K., here is some woman begging and she's pleading, Baby please don't dog me, when you know that you're doing wrong yourself. . . . Now that shoe might not fit my feet. That shoe might not fit your feet. But that shoe do fit somebody's feet. It's some woman out there is really thinking, she really feels the way that I'm singing about, what I'm talking about in this song. It's some woman somewhere really feels this way. These are the words she would like to say.[26]

Call-and-response persists in women's blues through the construction of fictional subjects who assert their sexuality in a variety of ways. Such subjects permit a vast array of individual women to locate themselves within a blues community without having to abstract themselves from their personal lives. Rainey and Smith sang songs about women who had numerous male lovers, women angry about male sexual behavior, and women who loved women. Moreover, individual women were able to respond to and comment on the problems of other women without having to reveal the autobiographical sources of their authority and wisdom.

"The widespread use of the call-and-response discourse mode among African-Americans," black feminist sociologist Patricia Hill Collins points out,

> illustrates the importance placed on dialogue. Composed of spon- taneous verbal and nonverbal interaction between speaker and listener in which all of the speaker's statements, or "calls," are punc-

tuated by expressions, or "responses," from the listener, this Black discourse mode pervades African American culture. The fundamental requirement of this interactive network is active participation of all individuals. For ideas to be tested and validated, everyone in the group must participate.[27]

Collins defines call-and-response discourse as an essential dimension of the "Afrocentric feminist epistemology" she proposes. While she invokes black women musicians like Billie Holiday and Aretha Franklin in her discussion of yet another dimension of this alternative epistemology, the ethic of caring, she does not discuss the musical roots of call-and-response discourse. Such a discussion—particularly in relation to blues women like Bessie Smith—would render her compelling argument even more powerful. Collins is concerned with the possibility of knowledge production that suppresses neither the individual at the expense of the general welfare, nor feelings at the expense of rational thought. The participatory character of the blues affirms women's community without negating individual feelings.

Without the assumption of such an imagined community, the advice song in women's blues simply could not work. Gertrude Rainey's "Trust No Man," composed by Lillian Hardaway Henderson, is one of the finest examples of the advice song:

I want all you women to listen to me
Don't trust your man no further than your eyes can see
I trusted mine with my best friend
But that was the bad part in the end

Trust no man, trust no man, no further than your eyes can see
I said trust no man, no further than your eyes can see
He'll tell you that he loves you and swear it is true
The very next minute he'll turn his back on you
Ah, trust no man, no further than your eyes can see.[28]

Singing "I want all you women to listen to me" in the first verse of the song, Rainey constructs an audience, an imagined community of women. It is clear on the recording that Rainey is inviting response—even to this mechanical reproduction of her live performance. Her advice is framed and delivered in such a way that any woman listening can discover a way to identify with her admonition. The appeal is so powerful that it is easy to imagine the responses that came forth during her live performances. As if to preclude any doubt as to the invitation to respond, Rainey included spoken words in the second chorus: "Say! Take Ma Rainey's advice! Don't trust *no* man. I mean, not even your own man!" She concludes this spoken session with the words: "Just don't trust nobody! You see where it got me, don't you? He sure will leave you."

Bessie Smith's "Safety Mama" is a song of advice that counsels women to take strong stands with the men with whom they are involved, and to take measures to guarantee their own economic independence:

> Let me tell you how and what one no-good man done to me
> He caught me pretty, young, and wild, after that he let me be
>
> He'd taken advantage of my youth, and that you understand
> So wait awhile, I'll show you, child, just how to treat a no-good man
>
> Make him stay at home, wash and iron
> Tell all the neighbors he done lost his mind
>
> Give your house rent shake on Saturday night
> Monday morning you'll hold collectors good and tight.[29]

This song's domestic imagery—and the gender reversal—have already been discussed in the first chapter. What is also striking about "Safety Mama" is that it emphatically counsels women to find ways of supporting themselves financially. Certainly, black women were compelled to work for a living, but for many decades following the abolition of slavery, the jobs that were available to them were limited to domestic work. "Safety Mama" suggests that rather than rely on their men—and perhaps also to avoid the perpetual servitude to which so many working black women were condemned—they organize rent parties in order to acquire funds to meet their landlords' demands. By the 1920s these "house rent shakes" had developed into a community institution in the urban North, aiding men and women alike to raise the money necessary to "hold collectors good and tight." The imagined women's community in this song is one that refuses to place women in sexual and economic subordination to men. It affirms working-class women's independence. Again, it is possible to envision the enthusiastic responses that came from Smith's female audiences.

Another advice song recorded by Bessie Smith—also previously discussed—is "Pinchback Blues." It proposes to arm women with the power to resist men who attempt to use sexual attractiveness to exploit women. As in "Safety Mama" and Rainey's "Trust No Man," "Pinchback" opens with an evocation of a female community. "Girls," Smith states in the spoken introduction, "I wanna tell you about these sweet men. These men goin' 'round here tryin' to play cute. I'm hard on you, boys, yes sir." She then proceeds to narrate an experience of having been lured into a relationship that led to marriage with a "sweet man" who then refused to get a job to support either his female partner or himself:

> I fell in love with a sweet man once, he said he loved me too
> He said if I'd run away with him what nice things he would do
>
> I'd travel around from town to town, how happy I would feel
> But don't you know, he would not work . . .

Universalizing the lesson drawn from these experiences, Smith offers direct advice to her female audience:

> . . . girls, take this tip from me
> Get a workin' man when you marry, and let all these sweet men be
> . . . .
> There's one thing about this married life that these young girls have got to know
> If a sweet man enter your front gate, turn out your lights and lock your door.[30]

The admonition "get a working man" is even more than a sound bit of advice to a woman who wishes to acquire a measure of material security. It suggests an identification with workers—and by extension, the values and perhaps also the collective consciousness associated with the working class. Women are urged to seek out solid working men and to learn how to resist the temptations of parasitic men who try to dazzle with their good looks and smooth talk.

It is interesting that Bessie Smith's appearance in the 1929 motion picture *St. Louis Blues*[31]—the only extant recording of her image on film—was in the role of a woman who did not take the advice offered in "Pinchback Blues." In this film, which incorporates an overabundance of racist and sexist stereotypes, the character she plays is abused and exploited by a handsome, light-skinned, disloyal, crapshooting man who has obviously attached himself to her for the sole purpose of taking her money. "Bessie," the character she plays in the film, has bought clothes for "Jimmy" (played by Jimmy Mordecai), allowed him to live in the hotel room she is renting, and provided him with money. He, in turn, is involved with a thin, light-skinned woman (played by Isabel Washington) who fits a Eurocentric definition of feminine beauty.

The plot of this film, superficially constructed around Bessie Smith's performance of W. C. Handy's "St. Louis Blues," is based on Jimmy's taunting abandonment of Bessie, who is so utterly mesmerized by him that she pleads with him to stay even as she lies on the floor after being battered by him. When the scoundrel returns—the setting for this scene is a luxurious Harlem nightclub—she experiences a momentary exhilaration. However, she is soon overcome with despair once more because, as it turns out, Jimmy's romantic invitation to dance is simply a ploy to steal the money she has hidden in her garter. The film concludes with the pinchback, Jimmy, in a posture of triumph, and the victimized woman, Bessie, in a state of paralyzing depression.

The choice of Bessie Smith for the part in the film has been attributed to W. C. Handy, who, as a collaborator on the film, suggested to the director, Dudley Murphy, that she be cast in the leading role. "She had made the definitive version of the title tune," Chris Albertson has pointed out, and her powerful voice was one of the few that could be heard over the projected accompaniment of a forty-two-voice mixed choir, jazz band, and strings.[32] It is not difficult to understand Smith's decision to make this film. During the late twenties, the popularity of blues had begun to wane and many leading blues singers—Alberta Hunter and Ethel Waters included—increasingly began to sing Tin Pan Alley products and to seek roles in musicals. Smith had starred in a Broadway production that had flopped, and she, like other black women entertainers, was eager to break into the revolutionary medium of talking pictures. But black singers who had been able to exercise a certain measure of autonomy and control over their music found that the new medium used and abused their talents at the whims of producers and directors.

St. Louis Blues deserves criticism not only for its exploitation of racist stereotypes but for its violation of the spirit of the blues. Its direct translation of blues images into a visual and linear narrative violates blues discourse, which is always complicated, contextualized, and informed by that which is unspoken as well as by that which is named. *St. Louis Blues*, the film, flagrantly disregards the spirit of women's blues by leaving the victimized woman with no recourse. In the film, the response is amputated from the call. Although the advice song "Pinchback Blues" evokes a male figure who bears a striking resemblance to the character of Jimmy in the film, "Pinchback" warns women to stay away from such con men. In other women's blues that allude to these men, even when the criticism is not open and direct, the female subjects are never left in a state of absolute despair. Such a posture violates the spirit of women's blues. It is precisely the presence of an imagined community of supportive women that rescues them from the existential agony that Smith portrays at the end of *St. Louis Blues*.

There are also a number of advice songs that suggest how women should conduct themselves in relationships with men who are worthy partners. A cover Bessie Smith recorded of Alberta Hunter's "A Good Man Is Hard to Find" is a typical woman-to-woman advice blues of this kind. It eventually became a standard. This song is unique in that it does not evoke an individual's experiences but rather is directed, in its entirety, to the female audience, articulating their collective experiences with their sexual partners. The persisting problems women encounter in their relationships are named: the unfaithful male lover whose actions provoke tumultuous feelings of jealousy in his female partner, as well as fantasies (if not realities) of violent assault. The main advice in this song is that if a woman does find a man who is loyal, respectful, and sensitive, she should know how to reciprocate:

> Lord, a good man is hard to find, you always get another kind
> Yes, and when you think that he's your pal
> You look and find him fooling 'round some old gal
> Then you rave, you are crazed, you want to see him down in his grave
>
> So if your man is nice, take my advice
> Hug him in the morning, kiss him at night
> Give him plenty lovin', treat your good man right
> 'Cause a good man nowadays sho' is hard to find.[33]

There is a series of songs among the recordings of Gertrude Rainey and Bessie Smith in which the woman who is experiencing difficulties in love shares her problems and her feelings with other women. These songs implicitly emphasize the dialectical relation between the female subject and the community of women within which this individuality is imagined. In an aesthetic realm, these songs construct a women's community in which individual women are able to locate themselves on a jagged continuum of group experiences. They encourage intimacy and familiarity between women. They contextualize particular events in the personal histories of the songs' subjects—often actions by their male partners that have wrought havoc in their lives—as stories they are sharing with their girlfriends. These girlfriends console them by implicitly confirming similar events in their own histories, thus providing emotional support and enabling women to confront such disruptive moments with attitudes that move from victimization to agency. Ma Rainey, for example, begins "Jelly Bean Blues" by asking, "Did you ever wake up with your good man on your mind?"[34] The song then proceeds to describe the subject's state of mind in the aftermath of her lover's desertion. The initial question establishes a relationship of intimacy and familiarity with her female audience.

Bessie Smith's version of Rainey's composition "Moonshine Blues" makes a few minor but significant changes, including the substitution in one stanza of "girls" for "lord." Smith thus explicitly conjures up a supportive female community. In Rainey's rendition:

I feel like screamin', I feel like cryin'
Lord, I been mistreated, folks, and don't mind dyin'.[35]

In Smith's version:

Girls, I feel like screamin', I feel like cryin'
I been mistreated, and I don't mind dyin'.[36]

Of course, Rainey, following the traditional patterns of blues discourse, is announcing her plight, publicizing her private woes, and thus, in this stanza, invokes her entire community—the folks—while directing her feelings of despair to the Lord. Smith, on the other hand, seeks solace not in the Lord but rather from the girls.

In "You Don't Understand," recorded by Bessie Smith in 1929, a collective female presence is invoked in the first line. The subject realizes that it is futile to try to persuade the man she loves to return to her: "Here I am, girls of mine, pleading but it's all in vain."[37] The entire text, with the exception of the opening phrase, is directed to the unresponsive man. Ma Rainey's "Titanic Man Blues" begins with a similar invocation: "Everybody fall in line, going to tell you 'bout that man of mine." From the story that follows, it is obvious that she is addressing herself to women. After this opening phrase, the female figure in the song proceeds to direct her comments to a lover she plans to leave, ending each verse with this statement: "It's the last time, Titanic, fare thee well."[38] It is as if she invites a community of women to be present at a ritualistic shunning. Invoking the presence of sympathetic women summons up the courage the woman needs in order to eject this man from her life.

Bessie Smith's "I Used to Be Your Sweet Mama" is one of the most stunning examples of sharing among women for the purpose of summoning up the emotional strength necessary to challenge male supremacy in personal relationships:

All you women understand
What it is to be in love with a two-time man
The next time he calls me sweet mama in his lovin' way
This is what I'm going to say

"I used to be your sweet mama, sweet papa
But now I'm just as sour as can be."

Again, this song anticipates the 1960s strategy of consciousness-raising. Affirming that the women in her listening audience have a common understanding of disloyal lovers, the protagonist creates, on the basis of that collective experience, a rehearsal space. One easily can imagine the testifying that punctuated Bessie Smith's performances of this song. She must have received enthusiastic shouts of encouragement from the women in her audiences as she sang, "This is what I'm going to say," and certainly as she informed her audience what she would tell "sweet papa":

"So don't come stallin' around my way expectin' any love from me
You had your chance and proved unfaithful
So now I'm gonna be real mean and hateful
I used to be your sweet mama, sweet papa
But now I'm just as sour as can be."

I ain't gonna let no man worry me sick
Or turn this hair of mine gray
Soon as I catch him at his two-time tricks
I'm gonna tell him to be on his way
To the world I scream, "No man can treat me mean
And expect my love all the time."
When he roams away, he'd better stay
If he comes back he'll find

"You've had your chance and proved unfaithful
So now I'm gonna be real mean and hateful

I used to be your sweet mama, sweet papa
But now I'm just as sour as can be."[39]

Such songs as this and Rainey's "Trust No Man," in part because they evoked enthusiastic, testifying responses from their female audiences, would have been considered distasteful by middle-class club women. Formally educated women assumed that such cultural expressions tended to confirm the dominant culture's association of black women with sexual license and immorality. As the club women went about their work of "defending our name," they disassociated themselves from working-class women's blues culture, and assumed the missionary role of introducing "true womanhood" to their less fortunate sisters. In fact, they were defending the name of the female contingent of the black bourgeoisie. It did not occur to them then—and may not be obvious to us today—that this women's blues community was in fact defending the name of its own members. And while the club women achieved great victories in the historical struggles they undertook against racism, and forcefully affirmed black women's equality in the process, the ideological terrain on which they operated was infused with assumptions about the inherent inferiority of poor—and especially sexually assertive—women. In hindsight, the production, performance, and reception of women's blues during the decade of the twenties reveal that black women's names could be defended by working-class as well as middle-class women. Women's blues also demonstrate that working-class women's names could be defended not only in the face of the dominant white culture but in the face of male assertions of dominance in black communities as well.

HERE COME MY TRAIN

Traveling Themes and Women's Blues

I'm dangerous and blue, can't stay here no more
Here come my train, folks, and I've got to go.

— "Traveling Blues"[1]

Live blues performances, as well as the widely distributed recordings of the 1920s, facilitated among black working-class women recognition of the social sources of ideas and experiences they encountered in their own lives. But this music accomplished much more. It permitted the women's blues community—performers and audiences alike—to engage aesthetically with ideas and experiences that were not accessible to them in real life. The imaginary was as important to the women's blues community and to its challenges to male dominance as real-life experiences.

One of the most salient of these imaginary themes was travel. Travel themes are ubiquitous in early women's blues. Gertrude Rainey—the "Mother of the Blues"—sings about women who were forever walking, running, leaving, catching trains, or sometimes aimlessly rambling. Their travels back and forth, away from and toward home, are frequently associated with the exercise of autonomy in their sexual lives. The subjects of Rainey's songs, like those of other blues women, make decisions to embark on various journeys because they have been hurt deeply by their sexual partners but refuse, even in their pain, to relinquish their own agency. They travel because they have lovers in other cities, or because they wish to find new lovers. As I pointed out in the first chapter, for people of African descent who were emerging from a long history of enslavement and oppression during the late nineteenth and early twentieth centuries, sexuality and travel provided the most tangible evidence of freedom. I have discussed the ways women's blues simultaneously were shaped by and helped to shape a new consciousness in the black community regarding female sexuality. This chapter will explore the ways in which blues representations of traveling women constructed a cultural site where masses of black women could associate themselves aesthetically with travel as a mode of freedom. Blues representations of women engaged in self-initiated and independent travel constitute a significant moment of ideological opposition to the prevailing assumptions about women's place in society. Notions of independent, traveling women enter into black cultural consciousness in ways that reflect women's evolving role in the quest for liberation. At the same time, dominant gender politics within black consciousness are troubled and destabilized.

Until the 1920s, for as long as African people had been present in North America, the majority had been confined to the environs of the plantations and the farms on which they worked. During slavery, their lives, extending in many instances even to their sexual partners, were dictated by their masters. Travel was the risky prerogative of runaways and fugitives. Many risked capture to join lovers. Although most accounts of fugitive travelers during slavery are found in narratives authored by men, there are a number of prominent cases of women joining the ranks of escaped slaves. Ellen Craft, who disguised herself as a white man while her husband posed as her slave, is one of the best-known of these women.[2] The most dramatic example of a woman runaway during slavery is detailed in the narrative of Harriet Brent Jacobs, who, as a fugitive slave, hid for seven years in a tiny crawl space above a storeroom in her grandmother's house before finally escaping the South.[3] However, the historical figure whose travel became most legendary was Harriet Tubman, leader of runaways and fugitives and the most successful conductor on the Underground Railroad. When slavery was finally abolished, mobility was no longer proscribed by law and the black community was offered the historically new experience of embarking upon personal journeys, journeys whose territorial and economic relocations occasioned and were occasioned by psychological repositionings. "As important as spacial mobility has been throughout American history for all segments of the population," Lawrence Levine has observed,

> it was a particularly crucial symbol for Afro-Americans to whom it had been denied throughout the long years of slavery. Freedom of movement, as Howard Thurman has argued, was for Negroes the "most psychologically dramatic of all manifestations of freedom." The need to move, the existence of places to go, and the ability to get there, constituted central motifs in black song after emancipation.[4]

This new historical experience of autonomous movement, however, was subject to the gender restrictions that reflected both the gender ideology of the dominant culture and its insinuation into the social structures and ideological perceptions of women's role in communities of newly freed slaves. While the universe of the newly freed male slaves was geographically and psychologically enlarged, women, in their overwhelming majority, remained territorially confined by the domestic requirements of family building. In Zora Neale Hurston's *Their Eyes Were Watching God*, Janie's grandmother tells her,

> Ah was born back due in slavery so it wasn't for me to fulfill my dreams of whut a woman oughta be and to do. . . . Freedom found me wid a baby daughter in mah arms, so Ah said Ah'd take a broom and a cook-pot and throw up a highway through de wilderness for her. She would expound what Ah felt. But somehow she got lost

offa de highway and next thing Ah knowed here you was in de world.[5]

Even as women were compelled to remain at home to care for the children they had borne—and at the same time to earn money by carrying out domestic tasks for white families in the vicinity—men often had no alternative to traveling in search of work. This was the genesis of a historical pattern of male travel within the African-American community. This economic catalyst for male travel also set the stage for the evolution of the country blues, an improvised musical form forged by southern black men wandering from town to town and from state to state. They moved—on foot or by freight train—carrying their banjos and guitars in search of work, or simply succumbing to the contagious wanderlust that was a by-product of emancipation. "Following emancipation," jazz writer Ben Sidran has observed,

freedom was equated with mobility, and thousands of Negroes took to the roads (establishing a pattern which was to become part of the black self-image in America). The traveling musician, who had taken on the role of truth-teller from the black Preacher, the role of trickster, or "bad nigger," from the Devil, became the ultimate symbol of freedom. Escape from the monotony and static hopelessness of black employment, combined with the potential for earning a living without having to rely on the white man—beating the white man at his own game, in other words—kept the musician's status high.[6]

Jazz musician and writer Julio Finn emphasizes the psychological meaning of travel within the lives of male blues musicians:

For the bluesman the road is a living being, a redoubtable character capable of heavenly sweetness and incredible cruelty. He tells it his problems, admonishes it for its caprices, cajoles it to treat him right, and complains to it when things go wrong. It is both a seductress who lures him back away from his loved ones and the fairy godmother who leads him back home.[7]

Like themes of sexuality, themes of travel in the blues reflected and gave expression to new social realities. However, unlike sexuality, which was so conspicuously absent in the music of slavery, travel could claim a solid place within black musical history. In a sense, it can be said that travel themes in the blues rearticulated the collective desire to escape bondage that pervaded the musical culture of slavery. Travel was one of the central organizing themes of the spirituals. Traveling liberators (as in "Go down, Moses / Way down in Egypt land / Tell old Pharaoh / To let my people go") and signposts for travel (as in "Follow the drinking gourd / And the old man is a-waiting / For to carry you to freedom / Follow the drinking gourd") are common subjects of the spirituals. Images of trains (as in "The gospel train is coming / Get on board, little children, get on board") and other traveling vehicles (as in "Swing low, sweet chariot / Coming for to carry me home") are also abundant in the spirituals. In his discussion of the agencies and models of transformation in the spirituals, black music scholar John Lovell, Jr., observes:

> Songs about trains are a minor miracle. The railroad train did not come into America until the late 1820s; it did not reach the slave country to any great extent until the 1830s and 1840s. Even then, the opportunities of the slave to examine trains closely were limited. Yet, before 1860, many spiritual poems exploited the train, its seductive sounds, speed and power, its recurring schedules, its ability to carry large numbers of passengers at cheap rates, its implicit democracy.[8]

In the spirituals, movement is rarely evoked simply to indicate territorial change. As Lovell insists, it is most often about structural transformation. Thus, images of rivers and oceans as sites of passage as well as "troubling" and cleansing can be found in spirituals such as "Wade in the

Water," which contains the line "God's gonna trouble the water." Spiritual and worldly desire are simultaneously inscribed in this religious music as compatible and noncontradictory. In the song "All God's Children Got Shoes (Wings)," the mundane requirements for walking away from slavery are situated in heaven:

I got shoes, you got shoes
All God's children got shoes
When I get to heaven
Gonna put on my shoes
Gonna walk all over God's heaven.[9]

This desire to travel is articulated within a Christian framework. When the blues extricated travel from the spirituals' religious context and rearticulated it as an overarching blues theme, representations of desire took on the dimensions of actuality. In the process, travel was individualized, secularized, and sexualized. Women's blues, recorded prolifically during the decade of the 1920s, brought a gendered perspective to this process.

Commenting on the blues, cultural critic Houston Baker has written:

Even as they speak of paralyzing absence and ineradicable desire, their instrumental rhythms suggest change, movement, action, continuance, unlimited and unending possibility. Like signification itself, blues are always nomadically wandering. Like the freight-hopping hobo, they are ever on the move, ceaselessly summing novel experience.[10]

The traveling blues man is a familiar image. But the traveling blues woman is not so familiar. Although travel was generally a distinctly male prerogative, there were some women who, because their lives were not primarily defined by their domestic duties, were as mobile as men. These women were among the first black performers in the embryonic black entertainment industry. They were members of minstrel troops and they performed in circuses and medicine shows. Gertrude "Ma" Rainey, who toured at the beginning of the century with the Georgia Smart Set, the Florida Cotton Blossoms, Shufflin' Sam from Alabam', and Tolliver's Circus and Musical Extravaganza, was destined to become the South's premier black entertainer. The most widely known company with which she toured, the Rabbit Foot Minstrels, often arranged its engagements to coincide with the harvests throughout the South:

> Sometimes the Rabbit Foot Minstrels followed the cotton harvest through Mississippi in the fall, spent the winter in Florida, and went back through the Carolinas in the spring; they traveled as far as the Georgia Sea Islands, Texas, Oklahoma, and even Mexico. . . .[11]

For Rainey and other black women who toured as entertainers from the turn of the century on, the interminable journeys around which they constructed their lives fundamentally challenged the normal social expectations surrounding female experience. These women disengaged themselves from the usual confines of domesticity. Although most of them did marry, few actually bore children and built families as the center of their lives. While women who operated in this tradition sometimes expressed regrets that they were unable to establish "normal" family lives—Bessie Smith and Billie Holiday, for example—there is often an emancipatory quality about their music that almost certainly would not have been present had their lives been fundamentally anchored in family pursuits.

As Rainey's career as a traveling entertainer brought a message confirming the end of slavery—like vast numbers of men, she was exercising the freedom to travel—her music also invited her female audience to glimpse for themselves the possibility of equaling their men in this new freedom of movement. Rainey's music presented women who did not have to acquiesce to men who set out on the road, leaving their female partners behind. The female characters in her songs also left home, and they often left their male partners behind. They were female subjects who were free of the new, postslavery fetters of domestic responsibilities and domestic service outside the home:

I'm running away tomorrow, they don't mean me no good
I'm running away tomorrow, they don't mean me no good
I'm gon' run away, have to leave this neighborhood.[12]

A perusal of some of Rainey's song titles suggests how much her music is permeated with travel: "Leaving This Morning,"[13] "Traveling Blues," "Walking Blues,"[14] and "Runaway Blues" (from which the above verse is taken).

Ma Rainey herself was apparently aware of the extent to which her music permitted her audience—especially the women who came out to see her—to partake vicariously of the experience of travel. During one phase of her career, she identified her favorite song as "Traveling Blues":[15]

Train's at the station, I heard the whistle blow
The train's at the station, I heard the whistle blow
I done bought my ticket and I don't know where I'll go

I went to the depot, looked up and down the board
I went to the depot, looked up and down the board
I asked the ticket agent, "Is my town on this road?"

The ticket agent said, "Woman, don't sit and cry."
The ticket agent said, "Woman, don't you sit and cry
The train blows at this station, but she keeps on passing by."

I hear my daddy calling some other woman's name
I hear my daddy calling some other woman's name
I know he don't need me, but I'm gonna answer just the same

I'm dangerous and blue, can't stay here no more
I'm dangerous and blue, can't stay here no more
Here come my train, folks, and I've got to go.[16]

When Ma Rainey sang this song, she dramatized the activity of travel, consciously attempting to evoke envy among members of her audience:

Baby, I came out on that stage, dressed down! I had on a hat and a coat and was carrying a suitcase. I put the suitcase down, real easy like, then stand there like I was thinking—just to let them see what I was about. Then I sing. You could just see them jigs wanting to go some place else.[17]

For women especially, the ability to travel implied a measure of autonomy, an ability to shun passivity and acquiescence in the face of mistreatment and injustice and to exercise some control over the circumstances of their lives, especially over their sexual lives. The railroad tracks were concrete evidence of something different, perhaps better, somewhere else. The protagonist of "Traveling Blues" does not know, in fact, where she is headed. Yet she has purchased her ticket and is certain of the fact that she has got to go wherever her travels may lead her. This song provides a powerful refutation of the blues cliché that "when a man gets the blues, he hops a train and rides, [but] when a woman gets the blues, she lays down and cries."[18]

The blues as a genre marked a point in African-American historical development when black communities seemed open to all sorts of new possibilities. It was a musical form whose implied celebration of exploration and transformation held a special meaning for African-American women. It offered them the possibility of challenging the social norms governing women's place within the community and within the society at large. Indeed, women also could embark upon the search for a more fulfilling, more creative life—not only for their people as a group, but for themselves as individuals. The subject who announces in "Runaway Blues" that "I'm running away tomorrow" also expresses the hope that "the sun's gonna shine someday in my backyard." In the meantime, rather than stabilize herself within a situation that involved domestic abuse—physical and emotional—she becomes a rebel, walking and wandering, unsure of what she seeks, but determined ultimately to find the sun. "Got my clothes in my hand, walk the streets all night."[19]

The project and destination of the woman in "Weeping Woman Blues" is less ambiguous: a journey leading to the southern natal land is undertaken in search of an absconding male lover:

Lord, this mean old engineer, cruel as he could be
This mean old engineer, cruel as he could be
Took my man away and blowed the smoke back at me

I'm going down South, won't be back 'til fall
I'm going down South, won't be back 'til fall
If I don't find my easy rider, ain't comin' back at all.[20]

"Weeping Woman Blues" is one of a series of songs in which the main characters embark on journeys in search of men who, for one reason or another, have abandoned them. Although the title of the song might lead one to believe that the posture assumed by the woman is one of dejection and resignation, the lyrics emphasize movement and agency rather than immobility and passivity. While most black women were powerless in face of an absconding male partner—who may have left in search of work or to flee responsibilities at home, or was simply lured by the temptations of the road—songs such as "Weeping Woman Blues" disrupted this common-sense notion of the stay-at-home woman.

Like Ma Rainey, Bessie Smith recorded a series of songs revolving around the theme of searching for an absconded lover, among which are "Lookin' for My Man Blues,"[21] "Frankie Blues,"[22] and "Mama's Got the Blues."[23] In the last song, the woman's response to the man who has abandoned her is a boastful proclamation that, in fact, she has nineteen other men: one in Alabama, three in Chattanooga, four in Cincinnati, five in Mississippi, and six in Memphis, Tennessee. Bragging about the accumulation of sexual partners in various cities and states was a posture often borrowed from male blues and adopted by the classic blues women. It attested to their extensive travels, and was a sign of their determination to redefine black womanhood as active, assertive, independent, and sexual.

Sandra Lieb considers "Walking Blues," performed and composed by Ma Rainey, to be "the finest expression of the wandering woman theme":[24]

Walked and walked 'til I, walked and walked 'til I almost lost my mind, hey,
    hey, hey
Walked and walked 'til I almost lost my mind
I'm afraid to stop walking, 'cause I might lose some time

> Got a short time to make it, short time to make it, and a long ways to go,
>   Lord, Lord, Lord
> Got a short time to make it, and a long ways to go
> Tryin' to find the town they call San Antonio.[25]

"Walking Blues," Lieb asserts, "shows indomitable will and strength rather than weepy self-pity." As she points out, "here, the reason for the break and the man's departure is not even mentioned, and the song describes the woman's monotonous, exhausting days on the road and her fruitless requests for information."[26] Still, there is an emancipatory quality about the woman's interminable walking. She is able to go out in pursuit of the object of her desire, an activity virtually inconceivable during previous eras of African-American history and beyond the realm of possibility for most black women of the time.

"Slow Driving Moan," with a few gender changes here and there, could easily be a male blues, based on the motif of the blues man's wanderlust. Ma Rainey's performance of this song, her own composition, renders it an explicit and powerful challenge to the prevailing notions of gender socialization:

> I've rambled 'til I'm tired, I'm not satisfied
> I've rambled 'til I'm tired, I'm not satisfied
> Don't find my sweet man, I gon' ramble 'til I die
> . . . .
> Oh, you've been feeling the same, I know our love is just the same
> And now you know mama'll be home some day, I'll hear you call my name
> I'm a common old rollin' stone, just got the blues for home sweet home.[27]

Usually, it is the man who leaves his woman in order to answer the call of the road. In this case, the woman becomes "the rolling stone," promising her man that she will eventually return home and settle down. The woman announces that she wishes to test the possibilities of freedom. In writing and singing "Slow Driving Moan," Ma Rainey performed an invaluable service for her female audience, raising them to new levels of consciousness about the unexplored realms of their own lives.

The experience of freedom is sought in the journey itself—it is mobility, autonomously constructed activity that brings with it a taste of liberation. There is no guarantee that the traveler will reach a satisfactory destination or that the process itself will not be painful. Although, contrary to popular belief, there is no all-consuming pessimism in the blues, blues consciousness also eschews the optimism so evident in the spirituals. "Lost Wandering Blues," another Rainey composition, provides a striking example of this nonteleological character of blues consciousness:

I'm leavin' this mornin' with my clothes in my hand
Lord, I'm leavin' this mornin' with my clothes in my hand
I won't stop movin' 'til I find my man

I'm standin' here wonderin' will a matchbox hold my clothes
Lord, I'm standin' here wonderin' will a matchbox hold my clothes
I got a trunk too big to be botherin' with on the road

I went up on the mountain, turned my face to the sky
Lord, I went up on the mountain, turned my face to the sky
I heard a whisper, said, "Mama, please don't die."

I turned around to give him my right han'
Lord, I turned around to give him my right han'
When I looked in his face, I was talking to my man

Lord, look-a yonder, people, my love has been refused
I said, look-a yonder, people, my love has been refused
That's the reason why mama's got the lost wandering blues.[28]

The lyrics of "Lost Wandering Blues" articulate a commitment to undertake an emotional journey, regardless of what the risks may be and despite the fact that the destination cannot be precisely conceptualized. The song announces a determination to explore all the myriad possibilities inherent in black women's new situation, regardless of the uncertainties and agonies that might be encountered. Here, religious enlightenment, sexual love, and psychological self-exploration are all intermingled. Initially, the goal of the journey is represented as "finding my man." However, the spiritual experiences and existential confrontations along the way affirm sexual desire without remaining imprisoned within it. The woman in this song may not have achieved clarity with respect to the goal she wishes to reach. Is she in search of self-understanding? Is she exploring the dilemmas created by the church's condemnation of sexual pleasure? Is she seeking a new social context within which she can function as a free and creative human being? All of these ends are possible, unarticulated motivations for her journey. What is absolutely clear, however, is that she is determined to keep on moving, to explore all the possibilities. Julio Finn's observations on the significance of the road for blues men may be applied equally to blues women: "To the bluesman the road may be likened to a song, the meaning of which becomes, spiritually speaking, the road within."[29]

Like most blues songs, Rainey's "Lost Wandering Blues" is an evocative, associative, and symbolic presentation rather than a sequential narrative. The imagery of the first stanza—"leavin' this mornin' with my clothes in my hand"—indicates an absolute rupture with the old conditions the protagonist is rejecting. This is reaffirmed in stronger terms in the second stanza, which transforms a recurring male blues image into one with a specifically female content. The evocation of the matchbox as baggage for the journey is often associated with impoverishment—the traveler does not possess more than will fit into a matchbox. Blind Lemon Jefferson's "Matchbox Blues," for example, contains this verse:

> I'm setting here wondering will a matchbox hold my clothes
> I'm setting here wondering will a matchbox hold my clothes
> I ain't got so many matches but I got so far to go.[30]

However, when Ma Rainey sings, "I got a trunk too big to be bothering with on the road," the matchbox emerges as a metaphor for the protagonist's conscious decision to strip herself down to the bare essentials, leaving behind everything that may have defined her place under former conditions. What once served as a sign of impoverishment and want becomes for

Rainey an emancipatory vehicle. In this sense, her use of this metaphor is similar in meaning to Leadbelly's matchbox in "Packing Trunk Blues," sung in the archaic AAA form:

> Sitting here wondering will a matchbox hold my clothes
> Sitting here wondering will a matchbox hold my clothes
> Sitting here wondering will a matchbox hold my clothes
>
> I don't want to be bothered with no suitcase on the road
> I don't want to be bothered with no suitcase on the road
> I don't want to be bothered with no suitcase on the road.[31]

Being a woman without roots and without ties meant something entirely different from being a man in a similar situation. In many ways, the African-American man of that era was compelled to take to the road— and he often developed an addiction to travel. Territorial mobility was a normal mode of male existence within the community of freed slaves. The woman who spent substantial periods of time on the road was exceptional and was no doubt compelled to question her own ability as a woman to sustain herself and to persevere, tormented as she must have been by the uncertainty of what lay ahead. "Lost Wandering Blues" evokes just such a moment of spiritual questioning: the protagonist ascends to a mountaintop, turns her attention to the heavens, and, it is implied, is racked by thoughts of death.

As is most often the case with the blues, no certain resolution is achieved in "Lost Wandering Blues." Nonetheless, this song furnishes an affirmation of the woman's determination to keep moving, to continue wandering, as "lost" as she may feel. Though her love has been refused, she herself refuses to move away from the new persona imparted to her by her journey. Sandra Lieb describes such songs as

> characterized by an emphasis on action rather than emotional excess. Less self-indulgent, the woman is in motion, on the streets instead of crying in her bed; she has left the house, moving away from solitary depression to activity in the world.[32]

Bessie Smith represents a new moment in black American history, reflecting the changed circumstances ushered in by the migration northward: the traveling themes in her songs often express either a longing to return home or a belief in the ultimate futility of wandering. There are, nonetheless, some songs that emphasize—like Rainey's "Lost Wandering Blues"—the process itself as potential salvation. "Sobbin' Hearted Blues," for example, evokes a woman who has been mistreated by her man and who takes to the road in hopes of emerging from her depression:

> I'm gon' start walkin' 'cause I got a wooden pair of shoes
> Gon' keep on walkin' 'til I lose these sobbin' hearted blues.[33]

A good number of Rainey's songs that evoke mobility and travel encourage black women to look toward "home" for consolation and inspiration. In these songs the activity of travel has a clear and precise goal. Travel is not synonymous with uncertainty and the unknown but rather is undertaken with the aim of bringing certainty and stability into the woman's life. "Home" is evocatively and metaphorically represented as the South, conceptualized as the territorial location of historical sites of resistance to white supremacy, aesthetically transformed into sites of resistance to male supremacy. "South Bound Blues," for example, explores the situation of a woman who has accompanied her man to the North, only to have him abandon her:

> Oh, you done me wrong, you throwed me down
> You caused me to weep and to moan
> I told him I'd see him, honey, some of these days
> And I'm going to tell him 'bout his low down dirty ways.

The woman's resistance is in returning home; in the concluding verse, she affirms and celebrates the voyage homeward, leaving unresolved the pleasure and pain of the return:

> Done bought my ticket, Lord, and my trunk is packed
> Goin' back to Georgia, folks, I sure ain't comin' back

My train's in the station, I done sent my folks the news
You can tell the world I've got those South bound blues.[34]

This song affirms African-American culture, rooted in the southern experience, as the source of black people's—and women's—creative energy and of their ability to defy the hardships visited upon them. As in virtually all of Gertrude Rainey's songs, the focal point is a sexual relationship, and the man in the relationship is evoked in an accusatory fashion. However, representations of pain suffered by women in their sexual relationships often also seem to be metaphorical allusions to pain caused by the material hindrances of sexism and racism. This blurring of the sexual and social runs parallel to the spirituals' blurring of the religious and the mundane. What is needed to survive, the song seems to imply, is the inspiration that comes from the knowledge that southern black culture recapitulates the resilience of Africans who survived the Middle Passage, the slavery awaiting them in this hemisphere, and the unleashed racism that followed emancipation. Women suffered not only as laborers, but also because of the sexual abuse of white men (and black men as well), the dismembering of families, forced breeding, and countless other forms of oppression. The actual return by train to Georgia described in "South Bound Blues" can be read as a spiritual identification with the black ethos of the South and the cumulative struggles black people have collectively waged over the centuries.

"South Bound Blues" voices the situation of black women who found themselves betrayed and mistreated by the men who had raised false hopes—men whom they had accompanied to an alien and hostile world. It encourages a spiritual identification with black southern culture, which produced a standard of womanhood based on self-reliance and independence. The song appeals to women to summon up within themselves the courage and independence of their foremothers. Movement backward into the African-American historical past becomes movement forward, progressive exploration.

"Bessemer Bound Blues" is another of Rainey's songs linking resistance to abusive treatment within a relationship to a return to the natal land. Bessemer, then a rural suburb of Birmingham, Alabama, is the destination of a woman who decides that experiencing the glitter of Chicago is not worth the trouble of being victimized by a mistreating man. Assertively informing her "papa" that "I won't be your dog no more," she announces the news that "mama's going home singin' those Bessemer Blues." During this era, the North still represented, in the eyes of most southern black people, palpable hope for a better life. But many who migrated north discovered that the bright lights of the city could not camouflage the poverty and alienation awaiting them. In women's blues the relationship gone sour in the North frequently serves as a way of articulating the frustrations, disappointments, and disillusionment black women suffered as a consequence of migration. The return to the South symbolizes a new measure of hope. As Rainey sings in "Bessemer Bound Blues":

> State Street's all right and lights shine nice and bright
> State Street's all right and lights shine nice and bright
> But I'd rather be in Bessemer reading by a candle light.[35]

In "Toad Frog Blues," the journey back to the South is a search for a harbor of refuge from the blues. The ubiquitous image of the train occurs in this song, again, like in the spiritual predecessors of the blues, as a symbol of hope and transformation:

> When you hear a frog croaking, you'll know they're cryin' for more rain
> When you hear a frog croaking, you'll know they're cryin' for more rain
> But when you hear me cryin', I'm cryin' because I can't ride a train
>
> . . . .
>
> If I don't lose these blues, I'll be in some undertaker's morgue
> If I don't lose these blues, I'll be in some undertaker's morgue
> I'm tired of eating one meal, hopping, too, just like a frog
>
> I can't get no higher, sure can't get no lower down
> I can't get no higher, sure can't get no lower down
> I got the toad frog blues and I'm sure Lordy Dixie bound.[36]

In Rainey's "Moonshine Blues," a woman whose partner has abandoned her turns to alcohol, proclaiming in a drunken stupor that she intends to head southward:

My head goes 'round and around, babe, since my daddy left town
I don't know if the river runnin' up or down
But there's one thing certain, it's mama's going to leave town

You'll find me wrigglin' and a-rockin', howlin' like a hound
Catch the first train that's runnin' South bound.[37]

Bessie Smith, who recorded this Rainey composition two and a half years before Rainey herself recorded it, had more experience with alcohol than Rainey.[38] Smith also had a broader grasp of the problems encountered by black women who migrated northward, since, as a native of Tennessee, she had decided to take up residence in Pennsylvania. Although Rainey spent much of her career on the road, she always maintained her residence in the South. The theme of disillusionment with the North is much more frequent in Smith's work than in that of her mentor. Smith's work resonated with the new experiences of black people in the urban North and her songs helped to forge for northern African-Americans a collective consciousness rooted in memories of the South but rearticulated with the northern black working-class experience. The forging of this consciousness was critically important as a buffer against the often traumatizing effects of the migration northward.

During slavery the North had been an enduring symbol of freedom and hope, frequently merged with visions of heaven in the spiritual music produced by slaves. The South, under the reign of an oppressive slaveocracy, was the geographic locus of black people's lifelong troubles, and site of the oppression from which millions of African Americans wished to escape — either home to Africa, a place also frequently merged with heaven in the spirituals, or to the promise of freedom in the North. The South did not change its symbolic geography after the Civil War, when black people were as impoverished as ever, and Jim Crow segregation brought murderous waves of racist terror. There was still all the reason in the world to bid the South goodbye, as Cow Cow Davenport insisted in his 1929 recording of the "Jim Crow Blues":

> I'm tired of this Jim Crow, gonna leave this Jim Crow town
> Doggone my black soul, I'm sweet Chicago bound
> Yes, I'm leavin' here, from this ole Jim Crow town
>
> I'm going up North, where they say—money grows on trees
> I don't give a doggone, if my black soul leaves
> I'm going where I don't need no BVDs.[39]

But, of course, money did not grow on northern trees, some of which, as in the South, even served as sites of lynching. Migrant black working people frequently discovered that times were harder in the North than in the southern towns and countryside they had left behind.

Conspicuously absent in the North were the cultural unity and extended family-support systems they had known in the South, by means of which they had succeeded in humanizing their environment. As the socioeconomic realities of the North shattered black immigrants' illusions, the historical meaning accorded the South was reconfigured and became associated with release from the traumas of migration. In expressing his optimistic ideas about life up North, Cow Cow Davenport did not fail to acknowledge that he might encounter disappointments that would motivate him to return to his southern homeland:

> Lord well, if I get up there—where they don't suit—
> I don't start no crying. Go tell that ole ma'am of mine
> Lord, I'm ready to come back to my Jim Crow town.[40]

"Far Away Blues," a duet Bessie Smith sang with Clara Smith in what is unfortunately one of her least successful recordings, expresses unmitigated disenchantment with the North—even to the point of predicting death from loneliness:

We left our southern home and wandered north to roam
Like birds, went seekin' a brand new field of corn
We don't know why we are here
But we're up here just the same
And we are just the lonesomest girls that's ever born.

The song concludes with these two lines:

Oh, there'll come a day when from us you'll hear no news
Then you will know that we have died from those lonesome far away
  blues.[41]

Bessie Smith's "Louisiana Low Down Blues" is, like "Far Away Blues,"
one of those rare instances in which allusions to personal relationships are
absent. It draws upon traditional imagery associated with the spirituals, yet
in an appropriately inverted fashion:

Lou'siana, Lou'siana, mama's got the low down blues
Lou'siana, Lou'siana, mama's goin' on a cruise

Tonight when I start walkin', although the road is hard
I'm gonna keep on walkin' 'til I get in my own backyard

Mississippi River, Mississippi River, I know it's deep and wide
Mississippi River, I know it's deep and wide
Won't be satisfied 'til I get on the other side

Gon' to keep on trampin', gon' keep on trampin' 'til I get on solid ground
Gonna keep on trampin' 'til I get on solid ground
On my way to Dixie, Lord, I'm Lou'siana bound

Got a low down feelin', a low down feelin', I can't lose my heavy load
Got a low down feelin', I can't lose my heavy load
My home ain't up North, it's further down the road.[42]

The imagery reminiscent of the religious slave songs is that of flight—ships, interminable walking and crossing rivers "deep and wide," on whose opposite shores freedom awaits. But whereas the freedom-seeking voyages of the spirituals point to northern destinations, "Louisiana Low Down Blues" tells of the return home to the South.

"Dixie Flyer Blues" restates the central phrase of "Louisiana Low Down Blues." The concluding line of the latter song, "My home ain't up North, it's further down the road," becomes part of the opening stanza of the former: "'Cause my home ain't here, it's a long way down the road." Like "Louisiana Low Down Blues," "Dixie Flyer Blues" avoids any reference at all to a personal relationship, concentrating instead on the theme of homecoming. In a rare allusion to family life, the woman of this song announces that she is returning to her mother:

> Here's my ticket, take it, please, conductorman.
> Here's my ticket, take it, please, conductorman.
> Goin' to my mammy way down in Dixieland.[43]

Bessie Smith performs this song with gusto, joyously celebrating the decision to leave the North behind—"wouldn't stay up North to save nobody's doggone soul"—and return to "Dixieland . . . the grandest place on earth."

The segregated conditions under which the journey home would be made were evoked in a song by Bessie Smith's rival, Clara Smith. "L. & N. Blues" explicitly calls attention to the racist policies of the South even as it praises the traveling woman. The Jim Crow policies of the railroad companies, as the last verse asserts, send black people into the segregated coaches as soon as they cross the Mason-Dixon line:

> I'm a ramblin' woman, I've got a ramblin' mind
> I'm a ramblin' woman, I've got a ramblin' mind
> I'm gonna buy me a ticket and ease on down the line
>
> Mason-Dixon line is down where the South begins
> Mason-Dixon line is down where the South begins
> Gonna leave a Pullman and ride the L. & N.[44]

Edward Brooks expresses astonishment that Bessie Smith would record a popular tune called "Muddy Water," another song of nostalgia for the South, whose lyrics seem to romanticize and thus trivialize the disastrous Mississippi floods:

> The lyrics of "Muddy Water (A Mississippi Moan)" . . . express nostalgia for an idealised South which would cause little serious objection if they did not also sentimentalise the recurrent Mississippi floods. Bessie presumably still had little control over her recording material[,] otherwise it is hard to explain why, having dealt with the theme sincerely in "Backwater Blues," a fortnight earlier, she now risks casting doubt upon this sincerity by entertaining such ludicrous, Tin Pan Alley words.[45]

These are the lyrics to which he refers:

> Dixie moonlight, Swanee shore
> Headin' homebound just once more
> To my Mississippi Delta home
>
> Southland has got grand garden spots
> Whether you believe it or not
> I hear those trees a-whispering, "Come on back to me."
>
> Muddy water 'round my feet
> Muddy water in the street
> Just God's own shelter
> Down on the Delta
> Muddy water in my shoes
> Reelin' and rockin' to them low down blues
>
> They live in ease and comfort down there, I do declare
> Been away a year today to wander and roam
> I don't care, it's muddy there
> But, see, it's my home

Got my toes turned Dixie way
'Round the Delta let me lay
My heart cries out for muddy water.[46]

These lyrics certainly reflect the banality of Tin Pan Alley assembly-line musical products and, as a written text, hardly measure up to the poetry of blues lyrics. A patchwork of discordant imagery, reflecting the South of white aristocrats with their "grand garden spots" and the home of working-class black people "reelin' and rockin' to them low down blues," "Muddy Water" appears to have been thrown together without any sensitivity to real social relations—racial and class—of the South. The most conspicuous example of this is the phrase—which was probably entirely unintentional—"I hear those trees a-whispering, 'Come on back to me.'" Although the literal reference is to the "grand garden spots," how many black people could listen to this evocation of whispering trees without being reminded of the thousands of lynchings in which trees became instruments of terror?

Why would Bessie Smith record such a song? Chris Albertson challenges critics' explanation for the recording session during which this song was produced—which consisted exclusively of popular songs, including "Alexander's Ragtime Band" by Irving Berlin—as an attempt to revitalize her popularity by recording "commercial" material. Brooks is probably right in pointing to her lack of control over this material. Albertson notes that during the time this session took place, Smith was appearing at the Lincoln Theater in Harlem in a show that was advertised as "Bessie Smith and Her Yellow Girl Revue." Albertson suggests that she probably had nothing to do with the production and billing of the show, because "she had always expressed monumental disdain for light-complexioned women."[47] What Albertson fails to indicate here is that it would not have been merely a question of prejudice on Smith's part. In fact, during that period, light-skinned showgirls were the only ones given work in most of Harlem's clubs and theaters.

It is interesting that the instrumentalists for this recording session were some of the most brilliant jazz musicians of the era—Fletcher Henderson, Joe Smith, and Coleman Hawkins. Albertson is quite correct in pointing out that, working with these musicians, Smith's "treatment of these songs offers delightful evidence of her talent for turning banal material into something special."[48] Moreover, because the first master of "Muddy Water" was damaged, Columbia later released the second take under the same record number. In the second take Smith adopts a very different mood toward her material, one which is more contemplative and complicated—as if she is summoning her audience toward a critical reading of the lyrics. In this Tin Pan Alley song whose lyrics create a minstrel-like caricature of the blues theme of the return home, Smith's performance foreshadows the transformative work that Billie Holiday, drawing virtually all of her material from Tin Pan Alley, would later undertake.

Blues scholar Paul Oliver described Bessie Smith's art in relationship to the great migrations in these terms:

> This was a period of great social change for the Negro and to a certain extent her art symbolized it. Attracted by the prosperity enjoyed by their brothers who had already moved into the northern industrial centres, streams of Negroes from the South continued to pour into Cleveland, Detroit, Chicago and Gary. Retaining some indications of their southern origins and habits, yet trying to assume a new way of life in a strange environment, they aggravated the housing problem and were the unintentional cause of many interracial and biracial disturbances. Many were homesick, unaccustomed to the teeming cities, the accelerated pace of living and the extreme climate. When they heard that Bessie Smith was in town, a singer who sang the blues and songs of their southern homeland but who was a part of the urban scene in the Negro North, they flocked to hear her.[49]

While nostalgia certainly figured in Bessie Smith's evocations of the South, and while vast numbers of the newly immigrant black population in the North were no doubt homesick for the South they had left behind, the celebrated blues artist did much more than cater to a wistful yearning for home. She assisted in the creation of a new consciousness of African-American identity, a consciousness that was critical of the experiences of exploitation, alienation—and for women, male dominance—in the North, which had been the focus of black people's hopes and dreams since the earliest days of slavery. Her songs, more than those of any other blues performer of the era, constructed aesthetic bridges linking places and time and permitting a collective *prise de conscience* encompassing both the unity and the hetereogeneity of the black experience.

BLAME IT
ON THE BLUES

BESSIE SMITH, GERTRUDE "MA" RAINEY,

AND THE POLITICS OF BLUES PROTEST

Can't blame my mother, can't blame my dad
Can't blame my brother for the trouble I've had
Can't blame my lover that held my hand
Can't blame my husband, can't blame my man
Can't blame nobody, guess I'll have to blame it on the blues.

— "BLAME IT ON THE BLUES"[1]

The lyrics of women's blues, as interpreted in the recorded performances of the classic blues singers, explore frustrations associated with love and sexuality and emphasize the simultaneously individual and collective nature of personal relationships. Sexuality is not privatized in the blues. Rather, it is represented as shared experience that is socially produced. This intermingling of the private and public, the personal and political, is present in the many thousands of blues songs about abandonment, disloyalty, and cruelty, as well as those that give expression to sexual desire and love's hopefulness. There is also a significant number of women's blues songs on work, jail, prostitution, natural disasters, and other issues that, when taken together, constitute a patchwork social history of black Americans during the decades following emancipation. Most often such themes are intertwined with themes of love and sexuality.

Bessie Smith recorded numerous songs invoking problems emanating from racism and economic injustice—crime, incarceration, alcoholism, homelessness, and the seemingly insurmountable impoverishment of the black community. In this sense, she further developed the legacy of Gertrude Rainey, whose socially oriented music constituted an aesthetically mediated community-building and assisted in developing a specifically African-American social consciousness. Rainey's work was inextricably linked to the experiences of black southerners, the vast majority of whom were still tied to agrarian life. Smith's art, while obviously rooted in black rural culture, also reflected the new historical experiences of the urban immigrant communities of the North.

The tendency among blues scholars and critics—evident, for example, in the work of Samuel Charters—has been to argue that the blues form, which demands an intensely personal perspective on the part of the composer or performer, is rarely compatible with social commentary or political protest. In his often-quoted 1963 study, *The Poetry of the Blues,* Charters writes:

> There is little social protest in the blues. There is often a note of anger and frustration; sometimes the poverty and the rootlessness in which the singer has lived his life is evident in a word or a phrase, but there is little open protest at the social conditions under which a Negro in the United States is forced to live. There is complaint, but protest has been stifled. . . .
>
> It is almost impossible for the white American to realize how tightly he has united against his black fellow citizens. The oppressive weight of prejudice is so constricting that it is not surprising to find little protest in the blues. It is surprising to find even an indirect protest.[2]

Charters's argument fails to consider the interpretive audience to which the blues is addressed, and treats potential protest as necessarily constructed in terms established by an imagined white oppressor. Like so many white scholars in the early 1960s who attempted to define their work as antiracist, Charters displays here notions of black subjectivity that reek of paternalism.

Paul Oliver develops an argument to explain the putative lack of protest themes in the blues. He peremptorily announces that black people are nothing more than the product of their material circumstances:

That the number of protest blues is small is in part the result of the Negro's acceptance of the stereotypes that have been cut for him. In rural areas where education is meagre and the coloured people have known no better environment, there is little with which to compare their mode of life. They are primarily concerned with the business of living from day to day, of "getting along" with the Whites, of conforming and making the best of their circumstances. As surely as the Southern White intends them to "keep their place" the majority of Negroes are prepared to accept it. They know that they cannot change the world but that they have to live in it. An apathy develops which the racial leaders find exasperatingly hard to break, and even when aggravation reaches the point where the spirit of revolt against the system arises, this is often soon dissolved in minor personal disruptions and eventual disregard.[3]

I am primarily concerned with Oliver's claim that a dimension of protest is rarely discovered in the blues, but the temptation to comment on his attitude toward the "masses" of southern black people at the beginning of the civil rights era is too great to resist. Oliver is British and considers himself culturally removed from the blues and its originators, but there is no excuse for representing southern black people as necessarily apathetic or any less politically mature than any other people. Such a position is especially offensive considering the fact that the era during which he wrote this book—the years following the Montgomery bus boycott—was the beginning of one of the most influential social movements in modern world history. It was precisely these black people whom Oliver characterizes as being more concerned with getting along with white people than with challenging the system who initiated revolutionary changes in the racist social structure of the United States.

In order to contest Charters's and Oliver's arguments that the blues lack a dimension of social protest, I use the recorded performances of Gertrude

Rainey and Bessie Smith in two ways. First, I will argue that, even when using these blues scholars' notions of what constitutes protest conscious-ness, such a consciousness is an integral part of the blues. I also argue that the inflexibility with which they define both what constitutes protest and what constitutes acquiescence prevents them from looking more deeply at the blues imagination. Central to both moments of my interpretation of women's blues as protest is the recognition that such earlier investigations of the blues as Charters's and Oliver's symptomatically fail to address the reign of male dominance as worthy of social protest. This failure is also true of more recent studies, which tend to treat women's blues as a marginal phenomenon. Even in Paul Garon's excellent study *Blues and the Poetic Spirit*, which highlights psychoanalytic analyses of desire, he considers only a handful of women blues singers. However, it should be pointed out that following a section of his study which furnishes examples of male supremacy in men's blues, Garon includes an extremely provocative, albeit short, section entitled "Liberation of Women." Quoting lyrics of songs recorded by such blues women as Ida Cox, Victoria Spivey, Sara Martin, and Memphis Minnie (but interestingly none by Ma Rainey or Bessie Smith), Garon argues:

> If there is implicit in the blues a "feminist" critique of society, linked to this is a broader critique of repressive civilisation, based not on any sex-specificity, nor even on the peculiar position of the black in American culture, although this characteristic is very likely the major force from which blues draws its unique perspective as well as its specific form. . . .[4]

Evaluations of the works of the classic blues singers must unfortunately be based largely on their recordings. They were, of course, primarily live performers, who relied on their records to attract audiences to their shows. Yet because no recordings exist of their live performances, we can only speculate—except in the few instances where we have firsthand accounts —about the full impact of those performances. Moreover, the material recorded by blues singers during the twenties was subject to the veto power of white record producers. In some rare instances the head of a company's "race" section was black, but his superior was certainly white. Paul Oliver observes that "amongst the record companies, precautions were generally taken to ensure that material likely to cause embarrassment and possible distress was rejected."[5] According to music critic Carman Moore, Bessie Smith sang a song during her live performances which included this verse:

All my life I've been making it
All my life white folks have been taking it.[6]

If indeed she sang this song, it may have remained unrecorded thanks to the censorship powers of Frank Walker, who headed Columbia's race records division. "In view of her forcible character," observes Edward Brooks,

it is, on the surface, strange that Bessie should always be so careful to avoid direct criticism of whites on record, but presumably the white shareholding [sic] and management of Columbia Records, the only company she recorded for, was responsible; significantly, her stage shows in which Albertson says she frequently alluded to the subject [sleeve notes to the 1970s reissues] were produced by Blacks in theatres owned by Blacks.[7]

More than a decade after the height of the classic blues era, Billie Holiday was unable to convince Columbia, which held her under contract, to permit her to record "Strange Fruit." They were unwilling to face the negative responses—particularly from white southerners—that inevitably would be provoked by the overtly antiracist content of her song. Eventually, Commodore Records, a new independent label whose management was far more audacious than Columbia's, agreed to record her powerful antilynching anthem.[8]

Anyone familiar with the 160 songs that comprise the extant work of Bessie Smith would unhesitatingly refer to "Poor Man's Blues" if asked about the role of social protest in her repertoire. In the same way, "Strange Fruit" has come to stand for social protest in Billie Holiday's work. Like "Strange Fruit," "Poor Man's Blues" has been viewed as an anomaly. How-

ever, this has as much to do with the definitions of social protest music as
with the explicitly racial and class evocations in the lyrics of the two songs.
"Poor Man's Blues" was composed by Bessie Smith and recorded in 1928.
Chris Albertson calls it "a poignant song of social protest" and designates it
as "Black Man's Blues." As critics would later define Billie Holiday as "apolitical," Albertson implies that Smith "had no interest in politics,"[9] that, in
other words, she was not capable of thinking about class relations—lines of
demarcation between rich and poor—but only about race relations—those
between white and black. However, the words of "Poor Man's Blues" refute
this narrative of Smith's political apathy.

> Mister rich man, rich man, open up your heart and mind
> Mister rich man, rich man, open up your heart and mind
> Give the poor man a chance, help stop these hard, hard times
>
> While you're livin' in your mansion, you don't know what hard times
>   means
> While you're livin' in your mansion, you don't know what hard times
>   means
> Poor working man's wife is starvin', your wife's livin' like a queen
>
> Please, listen to my pleading, 'cause I can't stand these hard times long
> Oh, listen to my pleading, can't stand these hard times long
> They'll make an honest man do things that you know is wrong
>
> Poor man fought all the battles, poor man would fight again today
> Poor man fought all the battles, poor man would fight again today
> He would do anything you ask him in the name of the U.S.A.
>
> Now the war is over, poor man must live the same as you
> Now the war is over, poor man must live the same as you
> If it wasn't for the poor man, mister rich man, what would you do?[10]

This song was recorded a year before the stock market crash ushered in
the era of the Great Depression. Its historical reference is to the post–

World War I period, when black people found themselves caught up in a web of painful economic circumstances that foreshadowed the Depression. In this song there is a sophisticated combination of realism, humor, and irony, with which Smith creates a complex portrait of class and race relations. "Poor Man's Blues" openly indicts the wealthy classes for the prevailing poverty—and not only in the black community—highlighting the extent to which their luxurious lifestyle renders them blind to the economic injustice they themselves have created. When Smith sings of the desperation that inevitably accompanies "hard times," she passionately explains the social roots of crime: "They'll make an honest man do things that you know is wrong." The stanza referring to the role played by poor men as combatants during World War I is an accurate observation on the working-class background of the frontline soldiers in virtually all wars conducted by the United States. The complexity of the statement "He would do anything you ask him in the name of the U.S.A." points to both gullibility and serious commitment, and she sings it with the appropriate irony. There are many reasons black people and working people of other ethnic backgrounds would take seriously the quest for freedom and democracy. After all, black people fought in the American Revolution, in the Civil War, and not only served as combatants in the two world wars, but militantly challenged the racist discrimination practiced by the military establishment as well. But Bessie Smith's voice also delivers a humorous critique of the superpatriotic stance assumed by some black and poor people.

According to prevailing notions of protest music, "Poor Man's Blues" can be seen as a venerable but forgotten ancestor of the social protest genre in black popular music. Its impassioned denunciation of injustice would be repeated time and time again across the continuum of black music—in blues, in jazz, in rhythm and blues, in funk, and in rap. This pioneering song established social protest themes as legitimate content for African-American popular music. The historical role of "Poor Man's Blues" obviously discredits arguments alleging the absence of protest in the blues, and in particular in the classic blues. But we need to go much further than this in our analysis. As is true of any artist's oeuvre, Bessie Smith's recorded legacy should not be interpreted simplistically as the mere sum of its parts.

It is true that "Poor Man's Blues" is strikingly different from most of her other songs. Precisely because it seems so dissimilar in its uncamouflaged social analysis and protest, the entire body of Bessie Smith's work needs to be reexamined with an eye to uncovering its social content and its political dimension of protest.

As explicit social protest, "Poor Man's Blues" does not stand entirely alone. Another twelve-bar blues recorded in August 1928—during the same session as "Poor Man's Blues"—also provides scathing social commentary in the traditional sense. In "Washwoman's Blues," Bessie Smith sang with stark simplicity about the economic conditions of many African-American women.[11] Her heartfelt presentation reveals the extent to which she identified with the countless numbers of black women for whom domestic service was the only available occupation. "Poor Man's Blues" can be taken literally as a song about poor men. Similarly, "Washwoman's Blues" is a song about poor women. Contrary to the employment trends for white women during the first decades of the twentieth century, most black women did work for a living. And the overwhelming majority of black working women cooked, cleaned house, did the laundry, or engaged in some other form of domestic service for well-off white people.

The first and second stanzas of "Washwoman" describe the stultifying impact of the labor to which so many black women were condemned. It was, in effect, slavery reincarnated:

All day long I'm slavin', all day long I'm bustin' suds
All day long I'm slavin', all day long I'm bustin' suds
Gee, my hands are tired, washin' out these dirty duds

Lord, I do more work than forty-'leven Gold Dust Twins
Lord, I do more work than forty-'leven Gold Dust Twins
Got myself a achin' from my head down to my shins.

After evoking the "Gold Dust Twins," a reference to a brand of washing powder during that period that was packaged in a box bearing the picture of two pickaninnies, the third stanza states the economic necessity that drove so many black women into domestic service:

Sorry I do washin' just to make my livelihood
Sorry I do washin' just to make my livelihood
Oh, the washwoman's life, it ain't a bit of good.[12]

Edward Brooks treats this song as a "mild social protest against the type of work blacks are forced into."[13] Brooks's comprehensive study, *The Bessie Smith Companion*, is largely concerned with analyzing her musical technique in conjunction with the instrumental accompaniment of each recording session, but some of his comments are revealing, because they typify conventional misconceptions both about the blues and about what constitutes "protest" in the blues. Criticizing the lyrics written by Spencer Williams, Brooks characterizes the song as "one of his less successful efforts."

The lyrics are jejune and lack authenticity with their use of such cultural anachronisms as "duds," "livelihood" and the archaic "scullion." As has been mentioned before, it is unusual for Bessie to use her songs as vehicles for social protest and here in the fourth chorus, the already innocuous remonstration is further weakened by sycophantic gestures towards those against whom it should be directed:

Rather be a scullion,
cooking in some white folks yard; (twice)
I could eat up (sic) plenty,
wouldn't have to work so hard.[14]

Brooks's critique is problematic because of its analysis of the "protest" as unsuccessful. He does not address Smith's performance except to comment on the seriousness with which she treats the material. For example, in reference to a series of bizarre chuckling notes emanating from the reed section after the third verse quoted above, he makes the following observation:

Whilst Bessie . . . generally makes sober observations upon the disagreeable life of a drudge, the reeds take an unsympathetically

Olympian view, the most offensive expression of which is the jeer-
ing "laugh" at the end of the third chorus.[15]

Brooks moves from an analysis of the language in the lyrics of "Washwoman's Blues," which he regards as anachronistic and "inauthentic," to a
much too literal and thus rather shallow reading of the content, which he
thinks is violated by the instrumentals. He attempts none of the historical
contextualization which is at the center of his reading of "Poor Man's
Blues." It is as if the evocation of black women's work is not even worth the
trouble of a discussion that connects this song with the historical conditions that were specific to women. Moreover, his characterization of the
song as consisting of "innocuous remonstrations" and "sycophantic gestures" ignores the importance of indirection, irony, and humor in the
blues.

The literal, semantic level of blues lyrics is often an invitation to mis-
reading. When the washwoman in the song declares that she would rather
be a scullion, these words do not affirm how welcome a cook's job would
be to a black washwoman. Instead, there is equivocation in these words, a
light and scathing irony—a hint of protest. The washwoman is saying that
her occupational possibilities are so restricted that the only other jobs available to her would also require her to be a servant. Her expressed desire to
work in "Mr. Charlie's" kitchen is reminiscent of the prison work song in
which the convict sings:

My buddy got a hundred years, I got ninety-nine
Wasn't I lucky when I got my time?[16]

In both instances, we hear veiled protest of the social conditions that create
such objective impasses in the lives of black people.

Brooks's claim about the instrumental phrase after the third verse is
equally misguided. There are ways of interpreting it that do not require us
to hear the laughter of the reeds as dismissive or demeaning of the washwoman's problems. His analysis fails to pose a key question: Who, indeed,
is laughing at this poor woman? Is it her sisters, most of whom share

the same plight? Is it her brothers, who often depend upon the pittance she brings in from such work as the only hope of the family's survival? Or is there another presence in this song? The taunting instrumental response mimics the ridicule directed toward the washwoman by her white employer and, in a larger sense, by the racist society. In that case, who, we must ask in this interpretation, is the trickster, and who is made the fool?

It is important to register what is not included in Brooks's analysis. Like "Poor Man's Blues," "Washwoman's Blues" reveals that blues do not always require an individual narrator who shares his or her personal experiences—that "the personal" can also be conveyed through "the social." Smith's recording of "Washwoman" also provides us with an example of the way she and other blues women addressed gendered social issues that were rarely, if ever, formally acknowledged elsewhere.

The absence of what Charters and Oliver would call "direct social protest" in blues songs can be explained without denying their powerful political content. "Protest" implies the existence of formal political channels through which dissent can be collectively expressed. In this context "protest" would suggest some strategic goal such as bringing black women domestic workers into organized trade unions. But such a historical possibility did not exist at the time.[17] "Protest," when expressed through aesthetic forms, is rarely a direct call to action. Nevertheless, critical aesthetic representation of a social problem must be understood as constituting powerful social and political acts. Samuel Charters might interpret such representation as "complaint," but public articulation of complaint—of which there are many instances in the blues—must be seen as a form of contestation of oppressive conditions, even when it lacks a dimension of organized political protest. "Washwoman's Blues" does not conclude with a call for the unionization of domestic work, but rather with a restatement of the worker's misery:

> Me and my ole washboard sho' do have some cares and woes
> Me and my ole washboard sho' do have some cares and woes
> In the muddy water, wringin' out these dirty clothes.[18]

"Washwoman's Blues," in my opinion, is a powerfully moving tribute to the countless numbers of African-American women whose toiling hands released their more prosperous white sisters from the drudgery of domestic work. During slavery, black women worked in the cotton fields alongside their men, performed their own domestic chores, and many of them were also charged with the responsibility of keeping the big house in order— preparing the meals, washing the clothes, scrubbing the floors. During the postslavery decades, the paid work most available to black women— the work that in fact was reserved for them—was housecleaning, child care, cooking, and clothes-washing. Until the late 1950s the majority of African-American women who worked outside their homes were maids and washerwomen.[19] Bessie Smith's rendition of "Washwoman's Blues" simultaneously memorializes these millions of women and issues a cry of condemnation against the conditions under which they have worked, as well as against the society that restricts them to this type of work.

"Poor Man's Blues" and "Washwoman's Blues" are only the most liter-ally explicit of the vast body of blues songs that name and explore oppres-sive social conditions defining life in the black community. A recurring theme in both female and male blues is imprisonment. Bessie Smith re-corded numerous songs on this theme: "Jail House Blues,"[20] "Work House Blues,"[21] "Sing Sing Prison Blues,"[22] "Send Me to the 'Lectric Chair."[23] But it is Ma Rainey's "Chain Gang Blues" that most incisively and realisti-cally addresses this omnipresent fact of life in the black community:

> The judge found me guilty, the clerk he wrote it down
> The judge found me guilty, the clerk he wrote it down
> Just a poor gal in trouble, I know I'm county road bound
>
> Many days of sorrow, many nights of woe
> Many days of sorrow, many nights of woe
> And a ball and chain, everywhere I go
>
> Chains on my feet, padlock on my hand
> Chains on my feet, padlock on my hand
> It's all on account of stealing a woman's man

It was early this mornin' that I had my trial
It was early this mornin' that I had my trial
Ninety days on the county road and the judge didn't even smile.[24]

Sandra Lieb points out that the lead sheet for this song contains a penultimate verse which was omitted in the recording:

Ain't robbed no train, ain't done no hanging crime
Ain't robbed no train, ain't done no hanging crime
But the judge said I'd be on the county road a long, long time.

As Lieb indicates, "the woman's crime was clearly minor."[25] But obviously
the point of the song is not her guilt or innocence but the experience of the
chain gang and the convict lease system, from which black women were
not exempt by virtue of their gender.

The convict lease system carried over the relations of slave labor into
the era of emancipation. Shortly after the Hayes-Rutherford Compromise
of 1877, which terminated the exciting transformations of Radical Reconstruction, southern states legislated the Black Codes, simultaneously
institutionalizing peonage and convict leasing. In 1878, Georgia's system
leased out 1,124 black people and 115 whites, charging an average of
$25,000 each.[26] Over forty years later, during the era of the classic blues,
this system seemed to be even more brutal than slavery. In a pamphlet
issued by the American Civil Liberties Union in 1921, William Pickens
described Georgia's convict labor system:

It can be readily understood why this system is so much more
vicious than was the old slave system. In a regular slave system, the
owner might have such selfish interest in the slave as any man may
have in the preservation of valuable property. But in the convict
lease system of Georgia, it is to the landlord's advantage to put the
least into the Negro and get the most out of him whom he owns for
a limited time only.[27]

The discourse of slavery had bestialized black labor, allowing for the assignment of women and men to work without regard to the gendered division of labor operative in the larger society.[28] This practice was carried over to the convict lease system:

> It is one of the greatest horrors of our history that colored women have been thus farmed out to work and live in stockades under the absolute control of brutal men. The multiple lynchings in Brooks and Lowndes Counties, Georgia, which were caused by this system in May, 1918, are among the most savage of such occurrences. The unspeakable vivisection of Mary Turner, a colored woman whose baby was to be born about four weeks later, was one in this carnival.[29]

Black people throughout the South who listened to Rainey perform "Chain Gang Blues," and who were all too familiar with the chain gang and convict lease systems, likely would have interpreted this song as a deeply felt protest aimed at the racism and sexism of the criminal justice system.

"Ma and Pa Poorhouse Blues," recorded by Ma Rainey and Papa Charlie Jackson in 1928, employs the broad humor associated with vaudeville routines to evoke the experience of poverty and the possibility of another form of incarceration—in the poorhouse. Despite the levity of their presentation, there could have been no doubt about the seriousness of this subject in the minds of Rainey's southern black audiences. The song opens with a comic dialogue spoken by the two performers, each relating their respective woes—Charlie has been forced to pawn his banjo and Ma's touring bus has been stolen. Each one informs the other that she or he is broke. When Charlie asks what they should do, Ma answers, "Let's both go to the poorhouse together."

> *Rainey:* Too bad, too bad, too bad, too bad, too bad
> Too bad, too bad, too bad, too bad, too bad
> I've lost all my money, lost everything I had

Jackson: Ma, being broke's all right when you know you got some more
money comin' in
Ah, being broke's all right when you know you got some more
money comin' in
But when you lose your money, that's when friendship ends

Rainey: Oh, here I'm on my knees
Pa, here I am, on my knees
I want the whole world to know mama's broke and can't be pleased

Jackson: When you had lots of money, you had plenty friends
Rainey: Lord, lost all my money, that was my end, oh, ain't got no money
now
Both: We better go to the poorhouse, and try to live anyhow
We better go to the poorhouse, and try to live anyhow.[30]

This is certainly an instance of laughing to keep from crying, an aesthetic strategy black people learned to use in the work songs of the slave era, which have continued to be sung in the prison work camps. Interwoven in the broad comedy of this piece is an all-important message about the perseverance and survival of the community. The key is togetherness and solidarity: "Let's both go to the poorhouse together. . . . We better go to the poorhouse, try to live anyhow."

One unavoidable consequence of poverty is the inability to meet the incessant demands of the landlord. "House Rent Blues," recorded by Bessie Smith, poignantly evokes this common dilemma. In the first two stanzas she conjures up the stark reality of impending homelessness, rendered even more dreadful by the fact that it is "on a cold dark and stormy night" that an eviction notice is nailed on her door. The last stanza sums up the situation:

Lordy, what a feelin', rent man comes a-creepin', in my bed a-sleepin'
He left me with those house rent blues.[31]

Again, social experiences rooted in the historical oppression of the African-American community are interwoven with experiences of sexuality—also inflected by collective oppression. The evicted protagonist in "House Rent Blues" appeals to a lover to oust his woman so that she herself may find shelter:

> See me comin', put your woman outdoors
> See me comin', put your woman outdoors
> You know I ain't no stranger, and I been here before.[32]

Here, as in blues discourse generally, the personal relationship stands both for itself and for unrealizable social aspirations and failed dreams. The blues as aesthetic form and practice must be understood as a means of testifying to and registering the lack of real, objectively attainable possibilities of social transformation. In this song the protagonist is willing to inflict her predicament on another woman as a means of saving herself from homelessness. Nevertheless, there is a dimension of protest here. The symbolic economy of the blues refutes and simply refuses to be subject to the symbolic economy governing mainstream American popular forms.

In other songs, the intrusion of the landlord, demanding his rent payments, complicates an already existing set of depressing sexual circumstances. In "I'm Down in the Dumps," Bessie Smith sings of having been abandoned by her lover. She goes on to inform us that:

> Someone knocked on my do' last night when I was sleep
> I thought it was that sweet man of mine making his 'fore day creep
> 'Twas nothin' but my landlord, a great big chump
> Stay 'way from my door, Mr. Landlord, 'cause I'm down in the dumps.[33]

And in "Baby, Won't You Please Come Home," the woman making this appeal wants her lover back because, among other reasons, she needs money to pay the rent:

> Landlord's gettin' worse
> I got to move May first
> Baby, won't you please come home, I need money
> Baby, won't you please come home.[34]

The blues idiom requires absolute honesty in the portrayal of black life. It is an idiom that does not recognize taboos: whatever figures into the larger picture of working-class African-American realities—however morally repugnant it may be to the dominant culture or to the black bourgeoisie—is an appropriate subject of blues discourse. There are, for example, numerous blues about prostitution, from both the male perspective—as procurer, as customer, or as the unfortunate man who falls in love with a prostitute—and from the perspective of the prostitute herself. As a rule, these songs do not criticize the institution, but simply treat it as an existing reality. Rainey's "Hustlin' Blues," while it is not a direct critique of prostitution as such, does portray a woman who decides to turn her pimp in to the police and who wants to leave the streets altogether:

It's rainin' out here and tricks ain't walkin' tonight
It's rainin' out here and tricks ain't walkin' tonight
I'm goin' home, I know I've got to fight

If you hit me tonight, let me tell you what I'm going to do
If you hit me tonight, let me tell you what I'm going to do
I'm gonna take you to court and tell the judge on you

I ain't made no money, and he dared me to go home
I ain't made no money, and he dared me to go home
Judge, I told him he better leave me alone

He followed me up and he grabbed me for a fight
He followed me up and he grabbed me for a fight
He said, "Oh, do you know you ain't made no money tonight?"

Oh, judge, tell him I'm through
Oh, judge, tell him I'm through
I'm tired of this life, that's why I brought him to you.[35]

Hazel Carby describes this song, which was co-composed by Rainey and Thomas Dorsey, as "the articulation of the possibility that women could leave a condition of sexual and financial dependency, reject male violence, and end sexual exploitation."[36] But there are also underlying racial implications and political contradictions in this song, which Rainey's black audience would have been able to read. The woman in this song is not only subject to the abusive and exploitative behavior of her pimp and to the general hazards of her trade. When she stands before the white judge as a black woman, she is already hypersexualized within a context of power relations defined by race. There is thus a tragic incongruity to this woman's plea, for she stands between a white male symbol of power and repression and a black male purveyor of abuse and exploitation. She has informed on her pimp, and in all likelihood, the judge will not only refuse to protect her from her procurer but will sentence her, rather than her pimp, to jail. This song invites audiences to fashion their own critique of the impact of racism on black life.

The inspiration for one of Bessie Smith's greatest compositions, "Backwater Blues," came from an encounter with a southern black community in the throes of a disastrous flood, and with the racism underlying the differential relief provided black and white victims. In the words of Bessie Smith's sister-in-law, Maud Smith:

> After we left Cincinnati, we came to this little town, which was flooded, so everybody had to step off the train into little rowboats that took us to where we were staying. It was an undertaker parlor next door to the theatre, and we were supposed to stay in some rooms they had upstairs there. And, after we had put our bags down, Bessie looked around and said, "No, no, I can't stay *here* tonight." But there was a lot of other people there, and they were trying to get her to stay, so they started hollerin' "Miss Bessie, please sing the 'Back Water Blues,' please sing the 'Back Water Blues,' " Well, Bessie didn't know anything about any "Back Water Blues," but after we came back home to 1926 Christian Street where we were living, Bessie came in the kitchen one day, and she had a pencil and paper, and she started singing and writing. That's when she wrote the "Back Water Blues"—she got the title from those people down South.[37]

Its timing made the recording of "Backwater Blues" extraordinarily successful. The song's 1927 release coincided with one of the most catastrophic and tragic floods of the Mississippi River in history. Twenty-six thousand square miles of land were inundated, causing over 600,000 people, more than half of whom were black, to lose their homes.[38]

> When it rains five days and the skies turn dark as night
> When it rains five days and the skies turn dark as night
> Then trouble's takin' place in the lowlands at night
>
> . . . .
>
> When it thunders and lightnin', and the wind begins to blow
> When it thunders and lightnin', and the wind begins to blow
> There's thousands of people ain't got no place to go
>
> . . . .
>
> Backwater blues done caused me to pack my things and go
> Backwater blues done caused me to pack my things and go
> 'Cause my house fell down, and I can't live there no mo'
>
> Mmmmmmmmmmm, I can't move no mo'
> Mmmmmmmmmmm, I can't move no mo'
> There ain't no place for a poor old girl to go.[39]

The seasonal rains causing the Mississippi River to flood its banks are part of the unalterable course of nature, but the sufferings of untold numbers of black people who lived in towns and the countryside along the river also were attributable to racism. Black people were often considered expendable, and their communities were forced to take the overflow of backwaters in order to reduce the pressure on the levees. While most white people remained safe, black people suffered the wrath of the Mississippi, nature itself having been turned into a formidable weapon of racism.

In 1927, between the months of April and June, hundreds of thousands of people lost everything they owned in the floods, with virtually no means of recovery. While relief services were free to white victims, black victims were often informed that they would have to pay cash for food and other necessities. Destitute, they were forced to take loans from plantation own-ers, who later forced them to work off their alleged debt.[40] According to John Barry, author of *Rising Tide: The Great Mississippi Flood of 1927 and How It Changed America*, Will Percy, the head of the flood relief commit-tee in Greenville, Mississippi, announced that "[n]o able-bodied negro is entitled to be fed at all unless he is tagged as a laborer." Moreover, Percy issued the following order:

> 1. No rations will be issued to Greenville negro women and chil-dren unless there is no man in the family, which fact must be certi-fied by a white person. 2. No negro man in Greenville nor their families will be rationed unless the men join the labor gang or are employed. 3. Negro men . . . drawing a higher wage [than $1 a day] are not entitled to be rationed.[41]

A minister from Greenville wrote to President Coolidge that black people were "being made to work under the gun, [whites] just bossing the colored men with big guns buckled to them. . . . All of this mean and brutish treat-ment of the colored people is nothing but downright slavery."[42]

After the relief operations ended, there were reports of mob violence and lynching in several of the states affected by the flood. The Colored Advisory Commission appointed by Herbert Hoover (whose successful campaign for the presidency was based in large part on his role as the national head of relief operations) reported that black "men were beaten by the soldiers and made to work under guns. That more than one wanton murder was committed by these soldiers. . . . [T]hat women and girls were outraged by these soldiers."[43] The intense coverage in the black press and the NAACP's antiracist campaign around the relief operations meant that the 1927 Mississippi flood was a major event in the lives of black people, both North and South.

The enormous sales of "Backwater Blues" attest to Bessie Smith's abil-ity to capture the sentiments of the thousands of people whose lives were touched by the Mississippi floods. Scores of blues songs were inspired by these floods, including "Rising High Water Blues"[44] by Blind Lemon Jef-ferson and "Mississippi Heavy Water Blues"[45] by Barbecue Bob. Sippie

Wallace, a blues woman like Bessie Smith, recorded "Flood Blues" in June of 1927.[46] In September of that year, Bessie Smith recorded "Homeless Blues," which accusingly addresses the Mississippi River as the bearer of responsibility for the protagonist's homelessness.[47] Charley Patton released "High Water Everywhere" in 1929.[48]

Bessie Smith's and Sippie Wallace's contributions, together with many other songs about the catastrophic effects of the floods on the lives of black people, preserve a tragic moment in the history of African Americans. They also preserve and reflect a cultural consciousness that was capable of transforming such tragedies into catalytic events, rather than consigning them to historical memory as merely private misfortunes. If not for the blues, many individual tragedies affecting black working-class communities might never have been recast as social, collective adversities. Such a course would have significantly diminished black people's ability to constitute themselves as a community in struggle.

Songs like "Backwater Blues" are much more than the folk history to which they are often relegated. Transforming individual emotions into collective responses to adversity, they transcend the particular circumstances that inspired them and become metaphors about oppression, while the aesthetic distance achieved through music forges a consciousness that imagines community among the people who share glimpses of the possibility of eventually moving beyond this oppression.

We would encounter many more blues with themes of critical social commentary if the artists had been allowed to record all the material they included in their live repertoires. But even if we were not able to document a single blues song that treated social issues directly, this, in itself, would not justify the argument that early blues avoided political engagement. Given its place within the African-American music tradition, the blues absorbed techniques from the music of slavery, in which protest was secretly expressed and understood only by those who held the key to the code. Gertrude "Ma" Rainey, who stands at the juncture of country blues and the professionally performed classic blues of artists like Bessie Smith, recorded a number of songs that contained coded references to the racial and economic oppression that afflicted black communities. "Blame It on the Blues" is an example of such a song:

I'm so sad and worried, got no time to spread the news
I'm so sad and worried, got no time to spread the news
Won't blame it on my trouble, can't blame it on the blues

Lord, Lord, Lord, Lordy Lord
Lord, Lord, Lordy, Lordy Lord
Lord, Lord, Lord, Lord, Lord, Lord

[Spoken] Lord, who'm I gonna blame it on then?

I can't blame my daddy, he treats me nice and kind
I can't blame my daddy, he treats me nice and kind
Shall I blame it on my nephew, blame it on that trouble of mine?

This house is like a graveyard, when I'm left here by myself
This house is like a graveyard, when I'm left here by myself
Shall I blame it on my lover, blame it on somebody else?

Can't blame my mother, can't blame my dad
Can't blame my brother for the trouble I've had
Can't blame my lover that held my hand
Can't blame my husband, can't blame my man
Can't blame nobody, guess I'll have to blame it on the blues.[49]

The blues represent experience as emotionally configured by an individual psyche, historically shaped by post–Civil War conditions and the emancipation of the slaves. These conditions are often simply designated as "the blues." The emotional responses to them are also called "the blues." "The blues" therefore designates both feelings and the circumstances that have provoked them. In Ma Rainey's "Blame It on the Blues," the protagonist exhaustively investigates the individuals who play central roles in her life in order to uncover the source of her difficulties. Her inability to blame any one of them implies that someone or something that cannot safely be named in the direct manner in which she has named her kin and sexual partners is responsible. Thus, she blames it on the blues. Many among her black working-class audiences could have understood this song to mean that "the white man"—in other words, the racist structure of the society in which they lived—was finally responsible for their troubles.

As discussed at the beginning of this chapter, blues scholar Samuel Charters argues that the blues allow for "complaint," but not for "protest."[50] Such a distinction is questionable, particularly when applied to the nascent period of the organized black liberation movement, which began with the founding in 1910 of the NAACP—of which W. E. B. Du Bois initially was the only black officer—and the founding of the Urban League in 1911. To reiterate a point made earlier in this chapter, in order for protest to acquire an explicitly political character, there must be an organized political structure capable of functioning as a channel for transforming individual complaint into effective collective protest. At the same time, social protest can never be made the exclusive or limiting function of art. Art may encourage a critical attitude and urge its audience to challenge social conditions, but it cannot establish the terrain of protest by itself. In the absence of a popular mass movement, it can only encourage a critical attitude. When the blues "name" the problems the community wants to overcome, they help create the emotional conditions for protest, but do not and could not, of themselves, constitute social protest.

If it is true that the linguistic origin of the term "blues" is in the eighteenth-century English term "blue devils," referring to a psychological state of depression,[51] then it underwent a significant transformation in the context of black culture. Black people's inflected appropriation of this term did not make such a rigorous distinction between a subjective, psychological state of depression and an objective, socially defined status of oppression. Indeed, it seems likely that in the African-American consciousness of the period of their origins, the blues were considered to be both a subjective state and an objective phenomenon. The verse with which Bessie Smith concludes "Jail House Blues" consists of these traditional and frequently recurring words:

Good mornin', blues, blues, how do you do, how do you do
Good mornin', blues, blues, how do you do
Say, I just come here to have a few words with you.[52]

Blues singers, regardless of their ethnic backgrounds, recognize the historical connection between blues music and black experience. As blues man Houston Stackhouse put it, "Hardworking people, been half mistreated and done around—I believe that's where the blues come from . . . well the blues come from Black people."[53] Lil' Son Jackson says:

> I think that the blues is more or less a feeling that you get from
> something that you think is wrong, or somebody did wrong to you,
> or something that somebody did wrong to some of your own people
> or something like that . . . and the onliest way you have to tell it
> would be through a song, and that would be the blues . . . but the
> blues is really aimed at an object of some kind or an indirect
> person. . . .[54]

Although Ma Rainey's "Slave to the Blues" contains a fleeting reference to a male partner, it addresses the blues anthropomorphically as a slavemaster:

> Ain't robbed no bank, ain't done no hangin' crime
> Ain't robbed no bank, ain't done no hangin' crime
> Just been a slave to the blues, dreamin' 'bout that man of mine
>
> Blues, please tell me do I have to die a slave?
> Blues, please tell me do I have to die a slave?
> Do you hear me pleadin', you going to take me to my grave
>
> I could break these chains and let my worried heart go free
> If I could break these chains and let my worried heart go free
> But it's too late now, the blues have made a slave of me
>
> You'll see me raving, you'll hear me cryin'
> Oh, Lord, this lonely heart of mine
> Whole time I'm grieving, from my hat to my shoes
> I'm a good hearted woman, just am a slave to the blues.[55]

Rainey herself was just one generation removed from slavery, and her unveiled references to the institution had to have evoked historical memories of the system that had kept preceding generations in bondage. Even though the blues that figuratively enslave the protagonist of this song arise from a romantic relationship ("Just a slave to the blues, dreamin' 'bout that man of mine"), the image of slavery throughout the lyrics is too stark not to resonate beyond the level of individual heartsickness. There is no consistent exploration of the love relationship referred to in the first verse as the source of the protagonist's blues. If "the blues have made a slave of me," it is because they constitute and express a state that is grounded in profound injustice. Allusions to the repressive character of the criminal justice system can be found in the first verse: the woman has not perpetrated a crime that justifies her punishment. The implication is that the blues at once stand in the place of the slaveocracy of previous times, and function as a means of registering the oppressive force now weighing on the black community.

Ma Rainey's "Yonder Come the Blues" also hints at the social underpinnings of the blues:

I worry all day, I worry all night,
Every time my man comes home he wants to fuss and fight
When I pick up the paper to read the news
Just when I'm satisfied, yonder come the blues

I went down to the river each and every day
Tryin' to keep from cryin' and do myself away
I walked and walked 'til I wore out my shoes
I can't walk no further, yonder come the blues

Some folks never worry, things all come out right
Poor me, lie down and suffer, weep and cry all night
When I get a letter, it never bring good news
Every time I see the mailman, yonder come the blues

Go back blues, don't come this way
Lordy, give me something else besides the blues all day
Every man I've loved, I've been misused
And when I want some lovin', yonder come the blues

People have different blues and think they're mighty bad
But blues about a man the worst I've ever had
I been disgusted and all confused
Every time I look around, yonder come the blues.[56]

Charters has called this song "one of the most vivid personifications of the blues . . . in which [Rainey] seems to suggest that the blues is a loiterer, lounging after her when she tries to ignore his presence."[57] According to Sandra Lieb, "The repetition of the refrain strengthens the sense of personification, an inheritance from folk blues: the blues become an entity that stalks the singer throughout the stanzas, and surrounds her by the end of the song."[58]

But if in this song the blues are a personification, they are also a symbol of an adversary—as pervasive and amorphous as Mr. Blues himself. The blues, which approach at every juncture, which influence every aspect of the woman's life, are certainly far more powerful than the lover who wants to "fuss and fight" or even all the men who have abused and misused her. It is significant that in the last verse, after having asserted that "blues about a man [are] the worst I've ever had," she confesses how confused she is. The omnipresent blues seem to symbolize, in a fundamental though generalized way, the mystifying, all-pervasive—and seemingly insurmountable—but obscure social forces that have created the overall context of misery and oppression. The reference in the third verse to "some folks" who are never tormented by the blues is equally general but can be heard as an allusion to white people, to well-to-do people in general, or even to black men.

Sandra Lieb considers Rainey's "Tough Luck Blues"[59] an expression of a "mood of self-defeat [that] is extended beyond love, and could be called absurdist in the contemporary sense." She argues that "the apparently nonsensical lyrics actually reveal a pattern of sardonic frustration and confusion."[60] But another way to interpret this song is as an aesthetic invocation of the social impasse and lethal incoherence of a society organized around the demented logic of racism.

When a black cat crosses you, bad luck I heard it said
When a black cat crosses you, bad luck I heard it said
One must've started 'cross me, got halfway and then fell dead

Things sure breakin' hard, worse than ever before
Things sure breakin' hard, worse than ever before
My sugar told me, speak to him no more

Yeah, my right hand's raised to the good Lord above
Yeah, my right hand's raised to the good Lord above
If they was throwin' away money, I'd have on boxing gloves

If it was rainin' down soup, thick as number one sand
If it was rainin' down soup, thick as number one sand
I'd have a fork in my pocket and a sifter in my hand

My friend committed suicide, while I was away at sea
My friend committed suicide, while I was away at sea
They want to lock me up for murder in first degree.[61]

Linked as she was to the strong folk tradition of the blues, Ma Rainey gave individual expression to problems that were the collective lot of black people. The images humorously evoked in this song capture the collective predicament of working-class African Americans, always the recipients of the worst of the worst. Black cats simply cross other people's paths, bringing them their rightful share of bad luck, but this very symbol of bad luck falls dead in front of black people. The social circumstances of black people's lives produce an endless series of calamities.

Even God—and this is especially interesting given most black people's deeply felt religious commitment—seems to participate in this conspiracy. Even though she has her hand raised toward God, he is of no assistance in ameliorating her economic plight or, by extension, that of her people. The images of wealth and food in abundance—money thrown away and soup raining down—of which the protagonist is unable to take advantage, evoke conditions of social injustice. Finally, the lyrics portray a familiar experience in the black community: fraudulent charges brought by the criminal justice system. Although her friend committed suicide while she was far away from the site of the tragedy, she nonetheless is charged with murder.

Sexuality, too, loses its emancipatory edge in "Tough Luck Blues," bringing tribulations that only add to life's difficulties. The narrator's lover has instructed her not to speak to him. Charters and Oliver might interpret "Tough Luck Blues" as a prime example of blues "complaint," and Lieb sees the song as simply affirming frustration and confusion. There is, however, latent protest in the song, inscribed by the process of humorously naming—in the African tradition of nommo—the difficult route black people have had to navigate in all aspects of their lives.

Gertrude Rainey's and Bessie Smith's recorded work reveals an abundance of socially significant themes approached from a number of different perspectives. In a few salient instances oppressive conditions are explicitly and literally denounced, while in other cases they are simply stated: the problem is named, whether it be eviction, prostitution, imprisonment, or homelessness brought on by floods and the resulting failure of the government to furnish emergency assistance to black people. Such issues were often stated in such a way that the mere naming of the problem was likely to provoke at least a rudimentary community consciousness of the need for eventual social transformation.

Finally, there are representations of adversity, whose relatively abstract character—often simply in the form of the blues—bears some measure of resemblance to abstract visual art in both European and African forms. The African-American community of that era did not need to be informed about the underlying social implications of such seemingly abstract notions. Their collective emotional experience of these themes almost certainly facilitated shared social interpretations. When Ma Rainey sang about soup raining from the sky, her listeners would not have found it difficult to extract a metaphorical evocation of the affluent society—especially since the protagonist, with a fork in her pocket and a sifter in her hand, is ill-equipped to partake of the surrounding abundance.

Lawrence Levine has insightfully pointed out:

The blues insisted that the fate of the individual black man or woman, what happened in their everyday "trivial" affairs, what took place within them—their yearnings, their problems, their frustrations, their dreams—were important, were worth taking note of and sharing in song. Stressing individual expression and group coherence at one and the same time, the blues was an inward-looking music which insisted upon the meaningfulness of black lives. In these respects it was not only the angry work songs but the blues as well, that were subversive of the American racial order and proved to be an important portent of what was to come in a very few decades.[62]

Seen in this light, Gertrude Rainey's and Bessie Smith's songs may be interpreted precisely as historical preparation for political protest. They are certainly far more than complaint, for they begin to articulate a consciousness that takes into account social conditions of class exploitation, racism, and male dominance as seen through the lenses of the complex emotional responses of black female subjects. While there may not be a direct line to social activism, activist stances are inconceivable without the consciousness such songs suggest.

PREACHING
THE BLUES

SPIRITUALITY AND SELF-CONSCIOUSNESS

Lord, I got the blues this morning
I want everybody to go down in prayer, Lord, Lord

Layin' in my bed with my face turned to the wall
Lord, layin' in the bed with my face turned to the wall
Tryin' to count these blues, so I could sing them all.

— "COUNTIN' THE BLUES"[1]

Music was central to the meaning of a culture of resistance during slavery. Likewise, the blues, the most important postslavery musical genre, encouraged forms of social consciousness that challenged the dominant ideology of racism. Women's blues, specifically, celebrated and valorized black working-class life while simultaneously contesting patriarchal assumptions about women's place both in the dominant culture and within African-American communities. I have argued that women's blues helped to construct an aesthetic community that affirmed women's capacities in domains assumed to be the prerogatives of males, such as sexuality and travel. In this chapter I contend that the construction of this women's community entailed bold challenges to institutions and ideologies within the African-American community, as well as in the dominant culture. Women's blues contested black bourgeois notions of "high" culture that belittled working-class popular music. They also challenged the most powerful African-American institution, the Christian church. In order for the blues to be extricated from a hierarchy that established Christianity as the community's overarching moral authority, they had to affirm, in a self-conscious manner, their own cultural integrity.

I have attempted to emphasize the complex political implications of the blues' postslavery historical context. This musical form reflected both continuities and ruptures with slave culture. The importance of gender-based structures and themes in the blues reflects a significant rupture with the musical culture of slavery. At the same time, even in the absence of cultural representations of women's place in slave music, the relatively equal social status of women within slave communities reveals a historical precedent for blues affirmations of black women's self-reliance and assertiveness. As I argued in *Women, Race, and Class*, the conditions of production under U.S. slavery—which required women to perform virtually the same labor tasks as men—established a distorted form of gender equality between African women and men. While this equality was in the first place an indication of the severity of oppression under slavery, it also led to gender politics within the slave community that were radically different from those operating in the dominant culture. Moreover, women's leadership in the domestic sphere—one of the only social spaces not subject to the overarching authority of the slave masters—meant that women played an especially important role in the community of slaves.[2]

Women's blues are such an important source of insights about African-American historical consciousness precisely because they do not attempt to eradicate the memory of an era of relatively egalitarian gender relations. Veteran New Orleans jazz musician Danny Barker's humorous description of Gertrude Rainey also evokes, I think, the historical respect accorded women:

Ma Rainey was Ma Rainey. When you said "Ma," that means Mother. "Ma," that means the tops. That's the boss, the shack bully of the house, Ma Rainey. She'd take charge. "Ma." Ma Rainey's coming to town, the boss blues singer. And you respect Ma. Grand "Ma,"

my "Ma," and ma"Ma." That's "Ma." That's something you respect.
You say Mother. That's the boss of the shack. Not papa, mama.[3]

In nationalist expressions of black middle-class—and later working-class—
cultural consciousness, the historical memory of slavery, the most painful
institutionalized oppression in African-American history, frequently has
been conflated with an ideologically distorted notion of black matriarchy.
According to this construction of slavery, slave women literally ruled over
slave men, sometimes collaborating with the white slaveholders. In the
1960s, as exemplified by the official government report authored by Daniel
Moynihan (*The Negro Family: The Case for National Action*), the allegedly
matriarchal structure of the black family was increasingly identified as the
main source of the community's impoverishment.[4] This hegemonic notion
that a dysfunctional matriarchal family and community structure was the
most pressing social problem in poor black communities was uncritically
appropriated in black nationalist articulations that equated patriarchal
dominance with black liberation.[5]

During the late 1960s, when cultural nationalist movements rose to
prominence in black communities, women were relegated to subsidiary
and decidedly inferior positions, both ideologically and organizationally.
In this context, male dominance was considered a necessary prerequisite
for black liberation. Similarly, the abstract emphasis on African heritage in
contemporary cultural representation often invokes a heroic, masculinist
past situated in an African imaginary which tends to displace the era of
slavery as the formative historical period for Americans of African descent.
In hip-hop culture, for example, black women are often portrayed as
"African queens," to be accorded respect by their men. What is frequently
implied by evocations of "queens," however, is that the ultimate authority
rests with the "kings." Along with the oppression associated with slavery,
this imagined masculinist past erases the relative equality of women characteristic of the slave community.

Like the music of slavery, the blues incorporated recast elements of
European musical culture as well as recognizable, but transformed, West
African features. Defying literal interpretation, this musical form—like
spirituals and work songs—contained secrets that the dominant white cul-

ture was unable to decipher. Failing to detect the complexities of the blues form and blues themes, some early white observers tended to consider this music "low," childish, irrational, and bizarre.[6] But the blues were not only perceived to be lowly and vulgar by those to whom their language was foreign. African Americans, whose social aspirations led them to disassociate themselves from the more impoverished members of their community, often condemned the blues as well.

During the Harlem Renaissance, even as black artists and intellectuals attempted to articulate—in often divergent ways—a uniquely black aesthetic, they almost entirely ignored the musical heart of African-American culture, the blues. There were two notable exceptions. Zora Neale Hurston, in both her scholarly and her creative work, affirmed the vitality and integrity of black folk culture, of which the blues was an integral part, and Langston Hughes used the blues as the very foundation of his poetics. Both artists tended to be shunned by black intellectuals who assumed that the "primitive" ingredients of poor and working-class black culture needed to be transcended if "great art" was to be produced by people of African descent. When Black Swan, the first black recording company, lined up the artists it wished to record, its producers chose music that had more in common with the music of the dominant culture than with the popular musical expressions of the African-American people. Bessie Smith's sound—as sophisticated and urban as it was in relation to Gertrude "Ma" Rainey's country blues sound—was rejected because it was considered too "raw" by Black Swan.[7]

The most pervasive opposition to the blues, however, was grounded in the religious practices of the historical community responsible for the production of the blues in the first place. The blues were part of a cultural continuum that disputed the binary constructions associated with Christianity. In this sense, they blatantly defied the Christian imperative to relegate sexual conduct to the realm of sin. Many blues singers therefore were assumed to have made a pact with the Devil. Among the many myths surrounding the legendary Delta blues man Robert Johnson is one that has him signing away his soul to Legba, or Elegua, the Yoruba orisha of the crossroads—represented in the black southern vernacular as a Devil-like figure.[8]

Blues singers were (and to a certain extent still are) associated with the Devil because they celebrated those dimensions of human existence considered evil and immoral according to the tenets of Christianity. But precisely because they offer enlightenment on love and sexuality, blues singers often have been treated as secular counterparts to Christian ministers, recognized by their constituencies as no less important authorities in their respective realms. However, from the vantage point of devout Christians, blues singers are unmitigated sinners and the creativity they demonstrate and the worldview they advocate are in flagrant defiance of the community's prevailing religious beliefs. According to Danny Barker, a veteran of that era, "some of them feared the stage. That's the Devil's work. They stay home, married, and had a family and still died with that attitude. That's the Devil's work, the stage. Make believe."[9]

A contemporary literary expression of this marginalization of the blues singer is the character Shug Avery in Alice Walker's novel *The Color Purple*. According to Celie's written account, when the community minister chooses to "take [Shug's] condition for his text":

He don't call no name, but he don't have to. Everybody know who he mean. He talk bout a strumpet in short skirts, smoking cigarettes, drinking gin. Singing for money and taking other women mens. Talk bout slut, hussy, heifer and streetcleaner.[10]

However, from the margins to which she is relegated, Shug sparks numerous transformations in the lives of Celie and Mr. ———, the main characters in the novel. Steven Spielberg's cinematic version of *The Color Purple* presents a rather contrived reconciliation between the blues woman and her minister father (a character created by Spielberg, not Walker) in which Shug leads a group of good-time, blues-loving people from the jook joint where they were partying on Saturday night into Sunday morning church services.[11]

Historically, the blues person has been an outsider on three accounts. Belittled and misconstrued by the dominant culture that has been incapable of deciphering the secrets of her art, she has been ignored and denounced in African-American middle-class circles and repudiated by the most authoritative institution in her own community, the church. Yet, at the same time, she has been loved, praised, and emulated by the masses of black people as her community's most intimate insider. Gertrude "Ma" Rainey was celebrated by black southerners as one of the great cultural figures of her time. Her contemporaries no doubt appreciated not only the fact that she sang the blues but also that, in face of the forces condemning them, she defended the vitality of the blues and their indispensable social role in the lives of African Americans.

Considering the cultural centrality of the blues during the formative decades of the construction of a "free" African-American working-class community, it is significant that the most widely known blues performer— and defender of the blues—was a woman. In the context of black Christianity's disdain for the blues, Rainey's work can be viewed as a female subversion of the male Christian ministry that equated blues and sexuality with the Devil and sin. This is not to imply that women have not played an important role in perpetuating the Christian discourse opposing the blues. Although they have been largely relegated to a subsidiary status within the church hierarchy, black women are and have always been a mainstay in the church and have sometimes defended and perpetuated the church's most backward positions. When Rainey herself retired as a blues performer, she joined the Friendship Baptist Church in Columbus, Georgia—a church where her brother, Thomas Pridgett, Jr., served as a deacon. She spent the last years of her life as a Christian devotee, refusing to sing the blues and fervently supporting the church and its institutions.[12]

Like Rainey, Ethel Waters would not sing the blues after she committed her life to the church. She did not, however, leave the stage entirely, for she continued to work as an actor and limited her singing to religious music. Many less-known blues women shunned the "make-believe" and sexually charged world of the blues during their latter years. Music critic Bruce Cook quotes a conversation with Annie Pavageau, the wife of a dead New Orleans jazz bassist and herself a former blues performer:

Any kind of music make you feel good—blues or church music. It's the sincereness of it—that's what make you feel good. It does seem to me, though, that you're bound to feel different when you sing

for Jesus than when you sing the blues, because *then* . . . you are
inspired by the Holy Spirit.[13]

Later in the conversation Pavageau justified her former involvement in the
blues life as a function of her youth and explained that during that period
"I wasn't a church member . . . not even a churchgoer." When she turned
to the church, she was compelled to give up the blues. "I didn't believe I
could play all that ragtime music and still serve God in truth and spirit. I
give all my time to the church today." Moreover, "you know you can't serve
two people. Jesus said that. You can't serve God and mammon, too. Everything that is not right is wrong. Everything that does not pertain to God is
sinful. We believe the way Christ did."[14] Veteran blues singer Ida Goodson
has a different perspective:

> I'm going to tell you something. This is no lie. I can be playing the
> blues . . . and when I play the blues I feel something going on and
> next thing I know I'm feeling good. . . . That's the devil in me
> then. . . . And then you go and play church songs and then that feel-
> ing come back, that Christian feeling coming back on you. You see,
> that's just the way it is. The Devil got his work and God got his work.[15]

Annie Pavageau's disdain for the blues, while articulated in religious
terms, resonates with the assumptions about high and low cultural productions that deem the blues an inferior music. Ma Rainey, on the other
hand, championed the blues in her performances, unafraid to affirm their
authority in overt defiance of both the church and the musical traditions of
the dominant culture. Her lusty rendition of "Down in the Basement," for
example, unhesitatingly upholds the "lowness" of music in the blues tradition, with its uncamouflaged sexual implications, as far more desirable
than the elite "highbrow" music of the dominant culture:

> I've got a man, piano hound
> Plays anything that's going around
> When he plays that highbrow stuff
> I shout, "Brother, that's enough!"

Take me to the basement, that's as low as I can go
I want something low down, daddy, want it nice and slow
I can shimmy from A to Z, if you'll play that thing for me
Take me to the basement, that's as low as I can go.[16]

Ma Rainey injects an uplifting meaning into the characterization of the blues as "low down," thereby contesting dominant assumptions about the inferiority of the blues as well as the ideologically constructed inferiority of black people. "Down in the Basement" memorializes black musical culture as well as the people who created it.

Bessie Smith sang a number of popular songs that pay tribute to the scores of unsung black musicians who, by the prevailing white musical standards, were refused recognition as the brilliant instrumentalists they were. "Trombone Cholly" is one such song:

Nobody else can do his stuff 'cause he won't teach 'em how
Oh, Cholly, blow that thing, that slide trombone
Make it talk, make it sing, Lordy, where did you get that tone?
. . . .
Oh, Cholly, make it sing, that slide trombone
You'll even make a king get down off his throne
And he would break a leg, I know, by doin' the Charleston while you blow.[17]

"Jazzbo Brown," the unschooled clarinet player from "Memphis Town," who is unable to read music and "don't play no classy stuff like them Hoffman Tales," nonetheless plays music that is "good enough for the Prince of Wales."[18] In recording such songs, Smith honored the blues source of African-American music, thus elevating both the blues people and the blues spirit.[19]

In one sense, Rainey and Smith are simply carrying forth a blues tradition that incorporates in the ritual of its creation a certain self-reflexivity that calls upon the blues artist to share with her or his audience the meaning of a blues vision. The blues aesthetic is an aesthetic of self-consciousness, after all. But, in a less obvious sense, the defense of the blues proposed by the classic blues artists I am exploring—Gertrude "Ma"

Rainey and Bessie Smith—has profound feminist implications. For in defending as well as in performing the blues, they were establishing it as a genre that belonged as much to women as to men. They were also implicitly defining the blues as a site where women could articulate and communicate their protests against male dominance.

One of the most explicit and most eloquent defenses of the blues spirit and the blues tradition can be found in one of Ma Rainey's own compositions, "Countin' the Blues," in which she invokes the spirit of the blues by naming them—or, in her formulation, by "counting" them—thus recapitulating the West African practice of nommo,[20] which conjures powers associated with things by ritually pronouncing their names. This song directly alludes to fourteen blues titles, many of which were recorded by Rainey and/or Smith. The blues she names (or "counts") are: "Memphis Blues," "Rampart Blues," "Beale Street Blues," "Graveyard Blues," "'Bama Bound Blues," "Stingaree Blues," "Southern Blues," "Down Hearted Blues," "Gulf Coast Blues," "Midnight Blues," "Jail House Blues," and finally, three of her best-known works, "Bad Luck Blues," "Bo-Weevil Blues," and "Moonshine Blues."

The importance of "Countin' the Blues" resides in the fact that, in its self-reflexivity, it challenges the notion that blues songs are unconscious and naive creations of primitive folk, catering to base instincts and prurient interests. This proud, self-conscious catalog questions the premises on which the blues have been dismissed by European-American culture, by the black working class and by the black church. "Countin' the Blues" is a deeply spiritual blues reflection on the sociopsychological function of the blues. This song is a blues affirmation of the blues, as self-conscious art and communicative act. The conscious reference to black spirituality is announced in the opening phrase, which is spoken: "Lord, I got the blues this mornin', I want everybody to go down in prayer, Lord, Lord." Rainey consciously refigures the blues as prayer. Indeed, she is conjuring through naming—again recalling the process of nommo—the African equivalent of Christian prayer, but, by virtue of its magical potential, even more powerful.[21] Nommo is more powerful than Christian prayer because it attributes to human beings the power of the "word," which, in the Judeo-Christian religion, is exercised by God alone. "In the beginning was the word," says the Bible "and the word was with God and the word was God." As God created, he named, and as he named, he created. This creative and transformative power, possessed not only by supernatural beings but by living women and men, is an important distinguishing characteristic of the philosophical discourse of traditional West African societies. It can also help us understand blues aesthetics, which linked postslavery African-American culture with its African antecedent. Rainey's "Countin' the Blues" carries forth this connection.

The sung section of "Countin' the Blues" opens with a typical blues posture: "Layin' in my bed with my face turned to the wall." This blues posture is described immediately following the spoken invocation, which calls upon people to "go down in prayer." Blues music performs a magical—or aesthetic—exorcism of the blues, those things that lead to unhappiness and despair. Ritually invoking the names of blues songs serves the purpose of preparing the blues woman for the process of conferring aesthetic form on her emotional troubles. By creating out of them a work of art, she is giving herself aesthetic control over the forces that threaten to overwhelm her. As she lies in bed with her face turned to the wall, she is "tryin' to count these blues, so I could sing them all." Having called the names of numerous blues songs, Rainey concludes by proclaiming that she is going to sleep, "to try to dream away my troubles, countin' those blues."[22] In this song Rainey speaks as the quintessential blues woman, establishing the realm of the blues, defending it, validating it, and celebrating it. By doing so, she countered the Christian monopolization of black spirituality and established herself as an equal to the church's patriarchs.

One of Bessie Smith's own compositions philosophically juxtaposes the spirit of religion and the spirit of the blues, and contests the idea of the incontrovertible separateness of these two spheres. In "Preachin' the Blues,"[23] Rainey's younger counterpart establishes the realm of the blues as spiritually coexistent with and simultaneously antithetical to Christian religious practices. While "Preachin' the Blues" is not technically a blues, it employs typical blues postures of humor and sarcasm in order to contest the marginalization of the blues spirit. In a lighthearted and unabashedly blasphemous tone, Smith defines the content of the blues as scripture, and its presentation as sermon. In this song, she playfully, but openly, defies the Christian piety that dismisses the blues as beyond the pale of spiritual discourse. As in Rainey's invocation to "go down in prayer," Smith declares that the blues should be preached and that thereby souls can be converted:

> Preach them blues, sing them blues, they certainly sound good to me
>
> . . . .
>
> Moan them blues, holler them blues, let me convert your soul.[24]

By turning the blues into a spiritual discourse about love, this song reveals an interesting affinity with West African philosophical affirmations of the connectedness of spiritual and sexual joy. Later in her career Bessie Smith recorded two gospel-related songs, "On Revival Day" and "Moan, You Mourners." In these she assumed a different posture, deploying religious references in a relatively orthodox way. The former ends with these lines:

> When that congregation starts to sing
> Nothin' in this world don't mean a thing
> Oh, glory hallelujah
> Makes you feel so peculiar
> The Devil cannot rule you on Revival Day.[25]

And in the latter, there is an admonition to

> . . . get down on your knee
> And let the good Lord hear your plea
> 'Cause if you want to rest with ease
> Moan, you mourners
> Just bend your head way down and pray
> To have the Devil chased away.[26]

Even in these two songs, however, religious content is conveyed through the vehicle of secular song.[27]

"Preachin' the Blues" has important contemporary implications in that it places women at the center of a blues aesthetic that advises women to take control of their sexuality and implicitly challenges the church's condemnation of sexuality. It contains these lines:

I will learn you something if you listen to this song
I ain't here to try to save your soul
Just want to teach you how to save your good jelly roll.[28]

At a time when the greatest institutional support of homophobia in the African-American community is channeled through the church, it may be helpful to look at cultural challenges to the church's denunciation of sexuality as they were historically formulated in women's blues. In one sense, the fear of homosexuality perpetuated by the church is related to a generalized fear of sexuality. This fear of sexuality takes on new meaning when considered in light of the fact that the freedom to choose sexual partners was one of the most powerful distinctions between the condition of slavery and the postemancipation status of African Americans. In this sense, the incorporation by the black church of traditionally Christian dualism, which defines spirit as "good" and body as "evil," denied black people the opportunity to acknowledge one of their most significant social victories. The church played a pivotal role in valorizing that aspect of racist ideology that sexualized the ascription of intellectual and spiritual inferiority to black people.

The racialization of sexuality and the sexualization of race as it worked its way into the evolution of dominant racist culture was thus facilitated by the black church's condemnation of sexuality and its representation and affirmation in the blues. Religiously justified homophobia—and the resulting intransigence concerning the AIDS epidemic—has also been influenced strongly by this historical position assumed by the church. Counter to this has been the historical affirmation of sexuality as a part of working-class oppositional consciousness in the black community. This was a defining characteristic of women's blues. This is not to ignore the extensive elaboration of sexual themes in male blues. However, the affirmation of autonomous sexuality by women was characterized by a complexity that was not present in men's blues. And women's blues influenced men's attitudes toward women even as they were influenced by the prevailing ideas of women as sexual objects rather than as subjects of their own experience. Also simply by virtue of the fact that women's blues were more extensively recorded than men's during the twenties, the former enjoyed wider exposure.

In Ralph Ellison's tribute to Jimmy Rushing, he points out that Rushing,

> along with the other jazz musicians whom we knew, had made a choice, had dedicated himself to a mode of expression and a way of life no less "righteously" than others dedicated themselves to the church. Jazz and the blues did not fit into the scheme of things as spelled out by our two main institutions, the church and the school, but they gave expression to attitudes which found no place in these and helped to give our lives some semblance of wholeness.[29]

Ellison evokes conversations about Jimmy Rushing among the youth of his neighborhood in Oklahoma City's East Side that designate band members in language mocking the church hierarchy that condemns the blues. At the same time, this parody illuminates the real similarities between the blues ritual and religious life:

> "Now, that's the Right Reverend Jimmy Rushing preaching now, man," someone would say. And rising to the cue another would answer, "Yeah, and that's old Elder 'Hot Lips' signifying along with him; urging him on, man." And, keeping it building, "Huh, but though you can't hear him out this far, Ole Deacon Big-un [the late Walter Page] is up there patting his foot and slapping on his big belly [the bass viol] to keep those fools in line." And we might go on to name all the members of the band as though they were the Biblical four-and-twenty elders, while laughing at the impious wit of applying church titles to a form of music which all the preachers assured us was the devil's potent tool.[30]

If a translation of this parody that replaces the men's names with those of women like Bessie Smith, Ma Rainey, Ida Cox, or even Memphis Minnie rings strange, it is only because of the deeply ingrained male dominance in the church. It is hard to imagine Ellison describing a performance by Bessie Smith in which she is mockingly referred to as "the Right Reverend Smith," not because she did not dedicate herself in a "righteous" way to the performance of the blues, but rather because of male supremacy in the church and in black music culture.

In "Preachin' the Blues," Bessie Smith evokes the milieu of the blues: the Deep South—Atlanta, Georgia—and more specifically, the jook joint or barrelhouse where people are "drinkin' corn and hollerin' hooray" and where there are "pianos playin' 'til the break of day." These sites where blues were produced and performed were also places of great sexual freedom. The abode of the blues, a vital center for the production of African-American musical culture, is also evoked in "Soft Pedal Blues"[31] (another Bessie Smith composition), which re-creates the atmosphere of the buffet flat. The buffet flat was an institutionalized house party in the urban black community of that era, combining celebratory music with sexual activities of all sorts. It was also a major component of the black gay subculture, particularly during the era of the Harlem Renaissance. The "soft pedal" here refers to the need to keep the piano music as low as possible, so as not to provoke a police raid on the party.

The blues realm is all-encompassing. In contrast to the condemnatory and censuring character of Christianity, it knows few taboos. As a cultural form that has long been a target of racist-inspired marginalization, the blues categorically refrains from relegating to the margins any person or behavior. Because the blues realm is open to discourse on every possible subject affecting the people who created it, it need not banish religion. Rather, what it rejects is religion's manner of defining the blues as an inferior expression of an inferior people. The openness of the blues realm—its repudiation of taboos of all sorts—is rendered possible by virtue of the fact that the blues always decline to pass judgment. Their nonjudgmental character permits ideas that would be rejected by the larger society to enter into blues discourse. That is why blues women are able to speak in an active and assertive voice not permitted in mainstream society. Smith's "Nashville Woman's Blues," for instance, celebrates that ability to say whatever is on one's mind:

> Down there, they strut they stuff
> The way they strut, it really ain't no bluff
> You can say what you choose
> I have got those Nashville woman's blues.[32]

In "Ya Da Do," Ma Rainey sings in a light and playful way about the attraction the blues hold for black people, but her message is profound:

> Every evenin' 'bout half past four
> Sweet piano playin' near my door
> And turn to raggin', you never heard such blues before
>
> There's a pretty little thing they play
> It's very short, but folks all say
> "Oh, it's a-pickin'," when they start to want to cry for more
>
> I don't know the name, but it's a pretty little thing, goes
>
> Ya da da do, ya da da do
> Fill you with harmonizing, minor refrain
> It's a no-name blues, but'll take away your pains
>
> Ya da da do, ya da da do
> Everybody loves it, ya da do do do.[33]

The power of the blues to exorcise black people's emotional anguish is zestfully and buoyantly praised here. While in "Countin' the Blues," Rainey emphasizes the ceremonious naming of the songs, "Ya Da Do" refers to a "no-name blues," which nonetheless receives its scatlike name, "ya da da do." There is a self-conscious character about this song, which announces that the music itself—its "harmonizing, minor refrain"—exerts that magical power of banishing the blues.

Bessie Smith's "Yodeling Blues" is similar. It bemoans the depressing situation of the protagonist, whose man has abandoned her for no apparent reason. After wondering "who put them jinx on me," she turns to the blues as a means of extricating herself from this unhappy predicament:

> I'm gonna yodel, yodel my blues away (YEE HOO!)
> I'm gonna yodel 'til things come back my way.[34]

"Yodeling Blues" is about the blues as both feeling and song, and song as an emancipatory process. "Yodeling Blues" confronts the blues with the blues, and uses the blues to drive the blues away. It enacts the potential convergence of the aesthetic dimension with psychosocial reality.

Blues singers acknowledge this central function of blues song. The blues are sung in order to drive the blues away. A recurring stanza in traditional twelve-bar blues—one which Bessie Smith borrows for her "Jail House Blues"—establishes the following confrontation:

> Good morning, blues, blues, how do you do, how do you do
> Good mornin', blues, blues, how do you do
> Say, I just come here to have a few words with you.[35]

Confronting the blues, acknowledging the blues, counting the blues, naming the blues through song, is the aesthetic means of expelling the blues from one's life. This is an expression of the historical role of African-American song, whether secular or religious. It also reveals how the blues spirit constantly contests the borders between "reality" and "art." In the work of Gertrude Rainey and Bessie Smith, blues song represents the collective woes of the community, along with the determination to conquer them. But, at the same time, it acquires a specifically female meaning, furnishing women with one of the rare vehicles through which their agonies, joys, and aspirations may be expressed.

In Rainey's "Memphis Bound Blues," composed by Thomas Dorsey, song itself is represented as a means of inspiring and giving shape to emotional responses that might otherwise turn inward and become self-destructive. In this particular instance the courage is generated through song to confront and express anger at a man who has run out on the female protagonist:

> I talk because I'm stubborn, I sing because I'm free
> My daddy's gone and left me, bound for Memphis, Tennessee.[36]

In another Dorsey composition, "Last Minute Blues," the self-conscious character of the song reinforces the social character of the blues. Until W. C. Handy became the first to publish a blues song he had written—"The Memphis Blues"—thereby acquiring the title "Father of the Blues,"[37] blues songs were never considered the personal property of their composers or the performers. They were the collective property of the black community, disseminated, like folktales, in accordance with the community's oral tradition. A blues sung by one person and heard, remembered, revised, and resung by another belonged as much to the second performer as to the first. This socializing character of the blues rendered conscious the shared nature of emotional experience as well as the collective character of the blues form itself. "Last Minute Blues" presents an individual female experience of pain within a relationship and transforms it into a collective naming of the social quality of black women's domestic experiences. As anonymous as it is intensely personal, this song memorializes the countless nameless women who suffered in similar ways. There is triumph in the way it offers the experience and its creative expression to whoever wishes to claim it. It affirms the women's blues community as it affirms the integrity of the blues itself:

> Minutes seem like hours, hours seem like days
> Minutes seem like hours, hours seem like days
> It seems like my daddy won't stop his evil ways
>
> Seem like every minute going to be my last
> Seem like every minute going to be my last
> If I can't tell my future, I won't tell my past

The brook runs into the river, river runs into the sea
The brook run into the river, river run into the sea
If I don't run into my daddy, somebody'll have to bury me

If anybody ask you who wrote this lonesome song
If anybody ask you who wrote this lonesome song
Tell 'em you don't know the writer, but Ma Rainey put it on.[38]

"Putting on" or performing the blues onstage was preeminently the achievement of the women who sang the blues during the decade of the twenties. Women like Rainey and Smith presided over blues gatherings, and they were respected for the backstage work they did to pull these often extravagant shows together. Alberta Hunter, who saw Bessie Smith perform several times, described her as wearing "a headress with a thousand feathers. . . . She was dressed very gaudily—of course she paid a lot of money for her clothes."[39] Among other preparations, they decked their bodies out with pearls, gold, and rhinestones. "For audiences accustomed to seeing black performers in mammy costumes, Bessie Smith presented a rare vision. In full Empress regalia, she was bold, beautiful, outrageously out of line, and impossible to forget."[40] But they were also acknowledged for the responsibility they assumed for booking their shows, paying their musicians and dancers, and transporting them from city to city week after week and month after month. As jazz musician Danny Barker put it, they had to be fighters, scientists, and bakers: "When you ran a show, a group of people depend[ed] on you for a living."[41]

In an era in which the church had provided the main source of autonomous social space for African Americans, women like Gertrude Rainey and Bessie Smith helped to carve out new space in which black working people could gather and experience themselves as a community. The tent shows in the South and the clubs and buffet flats in the North, where the Devil's music was performed by irrepressible and sexually fearless women, helped to produce a new feeling of community, one in which black culture was affirmed and the male dominance of the black church powerfully contested.

UP IN HARLEM
EVERY SATURDAY NIGHT

BLUES AND THE BLACK AESTHETIC

Up in Harlem every Saturday night
When the highbrows get together it's just too tight
They all congregates at an all night strut
And what they do is tut, tut, tut
Ole Hannah Brown from 'cross town
Gets full of corn and starts breakin' 'em down . . .
Check all your razors and your guns
Do the shim sham shimmy 'til the risin' sun
Gimme a reefer and a gang o' gin
Slay me, 'cause I'm in my sin.

— "GIMME A PIGFOOT"[1]

Gertrude Rainey established the blues as women's music and became a mentor for countless women musicians. Contemporary blues singer Koko Taylor listened constantly to Rainey's and other blues women's recordings as a child in a family of sharecroppers working a cotton farm. "I always said I would like to be like these people I'm hearing on these records," she says. "What these women did—like Ma Rainey—they was the foundation of the blues. They brought the blues up from slavery up to today."[2] Rainey's work remained solidly anchored in the rural culture of southern black people as they gradually emerged from the era of slavery. Born in 1886, she was only one generation removed from slavery. When she began to perform in 1900 at the age of fourteen, the postslavery system of racial segregation in the South had been firmly established.[3] Rainey made ninety-two records— most of them in Chicago—between 1923 and 1928 and, according to Sandra Lieb, although her performances were largely in southern tent shows, she in fact played many successful engagements in Chicago, and performed in Cleveland, Cincinnati, and other Ohio cities, Pittsburgh, Detroit, Indianapolis, Philadelphia, and Newark as well. Because she lived in Chicago, she was not a regular Harlem performer, but did appear at the Lincoln Theater in 1923 and in March 1926; most likely she gave other local performances when she recorded in New York in 1924 and 1925.[4]

Every study of Gertrude Rainey cites Sterling Brown's powerful poem, "Ma Rainey." I, too, want to quote it here because it so successfully conveys the southern flavor of her appeal:

I

When Ma Rainey
Comes to town,
Folks from anyplace
Miles aroun',
From Cape Girardeau,
Poplar Bluff,
Flocks in to hear
Ma do her stuff;

Comes flivverin' in,
Or ridin' mules,
Or packed in trains,
Picknickin' fools . . .
That's what it's like,
Fo' miles on down,
To the New Orleans delta
An' Mobile town,
When Ma hits
Anywheres aroun'.

II

Dey comes to hear Ma Rainey from de little river settlements
From blackbottom cornrows and from lumber camps;

Dey stumble in de hall, jes' a-laughin' an' a-cacklin',
Cheerin' lak roarin' water, lak wind in river swamps.

An' some jokers keeps dey laughs a-goin' in de crowded aisles,
An' some folks sits dere waitin' wid dey aches an' miseries,
Till Ma comes out before dem, a-smilin' gold-toofed smiles,
An' Long Boy ripples minors on de black an' yellow keys.

III

O Ma Rainey,
Sing yo' song;
Now you's back
Whah you belong,
Git way inside us,
Keep us strong . . .
O Ma Rainey,
Li'l an' low;
Sing us 'bout de hard luck
Roun' our do';
Sing us 'bout de lonesome road
We mus' go . . .

IV

I talked to a fellow, an' the fellow say,
"She jes' catch hold of us, somekindaway.
She sang Backwater Blues one day:
        'It rained fo' days an' de skies was dark as night,
        Trouble taken place in de lowlands at night.
        Thundered an' lightened an' the storm begin to roll
        Thousan's of people ain't got no place to go.
        Den I went an' stood upon some high ol' lonesome hill,
        An' looked down on the place where I used to live.'
An' den de folks, dey natchally bowed dey heads an' cried
Bowed dey heavy heads, shet dey moufs up tight an' cried
An' Ma lef' de stage, an' followed some de folks outside."

Gertrude "Ma" Rainey was a pioneer on the black entertainment circuit. She shaped a musical tradition for many generations of blues women and was celebrated by black southerners as one of the great cultural figures of her time. *(Frank Driggs/Archive Photos)*

For Rainey and other black women who toured as entertainers from the turn of the century on, the interminable journeys around which they organized their lives posed fundamental challenges to the normal social expectations surrounding female experience. A sampling of her song titles suggests how much her music is permeated with travel themes: "Leavin' This Morning," "Traveling Blues," "Walking Blues," and "Runaway Blues." *(Michael Ochs Archives/Venice CA)*

When Bessie Smith auditioned at Black Swan—the first black-owned record company—she was rejected because of her grassroots sound. The company's board of directors included W. E. B. Du Bois and John Nail, James Weldon Johnson's brother-in-law and the most prominent real estate broker in Harlem. *(Frank Driggs/Archive Photos)*

As much a legend as her mentor, Ma Rainey, Smith would become one of the most extraordinary personalities in the history of American popular culture.*(Frank Driggs/ Corbis-Bettmann)*

Smith's work allows us to make a case for female enunciators of a historical consciousness that elevates women's lives to a position of equal importance with men's.
(Frank Driggs/Corbis- Bettmann)

Bessie Smith figures in Harlem Renaissance history largely owing to Carl Van Vechten's desire to count her among the guests at his notorious parties. While his written accounts of her performances leave much to be desired, he made a remarkable series of photographs of her the year before she died. *(Courtesy of the Estate of Carl Van Vechten, Joseph Solomon, Executor, and the Yale Collection of American Literature, Beinecke Rare Book and Manuscript Library, Yale University)*

The performances of the classic blues women—especially Bessie Smith— were one of the few cultural spaces in which a tradition of public discourse on male violence was established in the 1920s. *(Frank Driggs/Archive Photos)*

Women's blues provided a cultural space for community building among working-class black women, as well as a space devoid of bourgeois notions of sexual purity and "true womanhood." *(Photofest)*

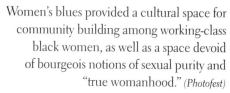

Smith created a musical caricature of domesticity that marked the beginnings of an oppositional attitude toward patriarchal ideology. *(Frank Driggs/Corbis-Bettmann)*

Of the various ways Billie Holiday's work remains connected to the blues tradition, one of the most striking is the intimate connection it reveals between love, sexuality, individuality, and freedom. *(Corbis-Bettmann)*

Although formal blues played a minimal role in Billie Holiday's repertoire, her music, deeply rooted in the blues tradition, recalled and transformed this cultural product of former slaves and used it to powerfully contest and transform prevailing popular song culture. *(Frank Driggs/Archive Photos)*

As a jazz musician who worked primarily within the idiom of white popular song, Lady Day transformed already existing material into her own form of modern jazz. In the process, she had a lasting influence on vocalists and instrumentalists alike. She is pictured here with Louis Armstrong on the set of the movie *New Orleans* in 1946. *(Culver Pictures, Inc.)*

"Strange Fruit", which Billie Holiday called her personal protest against racism, radically transformed her status in American popular culture.

(Robert Parent/Photofest)

Holiday's extraordinary cultural contributions as an artist are often overshadowed by her popular image as a woman whose private life was beset with personal tragedies. *(Michael Ochs Archives/Venice, CA)*

Lady Day's music proved that she was capable of negotiating entrances into mainstream popular culture while simultaneously forging sharp social critiques. *(Culver Pictures, Inc.)*

With the incomparable instrument of her voice, Holiday could completely divert a song from its composer's original and often sentimental and vapid intent. She was able to set in profound motion deeply disturbing disjunctions between overt statements and their aesthetic meanings. *(© Bob Douglas/Michael Ochs Archives/Venice, CA)*

Lady Day's genius was to give her life experiences an aesthetic form that recast them as windows through which other women could peer critically at their own lives. She offered other women the possibility of understanding the social contradictions they embodied and enacted in their lives—an understanding she never achieved in her own life.

(Courtesy of the Estate of Carl Van Vechten, Joseph Solomon, Executor, and the Yale Collection of American Literature, Beinecke Rare Book and Manuscript Library, Yale University)

Dere wasn't much more de fellow say:
She jes' gits hold of us dataway.[5]

Bessie Smith, who patterned herself after Rainey, was popular among both rural southern and urban northern audiences. As much a legend as the "Mother of the Blues," Smith would become one of the most extraordinary personalities in the history of U.S. popular culture. When Harlem emerged as the cultural capital of black America, Bessie Smith became the quintessential Harlem blues woman. And the audacious and innovative contributions of the premier blues woman of the twenties would inform the evolution of both jazz and popular song for the remainder of the century.

Following her first recording, "Down Hearted Blues,"[6] made in 1923, (simultaneously Columbia's first popular hit and its first "race record"), she sold millions of records and made hundreds of thousands of dollars. Bessie Smith, the "World's Greatest Blues Singer," the first real "superstar" in African-American popular culture, attracted a significant number of white people to her performances—in the South as well as in the North. Her work, however, was segregated into the "race music" market by the recording industry. The racialized classification of her 160 recordings ensured that her part and the role played by her peers in shaping the popular musical culture of the mainstream would never have to be acknowledged.

Initially—that is, before black music was commodified successfully by the recording industry—the location of the blues within a largely African-American cultural environment was simply due to the social conditions of its creation. This music sprang from the contradictory realities of black people's lives in the aftermath of slavery. However, during the 1920s, as blues music became the foundation of the fledgling recording companies' "race records" sections, it was identified and culturally represented not only as music produced by black people but as music to be heard solely by black people. As music entered its age of mechanical reproduction, blues were deemed reproducible only within the cultural borders of their site of origin. The racially segregationist distribution strategy of the recording industry implicitly instructed white ears to feel revolted by the blues and, moreover, to assume that this sense of revulsion was instinctive. Even those white Americans who wanted to break through barriers of racism, and who sincerely attempted to appreciate this music, tended to perceive it as primitive and exotic. Despite their intent to resist the racism that located the blues in a racially restricted cultural space, their Eurocentric perspective conferred upon the blues the very sense of inferiority they thought they were challenging. Carl Van Vechten, for instance, who played a pivotal role in expanding Bessie Smith's white audience, wrote about her

> strange rhythmic rites in a voice full of shouting and moaning and praying and suffering, a wild, rough, Ethiopian voice, harsh and volcanic, but seductive and sensuous, too, released between rouged lips and the whitest of teeth, the singer swaying lightly to the beat, as is the Negro custom.[7]

For Bessie Smith's black working-class audiences, she was a serious artist—not an exotic oddity—who courageously explored unknown terrains of the blues and honed and stretched the form to its very limits. Following a tradition established by the elder Rainey, Smith made the blues into women's music and a site for the elaboration of a black cultural consciousness that did not ignore the dynamics of gender. Her popularity was a result of the black community's ability to identify her greatness as an artist and to discover themselves and their lives—women and men alike—in her work.[8]

In later black cultural discourses, leadership—political, religious, cultural—is gendered as male. Bessie Smith's work allows us to make the case for female enunciators of a historical consciousness that elevates women's lives to a position of equal importance with men's. For masses of black people during the decade of the twenties—for those who remained geographically rooted in traditional southern culture as well as for migrant populations in the North and Midwest—Smith was an articulator and shaper of African-American identity and consciousness. Her songs at once reflected and conferred order upon the social experiences of black women and men and their emotional responses to those experiences. The themes of her music were the themes of working-class black people's lives, and the myriad emotional qualities with which her voice transmitted these themes—pathos or humor, aggressiveness or resignation, irony or straight-forwardness—were the various ways in which her working-class sisters and brothers lived the realities of these themes.

For the millions of women condemned to jobs involving domestic drudgery, there was "Washwoman's Blues,"[9] and for all those familiar with the monthly ritual of scraping together pennies to pay the landlord, there was "House Rent Blues."[10] "Jail House Blues"[11] acknowledged the inevitability of the prison experience in virtually every household of the black community, while "Backwater Blues"[12] was for those whose socially inflicted destitution was tragically compounded by floods and other natural disasters. And for all those who could be prodded to reflect upon the roots of their myriad pains of poverty, there was "Poor Man's Blues."[13]

This is not to say that Bessie Smith's musical messages coincided with the literal meaning of her lyrics. But the reality-oriented dimension of her songs—with all their secret allusions—rendered them easily accessible to her black audiences. As one jazz critic pointed out in a tribute to Smith five years after her death, "her art was real, she expressed the spirit of her people, to whom she remained faithful all her life. . . . Her message was mixed with pain, oppression and the horrors of lynch law—a panorama of a great race, and a cowardly foe."[14]

Bessie Smith knew how to ground her appeal in her own lived experiences as an African-American woman. Many of the songs she recorded directly address the circumstances of black women's lives: work, jail, physical abuse inflicted by male partners, and other injustices. The attitudes of the female subjects in the songs she sang encouraged black women to be as strong and independent as they were loving and caring. Bessie Smith's blues attitude foreshadowed the later development of feminist consciousness during the late 1960s and early 1970s. Her music issued an appeal as universal as the circumstances in which it was anchored were historically and culturally specific.

In the immediate aftermath of her death, John Hammond evaluated Smith's importance in this way:

To my way of thinking, Bessie Smith was the greatest artist American jazz ever produced; in fact, I'm not sure her art did not reach beyond the limits of the term jazz. She was one of those rare beings—a completely integrated artist capable of projecting her whole personality into music.[15]

Although her contributions are frequently ignored by the historians of jazz, she has been called "the first modern jazz performer—a performer of considerable influence on everyone from Louis Armstrong to Billie Holiday."[16] Richard Hadlock, who may be criticized for the sexism that led him to ignore other influential women musicians of that era, forcefully acknowledged the Empress. In Bessie Smith's work, he observes,

> instrumentalists recognized the sort of individuality they sought to express on their own horns and strings. Jazzmen heard, too, a thoughtful blend of precomposed song structures and Southern blues feeling, a blend close to their own ideas about how good jazz should sound.[17]

Formally unschooled in musical technique, Bessie Smith nevertheless developed many of the important technical elements that jazz musicians, vocalists and instrumentalists alike, would strive to perfect in the decades following her death.

The decade of Bessie Smith's artistic rise coincided with the Harlem Renaissance. Her music sought to accomplish the same goal as the visual and literary art associated with the Renaissance—the cultural articulation of African-American identities and consciousness. Yet she, and indeed the blues and jazz movements that reached their apogee during the twenties, were all but ignored by most of the leading figures of the Renaissance. The exception was Langston Hughes. As Steven Tracy points out in his important study *Langston Hughes and the Blues*, the premier poet of the Renaissance turned to the blues for formal and thematic inspiration.[18] His first published volume of work was entitled *The Weary Blues*.[19] As Hughes recalls in his first autobiography, *The Big Sea,* his relationship with the blues was so intense that even though he could not carry a tune, he sometimes attempted to sing his own blues poems aloud.

> The blues poems I would often make up in my head and sing on the way to work. (Except that I could never carry a tune. But when I sing to myself, I think I am singing.) One evening, I was crossing Rock Creek Bridge, singing a blues I was trying to get right before I put it down on paper. A man passing on the opposite side of the bridge stopped, looked at me, then turned around and cut across the roadway.
>
> He said: "Son, what's the matter? Are you ill?"
>
> "No," I said. "Just singing."
>
> "I thought you were groaning," he commented. "Sorry!" And went on his way.
>
> So after that I never sang my verses aloud in the street anymore.[20]

Langston Hughes paid tribute to the blues in numerous ways. In the narration of the pageant entitled "The Glory of Negro History," he represented the blues as a metaphor for black life: "The blues are sad songs, but with an undercurrent of hope and determination in them. Thus it was with Negro life for a long time, with pools of prejudice and segregation at the doorstep, but with hope and determination always there."[21] In the 1940 essay entitled "Songs Called the Blues," Hughes characterized the blues and the spirituals as "two great Negro gifts to American music." In his opinion, the three greatest singers of the blues were women: Mamie Smith, Clara Smith, and "the astounding Bessie Smith."[22] And in one of the "Simple" stories, which he called "Shadow of the Blues," there is a dialogue about the three Smiths in which Simple attempts to argue that he is younger than Hughes's narrator, based on the latter's familiarity with the classic blues singers.[23] However, when the discussion turns to Ma Rainey, Simple risks revealing his age in order to boast of his firsthand experience of Rainey's performances:

"Anyhow, to get back to the blues. Let me ask you about one more personality we forgot—Ma Rainey."

"Great day in the morning! Ma! That woman could sing some blues. I loved Ma Rainey."

"You are not as old as I am, you're older! I scarcely remember her myself. Ma Rainey is a legend to me."

"A who?"

"A myth."

"Ma Rainey were too dark to be a mist. But she really could sing the blues. I will not deny Ma Rainey, even to hide my age. Yes, I heard her! I am proud of hearing her! To tell the truth, if I stop and listen, I can still hear her."[24]

At this point Simple sings a few blues lyrics. He ultimately declares that giving away his age is a small price to pay for the privilege of announcing that he has heard Ma Rainey sing the blues firsthand.

Carl Van Vechten, one of the leading white patrons of the black literary renaissance, was equally interested in the black popular musical culture of the era. A former music critic for the *New York Times* and a regular contributor to *Vanity Fair*, Van Vechten reviewed concerts and recordings by blues and jazz musicians. In a letter to H. L. Mencken in 1924, he stated that "jazz, the blues, Negro spirituals, all stimulate me enormously for the moment."[25] Van Vechten, who took a decided interest in Bessie Smith's career, boasted that he had acquired "boxes and boxes" of her records, "which I played in the early Twenties and everybody who came to my apartment was invited to hear them. As a matter of fact, musicians arriving from Europe called on me especially to listen to these records."[26]

It is indeed ironic that if the personality of Bessie Smith figures into Harlem Renaissance history, it is largely due to Van Vechten's desire to count her among the guests at his notorious parties, which were attended alike by leading black intellectuals and white connoisseurs and consumers of black culture. Ethel Waters, one of Van Vechten's regular guests, said he "knew more about Harlem than any other white man except the captain of the Harlem police station."[27]

Some of the most widely circulated anecdotes from the Harlem Renaissance revolve around Bessie Smith's attendance at one Van Vechten party, where she performed while characteristically intoxicated. Smith is said to have physically assaulted Fania Marinoff, Van Vechten's wife, in order to ward off an unwanted kiss of gratitude.[28] Langston Hughes recounted in his autobiography that at this party Smith also complimented Marguerite D'Alvarez, the Metropolitan Opera singer, after her performance of an aria. "Don't let nobody tell you you can't sing!" Smith told D'Alvarez.[29] Perhaps the most interesting anecdote of all refers to her decision to sing "Work House Blues" at this gathering of what Smith might have called "highbrows."[30]

One of the familiar contemporary descriptions of Bessie Smith's work—from a *Vanity Fair* article in 1925 by Carl Van Vechten—has already been quoted. Its significance lies in the way it reveals the racist assumptions behind Van Vechten's and other powerful whites' appreciation of black cultural forms. His remarks were inspired by his attendance at a 1925 concert in Newark, New Jersey:

> As the curtain lifted, a jazz band, against a background of plum-colored hangings, held the full stage. . . . The hangings parted and a great brown woman emerged. She was at this time . . . very large, and she wore a crimson satin robe, sweeping up from her trim ankles, and embroidered in multicolored sequins in designs. Her face was beautiful with the rich ripe beauty of southern darkness, a deep bronze brown, matching the bronze of her bare arms. Walking slowly to the footlights . . . she began her strange rhythmic rites in a voice full of shouting and moaning and praying and suffering, a wild, rough, Ethiopian voice, harsh and volcanic, but seductive and sensuous, too, released between rouged lips and the whitest of teeth, the singer swaying lightly to the beat, as is the Negro custom. . . .
>
> Now, inspired partly by the expressive words, partly by the stumbling strain of the accompaniment, partly by the powerfully magnetic personality of this elemental conjure woman with her plangent African voice, quivering with passion and pain, sounding as if it had been developed at the sources of the Nile, the crowd burst into hysterical shrieks of sorrow and lamentation. "Amens" rent the air.[31]

Van Vechten admired Bessie Smith, yet he considered her "crude and primitive." She represented, in his opinion, "the true folk spirit of the race." Ethel Waters, he argued, was the superior artist. "She refines her comedy, refines her pathos, refines even her obscenities."[32]

Van Vechten's most valuable contributions to the historical preservation of Bessie Smith's life and works are the remarkable photographs he made of her the year before she died. (See the photographic section in this volume for one of these images.) He felt that the photographic session permitted him to get "nearer to her real personality than I ever had before." If one can ignore, for the moment, the presumptuousness of his words, it is possible to agree with his assessment that "the photographs, perhaps, are the only adequate record of [Bessie Smith's] true appearance and manner that exist."[33]

"[T]here was no 'Harlem Renaissance,' " Houston Baker writes in his study on *Modernism and the Harlem Renaissance,* "(and certainly not a 'voguish' one comprised of disparate artists lumped under a single heading) until *after* the event."[34] Baker's study examines the emergence of an African-American modernist *sound* as the distinctive feature of black intellectual history of that era. He persuasively argues that the problem with much of the scholarship on this period is that it has been informed by the uncritical acceptance of the failure of the Harlem Renaissance. His own conclusion is that

> "renaissancism" connotes something quite removed from a single, exotic set of "failed" high jinks confined to less than a decade. It signals in fact a resonantly and continuously productive set of tactics, strategies and syllables that takes form at the turn of the century and extends to our day.[35]

Beginning his analysis with Booker T. Washington, he argues that the climax of Renaissance modernism is reached with the publication of Sterling Brown's poem "Ma Rainey." In this widely reproduced (and already quoted) poem, written in black vernacular on the blues queen's powerful performances, Baker finds a "blending of class and mass—*poetic* mastery discovered as a function of deformative *folk* sound," which, he argues, "constitutes the essence of black discursive modernism."[36]

However, even as Baker focuses on the "deformative," in an effort to demonstrate the challenge posed by the Renaissance to the traditional European distinction between high and low art, his analysis — while focusing on the development of a new "sound" — tends to relegate music to the status of literary material. Moreover, while broadening the temporal and historical boundaries of the Renaissance, he restricts the Renaissance to the realm of literature. If, as Baker argues, the Renaissance cannot be evaluated accurately if it is assumed that impermeable historical borders confine it to the decade of the twenties, a similar argument can be made about its broader cultural context within that era. We should not marginalize the orature — the popular music — of that era by treating it simply as raw material for literary form or, to use Baker's term, for literary "deformation."

It is significant that the cover chosen for Baker's study is the most widely reproduced photograph of Ma Rainey. However, she figures in his analysis only as the subject of Sterling Brown's poem. Baker foregrounds the part blues women played in the Renaissance, but he fails to acknowledge their artistic agency and ends up with a masculinist analysis of black modernism.

In a conversation with Nathan Huggins, Eubie Blake maintained that music was at the center of the Harlem Renaissance. Much of the cultural interest in Harlem focused on the music that was being created during that era. "The white people," Blake told Huggins, "were coming up to Harlem to hear this music."[37] Yet black intellectuals associated with the Renaissance largely underestimated the value of African-American blues and jazz. Huggins points out that they tended to treat this music as a rather primitive folk art that needed to be elevated to the level of high art in order to take its place as a meaningful element of African-American culture:

> Harlem intellectuals promoted Negro art, but one thing is very curious, except for Langston Hughes, none of them took jazz — the new music — seriously. . . . [T]he promoters of the Harlem Renaissance were so fixed on a vision of *high* culture that they did not look very

hard or well at jazz. . . . Were it not for Langston Hughes, we would have almost no specific notice of [the blues] from the Harlem writers.[38]

Men like James Weldon Johnson and Alain Locke expected a race genius to appear who would transform their era's black music into *high* culture. Such was "the dream of Johnson's protagonist in *Autobiography of an Ex-Colored Man* as he fancied symphonic scores based on ragtime."[39] In his 1934 article entitled "Toward a Critique of Negro Music," Alain Locke argued that no great African-American music had as yet been created:

> It is time to realize that though we may be a musical people, we have produced few if any great musicians,—that though we may have evolved a folk music of power and potentiality, it has not yet been integrated into a musical tradition,—that our creativeness and originality on the folk level has not yet been matched on the level of instrumental mastery or that of creative composition,—and that with a few exceptions, the masters of Negro musical idiom so far are not Negro.[40]

Implicit in this analysis of black music is the assumption that it should develop in accordance with the criteria established by European "classical" music to become culturally equal to the serious music of other cultures. Alain Locke's attitude toward black American music reflected the ambivalence of many of the Renaissance writers and artists toward the music of their people. On the one hand, it was the one art form within black culture that had retained the vigor of the culture's historical realities. It furnished evidence of race identity and race consciousness. On the other hand, it was the target, like the culture as a whole, of racist characterizations such as "savage," "primitive," and "undeveloped."

In keeping with his disavowal of the blues, Locke's important essay entitled "The New Negro," which conveyed the philosophical and political complexities of the Harlem Renaissance, suggested that the spirituals and their development could be seen as a metaphor for the emergence of the "New Negro":

> Recall how suddenly the Negro spirituals revealed themselves; suppressed for generations under the stereotypes of Wesleyan hymn harmony, secretive, half-ashamed, until the courage of being natural brought them out. . . . Similarly the mind of the Negro seems suddenly to have slipped from under the tyranny of social intimidation and to be shaking off the psychology of imitation and implied inferiority. By shedding the old chrysalis of the Negro problem we are achieving something like a spiritual emancipation.[41]

However, in the article "The Negro Spirituals" that he contributed to *The New Negro*, he argued that these "natural" spirituals, this unadulterated folk music, should serve as the material for a "classic" music tradition. "A genius that would organize its distinctive elements in a formal way," he wrote, "would be the musical giant of his age."[42]

For Langston Hughes, however, the relationship between black music and the new, racially aware black American was more than metaphorical. He saw music as a potent social catalyst that could awaken to consciousness slumbering black intellectuals. And, indeed, in the final paragraph of his manifesto "The Negro Artist and the Racial Mountain," he specifically refers to the songs of Bessie Smith: "Let the blare of Negro jazz bands and the bellowing voice of Bessie Smith singing Blues penetrate the closed ears of the colored near-intellectuals until they listen and perhaps understand."[43] Jazz, for Hughes, was "one of the inherent expressions of Negro life in America," the most perfect manifestation of black people's cultural originality.[44] Hughes's appreciation of black music appears most strongly in the body of his poetry, much of which consists of poetic transpositions of the blues in both form and content.

Of all of the Renaissance intellectuals, he proved to be most receptive to the blues. This was perhaps because, more than anyone else, he attempted to incorporate the social realities of the masses of black people into his art. Of all of his Harlem contemporaries, Langston Hughes was the least influenced by the intelligentsia's bourgeois, anti-working-class attitudes. He realized that despite the unfolding urbanization of the black community and the crystallization of a black middle class and a black intelligentsia, it was essential to preserve the culture that had been born from the experiences of the masses. Even as the blues was being treated by most of the Harlem intellectuals as an indelicate stepchild, it was, nonetheless, being preserved.

As the circle of Harlem writers and artists took shape, the young recording industry was focusing its attention on female blues musicians who came to be known as the classic blues singers of the twenties. This process was initiated by the 1920 recording of Mamie Smith's performance of "Crazy Blues" on the Okeh label. Within one month's time, black people had purchased 75,000 copies at one dollar each.[45] Okeh's unanticipated success—this was one of the young company's first hits—motivated other firms to follow suit with their own recordings of female blues singers. These records, advertised and sold in the black community, constituted the "race records" sections of the recording companies.

In 1921, Harry Pace announced the formation of Black Swan Records, a company whose stockholders, employees, and artists all would be black. As Pace stated,

> Black Swan records are made to meet what we believe is a legitimate and growing demand. There are 12,000,000 colored people in the U.S. and in that number there is hid a wonderful amount of musical ability. We propose to spare no expense in the search for and developing of the best singers and musicians among the 12,000,000.[46]

The motto Pace chose for Black Swan was "The Only Genuine Colored Record—Others Are Only Passing."[47] However, when Bessie Smith auditioned at Black Swan, she was rejected because of her grassroots sound. The company's board of directors included W. E. B. Du Bois and John Nail, James Weldon Johnson's brother-in-law and the most prominent real estate broker in Harlem. William Grant Still, who was affiliated during that era with the Harlem Symphony, was Black Swan's musical director. Ethel Waters was chosen over Bessie Smith because her style seemed more compatible with that of the popular white singers of the day.[48] As with the Harlem Renaissance figures, the effort to assert an African-American identity and race consciousness was ambiguous at best, pervaded by the contradictions emanating from an uncritical acceptance of elitist cultural values.

Of the classic blues singers of the twenties, Ethel Waters was considered the most sophisticated, having consciously cultivated a sound from which many of the unfamiliar and inaccessible elements of black musical culture had been purged. According to Van Vechten,

> In her singing she exercises . . . subtle skill. Some of her songs she croons; she never shouts. Her methods are precisely opposed to those of the crude coon shouter, to those of the authentic Blues singer, and yet, not for once, does she lose the veridical Negro atmosphere. Her voice and her gestures are essentially Negro, but they have been thought out and restrained, not prettified, but stylized.[49]

To unschooled white ears as well as to successful black people who did not particularly relish musical reminders of their own social roots, Ethel Waters may have appeared to be the most accomplished blues singer of the period. But, as is universally recognized today, Bessie Smith was the real genius at her craft. She was not only the greater artist, she also more accurately represented the sociohistorical patterns of black people's lives.

Ethel Waters's sophisticated sound was a cultural product of urbanization that rapidly was transforming the black community and enticing those who were susceptible to the illusions of assimilation. Ethel Waters found receptive audiences outside the African-American cultural context—from the northern white population to European royalty. While Bessie Smith performed before ethnically integrated—and sometimes predominantly white—audiences, she did not feel the need to alter either her material or her mode of presentation. Whether Waters's brand of entertainment was aesthetically and historically faithful to the black American culture she professed to transmit to her white audiences is arguable. She herself recalled that during her Black Swan audition "there was much discussion of whether I should sing popular or cultural numbers."[50] According to historian David Levering Lewis,

> Black Swan records, after all, were intended to have class and reflect credit on the race. The directors did not want the company to appear too colored; and Bessie Smith, also auditioning . . . was rejected because of her unmistakable nitty-grittiness. . . . "They finally decided on popular," Waters said. "It was the right decision."[51]

In the eyes of the contemporary black middle class, Bessie Smith may not have appeared to "have class and reflect credit on the race," because her music, both in its style and its content, represented the experiences of the masses. "Successful blacks disliked Bessie," in the words of Elaine Feinstein,

> because they felt her behaviour endangered their own image of themselves. The crudity of her language, and the unpredictability of her moods, made her seem like a part of the street life they wanted to forget. Bessie continued to enjoy that life: its food, its home-made liquor and its uninhibited parties. Essentially, she was refusing to acknowledge the class system the blacks had set up which put the white world at the unreachable top of the tree.[52]

Bessie Smith maintained unashamed bonds with her own southern upbringing, preserving in her music African-American folk experiences that many black intellectuals associated with the racist-inspired stereotypes they were trying to transcend. Her blues—in the tradition of her mentor, Gertrude "Ma" Rainey—made numerous references, for example, to the African-based religious practice of hoodoo. From the vantage point of the dominant culture, hoodoo (or voodoo) was a primitive conglomeration of irrational superstitions. But for black people who believed in or performed the magical rituals of this religion—and often parallel to their Christian beliefs and practices—hoodoo was a vital if unrecognized link to the

African past. Among the literary figures associated with the Harlem Renaissance, it was primarily Zora Neale Hurston who explored the meaning of hoodoo.[53] Like Bessie Smith, Hurston was, however, relegated to the margins of the Renaissance. If she ultimately has become the most widely read black author associated with the Renaissance, her relatively recent popularity is in inverse relation to her status at the time she produced her work.

In retrospect, we can now see that Bessie Smith and Zora Neale Hurston were probing the heart of the problem of forging an African-American aesthetic. Smith sang about the experiences and sensibilities of the masses of black women and men—emanating, in part, from an African past, seasoned by slavery, and transformed by emancipation and migration. Hurston recorded, fictionalized, and analyzed those experiences, capturing both the form and content of what would later be seen as pivotal elements of African-American culture. The folk tales or "lies" Hurston wrote down and the spiritual power of hoodoo that she directly experienced as well as analyzed, together with the blues, hold the key to an understanding of the foundations of African-American popular culture.

Evidencing the genesis of the blues in the black culture of the rural South, the presence of folk traditions in the blues points to the preservation, in a transformed and frequently distorted fashion, of important elements of black people's African heritage. Because the slaveocracy had sought to extinguish the collective cultural memory of black people in order to confine them to an inferior social space, music, folktales, and hoodoo practices were always important ways black people could maintain connections—conscious or not—with the traditions of their ancestors.

In the aftermath of slavery, African Americans who still resided in the South could recognize and affirm the dailiness of their culture—with its often unacknowledged African roots—in the blues, in the folktales, and in the community's beliefs in the power of hoodoo. For the new immigrants to the cities, the blues were a way to keep alive a heritage that might otherwise have receded into the collective unconscious. The blues kept a sense of community alive and assisted it to transcend geographical boundaries. As a result of the feminist tendencies in the work of the blues women, this sense of community was not without its internal ruptures and challenges to black male dominance. As I have attempted to bring to light throughout this book, Bessie Smith's performances and recorded work were central to this process.

Because Bessie Smith was not influenced by prevailing concerns about "high art" or about making the African-American blues form palatable to white audiences, she unhesitatingly sang about such distinctively black folk practices as those of the hoodoo doctors or conjurers, which Zora Neale Hurston wrote about as a participant-observer. Bessie Smith exuberantly sang about fortune-tellers, healers, and other "two-headed" practitioners. Her songs present women as spiritual leaders in the community. As Hurston explains, and as Smith revealed in her performances, a good number of the hoodoo doctors specialized in male-female relationships. In "Red Mountain Blues," for example, the distraught subject of the song, who has been rejected by her partner, engages in suicidal reflections (incidentally an atypical posture for the women in Bessie Smith's blues). She consults a hoodoo doctor—"fortune-teller" in the language of the lyrics—who

. . . told me what I had to do
Get myself some snakeroot, start right in to chew

Got myself some snakeroot, John the Conqueror, too
Chewed them both together, I know what they will do
Took some in my pocket, put some in my boot
That don't make him love me, I'll start right in to shoot.[54]

There is an allusion here to what is generally considered the most potent root in conjuration, High John the Conqueror, named after a trickster figure of slave folklore who could always outwit the master:

The sign of this man was a laugh, and his singing-symbol was a drumbeat. . . . It was an inside thing to live by. It was most sure to be heard when and where the work was the hardest and the lot most cruel. It helped the slaves endure. They knew that something better was coming. So they laughed in the face of things and sang, "I'm so glad! Trouble don't last always." And the white people who heard them were struck dumb that they could laugh. . . .[55]

In Zora Neale Hurston's recapitulation of the folk history of this root, she explains that the "thousands upon thousands of humble people who still believe" in "John de Conquer,"

> that is, in the power of love and laughter to win by their subtle power, do John reverence by getting the root of the plant in which he has taken up his secret dwelling, and "dressing" it with perfume, and keeping it on their person, or in their houses in a secret place. It is there to help them overcome things they feel that they could not beat otherwise, and to bring them the laugh of the day. John will never forsake the weak and the helpless, nor fail to bring hope to the hopeless. This is what they believe, and so they do not worry. They go on and laugh and sing. Things are bound to come out right tomorrow. That is the secret of Negro song and laughter.[56]

High John the Conqueror, the root incorporating the spirit of hope—the hope of a woman whose man has abandoned her, the hope of a people still striving to be free—metaphorically captures the soul of Black American culture. Hope for the hopeless has been magically conjured up by the various trickster figures in black folklore. Hope for the hopeless has been conjured within the religious context—in Christianity as well as the more explicitly African-based practice of hoodoo. Hope for the hopeless has been conjured aesthetically by the blues women and blues men. If Bessie Smith was the "world's greatest blues singer," it was at least in part because, like John the Conqueror, she brought song and laughter as she evoked the harshest and cruelest experiences of black people in America, and she brought a promise that "the sun's gonna shine in my back door some day."

Zora Neale Hurston participated in, collected material on, and illuminated for the first time, through her discipline of anthropology, many aspects of southern black hoodoo practices. In this, she was a pioneer. On several occasions, she functioned as an apprentice to hoodoo doctors, thus acquiring firsthand information on this aspect of black culture that preserved collective memories of West African religious practices. In one instance, Hurston assisted the two-headed doctor, Eulalia—not insignificantly, a woman—to guarantee the consolidation of a love relationship. True, the man was married, but, insisted the customer, his wife was working roots on him in order to keep the marriage together. In the man's yard Hurston buried a lemon stuffed with gunpowder and a piece of paper on which the wife's name had been written nine times. Red pepper was placed in the stove.

> Then Eulalia took the [salt] bowl and went from corner to corner "salting" the room. She'd toss a sprinkling into a corner and say, "Just fuss and fuss till you part and go away." Under the bed was sprinkled also. It was all over in a minute or two. Then we went out and shut the kitchen door and hurried away. And Saturday night Eulalia got her pay and the next day she set the ceremony to bring about the marriage.[57]

In Bessie Smith's "I'd Rather Be Dead and Buried in My Grave," the protagonist attempts to ward off the influence of the man who has mistreated her, sending her to the brink of suicide, by "sprinkl[ing] salt around to keep him from around."[58] In the practices of conjuration, salt is thought to possess the power to remove the presence or influence of an undesirable person. Zora Neale Hurston relates a conversation between two women, one of whom informs the other that throwing salt at a woman who is after her will provide the protection she needs:

> You throw salt behind her everytime she go out of her gate. Do dat nine times and Ah bet she'll move so fast she won't even know where she's going. Somebody salted a woman over in Georgetown and she done moved so much she done wore out her furniture on de movin' wagon. . . .[59]

There are numerous other references to the practices of hoodoo in Bessie Smith's songs—for example in "Mama's Got the Blues,"[60] "Yodeling Blues,"[61] "Gin House Blues,"[62] and "Lady Luck Blues." In the last song the female protagonist relates measures she has taken after being deserted by a lover who left "with a girl I thought was my friend."

> I've got his picture turned upside down
> I've sprinkled goofer dust all around.[63]

In other words, she is attempting to use conjuring powers to send him to his death. While the significance of turning his picture upside down is obvious, the meaning of the allusion to "goofer dust" is rather esoteric, referring to soil from a gravesite, preferably from the grave of an infant. Hoodoo doctors, according to Zora Neale Hurston, were reluctant to use the dirt from an adult grave, because even though it is powerful as a means of bringing about someone's death, the spirit of this sinner "is likely to get unruly and kill others for the pleasure of killing. It is too dangerous to commission."[64]

As African-American literary, visual, and performing artists—and critics as well—would later realize, African-American religious practices based in the West African and especially Yoruba religion permeate the culture as a whole. The articulation of a specifically black aesthetic—the announced aim of the Harlem Renaissance—cannot locate itself in the living tradition of African-American culture without taking seriously the practices variously called conjure, voodoo, or hoodoo.

Bessie Smith and Zora Neale Hurston were similar in their respective attitudes toward hoodoo in that neither approached it as ungrounded superstition that needed to be purged from the cultural practices of the communities in which it was present. They were also alike in that they resisted the construction of hoodoo imposed by the dominant culture, which defined it as material to be exoticized and sensationalized. Zora Neale Hurston was able to combine effectively the knowledge she acquired through her lifelong exposure to African-American cultural practices with her scholarly work in the discipline of anthropology—a rare and challenging feat, given the traditional Eurocentric biases of her field. Bessie Smith sang about these practices in the immediacy of black people's daily lives, transcending the limitations of the segregated recording industry by selling millions of records during her career.

For her insistence upon centralizing folk culture in her work, and for her refusal to conform to the behavioral dictates of the Renaissance strategists, Hurston was vastly underread and underappreciated during her lifetime. Yet, she has emerged more than half a century later as perhaps the most important—and, finally, the most widely read—writer associated with the Harlem Renaissance, and her contributions to the preservation of African-American culture are unsurpassed by any of her peers of that era.

From a historical vantage point, Bessie Smith—whose work also centralized black folk culture—has occupied a space not unlike that from which Zora Neale Hurston has only fairly recently been retrieved; the decidedly black feminist consciousness that pervades Smith's work would situate her as something of an anachronism in the period that separated her career from the rise of black studies and women's studies as scholarly disciplines, and the majority of her contributions unfortunately escaped notice by many of the music critics who would examine her life and work during those years. Precisely at a moment like the present one, when questions of race, class, gender, and sexuality are being contested at every turn in our society, an artist like Bessie Smith can be given her full due. Not only for her musical contributions, but for her vital impact on the collective conscience of her live audiences and those who bought her records during her lifetime—as well as upon African-American culture generally—Smith deserves recognition. The challenge is ours to embrace the Empress of the Blues on all of these fronts, to begin honoring her memory in the same manner in which we have that of Zora Neale Hurston.

WHEN A WOMAN
LOVES A MAN

SOCIAL IMPLICATIONS OF
BILLIE HOLIDAY'S LOVE SONGS

Maybe he's not much, just another man, does what he can
But what does she care when a woman loves a man?
She'll just string along all through thick and thin, till his ship comes in
It's always that way when a woman loves a man.

— "WHEN A WOMAN LOVES A MAN"[1]

Ralph convinced Schiffman to come and catch me. When Schiff-
man asked Cooper what style I had, Cooper was stumped.

"You never heard singing so slow, so lazy, with such a drawl," he told
him. But he still couldn't put any label on me.

This, I figured, was the biggest compliment they could pay me.
Before anybody could compare me with other singers, they were com-
paring other singers with me.

"It ain't the blues," was all Cooper could tell him. "I don't know
what it is, but you got to come hear her."

— BILLIE HOLIDAY, LADY SINGS THE BLUES[2]

Although formal blues played a minimal role in Billie Holiday's repertoire, her music, deeply rooted in the blues tradition, recalled and transformed this cultural product of former slaves and used it to powerfully contest and transform prevailing popular song culture. What Ralph Ellison said about Jimmy Rushing is equally true of Lady Day: "[A]s a singer of ballads, [he] brought] to them a sincerity and a feeling for dramatizing the lyrics in the musical phrase which charged the banal lines with the mysterious potentiality of meaning which haunts the blues."[3] Holiday's remarkable ability as a jazz vocalist to appropriate inconsequential love songs—which without her interventions probably would have ended up in Tin Pan Alley trash cans—as occasions for evoking and exploring complex emotional meanings is celebrated abundantly in the literature on her life and career. What has remained unarticulated, however, is what I consider the most challenging problematic of her art: the social implications of this transformative aesthetic process. Thus, "Strange Fruit" is viewed almost universally as an anomaly in her vast recorded legacy. It is generally assumed that the song that became her signature is a unique and unparalleled production on her part, within the body of her work, with the possible exception of "God Bless the Child."

What is most immediately evident about these two selections is that, unlike the overwhelming majority of songs Lady Day performed and recorded, they contain no explicit allusions to love or sexuality. While "Strange Fruit" undoubtedly had the most forceful impact on her career— and, as I will discuss in the final chapter, brought previously unexplored dimensions of race, violence, and, implicitly, sexuality into the nightclub and concert hall—it should not be assumed that social content can be present only when themes of love and sexuality are absent. Of the various ways Holiday's work remains connected to the blues tradition, one of the most striking is the intimate connection it reveals between love, sexuality, individuality, and freedom.

Billie Holiday often referred to herself as a "race woman."[4] Her earliest biographer, John Chilton, alludes to the fact that she participated in a benefit concert for the Associated Communist Clubs of Harlem in May of 1944,[5] but significantly, he neglects to make any further comment on this moment in her career. In a study entitled *Communists in Harlem During the Depression*, Mark Naison includes a passing allusion to a "Communist anti-war song" Holiday included in her nightclub repertoire until FBI intervention forced her to remove it from her act.[6] One can only speculate as to whether or not she intended her performances to be a statement of partisan support, but her own words indicate that she had a deep appreciation of poor and working-class people—and especially African Americans. In a 1953 interview with *Tan* magazine, Holiday said:

There was nothing about living on the sidewalks that I didn't know. I knew how the gin joints looked on the inside; I had been singing in after-hours joints, damp, smoky cellars, in the backs of barrooms.

It was slow, this attempt to climb clear of the barrel. But as I grew older, I found those trying to keep me in it were not always the corner hoodlum, the streetwalker, the laborer, the numbers runner, the rooming-house ladies and landlords, the people who existed off the twenty-five and thirty-dollars-a-week salaries they were paying in those days.

They, I found, were the ones who wanted to see me "go," to get somewhere. It was their applause and help that kept me inspired. These "little people," condemned as I have been ever since I can remember, gave me my chance long before the mink-coated lorgnette crowd of Fifth Avenue and Greenwich Village ever heard of me.[7]

Yet, even if there were nothing in Billie Holiday's life to suggest a self-conscious social awareness, this would not justify the almost universal neglect of the politics of her music. She was much more than an artist who provided innovative jazz interpretations of the popular love songs of her era. That she did brilliantly, but the question remains: How can we interpret the creation of complex works of art that work with and against the platitudinous ideological content of undistinguished contemporary love songs? By and large, critics who appreciate Holiday's work have delved no more deeply into its meaning than to demonstrate her pivotal contributions to the evolution of modern jazz. I want to examine her work as an effort to transform social relations aesthetically beyond the shallow notions of love contained in the songs she remade through her art. Regardless of her conscious intent, her musical meditations on women's seemingly interminable love pains illuminated the ideological constructions of gender and the ways they insinuate themselves into women's emotional lives.

In examining Billie Holiday's love songs, I find it useful to employ Herbert Marcuse's notion of the "aesthetic dimension," first explored in his work *Eros and Civilization*[8] and later elaborated in *The Aesthetic*

Dimension.[9] "The political potential of art," he argued in the latter work, "lies only in its own aesthetic dimension."[10] He uses this concept to challenge, among other things, the assumption that "the political and the aesthetic, the revolutionary content and the artistic quality, tend to coincide."[11] While Marcuse's notion of "aesthetic form" is anchored in a conception of "authentic" or "great" art[12] informed by eighteenth- and nineteenth-century European literature, aspects of his theory of the subversive potential of art, developed as a critique of orthodox Marxist aesthetics, can be invoked not for the purpose of assimilating Holiday's music into the canon of "great" art, but rather as a way of understanding the persisting power and appeal of her performances. This, despite the fact that the songs she sang are lyrical inscriptions of an era during which male dominance went uncontested within dominant popular culture. "The radical qualities of art," according to Marcuse,

> are grounded precisely in the dimensions where art transcends its social determination and emancipates itself from the given universe of discourse and behavior while preserving its overwhelming presence. Thereby art creates the realm in which the subversion of experience proper to art becomes possible: the world formed by art is recognized as a reality which is suppressed and distorted in the given reality.[13]

My use of Marcuse's notion of the aesthetic dimension rejects its association with "transhistorical," "universal" truths.[14] I propose instead a conceptualization of "aesthetic dimension" that fundamentally historicizes and collectivizes it. Rather than a unique product of the solitary artist creating an "individual" aesthetic subversion, I want to argue that the "aesthetic dimension" of Billie Holiday's work represents a symbiosis, drawing from and contributing to an African-American social and musical history in which women's political agency is nurtured by, and in turn nurtures, aesthetic agency. It is this "aesthetic dimension" of Lady Day's songs which accounts for their undiminished appeal, for their simultaneous ability to confirm and subvert racist and sexist representations of women in love. It is this aesthetic dimension that demands close listening to and reading of her love songs for the purpose of proposing feminist reinterpretations. Such careful study will give her work an important place in the complex and continually evolving feminist consciousness associated with women of color.

Billie Holiday's project—as that of a jazz musician who worked primarily with the idiom of white popular song—consisted largely in transforming already existing material into her own form of modern jazz. It may be argued that what Marcuse called the aesthetic dimension resulted, in her work, from the way in which she utilized the formative power of her jazz style to refigure the songs she performed and recorded, the great majority of which were produced on the Tin Pan Alley assembly line according to the contrived and formulaic sentimentality characteristic of the era. When she transformed these sentimental love songs into works that would become jazz standards, she relocated them in a specifically African-American cultural tradition and simultaneously challenged the boundaries of that tradition. Her work, together with that of tenor saxophonist Lester Young, opened the way for new musical directions in modern jazz. Her approach to the lyrics both borrowed from and transformed ways of representing black female sexuality associated with classic blues women like Alberta Hunter and Bessie Smith. The complex negotiations she performed are reminiscent of the literary feat of Harriet Jacobs, whose narrative, *Incidents in the Life of a Slave Girl*, appropriated and transformed the nineteenth-century sentimental novel and, in the process, revealed new ways of thinking about black female sexuality.[15]

One way to explore Billie Holiday's awesome ability to transmute musical and lyrical meaning in the popular songs she performed is to think about her relationship to her musical material as analogous to African Americans' historical appropriation of the English language.[16] A new and unfamiliar language was imposed repressively on the Africans who had the misfortune to be transported from their native lands and deposited as slaves on the farms and plantations of European colonizers in America. Africans often were configured into labor forces in ways that prevented members of the same language groups from communicating with each other. English was a language they were powerless to reject, for in rejecting it, they effectively would have denied themselves the possibility of communicating with one another. June Jordan's work on black English indicates that, in accepting this language, Africans found ways to transform it, and thus to appropriate it in accordance with their own historically informed cultural and political needs.[17] Evolving over several centuries, black English reflects an attitude toward speech, poetry, and song that bears witness to the African experience within the North American context. For Billie Holiday, the very prospect of producing her music was contingent on her acceptance of a kind of song that not only represented a different musical tradition from the one in which she placed herself—she wanted Bessie Smith's big sound and Louis Armstrong's feeling—but that was imposed upon her repressively by the popular culture market.[18] Had she rejected the often insipid Tin Pan Alley material, she would have denied herself the possibility of song and thus of offering her musical originality to the black community, to the dominant culture, and to the world. Black people did not embrace the spoken English language without fiercely challenging the cultural oppression it implied and without incorporating this challenge into their daily speech. Billie Holiday did the same with the words and concepts of the songs imposed upon her, insinuating that battle into every musical phrase and making that battle the lyrical and dramatic core of her performances.

In the black American cultural context, speech is not taken for granted. It is not assumed that there are direct and undeviating correspondences between words and the objects, ideas, and feelings they purport to represent. In daily speech as well as in the aesthetic dimension, language has always been rewrought and recast, playfully coaxed toward new meanings, and sometimes ironically made to signify the opposite of its literal meaning. Distinctive patterns both of everyday speech and of slave songs manifested cultural connections between West African linguistic customs and African-American English as it was forged within and often against the system of slavery. While these patterns were ritualized in the musical tradition, from the field hollers and work songs to spirituals and the blues, daily speech patterns acquired a decidedly aesthetic character. "Playing the dozens," for example, reveals, beneath its misogynist overtones, the impulse to create poetry out of the language of everyday life.[19] Such an attitude toward language, based on a creative tension between the speaker and the spoken word, is one of the most salient characteristics of the evolution of African-American music, permitting song to speak the unspeakable, to communicate ideas otherwise banned by the oppressors from the realm of language. Black people, Sidney Finkelstein asserted,

> have had a powerful and terrible story to tell, the telling of which in more explicit languages has been denied to them by repression and censorship. Jazz is a music of protest against discrimination and Jim Crow. It expresses anger at lynchings and at direct or indirect slavery, resentment of poverty. It expresses the hope and struggle for freedom, the vitality which enables a people to wrest joy out of misery and to assert the triumph of human beings over the obstacles which would grind them down.[20]

This characteristic of jazz has its roots in the vocal music that stands at the beginning of the African-American music tradition. Initially, slave music was made by the unaccompanied human voice, because the primary musical instrument associated with various West African cultures—the drum—was banned by the slave owners, who knew that clandestine communication could be transmitted by its rhythms. The musicalization of speech arose as both aesthetic impulse and political impulse, incorporating African customs and expressing emancipatory yearnings. Through field hollers and work songs, black people communicated to one another a sense of membership in a community that challenged their collective identity as slaves. They created a language whose meanings were indecipherable to everyone who was not privy to the required codes. And, indeed, white slave owners and overseers often assumed that work songs revealed an acquiescence to slavery. In fact, slaves often used these songs to hurl aesthetic assaults at the slave masters and to share with one another a deep yearning for freedom. The language of the spirituals likewise was encoded in a way that permitted slaves to communicate specific modes of resistance through metaphors based on biblical teachings. While the slave-owning class assumed that the communicative potential of the English language was severely restricted by the peculiarities of slave speech, and that slave songs were "primitive" and thus nonsymbolic, in reality communication was expanded greatly and black song became potentially subversive.

This capacity to speak the unspeakable, to convey meanings that differed from and sometimes contradicted the particular terms employed to express them, would later be incorporated into the blues idiom of the post-slavery era. Although she worked only tangentially with the blues, Billie Holiday's music nonetheless was rooted in the blues tradition, and specifically that of the blues women of the twenties. Jazz musician and writer Benny Green has noted that because she was "cut off from the rich poetic imagery of the blues" and "chained by circumstance to the jingles of Tin Pan Alley," far greater transformative powers were required of her than of her musical predecessors.[21] She embarked upon her singing career at a time when popular music rapidly was becoming a highly specialized business, subject to the rigid requirements of the market.[22] This commodification of music led successful and would-be-successful songwriters to turn out, with almost factorylike uniformity, countless numbers of mediocre songs, composed around what were considered marketable formulas. As David Ewen has pointed out, "The sole yardstick by which Tin Pan Alley measured its success was the number of copies sold of the sheet music. . . ."[23] This is not to say that there were no flashes of brilliance in the songs produced during this era—it was, after all, the era of Irving Berlin, Cole Porter, Jerome Kern, and George and Ira Gershwin. However, black musicians generally received the worst material.

Billie Holiday's first recording session—with Benny Goodman and the Teagardens—produced two pieces, "Your Mother's Son-in-Law"[24] and "Riffing the Scotch,"[25] whose lyrical inanities would be utterly embarrassing if rendered by any singer but Lady Day. In 1935, a year and a half after the Goodman session, she began to record regularly with the prominent black jazz pianist Teddy Wilson, and had to content herself with the selections chosen by the recording company for the purpose of selling discs to jukebox operators in black urban areas.[26] During the Depression, few black people could be expected to purchase records for private listening at home. Needless to say, unlike the recording practices with which the blues women had to contend, the songs were not chosen with any regard for the prevailing tastes of the black community. More often than not, they were discards, sometimes blatantly ridiculous tunes. The most outrageous examples were "Yankee Doodle Never Went to Town"[27] and "Eeny Meeny Miney Mo."[28] Burnett James, who writes on jazz and classical music, has observed that all her life Billie Holiday was "congenitally incapable of skating over the surface of life or art, and in that respect she was a contradiction of and a reproach to the world of popular song from which she drew so much of her material."[29] She therefore was able to create gems like "You Let Me Down" in which she established an almost magical control of the tired words, revitalizing them and pushing them toward a criticism of the very cultural context out of which they were born:

> You told me that I was like an angel
> Told me I was fit to wear a crown
> So that you could get a thrill
> You put me on a pedestal
> And then you let me down, let me down
>
> You told me that I'd be wearing diamonds
> I would have the smartest car in town
> Made me think that I'm the top
> And then you let the ladder drop
> You know you let me down, let me down
>
> I walked upon a rainbow
> I clung onto a star
> You had me up in heaven
> That's why I had to fall so far
>
> I was even looking for a cottage
> I was measured for a wedding gown
> That's how I got cynical
> You put me on a pinnacle

And then you let me down, let me down
How you let me down.[30]

She transformed the song, which was full of clichéd images conjuring up propagandistic idealizations of spurned love, into a critique of its own content, a rupture exposing black people's status in a culture infused with the attitudes expressed in the song. Yet, this is a song that also reached across racial and class boundaries in its exposure of the futility of masculinist notions of romantic love.

In her recording of this song, Billie Holiday does not sound like she is attempting to represent a gullible, disillusioned young woman in love, who had been promised marriage and riches by a deceitful lover. Rather, she sounds as though she is protesting something more than the fickleness of an individual lover, thus transforming the song into an indictment. Of all the early pieces, this one most perfectly foreshadows her later style, which seemed to challenge through the musical form—the aesthetic dimension—the social conditions implied by the lyrics of the songs she sang. Her performance of "You Let Me Down" pushes the ideological content of the song to the surface, subjecting to a process of demystification the portrayal of women as "angels" wearing "crowns" and "diamonds" and being placed on "pedestals." At the same time, there are hints in the shadows of her voice that point to historical disappointment, to the recognition and coded indictment stemming from the fact that white racist society "let us down." The last phrase, "How you let me down," seems to reach out and encompass a host of grievances, personal and political, inviting listeners to reflect on loss and on possibilities of moving beyond that loss. "You Let Me Down," along with "What a Little Moonlight Can Do," unveiled, at the very beginning of her career, Billie Holiday's ability to use song—even of the most conventional and commercial kind—as a catalyst for social consciousness. Burnett James's essay "Billie Holiday and the Art of Communication" points out that

> Billie's musical style and emotional sensibility were not of the sort likely to prosper with the more rigid form of the classic blues. She needed the kind of tunes she could work her will on, those she

could take and refashion to her own musical and emotional ends, and out of which she could create something personal rather than social or racial. Her art was always looking inward, into her own heart, and discovering there deep and simple truths.[31]

James is accurate in his observation that the classic blues form with which Bessie Smith worked such wonders was too self-contained to allow Billie Holiday to explore the range of emotions necessary for her art. But the reason for this incompatibility goes beyond the stylistic. Billie Holiday represents not simply a new moment in the development of African-American music (the transition from the blues to modern jazz). Her work bears the mark of a new moment in African-American history, a moment characterized by an accelerated process of individualization in the black community. The moment was brought on by the migration northward and the resulting urbanization of the black community, by the entrance of a substantial number of African Americans into the middle classes, and, perhaps most significantly, by the tensions and dilemmas in the consciousness of class difference. The heterogeneity of her black audiences reflected this developing class stratification and the seduction of racial and cultural assimilation, combined with the persisting intransigence of racism.

Billie Holiday's songs were subversive in that they offered special and privileged insights to black people about the dominant culture. She sang songs produced by its rapidly developing popular-culture industry. Unlike Gertrude Rainey and Bessie Smith, she did not concentrate on the musical creations of black culture. Rather, she boldly entered the domain of white love as it filtered through the commodified images and market strategies of Tin Pan Alley. She revealed to her black audiences what the world of white popular culture was about and invited them to discover how white people acquired a consciousness of love and sexuality that was overdetermined by ideologies of male dominance and heterosexism. Familiarity with the work of blues women like Alberta Hunter, Ida Cox, and Bessie Smith, whose representations of personal relationships—lesbian as well as heterosexual—reflected lived experiences of black women and an appreciation of their subjectivity, rendered black audiences receptive to the cultural critique implicit in Lady Day's performances.

The rising black middle class was able to hear in Billie Holiday's renditions of the songs produced by the alluring dominant culture a note of warning. Her performances suggested that members of the new black middle classes proceed with caution lest they lose their moorings and become utterly disoriented in culturally alienating forms of consciousness. Indeed, her own music proved that she was capable of negotiating an entrance into the dominant culture that did not disconnect her from her people. She was able to recast for her own ends the very elements of that culture that might have devoured her talents and her identity. Because she brought an original vision of popular song to the world and at the same time expanded the world of jazz, she communicated critical social meanings—across racial and class boundaries—to the populations, and especially to the women, of both worlds.

The consensus among critics is that the young Billie Holiday, who sang primarily up-tempo tunes with a youthful buoyancy that seemed to transcend the troubles of society and the individual, was a more impressive artist than the mature Billie Holiday. This opinion fails to acknowledge the degree to which her art became increasingly communicative, even as her technical skills may have waned with the increasing depth and destructive intensity of her own life experiences. Perhaps, too, many critics simply do not want to confront and examine the complex social and psychological messages of her later work. I would argue that those who lavish praise on the youthful Billie Holiday, and respectfully approach the older artist only out of deference to her earlier work, fail to understand the degree to which the seeds of the later work are very much in evidence in the "golden years."

There is an impassioned, utopian quality about many of Lady Day's love songs, affirming eros as a potentially transformative force, thus resonating with Audre Lord's theory of the erotic as power.[32] "Some Other Spring," recorded in 1939, was, according to Billie Holiday, her favorite song.

> Some other spring, I've tried to love
> Now I still cling to faded blossoms
> Fresh when worn, left crushed and torn

Like the love affair I mourn
Some other spring when twilight falls
Will the nights bring another to me?
Not your kind, but let me find
It's not too late, love is blind
Sun shines around me
But deep in my heart it's cold as ice
Love, once you found me
But can that story unfold twice?
Some other spring will my heart wake
Stirring to sing love's magic music
Then forget the old duet
And love with some other spring.[33]

She sang this song, where the tension between form and content is played out in a less oppositional way than in others, with an understated nostalgia but eloquent conviction. Her performance emphatically represents the power of eros—the "erotic as power"—even when, and perhaps especially when, it remains beyond reach: a mournful past love that can no longer be rekindled, or a fantasized future love that may never become a reality. Lady Day's rendition of "Some Other Spring" expresses hope that is so passionately articulated that it seems to speak not only about a sexual partnership but about other dreams as well—our own dreams of better, happier, and more love-filled lives for ourselves, our families, and our communities.

Billie Holiday could sing with prophetic conviction about the transformative power of love because it may have come to represent for her all that she was unable to achieve in her own life. In a more complex racial and cultural context, she was able to carry on a tradition established by the blues women and blues men who were her predecessors: the tradition of representing love and sexuality as both concrete daily experience and as coded yearning for social liberation.

In an interview in 1956,[34] when Tex McCleary asked her about her favorite "happy" song, she responded that it was "Yesterdays" by Jerome Kern:

Yesterdays, yesterdays
Days I knew as happy, sweet sequestered days
Olden days, golden days
Days of mad romance and love
Then gay youth was mine
Then truth was mine
Joyous, free and flaming life
Then sooth was mine
Sad am I, glad am I
For today, I'm dreaming of yesterdays.[35]

Her interpreting a song as "happy" that most people would unhesitantly classify as "sad" suggests something about her approach to her art. In this interview McCleary asks her to speak the words of this song she had performed and recorded so many times. What is so striking about this spoken performance—and indeed about her singing—is the fluid boundaries between speech and music. In this sense, she can be said to have drawn upon a cultural tradition rooted in West African histories in which the communicative power of speech is grounded in and enhanced by its "musical" structure, and in which the communicative power of music is grounded in and enhanced by its relation to speech.[36] It is within such a context that different meanings are not necessarily mutually exclusive, that "sad" lyrics may become "happy," depending on their musical context. Her attitude toward this piece and her ability to rework it transformatively is reminiscent of other modernist aesthetic projects, such as that of Marcel Proust to recover and reorder his past and thereby create a new universe of subjectivity for himself.

In her rendition of "You're My Thrill," there is a haunting, spiritual, eerily otherworldly quality working against and in sharp contrast to the overt contents of the lyrics, which ostensibly describe a woman's infatuation with a man.[37] As she sings about a romantic attraction having rendered the female protagonist utterly out of control, Billie Holiday exercises consummate artistic control. Her delivery is at once rigorously disciplined and effortless. Listening to the song, it is possible to truly understand what Carmen McRae meant when she said that Lady Day was only truly happy when she was singing.

> Singing is the only place she can express herself the way she'd like to be all the time. The only way she's happy is through a song. I don't think she expresses herself as she would want to when you meet her in person. The only time she's at ease and at rest with herself is when she sings.[38]

In "You're My Thrill," even as she sings about being at the mercy of an emotional attraction for someone else, the artist achieves a state of autonomy and control that re-forms and reshapes those emotions into a unique critique of the "out of control" woman in love. This rendering represents a juxtaposition and performance of the conflict between representations of women's sexuality in the dominant popular musical culture and those in the blues tradition—the former denying female agency, the latter affirming the autonomous erotic empowerment and independent subjectivity of female sexuality.

With the incomparable instrument of her voice, Billie Holiday could completely divert a song from its composer's original and often sentimental and vapid intent. In "Lover, Come Back to Me," her voice is saying, "Lover, please stay away—I am immensely enjoying this state of freedom from the vagaries of love constructed according to male dominance":

The sky is blue and high above
The moon is new and so is love
This eager heart of mine is singin'
Lover, come back to me
The sky is blue, the night is cold
The moon is new, but love is old
This achin' heart of mine is sayin'
Lover, where can you be?
When I remember every little thing you used to do

I grow lonely
Every road I walk along, I walk along with you
No wonder I'm lonely
The sky is blue and high above
The moon is new, but love is old
And while I'm waiting here this heart of mine is singin'
Lover, come back to me.[39]

She seems to sense that these mediocre lyrics about blue skies, new moons, and lost love violate the seriousness of the subject they purport to explore, and that a serious rendition would be a violation of real emotions. She therefore chooses to sing it playfully and mockingly. By playing with the lyrics, she ventures a serious statement about the possibilities of women's independence. The lyrics reverse the response a woman is expected to have when deserted by a lover. Instead of mourning her loss by wallowing in her suffering, Lady Day's voice conveys a sense of deliverance and release, as if she were challenging the accepted gender roles within love relationships. She was able to project in her music the female strength she seemed chronically incapable of achieving in her own life. The visions of women's independence and autonomy that flow from her music may indeed have helped—at a time when feminist consciousness had not been popularly and extensively articulated—awaken women to their worth and the potential the prevailing society denied them.

In yet another example of her ability to challenge the superficial literal meaning of her songs' lyrics, her restrained, bittersweet rendition of the ebullient love song "There Is No Greater Love" captures the complexity of real situations in real life—their highs and lows, tantalizing attractions, and inevitable animosities:

There is no greater love than what I feel for you
No greater love, no heart so true
There is no greater thrill than what you bring to me
No sweeter song than what you sing to me
You're the sweetest thing I have ever known
And to think that you are mine alone

There is no greater love in all the world, it's true
No greater love than what I feel for you.[40]

As she sings the words "there is no greater love," the timbre of her voice undermines their literal meaning, and summons a critical examination of the social relationships taken so for granted by the very nature of the popular song. The complexity of such a perspective and its emotional range account for why people are touched so profoundly—and in ways they have difficulty expressing—by Billie Holiday's music.

Many of Holiday's songs are pervaded by loneliness and gloom—and she remains unequaled in her ability to re-create these emotions musically. By the subtleties of her phrasing and her flawless sense of swing, she offers us a glimpse into the human emotion of despair. No other voice has ever given it such honest, intimate, and profound expression. It is a woman's vision she presents, and as women's realities filter through the prism of her music, we are educated and enlightened about our interior emotional lives. Her message is able to escape the ideological constraints of the lyrics. In the music, in her phrasing, her timing, the timbre of her voice, the social roots of pain and despair in women's emotional lives are given a lyrical legibility.

"My Man" is frequently presented as evidence of female masochism, and, in a facile conflation of art and biography, of Lady Day's own masochistic investment in relationships characterized by male dominance:

It cost me a lot
But there's one thing that I've got
It's my man, it's my man
Cold or wet, tired, you bet
All of this I'll soon forget
With my man

He's not much on looks
He's no hero out of books
But I love him, yes, I love him
Two or three girls has he

That he likes as well as me
But I love him

I don't know why I should
He isn't true, he beats me too
Oh my man, I love him so
He'll never know
All my life is just despair
But I don't care
When he takes me in his arms
The world is bright, all right

What's the difference if I say
I'll go away
When I know I'll come back
On my knees someday
For whatever my man is
I'm his forevermore.[41]

The lyrics shock in the extravagance and intensity of their masculinist point of view and the complacent dominance of male self-regard they seem to countenance and encourage. Black feminist cultural critic Michele Wallace observed that this approach to love has not endeared Billie Holiday to feminists. However, Wallace argues, black women across several generations are able to discover themselves in this and other performances by Lady Day, because of the "existential truths" her singing reveals about black women's lives.[42] "My Man" has retained its appeal not because of its content, which represents women in a mode of victimization, but because its aesthetic dimension reworks that content into an implicit critique. In Holiday's performance of "My Man," an ironic edge in her voice warns against a facile, literal interpretation. And in case this is missed, the slow tempo with which she sings the words—expressing uncertainty as to whether she should love him because "he isn't true, he beats me too"—emphasizes an ambivalent posture rather than an acquiescence to the violence described. The way Billie Holiday sings "My Man"—now playfully, now mournfully, now emphatically, and now frivolously—highlights the contradictions and ambiguities of women's location in love relationships and creates a space within which female subjectivity can move toward self-consciousness. While, as Michele Wallace points out, black women have developed a special relationship to Billie Holiday through such performances—an appeal that transcends generational differences, social class, educational levels, and sexual orientation—her female (and male) audiences have always been and are becoming increasingly cross-cultural.

In her rendition of "When a Woman Loves a Man," Holiday sings quietly and introspectively, as if to question the power relationships played out in love partnerships:

> Maybe he's not much, just another man, does what he can
> But what does she care when a woman loves a man?
> She'll just string along all through thick and thin, till his ship comes in
> It's always that way when a woman loves a man
> She'll be the first one to praise him when he's going strong
> The last one to blame him when everything's wrong
> It's such a one-sided game that they play
> But women are funny that way
> Tell her she's a fool, she'll say yes, I know, but I love him so
> But that's how it goes when a woman loves a man.[43]

Certainly, her own life experiences—her relationships with Jimmy Monroe, Louis McKay, John Levy—revealed how destructive this "one-sided" love could be. As her autobiography reveals, she never managed to assert herself within these relationships.[44] In her art, however, she raised questions that encourage awareness of the political character of sexuality. Her genius was to give her life experiences an aesthetic form that recast them as windows through which other women could peer critically at their own lives. She offered other women the possibility of understanding the social contradictions they embodied and enacted in their lives—an understanding she never achieved in her own life.

Her style was to forge an independent meaning for her vocals out of their relation to the instrumental accompaniment and apart from the literal signification of the lyrics. She was able to set in profound motion deeply disturbing disjunctions between overt statements and their aesthetic meanings. The listener is made to feel that the instrumentals represent the relatively easy existence a man can enjoy within a love relationship—the instruments were all played by men—while her voice establishes its female persona as an equal participant, all the while raising questions about such unquestioned inequality.

The conclusion of "When a Woman Loves a Man" reinforces the critical dimension of the song: repeating the phrase "and that's how it goes when a woman loves a man," her voice ascends at the end, sounding a question. If that is how it goes, must it always be this way? This aesthetic challenging of the finality of the lyrics, moving them from affirmative statements toward open-ended interrogations, creates the space for a liberating—though not liberated—female subjectivity. It is still possible to glean this kind of meaning from Holiday's art, many decades after it was performed and recorded, because Lady Day's art expressed and embodied a critical stance, in an aesthetic context, toward social relations that at the time were not popularly experienced as capable of historical transformation. We remain moved by her songs because we experience in them the anticipated, inchoate presence of a vantage point later produced and systematically elaborated by social movements that would insist upon historical transformations of gender, race, and class relations.

"STRANGE FRUIT"

MUSIC AND SOCIAL CONSCIOUSNESS

Southern trees bear a strange fruit
Blood on the leaves, blood at the root
Black bodies swinging in the Southern breeze
Strange fruit hanging from the poplar trees
Pastoral scene of the gallant South
The bulging eyes and the twisted mouth
Scent of magnolia sweet and fresh
Then the sudden smell of burning flesh
Here is a fruit for the crows to pluck
For the rain to gather, for the wind to suck
For the sun to rot, for the tree to drop
Here is a strange and bitter crop.

— "STRANGE FRUIT"[1]

This song, which Billie Holiday called her "personal protest"[2] against racism, radically transformed her status in American popular culture. She previously had been acknowledged by her contemporaries on the jazz scene as a brilliant and innovative musician, but her performance of "Strange Fruit" firmly established her as a pivotal figure in a new tendency in black musical culture that directly addressed issues of racial injustice. Though she was only twenty-four years old when she recorded this song in 1939 and integrated it into her repertoire, she had already been striving for some time to reach a mass audience and thus to achieve recognition beyond the circles of musicians and jazz cognoscenti who so unanimously praised her work.[3] She would not—or perhaps could not—perform the Tin Pan Alley material that made up her repertoire in the commercial vein that might have won her the popular success she desired. John Chilton recounts a conversation between Holiday and Dave Dexter, then associate editor of *Down Beat* magazine, in which she said that

> she would quit the singing game if she failed to gain national promi-nence — "with the public as well as musicians and jazz fans," by the time she was 26. She admitted that she was aware of the great respect that musicians had for her, but said that she was discouraged "after nine years of hard work" and felt "at a loss as to why the public at large had failed to respond" to her.[4]

Holiday's own autobiographical reflections about that moment in her life, interestingly, draw a distinction between the mass recognition she had already achieved and the financial success she desired:

> I opened Café Society as an unknown; I left two years later as a star. But you couldn't tell the difference from what I had in my sock. I was still making that same old seventy-five dollars a week. I had made more than that in Harlem. I needed the prestige and publicity all right, but you can't pay rent with it.[5]

It was at Café Society, the newly opened interracial nightclub in Green-wich Village, that she premiered the song that, at first, seemed almost anti-thetical to her quest for financial success. Holiday never had a best-selling recording — neither during her lifetime nor after her death.[6] But what fame and commercial fortune she did enjoy would become inextricably, if ambiguously, tied to "Strange Fruit." Prior to her decision to sing "Strange Fruit," her work consisted almost exclusively of original and often sub-versive renderings of the conventional and formulaic popular love songs offered her by her record producers. In "Strange Fruit" she had a song with urgent and far-reaching social implications — a song about the hate, indignities, and eruptions of violence that threatened black people in the United States, a song that was able to awaken from their apolitical slumber vast numbers of people from diverse racial backgrounds. At the same time, it was not a song that could be counted upon for popular success. In fact, it seemed ready-made to damage her career and to further diminish her status as a popular singer. Nonetheless, once she decided to sing "Strange Fruit," she became obsessed with it. "I worked like the devil on it," she wrote, "because I was never sure I could put it across or that I could get across to a plush nightclub audience the things that it meant to me."[7]

As long as Holiday's work appeared to be without manifest social content, she was praised lavishly by critics. Their insistence on the nonracialized "universality" of art prohibited serious consideration of her work's relation to the collective struggles of black people. Since "Strange Fruit" was designed unambiguously to prick the consciences of those who were content to remain oblivious to racism, it was inevitable that many critics would dismiss it as propaganda.[8] But Holiday realized, to the contrary, that "Strange Fruit" would afford her a mode of expression that merged her own individual sensibility, including her hatred of racist-inspired brutality, with the rage of a potential community of resistance. Art never achieves greatness through transcendence of sociohistorical reality. On the contrary, even as it transcends specific circumstances and conventions, it is deeply rooted in social realities. As Herbert Marcuse has pointed out, it is at its best when it fashions new perspectives on the human condition, provokes critical attitudes and encourages loyalty "to the vision of a better world, a vision which remains true even in defeat."

> In the transforming mimesis, the image of liberation is fractured by reality. If art were to promise that at the end good would triumph over evil, such a promise would be refuted by the historical truth. In reality it is evil which triumphs, and there are only islands of good where one can find refuge for a brief time. Authentic works of art are aware of this: they reject the promise made too easily; they refuse the unburdened happy end. They must reject it, for the realm of freedom lies beyond mimesis.[9]

"Strange Fruit" evoked the horrors of lynching at a time when black people were still passionately calling for allies in the campaign to eradicate this murderous and terroristic manifestation of racism. While she never sang "Strange Fruit" exactly the same way twice, each time Holiday performed it she implicitly asked her audiences to imagine a dreadful

lynching scene, and to endorse and identify with the song's antilynching
sentiments. Yet her performance of this song did much more. It almost
singlehandedly changed the politics of American popular culture and
put the elements of protest and resistance back at the center of contemporary black musical culture. The felt impact of Holiday's performance of
"Strange Fruit" is as powerful today as it was in the 1940s. By placing this
song at the center of her repertoire, Holiday firmly established the place of
protest in the black popular musical tradition. Her use of this work in her
career helped dismantle the opposition, firmly entrenched until her singing of this song, between fame and commercial success on the one hand
and social consciousness in music on the other.

The most common portraits of Billie Holiday highlight drug addiction,
alcoholism, feminine weakness, depression, lack of formal education, and
other difficulties unrelated to her contributions as an artist. In other words,
the image she has acquired in U.S. popular culture relies on biographical
information about Holiday's personal life at the expense of acknowledging
her role as a cultural producer, which is, after all, the reason for her enduring importance. This is the approach taken by the Motown film based on
her autobiography, *Lady Sings the Blues*. This image of Lady Day, who is
played by Diana Ross, tends to imply that her music is no more than an
unconscious and passive product of the contingencies of her life.[10] If one
accepts this construction of Holiday, "Strange Fruit" appears to be an
anomaly. In fact, John Chilton explains her encounter with Lewis Allen,[11]
who composed the lyrics, in language that emphasizes Allen's active role —
although Allen never did this himself — and that of the white men who
owned and operated Café Society, while utterly downplaying Holiday's
part in deciding to sing the song:

> Poet Lewis Allen, then working as a schoolteacher, approached Bar-
> ney Josephson [the owner of Café Society] and Robert Gordon
> (who helped organize the floor-shows) with a set of lyrics that he
> had adapted from his own poetry; they recommended that Allen
> should meet Billie and offer the song to her. At first, Lady was slow

to understand the song's imagery, but her bewilderment decreased as Allen patiently emphasised the cadences, and their significance. After a few readings, Billie was "into" the song, but was unconvinced that the material was suitable for her. Her incredibly gifted interpretations of lyrics had enhanced many songs, but these songs, for all the varying skills of their composers and lyricists, had only dealt with the problems of love, unrequited or otherwise, skies blue and June moons. Here, Billie was being asked to provide a musical commentary on an issue raw enough to be unmentionable in urban New York.[12]

In Barney Josephson's own description of Holiday's initial encounter with "Strange Fruit," he takes all the credit for her decision to sing it:

A young man came in one evening with a song and showed it to me. Not reading music, I could read, so I read the lyrics. I read these lyrics and was just floored by them. I said, "What do you want to do with this?" He said, "I'd like to have Billie sing this song." So he sings the song to her. She looked at me and said, after he finished it, "What do you want me to do with that, man?" And I said, "It would be wonderful if you'd sing it—if you care to. You don't have to." "You wants me to sing it. I sings it." And she sang it. And that song was "Strange Fruit."[13]

Chilton describes Holiday as being "bewildered" by the imagery of "Strange Fruit," implying that she could not comprehend metaphorical presentations of anything other than women in love or spurned by lovers. According to Chilton's interpretation, Allen not only offered her the lyrics but taught her how to sing them. But it is more plausible to argue that Holiday translated an antiracist literary text into a dynamic musical work whose enduring meaning stemmed from the way she chose to render it as song. Josephson's description is nothing short of embarrassing. As important a figure as he may have been in opening New York's first truly interracial nightclub—where people of color were welcome in the audience as well as onstage—Josephson's depiction of Billie Holiday is problematic at best: he paints her as an illiterate, ignorant, and passive woman, willing to sing "Strange Fruit" simply because he asked her to do it. His attempt to recapture her speech—"You wants me to sing it. I sings it"—is reminiscent of the worst kind of minstrel caricatures of black "dialect."

Stuart Nicholson published a biography in 1995 entitled *Billie Holiday*.[14] It is to his credit that he omits these stories that foreground white men as the responsible parties in Holiday's decision to sing "Strange Fruit." However, Donald Clarke, Holiday's most recent biographer, further develops this narrative, emphasizing her alleged illiteracy. "Lady was nonpolitical; when she first looked at 'Strange Fruit' she didn't know what to make of it. She never read anything but comic books—promoter Ernie Anderson once brought her bundles of them—and she was used to learning songs, not reading poetry."[15] To bolster this interpretation he quotes Josephson, who said in an interview, "At first I felt Billie didn't know what the hell the song meant."[16] Clarke also quotes Arthur Herzog, whose memories of Holiday's initial encounter with "Strange Fruit" represent her as not understanding the song's meaning, which later "hit" her—as if her comprehension were entirely external to her own allegedly backward mental processes: "When she first started singing this song, I really don't believe she knew what she was doing or that the impact hit her. . . . My recollection is that the song didn't have much punch at first, and suddenly the impact of it hit her, and she put herself into the song."[17]

Compare Clarke's, Chilton's, and Josephson's accounts of the meeting between Holiday and Allen with her own (as transcribed by William Dufty in *Lady Sings the Blues*):

> It was during my stint at Café Society that a song was born which became my personal protest—"Strange Fruit." The germ of the song was in a poem written by Lewis Allen. I first met him at Café Society. When he showed me that poem, I dug it right off. It seemed to spell out all the things that had killed Pop.
>
> Allen, too, had heard how Pop died and of course was interested in my singing. He suggested that Sonny White, who had been my accompanist, and I turn it into music. So the three of us got together and did the job in about three weeks.[18]

Her father, jazz guitarist Clarence Holiday, had inhaled poisonous gases during a battle in World War I. He developed chronic lung problems, and in March of 1937, while on tour in Texas with Don Redman's band, he contracted a chest cold for which he received no treatment because of segregated hospitals in that state. By the time the band reached Dallas, where he was able to seek medical attention, his condition had progressed to pneumonia, and he died of a hemorrhage in the Jim Crow ward of the Veterans' Hospital.[19] According to Holiday's account, the antilynching theme of "Strange Fruit" resonated with her own anger about her father's death and with her desire to protest the racism that had killed him.

I have considered these conflicting accounts of the genesis of Billie Holiday's "Strange Fruit" because they reveal—even in the narratives of those whose relationships to her should have afforded them special insight into her musical genius—the extent to which her stature as an artist and her ability to comprehend social issues were both disparaged and defined as results of plans conceived by savvy white men. Chilton's, Clarke's, and Josephson's stories capture Holiday in a web of gendered, classed, and raced inferiority and present her as capable of producing great work only under the tutelage of her racial superiors. The importance Holiday herself accorded "Strange Fruit" is revealed not only by the fact that she reconstructed her entire repertoire around it, but also by her thwarted decision to name her autobiography *Bitter Crop*, the last two words of the lyrics.[20] *Lady Sings the Blues* was deemed a more marketable title by her publishers.

In order to suggest the historical context and impact of "Strange Fruit" and to comprehend the ease with which Holiday could compare the metaphorical lynching scene evoked by the song's lyrics with the Jim Crow death of her father, it is important to examine the debate around lynching during that period. Billie Holiday first sang "Strange Fruit" in 1939. During the preceding decade—the Depression years—public consciousness regarding lynching grew even as the numbers of lynching victims began to decline. While it was true that the lives of black people were no longer systematically consumed by mob violence in numbers that mounted into the thousands—as had been the case during the decades following emancipation—this did not mean that the scores of contemporary lynching victims could be dismissed as insignificant. According to one historian, during the four years following the stock market crash in 1929, 150 black people were lynched.[21] Black feminist historian Paula Giddings points out that

> [t]he lynching of twenty Black men in 1930 amounted to nowhere near the numbers at the turn of the century, or even in the immediate aftermath of World War I. But the news reports of the horrible crimes were made more vivid by the technological advances in communication and photography, and the sensationalism of yellow journalism.[22]

In the fall of 1934, a mere five years before Lady Day's encounter with the poem "Strange Fruit," a particularly brutal and well-publicized lynching occurred in Florida. A newspaper described the event:

> An eye-witness to the lynching . . . said that [Claude] Neal had been forced to mutilate himself before he died. The eye-witness gave the following account of the event which took place in a swamp beside the Chattahoochee River:
>
> . . . First they cut off his penis. He was made to eat it. Then they cut off his testicles and made him eat them and say he liked it.
>
> Then they sliced his sides and stomach with knives and every now and then somebody would cut off a finger or toe. Red hot irons were used on the nigger to burn him from top to bottom. From time to time during the torture a rope would be tied around Neal's neck and he was pulled over a limb and held there until he almost choked to death, when he would be let down and the torture begun all over again. After several hours of this punishment, they decided just to kill him.
>
> Neal's body was tied to a rope on the rear of an automobile and dragged over the highway to the Cannidy home. Here a mob estimated to number somewhere between 3,000 and 7,000 people from eleven southern states was excitedly waiting his arrival. . . . A

woman came out of the Cannidy house and drove a butcher knife into his heart. Then the crowd came by and some kicked him and some drove their cars over him. What remained of the body was brought by the mob to Marianna, where it is now hanging from a tree on the northeast corner of the courthouse square.

Photographers say they will soon have pictures of the body for sale at fifty cents each. Fingers and toes from Neal's body are freely exhibited on street-corners here.[23]

Historian John Hope Franklin describes a lynching in 1934 when he was a student at Fisk University in Nashville, Tennessee. Cordie Cheek, who lived in a Fisk-owned house on the edge of the campus, was lynched by a white mob after he struck a white child while riding his bicycle. The child was only slightly wounded. "As president of the student government I made loud noises and protests to the mayor, the governor, and even President Franklin D. Roosevelt, but nothing could relieve our pain and anguish or bring Cordie Cheek back."[24]

"Strange Fruit" rose out of sociohistorical circumstances that provided the most resonant background since the brief era of Radical Reconstruction for the reception of an impassioned plea for racial justice. The Harlem Renaissance of the 1920s had stimulated an expanding awareness of African-American art and culture in the wider population even though this awareness was marred by racist conceptions of black culture as "primitive" and "exotic." The 1930s saw the emergence of important multiracial political alliances. Organized challenges to lynching dated back to the turn-of-the-century efforts of Ida B. Wells and the antilynching campaign developed by the NAACP during its early years. However, white public opinion of the period through World War I and well into the 1920s was so poisoned by racism that it was difficult to draw substantial numbers of white people into antilynching campaigns. With the upsurge of mass movements during the thirties, white people began to take a more active role in antilynching efforts. Although the case of the Scottsboro Nine did not involve an extralegal lynching, it came to symbolize the pressing need to resist the racist ideology that so easily justified lynching. Lillian Smith, who allied herself with the Association of Southern Women for the Prevention of Lynching, was inspired by Holiday's song to write a novel, *Strange Fruit,* exploring inflammatory themes of race, sex, and violence. In 1936 the ASWPL had been endorsed by over 35,000 white southern women.[25] Billie Holiday's "Strange Fruit" echoed through circles of people who had been sensitized both by the transracial economic and social tragedies of the Great Depression and by the multiracial mass movements seeking to redress the grievances of blacks and whites alike.

Before the vast movements of the 1930s and the consequent radicalization of large sectors of the population, the phenomenon of "Strange Fruit" would have been inconceivable. Indeed, New York's interracial Café Society, where the song first was performed, could not have existed earlier. Barney Josephson, who opened the club at a time when even in Harlem black and white people could not listen to jazz under the same roof, told Holiday that "this was to be one club where there was going to be no segregation, no racial prejudice."[26] And, in fact, according to Holiday's biographer, John Chilton, "the liberal atmosphere of the club, with its clientele of 'New Dealers,' and the humanitarian principles of its owner, made it a receptive setting for the presentation of the song's dramatic anti-lynching lyrics."[27]

If white people had developed a greater sensitivity to the plight of African Americans, it was perhaps because enormous numbers of them had experienced in one form or another the devastation of the Great Depression. Workers' wages were cut almost in half, and by the last crisis year 17 million people were unemployed. Even more important to the development of this sensitivity were the great mass movements of the 1930s—the campaign against unemployment and the extensive organizing of industrial unions associated with the CIO. The Communist Party, the Young Communist League, and the Trade Union Unity League joined forces to establish the National Unemployed Councils, which were responsible for spectacular demonstrations throughout the country. On March 6, 1930, well over a million people participated in hunger marches in major urban centers—110,000 in New York, 100,000 in Detroit. In December of 1931 and early 1932, national hunger marches to Washington dramatized demands for unemployment insurance and other means of bringing relief to the unemployed.[28]

Such mass opposition to the antiworker policies of the Hoover administration played a pivotal role in the election of Franklin D. Roosevelt and the subsequent inauguration of the New Deal. Far from pacifying those who suffered the effects of the Great Depression, the New Deal served as a further catalyst for the organization of multiracial mass movements. Black people in particular were dissatisfied with the sedatives offered them by the New Deal legislation. One of the most consequential of the mass organizations initiated during the Roosevelt years was the American Youth Congress, founded in 1934. Although the government was responsible for the inception of the AYC, the more than four and a half million young people who joined it before the outbreak of World War II in 1939 made it into an organizing force beyond anything imagined by its government sponsors. Young African Americans, especially in the South, played an indispensable role in developing the strategic direction of this organization. The Southern Negro Youth Congress, according to William Z. Foster, was "the most important movement ever conducted by Negro Youth"[29] before the era of the civil rights movement. According to Robin D. G. Kelley, in his remarkable study of Alabama Communists during the Depression,

> Black Communists in SNYC promoted their own Double V program of action despite the Party's official opposition to the slogan. The Youth Congress fought racial discrimination in the armed forces, expanded its voter registration drive, continued to investigate police brutality cases and civil liberties violations, collected a mountain of data on discrimination for the FEPC [Fair Employment Practices Committee] hearings in 1943, and even waged a campaign in Birmingham to end segregation on buses.[30]

As a result of the work of organizations like the NAACP, the American Youth Congress, and the National Association of Colored Women, the issue of federal antilynching legislation was placed on the national political agenda for the first time in this century since the thwarted efforts of the NAACP to secure passage of an antilynching bill in 1921. Although the Costigan-Wagner bill, introduced in 1935, was passed by the House, it was defeated in the southern-dominated Senate. Nonetheless, when Billie

Holiday first sang "Strange Fruit" in 1939, her message fell on many ears rendered receptive by mass demands that the Roosevelt administration support the enactment of a law against lynching.

This is not to say that Billie Holiday herself was directly involved in the political developments of the thirties that served as the backdrop for her own cultural contributions. She was among a host of artists who moved into the stream of political radicalization by following paths carved out by their art, rather than by explicit political commitments. The thirties, according to cultural critic and socialist organizer Phillip Bonosky, constituted "a watershed in the American democratic tradition. It is a period," he continues,

> which will continue to serve both the present and the future as a reminder and as an example of how an aroused people, led and spurred on by the working-class, can change the entire complexion of the culture of a nation. This period, for the first time in American history, saw the fundamental placing of the Negro and Jewish questions, which brought them out of the murky realm of private and personal ethics to their real roots in a class society. . . . [It] saw a dramatic change in every aspect of culture — its most characteristic feature being the discovery of the organic relationship between the intellectual and the people — the workers first of all. . . .[31]

Billie Holiday was not directly associated with the artists' and cultural workers' movements related to the Works Progress Administration, but she clearly was conscious of the need for radical change in the status of black people in U.S. society. On countless occasions she herself was the target of vitriolic expressions of racism. As a vocalist with Artie Shaw's all-white band, she encountered the crassness of Jim Crow on a daily basis when the band toured the southern states. In Kentucky, for example, a small-town sheriff who tried his best to prevent her from performing finally came up to the bandstand and asked Shaw, "What's Blackie going to sing?"[32] In St. Louis, the man who had hired the band to play in one of the city's largest ballrooms contested her presence by saying, "What's that nigger doing there? I don't have niggers to clean up around here."[33] Needless to say, there were numerous incidents concerning hotel rooms and the eating establishments where she attempted to dine. "It got to the point," she wrote, "where I hardly ever ate, slept or went to the bathroom without having a major NAACP-type production."

> Sometimes we'd make a six-hundred-mile jump and stop only once. Then it would be a place where I couldn't get served, let alone crash the toilet without causing a scene. At first I used to be ashamed. Then finally I just said to hell with it. When I had to go I'd just ask the bus driver to stop and let me off at the side of the road. I'd rather go in the bushes than take a chance in the restaurants and towns.[34]

Billie Holiday experienced more than her share of racism. While she did not tend to engage in extended political analyses, she never attempted to conceal her loyalties. "I'm a race woman," she proclaimed on numerous occasions.[35] According to Josh White, who became her friend after an initial collision over his performance of "Strange Fruit," "she had more thought for humanity and was more race-conscious than people thought."[36]

Billie Holiday never witnessed a lynching firsthand. The fictionalized scene in the film *Lady Sings the Blues,* in which she sees a black man's body swinging from a tree, is a gross oversimplification of the artistic process. This scene suggests that Holiday could only do justice to the song if she had experienced a lynching firsthand. The film dismisses the connections between lynching—one extreme of racism—and the daily routines of discrimination which in some way affect every African American. Holiday's own description of the process that led her to embrace "Strange Fruit" recalls the perspective outlined by Frantz Fanon when he writes:

> One cannot say that a given country is racist but that lynchings or extermination camps are not to be found there. The truth is that all that and still other things exist on the horizon. These virtualities, these latencies circulate, carried by the life-stream of psycho-affective, economic relations.[37]

Fanon's observation also works in reverse: the specter of lynchings inevitably conjures up other forms of racism. Thus, the lyrics of "Strange Fruit" led Holiday to reflect upon the circumstances of her father's death.

Billie Holiday's gift of aesthetic communication did not consist simply in her ability to render in song the profound emotions underlying her own private woes. However skillful she may have been in musically conveying her own state of mind, she also achieved a mode of expression that forged community even as it remained deeply personal. Her songs acted as a conduit permitting others to acquire insights about the emotional and social circumstances of their own lives. For black people and their politically conscious white allies, "Strange Fruit" publicly bore witness to the corporeal devastation occasioned by lynching, as well as to the terrible psychic damage it inflicted on its victims and perpetrators alike. Her song also signified possibilities of ending this violence and the web of racist institutions implicated in the culture of lynching. For those who had not yet grasped the meaning of American racism, "Strange Fruit" compellingly stated the fact of lynching and passionately contested its cultural permanency. As critic Burt Korall said of Billie Holiday, she "so illuminated human situations as to give the listener a rare, if frightening, glimpse into the realities of experience. Where others fear to tread, she reached out and touched, where others mask their eyes, she defiantly kept hers open."[38]

"Strange Fruit" is a song that poses serious problems for its singer. Its metaphors are so forceful that an overly dramatic rendition might have transformed its powerful emotional content into histrionics. The intent behind the song—both Allen's and Holiday's—was to evoke solidarity in its listeners. This kind of art sometimes misses its aim and occasions pity instead. If those who were touched by "Strange Fruit" were left feeling pity for black victims of racism instead of compassion and solidarity, this pity would have recapitulated rather than contested the dynamics of racism. It would have affirmed rather than disputed the superior position of whiteness. But unless one is an incurable racist, it is difficult to listen to Billie Holiday singing "Strange Fruit" without recognizing the plea for human solidarity, and thus for the racial equality of black and white people in the process of challenging racist horrors and indignities. Her song appeals to listeners of all ethnic backgrounds to identify the "black bodies swinging in the southern breeze" as human beings with the right to live and love. Jack Schiffman, son of Apollo Theatre owner Frank Schiffman, who initially argued against the inclusion of "Strange Fruit" in her Apollo show, described its impact on the audience when she sang it there for the first time. Following her performance there was "a moment of oppressively heavy silence . . . and then a kind of rustling sound I had never heard before. It was the sound of almost two thousand (black) people sighing."[39]

But, predictably, some listeners were impervious to her message. In a Los Angeles club a woman requested that Holiday sing "Strange Fruit" by saying, "Why don't you sing that sexy song you're so famous for? You know, the one about the naked bodies swinging in the trees."[40] Most accounts of this story simply point out that she refused to sing it. However, what is interesting about this anecdote that seems permanently fixed to the story of Holiday's relationship with "Strange Fruit" is the bizarre and racialized way the woman links the song with the ubiquitous engagement with sexuality in Holiday's work. Indeed, there is a silent dialectic throughout her body of work between pain and pleasure, love and death, destruction and the vision of a new order.[41] In the popular imagination, lynching was the established order's ideological affirmation and corporeal destruction of black hypersexuality. Because of the historical linkage of sexuality and freedom in black culture, Holiday's decision to foreground "Strange Fruit" in her musical oeuvre accorded her love songs a richly textured historical meaning.

Although Billie Holiday made "Strange Fruit" a permanent part of her repertoire soon after her decision to sing it at Café Society, she was unable to convince Columbia, the recording company with which she was under contract, to let her record it. "They won't buy it in the South" was the company's excuse. "We'll be boycotted. . . . It's too inflammatory."[42] Holiday persisted, and eventually Columbia released her for one recording date on Milt Gabler's Commodore label.

Billie Holiday's recording of "Strange Fruit" achieved something far greater than the permanent preservation of her most important song, the aesthetic centerpiece of her career. Eventually, millions heard her sing this haunting antilynching appeal—more people than she herself would ever have imagined. She could not have predicted that "Strange Fruit" would

impel people to discover within themselves a previously unawakened calling to political activism, but it did, and it does. She could not have fore-
seen the catalytic role her song would play in rejuvenating the tradition
of protest and resistance in African-American and American traditions of
popular music and culture. Nevertheless, Billie Holiday's recording of
"Strange Fruit" persists as one of the most influential and profound
examples—and continuing sites—of the intersection of music and social
consciousness.

"Strange Fruit" was a frontal challenge not only to lynching and racism but
to the policies of a government that implicitly condoned such activities,
especially through its refusal to pass laws against lynching. The song was
thus an undisguised rallying cry against the state. "The message of Lewis
Allen's poem," in the words of jazz critic Leonard Feather,

> had a meaning more vital than any of the soufflé songs [Holiday]
> had been handed by record producers. This was the first significant
> protest in words and music, the first unmuted cry against racism. It
> was radical and defiant at a time when blacks and whites alike
> found it dangerous to make waves, to speak out against a deeply
> entrenched status quo.[43]

Jazz critic Joachim Berendt called it "the most emphatic and most impassioned musical testimony against racism to become known before Abbey
Lincoln's interpretation of Max Roach's 'Freedom Now Suite' of 1960."[44]

By transforming Lewis Allen's poem into an unsettling protest song
and making it so central to her repertoire that it became her signature
work, Holiday pioneered a tradition later taken up by musicians like Nina
Simone, who would unabashedly incorporate into their musical creations
explicit social critiques.[45] As a stylist, Holiday brought into popular musical
culture a new and original approach to singing; with "Strange Fruit," her
extraordinary interpretive capabilities blended with her consciousness as a
black woman to create a particularly challenging brand of popular music
that would be echoed by scores of singers and musicians who followed her,

and across a range of genres. "Strange Fruit" stood out from the rest of Holiday's repertoire in so pronounced a manner as to irretrievably prick the collective conscience of her listeners, both her contemporaries and subsequent generations. By disrupting the landscape of material she had performed prior to integrating "Strange Fruit" into her repertoire, she reaffirmed among her musical colleagues the import of employing their medium in the quest for social justice, thus perpetuating its musical voice.

At the same time, Holiday was following in the footsteps of a host of black artists who preceded her, including Ma Rainey and Bessie Smith, who to varying degrees—and against the social conventions and expectations of the dominant culture, including the music industry itself—incorporated into their music their own brand of critical social consciousness. Holiday hardly forged this tradition—indeed, its roots lie in the early days of slavery—but she most decidedly stands as a bridge between the past and the present, with her career as a galvanizing transition between her musical ancestors and descendants. It is in Billie Holiday that we can identify links, for example, between the classic blues of Bessie Smith and the contemporary rhythm and blues of artists such as Tracy Chapman and Erykah Badu. Chapman is known first and foremost for the sociopolitical character of her songs, while Badu, also known as a socially conscious artist, has been explicitly compared to Billie Holiday for her musical phrasing. Whatever the merits of her music, Badu's occasional vocal resemblance to Holiday is an oft-articulated reason for her popularity among young people today. Such evocations of Holiday—both Badu's emulation and her fans' referencing of Lady Day—are a testament to the staying power of Billie Holiday's legacy, and indeed to her impact upon black popular culture as a whole.

Lyrics to Songs

Recorded by

GERTRUDE "MA" RAINEY

ARMY CAMP HARMONY BLUES (*Hooks Tilford and Gertrude Rainey*)

My man is leavin', cryin' won't make him stay
Lord, my man is leavin', cryin' won't make him stay
If cryin'd do any good, I'd cry my poor self away

If I had wings, I'd fly all over this land
If I had wings, I'd fly all over this land
When I stop flyin', I'm right there over my man.

BAD LUCK BLUES (*Lovie Austin*)

Hey, people, listen while I spread my news
Hey, people, listen while I spread my news
I want to tell you people all about my bad luck blues

Did you ever wake up, just at the break of day
Did you ever break up, just at the wake of day
With your arms around the pillow where your daddy used to lay?

Lord, look where the sun done gone
Lord, Lord, look where the sun done gone
Hey, Lord, there's something going on wrong

What's the use of living, you can't get the man you love
What's the use of living, you can't get the man you love
You might as well to die, give your soul to the Maker above.

BARREL HOUSE BLUES (*Lovie Austin*)

Got the barrel house blues, feelin' awf'ly dry
Got the barrel house blues, feelin' awf'ly dry
I can't drink moonshine, 'cause I'm 'fraid I'd die

Papa likes his sherry, mama likes her port
Papa likes his sherry, mama likes her port
Papa likes to shimmy, mama likes to sport

Papa likes his bourbon, mama likes her gin
Papa likes his bourbon, mama likes her gin
Papa likes his outside women, mama like her outside men.

BESSEMER BOUND BLUES *(Everett Murphy)*

Woke up this morning looking for my diamond jewels
I woke up this morning looking for my diamond jewels
'Cause mama's goin' home singin' those Bessemer blues

Papa, sugar papa, how come you do me like you do?
Papa, sugar papa, how come you do me like you do?
I've done everything you asked me, tryin' to get along with you

I wade in the water, walk through the ice and snow
I wade in the water, I walk through the ice and snow
But from now on, papa, I won't be your dog no more

State Street's all right and lights shine nice and bright
State Street's all right and lights shine nice and bright
But I'd rather be in Bessemer reading by a candle light.

BIG BOY BLUES *(Gertrude Rainey)*

Oh, run here, daddy, tell me what's on your mind
Oh, run here, daddy, tell me what's on your mind
Oh, keeps me worried, grieving all the time

There's two things I can't understand
There's two things I can't understand
Why these married women crazy 'bout the back door man

[SPOKEN]
Lord, toot it, big boy, toot it
Lord, that's my back door man

[SUNG]
I'm goin' up on the mountain, goin' by the railroad tracks
Lord, going up on the mountain, going by the railroad tracks
I lost my daddy and I can't turn back

I got a letter this morning, it didn't read just right
I got a letter this morning, it didn't read just right
That means I'm leaving to walk the streets all night.

BIG FEELING BLUES (*Selma Davis and Gertrude Rainey*)

[SPOKEN]
>   All these many years I been pleadin' for a man
>   How come I can't get me a real monkey man?
>   I'm not no triflin' woman

[SUNG]
>   I've been looking for a man I can call my own
>   Been married many times, but they left my home
>
>   Ah, big feeling blues, worst I ever had
>   I've got the big feeling blues, I mean I've got 'em bad

Charlie Jackson: If you looking for a brown, come get this chocolate queen
                   I'm a big kid man, just out of my teens

Rainey: Ah, big feeling blues, worst I've ever had
             I've got the big feeling blues, I mean I've got 'em bad

             Unlucky with my yellow, unlucky with my brown
             The blacks they just keep on throwing me down

             Ah, big feeling blues, worst I've ever had
             I've got the big feeling blues, I mean I've got 'em bad

Jackson: If you need a good man, why don't you try me?
             I sho can put you out of your misery

Rainey: Ah, big feeling blues, worst I've ever had
             I've got the big feeling blues, I mean I've got 'em bad

             There's a whole lot left, what's left is good
             Gimme a chance, honey, I'll make you change your neighborhood

             Ah, big feeling blues, worst I've ever had
             I've got the big feeling blues, I mean I've got 'em bad.

BLACK CAT HOOT OWL BLUES (*Thomas Dorsey*)

Black cat on my doorstep, black cat on my windowsill
Black cat on my doorstep, black cat on my windowsill
If one black cat don't cross me, another black cat will

It's bad luck if I'm jolly, bad luck if I cry
It's bad luck if I'm jolly, bad luck if I cry
It's bad luck if I stay here, it's still more bad luck if I die

Last night a hootin' owl come and sit right over my door
Last night a hootin' owl come and sit right over my door
A feeling seemed to tell me I'd never see my man no more

I feel my left side a-jumping, my heart a-bumping, I'm minding my p's and q's
I feel my brain a-thumping, I've got no time to lose
Mama's superstitious, trying to overcome those blues.

BLACK DUST BLUES (*Selma Davis and Gertrude Rainey*)

It was way last year when my trouble began
It was way last year when my trouble began
I had a fuss with a woman, she said I took her man

She sent me a letter, says she's gonna turn me down
She sent me a letter, says she's gonna turn me down
She's gonna fix me up so I won't chase her man around

I begin to feel bad, worse than I ever before
I began to feel bad, worse than I ever before
Started out one morning, found black dust all 'round my door

I began to get thin, had trouble with my feet
I began to get thin, had trouble with my feet
Throwing stuff out my mouth whenever I tried to eat

Black dust in my window, black dust on my doormat
Black dust in my window, black dust on my doormat
Black dust got me walking on all fours like a cat.

BLACK EYE BLUES (*Thomas Dorsey*)

Down in Hogan's Alley lived Miss Nancy Ann
Always fussin', squabbling with her man
Then I heard Miss Nancy say
"Why do you treat your gal that way?"

I went down the alley, other night
Nancy and her man had just had a fight
He beat Miss Nancy 'cross the head
When she rose to her feet, she said

"You low down alligator, just watch me
Sooner or later gonna catch you with your britches down
You 'buse me and you cheat me, you dog around and beat me
Still I'm gonna hang around

"Take all my money, blacken both of my eyes
Give it to another woman, come home and tell me lies
You low down alligator, just watch me
Sooner or later gonna catch you with your britches down
I mean, gonna catch you with your britches down."

BLAME IT ON THE BLUES (*Thomas Dorsey*)

I'm so sad and worried, got no time to spread the news
I'm so sad and worried, got no time to spread the news
Won't blame it on my trouble, can't blame it on the blues

Lord, Lord, Lord, Lordy Lord
Lord, Lord, Lordy Lordy Lord
Lord, Lord, Lord, Lord, Lord, Lord

[Spoken] Lord, who'm I gonna blame it on, then?

I can't blame my daddy, he treats me nice and kind
I can't blame my daddy, he treats me nice and kind
Shall I blame it on my nephew, blame it on that trouble of mine?

This house is like a graveyard, when I'm left here by myself
This house is like a graveyard, when I'm left here by myself
Shall I blame it on my lover, blame it on somebody else?

Can't blame my mother, can't blame my dad
Can't blame my brother for the trouble I've had
Can't blame my lover that held my hand
Can't blame my husband, can't blame my man
Can't blame nobody, guess I'll have to blame it on the blues.

BLUES, OH BLUES *(Gertrude Rainey)*

[*SPOKEN*]
Now it's the blues, boys, play 'em whilst I sing 'em

[*SUNG*]
Oh blues, oh blues, oh blues
Oh blues, oh blues, blues, oh blues
I'm so blue, so blue, I don't know what to do
Oh blues, oh blues, oh blues

I'm going away, I'm going to stay
I'm going away, I'm going to stay
I'm going away, oh, mama's going to stay
I'm going to find the man I love some sweet day

[*SPOKEN*]
Lord, b'lieve it, I've changed my mind

[*SUNG*]
Oh blues, oh blues, oh blues
Oh blues, oh blues, blues, oh blues
I'm so blue, so blue, oh, mama don't know what to do
Oh blues, I'm blue, oh blues.

BLUES THE WORLD FORGOT, PART I
   (Composer unknown)

[*ENTIRELY SPOKEN*]
Rainey: Lord, Lord, Lord, I got the blues this mornin' and don't care who
            know it. I want all you boys to lock your doors, and don't let nobody
            in but the police.

Unknown man: Look here, Ma.

Rainey: What is it?

Man: What's the matter with you?

Rainey: I got the blues.

Man: What kinda blues?

Rainey: The blues that the world forgot.

Man: Woman, I believe you is drunk.

Rainey: Drunk? Don't gimme no hambone! Mm, mm, mm, mm. Lord have mercy! The way I feel this morning, I don't mind going to jail!

Man: Ma, don't talk so loud! Don't you see the sergeant standing out there on the corner?

Rainey: Tell the sergeant I said come on in, and bring all the corn mash he have with him! Lord have mercy! Now, that does it!

Man: Lookit here, Ma.

Rainey: What is it?

Man: They done turn all them black cats loose there in that alley.

Rainey: Turn all the cats loose? What do I care if they turn them cats loose? Let them bring all the drunken cats! Where is the bootlegger? Tell him I'm going to drink all the whiskey he made this week! I feel like going to jail!

Man: Uh-oh!

Rainey: What is it?

Man: Uh-oh!

Rainey: What's the matter?

Man: Old Tack Annie's done cut her old man's head again.

Rainey: Cut her old man's head? Tell Tack Annie t'come on down here! I ain't scared of her! Bring all the Tack Annies! The way I feel this morning, I'll tackle any Tack Annie! I wouldn't mind seein' Tack Annie!

Man: Well, it won't be long now.

Rainey: I know'd it, I know'd it, I know'd it; we'll all land up in jail. I'm going to tell the judge I don't know a thing about it!

Man: Well, it wasn't me!

BLUES THE WORLD FORGOT, PART II
(*Composer unknown*)

[*SPOKEN*]

Rainey: I told that judge I didn't know a thing about it.

Unknown man: Yeah, but you're doin' time right here with me, sister. Huh!

Rainey: All right, but I'm doin' my time for nothin'.

Man: Yeah, I heard that before.

Rainey: Everybody said I wasn't a little old drunk.

Man: No, you don't get drunk.

Rainey: How I feel this week, brother, I'm gonna tell you right now.

Man: Until Thursday. You go to jail every Friday mornin'.

Rainey: That's all right.

Man: Biggest whiskey head in town.

[*RAINEY SINGS, MAN SPEAKS*]

Rainey: Everybody cryin' mercy, tell me what mercy means.

Man: Now, ain't that one evil woman?

Rainey: Everybody cryin' mercy, tell me what mercy means.

Man: Mm, mm, mm, mm!

Rainey: If it means feelin' good, Lord, have mercy on me.

Man: Aw, that's what I thought.

Rainey: When your man start to quit you, you know there's somethin' goin' on
            wrong.

Man: That's it? That's it! Got one of them things in the bag.

Rainey: When your man start to quit you, somethin' goin' on wrong.

Man: Ought to take that graveyard dust out your pocket!

Rainey: Lay down in your bed, can't sleep all night long.

[*BOTH SPEAK*]

Rainey: Well, I'm drunk all right now, but I know just what I'm doin'!

Man: Yeah, yeah, woman, yeah! Stop shaking that mess in here!

Rainey: Yeah, well, look like the time ain't gonna be long now!

Man: You goin' back to jail again if you don't stop shakin' that thing here.
          Don't allow that in here!

Rainey: Can anybody come help poor little bitty old me? Lord, Lord.

Man: 'Round here carryin' a groundhog in your pocket.

Rainey: Oh, how I feel this evening!

Man: Aw! Somebody come here! Ma! Have you . . . have you completely
             lost your head?
Rainey: I'm drunk!

BOOZE AND BLUES (*J. Guy Suddoth*)

Went to bed last night and, folks, I was in my tea
I went to bed last night and I was in my tea
Woke up this morning, the police was shaking me

I went to the jail house, drunk and blue as I could be
I went to the jail house, drunk and blue as I could be
But the cruel old judge sent my man away from me

They carried me to the courthouse, Lordy, how I was cryin'
They carried me to the courthouse, Lordy, how I was cryin'
They give me sixty days in the jail and money couldn't pay my fine

Sixty days ain't long when you can spend them as you choose
Sixty days ain't long when you can spend them as you choose
But they seem like years in a cell where there ain't no booze

My life is all a misery when I cannot get my booze
My life is all a misery when I cannot get my booze
I can't live without my liquor, got to have the booze to cure those blues.

BO-WEEVIL BLUES (*Gertrude Rainey*)

Hey, hey, bo-weevil, don't sing them blues no more
Hey, hey, bo-weevil, don't sing them blues no more
Bo-weevils here, bo-weevils everywhere you go

I'm a lone bo-weevil, been out a great long time
I'm a lone bo-weevil, been out a great long time
I'm gonna sing these blues to ease the bo-weevil's lonesome mind

I don't want no man to put no sugar in my tea
I don't want no man to put no sugar in my tea
Some of 'em so evil, I'm 'fraid he might poison me

I went downtown, and bought me a hat
I brought it back home, I laid it on the shelf
Looked at my bed, I'm gettin' tired sleepin' by myself.

BROKEN HEARTED BLUES (*Gertrude Rainey*)

Lord, I wonder, what is it worryin' me
Lord, I wonder, what is it worryin' me
If it ain't my regular, must be my used to be

I'm going to buy me a pair of meat hounds to lead this lonesome trail*
I'm going to buy me a pair of meat hounds to lead this lonesome trail
If I don't find my good man, I'll spend the rest of my life in jail

Good morning, judge, Mama Rainey's done raised sand
Good morning, judge, Mama Rainey's done raised sand
She killed everybody, judge, she's even killed her man.

This section is virtually inaudible.

BROKEN SOUL BLUES (*H. Strathedene Parham*)

My soul is broken, my heart aches too
Days I spend longing, daddy, for you
Nights I spend weeping, weeping for you
You gonna miss the day you took your love away
Then you'll know just how it feels
When you got the broken soul blues

You made me love you, you made your mama care
You demanded money, I didn't scold
When you asked for loving, I give you my soul
I'm crying now, but still I feel somehow
You'll be laughing, dearie
When I got the broken soul blues

[SPOKEN]
Ah, my soul is broken
Seems the whole world's gone back on me

I'm crying now, but still I feel somehow
I'll be laughing, dearie
When you got the broken soul blues.

CELL BOUND BLUES (*Gertrude Rainey*)

Hey, hey, jailer, tell me what have I done
Hey, hey, jailer, tell me what have I done
You've got me all bound in chains, did I kill that woman's son?

All bound in prison, all bound in jail
All bound in prison, all bound in jail
Cold iron bars all around me, no one to go my bail

I've got a mother and father, livin' in a cottage by the sea
I've got a mother and father, livin' in a cottage by the sea
Got a sister and brother, wonder do they think of poor me

I walked in my room the other night
My man walked in and begin to fight

I took my gun in my right hand,
"Hold him, folks, I don't wanta kill my man."

When I did that, he hit me 'cross my head
First shot I fired, my man fell dead

The paper came out and told the news
That's why I said I got the cell bound blues
Hey, hey, jailer, I got the cell bound blues.

CHAIN GANG BLUES (*Charles J. Parker and Thomas Dorsey*)

The judge found me guilty, the clerk he wrote it down
The judge found me guilty, the clerk he wrote it down
Just a poor gal in trouble, I know I'm county road bound

Many days of sorrow, many nights of woe
Many days of sorrow, many nights of woe
And a ball and chain, everywhere I go

Chains on my feet, padlock on my hand
Chains on my feet, padlock on my hand
It's all on account of stealing a woman's man

It was early this mornin' that I had my trial
It was early this mornin' that I had my trial
Ninety days on the county road and the judge didn't even smile.

COUNTIN' THE BLUES (*Gertrude Rainey*)

[SPOKEN]
Lord, I got the blues this mornin'
I want everybody to go down in prayer, Lord, Lord

[SUNG]
Layin' in my bed with my face turned to the wall
Lord, layin' in the bed with my face turned to the wall
Tryin' to count these blues, so I could sing them all

Memphis, Rampart, Beale Street, set them free
Lord, Memphis, Rampart, Beale Street, set them free
Graveyard and 'Bama Bound, Lord, Lord, come from Stingaree

Lord, sittin' on the Southern, gonna ride, ride all night long
Lord, sittin' on the Southern, gonna ride all night long
Down Hearted, Gulf Coast, they was all good songs

Lord, 'rested at Midnight, Jail House made me lose my mind
Lord, 'rested at Midnight, Jail House made me lose my mind
Bad Luck and Bo-Weevil made me think of old Moonshine

Lord, going to sleep, boys, mama's just now got bad news
Lord, going to sleep now, just now I got bad news
To try to dream away my troubles, countin' these blues.

DADDY GOODBYE BLUES (*Gertrude Rainey*)

Left my man this mornin', standin' in my door
When I got back he said, "I don't want you no more."
Goodbye, goodbye, daddy, goodbye

Can't always tell when you ain't treated right
Your man go out from you, stay out all day and night
Goodbye, goodbye, daddy, goodbye

Now daddy wrote me a letter, said, "Mama please come home."
When I got home last night, I found my man had gone
Goodbye, goodbye, daddy, goodbye

Da, da, da, da, da, da, da, da, da, da, da
Goodbye, goodbye, daddy, goodbye

Ain't got nobody to tell my troubles to
Laid down in my bed, cried all night 'bout you
Goodbye, goodbye, daddy, goodbye

Goodbye, daddy, daddy, please tell me goodbye
If you don't want me, daddy, mama'll sure lay down and die
Goodbye, goodbye, daddy, goodbye

Da, da, da, da, da, da, da, da, da, da
Goodbye, goodbye, daddy, goodbye.

DAMPER DOWN BLUES (*Composer unknown*)

Lord, Lord, Lord Lord Lord
Lord, Lord Lord, Lord Lord Lord Lord
The man I'm lovin' treats me like a dog

I woke up this mornin', trouble all 'round my bed
I woke up this mornin', trouble all 'round my bed
I had the blues so bad, I couldn't hold up my head

Lord, ain't gwine cry no more
Lord, ain't gwine cry no more
I cried here, cried everywhere I go

If I had wings, I'd fly all over this town
If I had wings, I'd fly all over this town
When I'd found my man, I'd turn his damper down

Lord, ain't gwine cry no more
Lord, ain't gwine cry no more
I cried here, cried everywhere I go.

DEAD DRUNK BLUES (*George W. Thomas*)

[SPOKEN]
My man is friggin' drunk this morning, daddy, say, be yourself!

[SUNG]
Oh, give me Houston, that's the place I crave
Oh, give me Houston, that's the place I crave
So when I'm dry, I drink whiskey's just made

Oh, whiskey, whiskey is some folks' downfall
Oh, whiskey, whiskey is some folks' downfall
But if I don't get whiskey, I ain't no good at all

When I was in Houston, drunk most every day
When I was in Houston, drunk most every day
[Spoken] Lord, where the police?
[Sung] I drank so much whiskey, I thought I'd pass away

Have you ever been drunk, slept in all your clothes
Have you ever been drunk, slept in all your clothes
And when you wake up, feel like you've had a dose?

Daddy, I'm going to get drunk just one more time
[Spoken] Where's the whiskey bottle?
[Sung] Honey, I'm going to get drunk, papa, just one more time
'Cause when I'm drunk, nothing's gonna worry my mind.

DEEP MOANING BLUES (*Gertrude Rainey*)

Mmmm Mmmm Mmmm
Mmm Mmmm Mmm
Mmmm Mmm Mmmm

My doorbell this morning, don't know whichaway to go
My bell rang this morning, didn't know whichaway to go
I had the blues so bad, I set right down on my floor

I felt like going on the mountain, jumping over in the sea
I felt like going on the mountain, jumping over in the sea
When my daddy stay out late, he don't care a thing 'bout me

Mmmm Mmm Mmm
Mmm Mmm Mmm

[Spoken] Lord, where I'm gonna stay at tonight?

Mmm Mmm Mm Mm

Daddy, daddy, please come home to me
Daddy, daddy, please come home to me
I'm on my way, crazy as I can be.

DON'T FISH IN MY SEA (*Bessie Smith and Gertrude Rainey*)

My daddy come home this mornin', drunk as he could be
My daddy come home this mornin', drunk as he could be
I know my daddy's done gone bad on me

He used to stay out late, now he don't come home at all
He used to stay out late, now he don't come home at all
[Spoken] Won't kiss me, either*
I know there's another mule been kickin' in my stall

If you don't like my ocean, don't fish in my sea
Don't like my ocean, don't fish in my sea
Stay out of my valley and let my mountain be

I ain't had no lovin' since God knows when
I ain't had no lovin' since God knows when
That's the reason I'm through with these no-good triflin' men

Never miss the sunshine 'til the rains begin to fall
Never miss the sunshine 'til the rains begin to fall
You never miss your ham 'til another mule's in your stall.

*The speaking voice sounds to be that of Bessie Smith, who may very well have been present at this
recording session on an informal basis. Recording made in Chicago, December 1926.

DOWN IN THE BASEMENT (*H. Strathedene Parham*)

[SPOKEN]
Oh, this is one of my low down days, boys. Take me to the basement.

[SUNG]
I've got a man, piano hound
Plays anything that's going around
When he plays that highbrow stuff
I shout, "Brother, that's enough!"

Take me to the basement, that's as low as I can go
I want something low down, daddy, want it nice and slow
I would shimmy from A to Z, if you'll play that thing for me
Take me to the basement, that's as low as I can go

Take me to the basement, that's as low as I can go.
I want something low down, daddy, want it nice and slow
I can shimmy from A to Z, if you'll play that thing for me
Take me to the basement, that's as low as I can go.

DREAM BLUES (*Gertrude Rainey*)

Had a dream last night and the night before
Had a dream last night and the night before
Gonna get drunk now, I won't dream no more

Dreamed my man didn't treat me right
Lord, I dreamed my man didn't treat me right
Packed my clothes in a corner and walked the streets all night

I saw my man fall on his knees and cry
Lord, I saw my man fall on his knees and cry
"Take me back, mama, or else I'll die."

Lord, I wonder, what am I to do
Lord, Lord, I wonder, what am I to do
When everybody try to mistreat you

My heart is aching, mama feel like cryin'
Lord, my heart is aching, mama feel like cryin'
Since I had that dream last night, mama don't mind dyin'.

EXPLAINING THE BLUES (*Thomas Dorsey*)

Whole world seems against me, if I could just explain
Whole world seems against me, if I could just explain
Man I love left me, 'cause I called another man's name

Too sad to whistle, too broken hearted to sing
Too sad to whistle, too broken hearted to sing
Let me explain the trouble that a jealous man will bring

Explain why you left me, and tell me why you went away
Explain why you left me, and tell me why you went away
And I'll explain why I need you and want you back today

I'm goin' on that island where women never hear bad news
I'm goin' on that island where women never hear bad news
Then I'll never be down hearted, tryin' to explain these blues.

FAREWELL DADDY BLUES (*Gertrude Rainey*)

I'm wild about my daddy, I want him all the time
Wild about my daddy, I want him all the time
But I don't want you, daddy, if I can't call you mine

Got the farewell blues, see, and my trunk is packed
Got the farewell blues, see, and my trunk is packed
But I don't want no daddy because'n I ain't comin' back

Oh, fare you well, daddy, honey, it's your turn now
Fare you well, daddy, honey, it's your turn now
After all I've done, you mistreated me anyhow

Going through the wood field feeling sad and blue
Going through the wood field feeling sad and blue
Lord, I jumped a rabbit, said, "Mama, I've got 'em too."

Pig starts to singin', oh, how his voice could ring
Pig starts to singin', oh, how his voice could ring
He says, "I'm no yellow jacket, but lord how I can sting."

Since my man left me, the others can't be found
Since my man left me, others can't be found
But before he left me, the other men was hangin' around

So fare you well, daddy, someday you'll hear bad news
So farewell, daddy, someday you'll hear bad news
When you look for your mama, she's gone with the farewell blues.

'FORE DAY HONRY SCAT (*Billie McOwens and Gertrude Rainey*)

Yes, I'm mad, I feel so blue, I don't know what to do
My man left me this mornin', every cloud was black and blue
He got up and packed his grip
And he'll be gone a long, long time

I went to the fortune-teller to find my man, because he's layin' heavy on my
     mind
He said: "Your man has caught that 'fore day scat
And left here tipping like a Maltese cat
Poor girl, I know your man has done you wrong
Hit high timber, now he's long, long gone."

He left here ridin' that Cannonball
He was so handsome, and so long and tall
I want all you women to spread the news
Want you to tell 'em to who you choose
My man left me with them 'fore day honry blues, I said blues

He said: "Your man has caught that 'fore day scat
And left here tipping like a Maltese cat
Poor girl, I know your man have done you wrong
Hit high timber, now he's long, long gone."

He left here ridin' that Cannonball
He was so handsome, and so long and tall
Want all you women to spread the news
Want y'all to tell them to who you choose
My man left me with the 'fore day honry blues.

GEORGIA CAKE WALK (*Composer unknown*)

[ENTIRELY SPOKEN]

Unknown man: Say, Ma.

Rainey: What is it?

Man: Where'd you get that primrose from?

Rainey: From a cake walk last night.

Man: Down at where?

Rainey: Cake walk last night.

Man: What you know about a cake walk, woman?

Rainey: At the Georgia camp meetin' cake walk.

Man: Georgia camp meetin'?

Rainey: Yes.

Man: Ha! Say, you must be from Gaston, Georgia.

Rainey: I don't care where I'm from, I can cake walk all right!

Man: I guess you can cake walk.

Rainey: Yes.

Man: Well, let me see you.

Rainey: All right, you believe I can cake walk?

Man: Yeah, go ahead.

Rainey: Here I go. Oh, do it.

Man: Look at that fool dance! Ma, you done lost your head, haven't you?

Rainey: No, I'm just cake walkin', boy.

Man: Well, it's one thing, I'm gonna cake walk with you.

Rainey: Ah, do it. Turn the other way.

Man: If you shimmy in here, you gon' waffle outside. Here, here, woman, here, here. Stop that mess in here, you can't do that in here! Look out, Ma, here comes Big Dixon Middleton.

Rainey: Let him come on.

Man: I'm goin' home, Ma. You gon' get this place raided. Oh, shake it, Ma, shake it, honey. Ma, you going home with me?

Rainey: Yes.

Man: Well, let's go. Ah, do that thing, Ma, do that thing. Ah, shake it now.

GONE DADDY BLUES (*Gertrude Rainey*)

[KNOCKING]

[SPOKEN]
Unknown man: Who's that knockin' on that door?
Rainey: It's me, baby.
Man: Me who?
Rainey: Don't you know I'm your wife?
Man: What?! Wife?!
Rainey: Yeah!
Man: Ain't that awful? I don't let no woman quit me but one time.
Rainey: But I just quit one li'l old time, just one time!
Man: You left here with that other man, why didn't you stay?
Rainey: Well, I'll tell you why I didn't stay, baby. I got home and I had to come
          on back home to you!
Man: Well, I'm leavin' here today, what have you got to say?
Rainey: Well, all right, I'll tell it, baby.
Man: Talk fast, then.

[SUNG]
I'm going away, I'm going to stay
I'll find the man I love some day
I've got my ticket, clothes in my hand
Trying to find that South bound land

I'm gonna ride 'til I find that South bound land
I'm gonna ride 'til I find that South bound land
Gon' keep on ridin' 'til I shake hands with my man

I'm going away, I'm going to stay
I'll come back for my daddy someday
But, dad, you'll never know how much I've missed you 'til I'm gone

I'm going away, I'm going to stay
I'll long for my daddy some day
But, dad, you'll never know how much I've missed you 'til I'm gone.

GOODBYE DADDY BLUES (*Gertrude Rainey*)

Sitting in my room, all by myself
Sitting in my room, all by myself
Thinkin' the man I love might be with someone else

Daddy, when you left me all cold in mind
Daddy, when you left me all cold in mind
If you knowed how much I love you, you'd stay home all the time

When your daddy kisses you, and looks you in your eye
When your daddy kisses you, and looks you in your eye
Then he left with your heart, and that man's kiss means goodbye

Lord, goodbye, dad, mama'll soon be gone
Lord, goodbye, dad, mama'll soon be gone
She's gotta find another daddy to show her right from wrong

Every woman's got a dad, some dads tells them lies
Every woman's got a dad, some dads tells them lies
You can give your man your money, but his love you cannot buy

Lord, goodbye, dad, someday you'll bring good news
Lord, goodbye, dad, someday you'll bring good news
But he kills me with his lovin', tryin' to bring goodbye daddy blues.

GOODBYE MAMA FOREVER BLUES (*Gertrude Rainey*)

Here comes that train to take my man away
Here comes that train to take my man away
I'm gonna stay right here, he might come back some day

Mr. Conductor, why do you treat me so bad?
Mr. Conductor, why do you treat me so bad?
You've got the man I love, the only man I've ever had

My heart's on fire, I'm going round and round
My heart's on fire, I'm going round and round
It's the man I love, he leaves 'em burning down.

GRIEVIN' HEARTED BLUES (*Composer unknown*)

You throwed me away, you treated me mean
I love you better than any man I've seen
My heart is grievin', I've been refused
I've got those grievin' hearted blues

You'll find you love me, daddy, some sweet day
You'll find you love me, daddy, some sweet day
It's true I love you, but I can't take mistreatment thisaway

Lord, I wants my ticket, show me my train
I wants my ticket, show me my train
I'm gonna ride till I can't hear them call your name

I'm gon' start cryin', my love's been refused
Gon' start cryin', my love's been refused
Gon' keep on cryin' till I lose these grievin' hearted blues.

HEAR ME TALKIN' TO YOU (*Gertrude Rainey*)

Ramblin' man makes no change in me
I'm gonna ramble back to my used to be

Ah, you hear me talkin' to you, I don't bite my tongue
You want to be my man, you got to fetch it with you when you come

Eve and Adam, in the garden takin' a chance
Adam didn't take time to get his pants

Ah, you hear me talkin' to you, don't bite my tongue
You want to be my man, you got to fetch it with you when you come

Our old cat swallowed a ball of yarn
When the kittens was born, they had sweaters on

Ah, you hear me talkin' to you, I don't bite my tongue
You want to be my man, you got to fetch it with you when you come

Hello, Central, give me 609
What it takes to get it in these hips of mine

Ah, you hear me talkin' to you, I don't bite my tongue
You want to be my man, you got to fetch it with you when you come

Grandpa got grandma told
He says her jelly roll was 'most too old

Ah, you hear me talkin' to you, I don't bite my tongue
You want to be my man, you got to fetch it with you when you come.

HONEY, WHERE YOU BEEN SO LONG? (*Fred Fisher*)

My honey left me, he's gone away
I've had the worried blues all day

My heart is aching about that man
What makes me love him, I can't understand

He'll soon be returning and glad tidings he will bring
Then I'll throw my arms around him, then begin to sing

Honey, where you been so long?
Honey, where you been so long?

Ever since the day, the day you went away
I been crying, felt like dying, I'm not ashamed to say

Never thought you'd treat me wrong
Look how you have dragged me down

I have been almost insane
But I'm so glad to see you home again

Honey, where you been so long?
Never thought you would treat me wrong
Look how you have dragged me down

I have been almost insane
But then I'm so glad to see you home again
Honey, where you been so long?

HUSTLIN' BLUES (*Malissa Nix and Thomas Dorsey*)

It's rainin' out here and tricks ain't walkin' tonight
It's rainin' out here and tricks ain't walkin' tonight
I'm goin' home, I know I've got to fight

If you hit me tonight, let me tell you what I'm going to do
If you hit me tonight, let me tell you what I'm going to do
I'm gonna take you to court and tell the judge on you

I ain't made no money, and he dared me to go home
I ain't made no money, and he dared me to go home
Judge, I told him he better leave me alone

He followed me up and he grabbed me for a fight
He followed me up and he grabbed me for a fight
He said, "Oh, do you know you ain't made no money tonight?"

Oh, judge, tell him I'm through
Oh, judge, tell him I'm through
I'm tired of this life, that's why I brought him to you.

JEALOUS HEARTED BLUES (*Lovie Austin*)

You can have my money and everything I own
But for God's sakes, leave my man alone

'Cause I'm jealous, jealous, jealous hearted me
Lord, I'm just jealous, jealous as I can be

It takes a rocking chair to rock, a rubber ball to roll
Takes the man I love to satisfy my soul

Yes, I'm jealous, jealous, jealous hearted me
Lord, I'm just jealous, jealous as I can be

Got a range in my kitchen, cooks nice and brown
All I need is my man to turn my damper down

Yes, I'm jealous, jealous, jealous hearted me
Lord, I'm just jealous, jealous as I can be

Gonna buy me a bulldog to watch him while I sleep
To keep my man from making his midnight creep

Yes, I'm jealous, jealous, jealous hearted me
Lord, I'm just jealous, jealous as I can be.

JEALOUSY BLUES (*Glasco and Glasco*)

All the days have passed and gone, still my blues they lingers on
Used to be da-daddy, used to be da-daddy, your used to be baby's blue for you

Jealousy, jealousy, that's who stole my daddy, my loving sweet daddy from me
Jealousy, oh me, oh my, poor me, I've got the cruel jealousy blues

If all the world is evil, all the world is evil, oh jealousy is the worst of all
It'll make you mad and lonely, your sweet love will feel so pale
It'll steal your loving daddy, have many folks in jail

Jealousy, oh me, oh my, poor me, I've got the cruel jealousy blues.

JELLY BEAN BLUES (*Lena Arrant*)

Did you ever wake up with your good man on your mind?
Did you ever wake up with your good man on your mind?
My daddy left me this morning, that's why I moan and cry

He'll make you laugh, he'll make you cry, to drive those blues away
You'll sit right down, you'll weep and moan and then you'll finally say
Lord, I've been wonderin' where my jelly bean done gone

I can sit right here and look a thousand miles away
I just can't remember what my baby had to say
He said see, see rider, today I'm going away
And I won't be back until you change your ways

So fare thee well, heartache
Today that means goodbye
If you did not want me you had no right to lie.

LAST MINUTE BLUES (*Thomas Dorsey*)

Minutes seem like hours, hours seem like days
Minutes seem like hours, hours seem like days
It seem like my daddy won't stop his evil ways

Seem like every minute going to be my last
Seem like every minute going to be my last
If I can't tell my future, I won't tell my past

The brook runs into the river, river runs into the sea
The brook run into the river, river run into the sea
If I don't run into my daddy, somebody'll have to bury me

If anybody ask you who wrote this lonesome song
If anybody ask you who wrote this lonesome song
Tell 'em you don't know the writer, but Ma Rainey put it on.

LAWD, SEND ME A MAN BLUES (*Gertrude Rainey*)

Who gonna pay my board bill now?
Had a good man, and he turned me down
Landlord comin', knock on my door
I told him my good man don't stay here no more

Girls, take my advice
Ask the good Lord to help you twice

Oh, Lord, send me a man
I'm the loneliest woman in the land
I work hard both night and day
Tryin' to find a good man to come my way

Send me a Zulu, a voodoo, any old man
I'm not particular, boys, I'll take what I can
I've been worried, almost insane
Oh, Lordy, send me a man
Oh, Lordy, send me a man

Oh, Lord, send me a man
I'm the loneliest woman in the land
I work hard every night and day
Tryin' to find a good man to come my way

Send me a Zulu, a voodoo, any old man
I'm not particular, boys, I'll take what I can
I've been worried, almost insane
Oh, Lordy, send me a man
Oh, Lordy, send me a man.

LEAVIN' THIS MORNING (*Selma Davis and Gertrude Rainey*)

See me reelin' and rockin', drunk as I can be
Man I love tryin' to make a fool of me
I'm leavin' this mornin', I'm leavin' this mornin'
I'm leavin', tryin' to find a man of my own

When I get through drinkin', gon' buy a Gatlin gun
Find my man, he better hitch up and run
'Cause I'm leavin' this mornin', I'm leavin' this mornin'
I'm going to Kansas City to bring Jim Jackson home

I give him all my money, treat him nice as I can
Got another woman, wait 'til I find my man
Lord, I'm leavin' this mornin', I'm leavin' this mornin'
I'm leavin', tryin' to find a man of my own

I went up Eighteenth Street, found out where the other woman stays
Cure my man of his triflin' ways
'Cause I'm leavin' this mornin', honey, I'm leavin' this mornin'
I'm goin' to Kansas City to bring Jim Jackson home

I walked down the street, didn't have on no hat
Asking everybody I see where my daddy's at
I'm leavin' this mornin', honey, I'm leavin' this mornin'
I'm leavin', tryin' to find a man of my own.

LEVEE CAMP MOAN (*Composer unknown*)

My man has left me and he's gone away
Back to the levee, where he used to stay
I miss his huggin' and his kissin' too
I feel so lonesome and awf'ly blue
That's the reason, hear my lonesome cry, can't help but cry

Mmmmmmmmmmmmmmmm, mmmmmmmmmmmmmmmm
Each night and morning I might go roaming
Back to the levee where my man's home*
That's the reason I'm hummin' the levee camp moan

Mmmmmmmmmmmmmmm, mmmmmmmmmmmmmmmm
I miss his huggin', I miss his kissin'
And that ain't all that I've been missin'
That's the reason you hear me moan the levee camp moan

Mmmmmmmmmmmmmmm, mmmmmmmmmmmmmmmm
He called me honey, took all my money
Lord, he's a mean ol' dog*
That's the reason you hear me moanin' the levee camp moan.

Virtually inaudible.

LITTLE LOW MAMA BLUES (*Gertrude Rainey*)

Mmmm, Lordy Lordy Lord
Mmmm, Lordy Lordy Lord
The man I'm loving treats me like a dog

I know I've been your dog since I've been your gal
I been your dog since I've been your gal
I loves you, pretty papa, follow you everywhere

If you don't want me, papa, why don't you tell me so?
If you don't want me, papa, why don't you tell me so?
I'm little and low, can get a man anywhere I go

I'm gonna build me a scaffold, papa, to hang myself
I'm gonna build me a scaffold, papa, to hang myself
Can't get the man I love, don't want nobody else

Aiii, Lord Lord Lord
Aiii, Lordy Lordy
Aiii, Lord, ain't gonna sing no more.

LOG CAMP BLUES (*Thomas Dorsey and Gertrude Rainey*)

Down in Mississippi, where the air is low and damp
Down in Mississippi, where the air is low and damp
Low down on the Delta is a great big logging camp

I can see my daddy, jumpin' 'round from log to log
I can see my daddy, jumpin' 'round from log to log
And down in Onacaga* everybody's on the hog

Throw away your pinchback, burn up your Prince of Wales
Throw away your pinchback, burn up your Prince of Wales
Get your overalls and jumpers, start to rolling cotton bales

Meal is in my meat-box, chickens runs around my yard
Meal is in my meat-box, chickens runs around my yard
Yearlings in my cowpen, I never knowed that times was hard

If I can't get no ticket, put on my walking shoes
If I can't get no ticket, put on my walking shoes
I'm going to Mississippi, singing those logging camp blues.

This word is virtually inaudible, but likely is the name of a small Delta town.

LOST WANDERING BLUES (*Gertrude Rainey*)

I'm leavin' this mornin' with my clothes in my hand
Lord, I'm leavin' this mornin' with my clothes in my hand
I won't stop movin' 'til I find my man

I'm standin' here wonderin' will a matchbox hold my clothes
Lord, I'm standin' here wonderin' will a matchbox hold my clothes
I got a trunk too big to be botherin' with on the road

I went up on the mountain, turned my face to the sky
Lord, I went up on the mountain, turned my face to the sky
I heard a whisper, said, "Mama, please don't die."

I turned around to give him my right han'
Lord, I turned around to give him my right han'
When I looked in his face, I was talkin' to my man

Lord, look-a yonder, people, my love has been refused
I said, look-a yonder, people, my love has been refused
That's the reason why mama's got the lost wandering blues.

LOUISIANA HOODOO BLUES (*Gertrude Rainey*)

Going to Louisiana bottom to get me a hoodoo hand
Going to Louisiana bottom to get me a hoodoo hand
Gotta stop these women from taking my man

Down in Algiers where the hoodoos live in their den
Down in Algiers where the hoodoos live in their den
Their chief occupation is separating women from men

The hoodoo told me to get me a black cat bone
The hoodoo told me to get me a black cat bone
And shake it over their heads, they'll leave your man alone

Twenty years in the bottom, that ain't long to stay
Twenty years in the bottom, that ain't long to stay
If I can keep these tush-hog women from taking my man away

So I'm bound for New Orleans, down in goofer dust land
So I'm bound for New Orleans, down in goofer dust land
Down where the hoodoo folks can fix it for you with your man.

LUCKY ROCK BLUES (*Katie Winters and Lovie Austin*)

Feelin' kind of melancholy, made up my mind to go away
And though some folks says it's folly, sometimes it helps and sails away

You'll forget the man you love, although he may be mean
Goodbye, folks, I'm on my way, way down to New Orleans

Goin' to New Orleans to find that lucky rock
Goin' to New Orleans to find that lucky rock
Tryin' to rid myself of this bad luck I've got

On my way to find that lucky rock
Oh, I'm on my way to find that lucky rock
Just to ease my mind of all this trouble I've got.

MA AND PA POORHOUSE BLUES (*Selma Davis and Gertrude Rainey*)

[SPOKEN]

Rainey: Hello there, Charlie.

Jackson: Hello, Ma.

Rainey: Charlie, where's that big banjo you had?

Jackson: Oh, that big banjo's in pawn.

Rainey: In pawn?

Jackson: Yes, ma'am.

Rainey: Too bad, Jim.

Jackson: Hello, Ma.

Rainey: All right, Charlie.

Jackson: What become of that great big bus you had?

Rainey: Child, somebody stole that bus.

Jackson: Stole it?

Rainey: Yes.

Jackson: Mmmmmmmmmmm.

Rainey: Charlie, do you know I'm broke?

Jackson: Ma, don't you know I'm broke, too?

Rainey: I tell you what let's do.

Jackson: What we gonna do?

Rainey: Let's both go to the poorhouse together.

Jackson: All right, let's go.

[SUNG]

Rainey: Too bad, too bad, too bad, too bad, too bad
           Too bad, too bad, too bad, too bad, too bad
           I've lost all my money, lost everything I had

Jackson: Ma, being broke's all right when you know you got some more money
           comin' in
           Ah, being broke's all right when you know you got some more money
           comin' in
           But when you lose your money, that's when friendship ends

Rainey: Oh, here I'm on my knees

Jackson: [Spoken] Don't worry, Ma, I'll soon be down on my knees with you

Rainey: Pa, here I am, on my knees
           I want the whole world to know mama's broke and can't be pleased

Jackson: When you had lots of money, you had plenty friends
Rainey: Lord, lost all my money, that was my end, oh, ain't got no money now
Jackson: [Spoken] Oh, moan it, Ma!
Both: We better go to the poorhouse, and try to live anyhow
           We better go to the poorhouse, and try to live anyhow.

MA RAINEY'S BLACK BOTTOM (*Gertrude Rainey*)

[SPOKEN]
Unknown man: Now, you've heard the rest. Ah, boys, I'm gonna show you the
               best. Ma Rainey's gonna show you her black bottom!

[SUNG]
Rainey: Way down South in Alabamy
           I got a friend they call dancin' Sammy
           Who's crazy about all the latest dancin'
           Black bottom stomps and the new baby prancin'

           The other night at a swell affair
           Soon as the boys found out that I was there
           They said, "Come on, Ma, let's go to the cabaret."
           When I got there, you ought to hear me say

           Want to see the dance you call the black bottom
           I wanna learn that dance
           Want to see the dance you call your big black bottom
           They put you in a trance.

           All the boys in the neighborhood
           They say your black bottom is really good
           Come on and show me your black bottom
           I want to learn that dance.

           I want to see the dance you call the black bottom
           I want to learn that dance
           Come on and show that dance you call your big black bottom
           It puts us in a trance.

Early last morning 'bout the break of day
Grandpa told my grandmama, I heard him say
"Get up and show your good old man your black bottom
I want to learn that dance."

Now I'm gon' show you all my black bottom
They stay to see that dance
Wait until you see me do my big black bottom
It'll put you in a trance

[SPOKEN]
Man: Ah, do it, Ma, do it, honey. Look out, now, Ma, you's gettin' kinda
         rough there! You bet' be yourself, now, careful now, not too strong,
         not too strong, Ma!

[SUNG]
Rainey: I done showed y'all my black bottom
         You ought to learn that dance.

MA RAINEY'S MYSTERY RECORD (*Guy Early and Thomas Dorsey*)

Lord, I'm down with the blues, blue as I can be
Lord, I'm down with the blues, blue as I can be
Nobody knows my trouble but the good Lord and me

Ooh, there's something going all wrong
Ooh, ooh, there's something going all wrong
The way I'm thinking, I know I can't last long

I've had the blues a solid week, every night and day
Had the blues a solid week, every night and day
Man I love broke my heart, and I'm 'bout to pass away

I'm down with the blues, just as blue as I can be
I'm down with the blues, blue as I can be
I think I hear an angel singing "Nearer My God to Thee."

MEMPHIS BOUND BLUES (*Thomas Dorsey*)

You got your grip to leave me, you're going to leave your home today
You got your grip to leave me, you're going to leave your home today
But drop it for a minute, and listen to what I've got to say

You can fly up high, you can spread your feathers all around
You can fly up high, you can spread your feathers all around
But when you get in trouble, you got to fall back to the ground

Some folks born with riches, some folks born with pain
Some folks born with riches, some folks born with pain
But I'm here to tell you, when you leave they all leave the same

I talk because I'm stubborn, I sing because I'm free
I talk because I'm stubborn, I sing because I'm free
My daddy's gone and left me, bound for Memphis, Tennessee.

MISERY BLUES (*Gertrude Rainey*)

I love my brownskin, indeed I do
Folks I know used to me being a fool
I'm going to tell you what I went and done
I give him all my money just to have some fun

He told me that he loved me, loved me so
If I would marry him, I needn't to work no mo'
Now I'm grievin', almost dyin'
Just because I didn't know that he was lyin'

I've got the blues, I've got the blues
I've got those misery blues
Love my brownskin, he's done left town
Goodbye, dearie, you used to be so cheery
Hold on, honey, took all my money
I worry, worry so

I've got the blues, down in my shoes
I've got those misery blues
I've got to go to work now, get another start
Work is the thing that's breaking my heart
I've got those mean old misery blues

I've got the blues, I've got the blues
I've got those misery blues
I've got to go to work now, get another start
Work is the thing that's breaking my heart
I've got those mean old misery blues.

MOONSHINE BLUES (*Gertrude Rainey*)*

[SPOKEN]
Hold it, Luke, it might be a bootlegger!

[SUNG]
I been drinkin' all night, babe, and the night before
But when I get sober, I ain't gonna drink no more
'Cause my friend left me, standin' in my door

My head goes 'round and around, babe, since my daddy left town
I don't know if the river runnin' up or down
But there's one thing certain, it's mama's going to leave town

You'll find me wrigglin' and a-rockin', howlin' like a hound
Catch the first train that's runnin' South bound

Oh, stop, you'll hear me say, stop right to my brain
Oh, stop that train, so I can ride back home again

Here I'm upon my knees, play that again for me
'Cause I'm about to be losin' my mind

Boys, I can't stand up, can't sit down
The man I love is done left town

I feel like screamin', I feel like cryin'
Lord, I've been mistreated, folks, and don't mind dyin'

I'm going home, I'm going to settle down
I'm going to stop my running around

Tell everybody that come my way
Lord, I got the moonshine blues, I say
I got the moonshine blues.

---

*This is a transcription of the 1923 recording of "Moonshine Blues." The 1927 version has slightly
different lyrics.

MORNING HOUR BLUES (*Gertrude Rainey and Bessie Smith*)

I woke up this morning, something was worrying me
I woke up this morning, something was worrying me
Must have been the man I love, that man I'll never see

I went to the graveyard, cried, "Gravedigger, please . . ."
I went to the graveyard, cried, "Gravedigger, please . . .
Show me the grave, the grave of my used to be."

Lord, look where the sun's done gone
Lord, see now, I just said it, look where the sun's done gone
You made me love you, now you love some other one

[Spoken] That's all right!

The man I got here, he's so cruel to me
The man I got here, he's so cruel to me
There'll never be a man to love me like Stingaree.

MOUNTAIN JACK BLUES (*Sid Harris*)

Early this morning, everything was still
Early this morning, everything was still
I spied my good man goin' over the hill

He said, "I'm goin', sweet mama, cryin' won't make me stay."
He said, "I'm goin', sweet mama, cryin' won't make me stay
The more you cry, the further you drive me away."

If I could holler just like a mountain jack
If I could holler just like a mountain jack
I'd go up on the mountain, call my good man back

Sometimes I want to crown him, but I know it's wrong
Sometimes I want to crown him, but I know it's wrong
I'd rather air out and leave you to weep and moan

You think I want every man I see
You think I want every man I see
That's why you nag and squabble with me

Now I've run my man away, I don't know what to do
Now run my man away, don't know what to do
My heart is achin', babe, I'm so sad and blue.

NIGHT TIME BLUES (*Gertrude Rainey and Thomas Dorsey*)

[SPOKEN]
It's three o'clock in the morning, and my man hasn't come home yet!

[SUNG]
Nighttime's falling, the day is almost gone
Nighttime is falling, the day is almost gone
My man leaves at midnight, folks, and don't come back 'til early morn

The night is dark and dreary, I can't see what to do
The night is dark and dreary, I can't see what to do
I wonder why he leave me, to roll and cry the whole night through

[SPOKEN]
Lord have mercy!

[SUNG]
It's three o'clock in the morning, by the clock hanging on the wall
It's three o'clock in the morning, by the clock hangin' on my wall
He used to come at midnight, but now he don't come home at all

When day starts to breaking, it seems to bring good news
When day starts to breaking, it seems to bring good news
It finds me broken hearted, trying to overcome these blues.

OH MY BABE BLUES (*Gertrude Rainey*)

Some of these days I'm going to leave my home, oh my babe
Now I know I'm going and it won't be long
If I go, let me go, if I stay, let me stay
Maybe I'll ask let me come back home

Tell my dad I won't be home tonight, oh my babe
My heart aches and I'm not treated right
My heart's down, it's a shame, and I just can't call his name
Still I'll ask to let me come back home

Lordy Lord, have mercy on poor me, oh my babe
Tell somebody to let my heart go free
When I go, leave me alone and still I'll stay from now on
Tell my dad I want to come back home

I'm feelin' now I'm sorry we have to part, oh my babe
'Cause you tried to break my aching heart
But someday you will say, "Come back home, babe, and stay."
Then I'll know my dad wants me back home.

OH PAPA BLUES (*E. Herbert and W. Russell*)

Just like a rainbow I am faded away
My daddy leaves me 'most every day
But he don't mean me no good, why?
Because I only wish he would
I've almost gone insane
I'm forever tryin' to call his name

Oh, papa, look what you doin', look what you doin'
Oh, papa, you caught me ruinin', you caught me ruinin'
All my money, I give you
You treat me mean and made me awfully blue
When you miss me, you're going to kiss me
You'll regret the day that you ever quit me

Oh, papa, think when you away from home
I give you money, don't want me nohow
But you will love me someday, not now
Papa, papa, now you won't have no mama at all

Oh, papa, look what you doin', look what you doin'
Oh, papa, you caused me ruinin', you caused me ruinin'
All my money, I give you

You treat me mean and make me feel so blue
You're going to miss me, you'll long to kiss me
You'll 'gret the day that you ever quit me

Oh, papa, think when you away from home
You just don't want me now, wait and see
You'll find some other man makin' love to me, now
Papa, papa, you ain't got no mama now.

PROVE IT ON ME BLUES (*Gertrude Rainey*)

Went out last night, had a great big fight
Everything seemed to go on wrong
I looked up, to my surprise
The gal I was with was gone

Where she went, I don't know
I mean to follow everywhere she goes
Folks say I'm crooked, I didn't know where she took it
I want the whole world to know

They said I do it, ain't nobody caught me
Sure got to prove it on me
Went out last night with a crowd of my friends
They must've been women, 'cause I don't like no men

It's true I wear a collar and a tie
Make the wind blow all the while
'Cause they say I do it, ain't nobody caught me
They sure got to prove it on me

Say I do it, ain't nobody caught me
Sure got to prove it on me
I went out last night with a crowd of my friends
They must've been women, 'cause I don't like no men

Wear my clothes just like a fan
Talk to the gals just like any old man
'Cause they say I do it, ain't nobody caught me
Sure got to prove it on me.

ROUGH AND TUMBLE BLUES (*Gertrude Rainey*)

I'm going to the Western Union, type the news all down the line
I'm going to the Western Union, type the news all down the line
'Cause mama's on the warpath this mornin' and don't mind dyin'

My man's so good lookin' and his clothes fit him so cute
My man's so good lookin' and his clothes fit him so cute
I cut up his box-back and bought him a struttin' suit

Then every little devil got on my man's road
Then every little devil got on my man's road
Mama Tree Top Tall and Miss Shorty Toad

Tree Top Tall give a stomp as I stepped in the door
Tree Top Tall give a stomp as I stepped in the door
Miss Shorty Toad and my man was shimmying down to the floor

I got rough and killed three women 'fore the police got the news
I got rough and killed three women 'fore police got the news
'Cause mama's on the warpath with those rough and tumble blues.

RUNAWAY BLUES (*Gertrude Rainey*)

I'm running away tomorrow, they don't mean me no good
I'm running away tomorrow, they don't mean me no good
I'm gon' run away, have to leave this neighborhood

Ah, the sun's gonna shine someday in my backyard
Ah, the sun's gonna shine someday in my backyard
I got my man, but I had to work so hard

Lord, what's the matter, mama can't be treated just right
Lord, what's the matter, mama can't be treated just right
Got my clothes in my hand, walk the streets all night.

SCREECH OWL BLUES (*J. Sammy Randall and Gertrude Rainey*)

When a hog makes a bed, you know the storm is due
When a hog makes a bed, you know the storm is due
When a screech owl hollers, mean bad luck for you

Screech owl hollered this mornin', twice in front of my back door
Screech owl hollered this mornin', twice in front of my back door
I know when he hollered, bad luck comin' back once more

I got a taxi, begged the driver to show me some speed
I got a taxi, begged the driver to show me some speed
Screech owl brought me bad luck, money's what my baby needs

I called all over town, tryin' to find that good brown of mine
I called all over town, tryin' to find that good brown of mine
He called me from the station, said, "Fifty dollars was my fine."

When I got to the station, bad luck was waitin' there too
When I got to the station, bad luck was waitin' there too
When they need more money, "We've got a warrant for you."

SEE SEE RIDER BLUES (*Gertrude Rainey*)

I'm so unhappy, I feel so blue
I always feel so sad

I made a mistake, right from the start
Lord, it seems so hard to part

Oh, but this letter that I will write
I hope he will remember, when he receives it

See, see, rider, see what you done done, Lord, Lord, Lord
Made me love you, now your gal done come
You made me love you, now your gal done come

I'm going away, baby, won't be back 'til fall, Lord, Lord, Lord
Goin' away, baby, won't be back 'til fall
If I find me a good man, I won't be back at all

I'm gonna buy me a pistol, just as long as I am tall, Lord, Lord, Lord
Gonna kill my man and catch the Cannonball
If he don't have me, he won't have no gal at all.

SEEKING BLUES (*L. McCallister*)

My daddy left me crying, I hate to see him go
My daddy left me crying, I hate to see him go
I can't live without him, 'cause I love him so

I walked on the railroad, stood up on the tracks
I walked on the railroad, stood up on the tracks
I wondered if my daddy would take me back

Oh, daddy, please come back to me
You know I'm lonesome as can be
You left me and why you broke up my fun
You left me to fight for myself alone
That's why I've got those mean ole seeking blues

Oh, my daddy, please come back to me
You know I'm lonesome as can be
You left me but why you broke up my fun
You left me to fight for myself alone
That's why I've got those mean ole seeking blues.

SHAVE 'EM DRY (*Gertrude Rainey and William Jackson*)

There's one thing I don't understand
Why a good lookin' woman likes a workin' man
Hey, hey, hey, daddy, let me shave 'em dry

Goin' away to where you off my mind
You keep me hungry and broke, daddy, all the time
Hey, hey, hey, daddy, let me shave 'em dry

Don't see how you hungry women can sleep
They shimmies all day without a bite to eat
Hey, hey, hey, daddy, let me shave 'em dry

Going downtown to spread the news
State Street women wearin' brogan shoes
Hey, hey, hey, daddy, let me shave 'em dry

If it wasn't for their powder and their store-bought hair
State Street gals couldn't go nowhere
Hey, hey, hey, daddy, let me shave 'em dry

There's one thing I can't understand
Some women drivin' State Street like a man
Hey, hey, hey, daddy, let me shave 'em dry

Went to the show the other night
Everybody on State Street was tryin' to fight
Hey, hey, hey, daddy, let me shave 'em dry

Ain't crazy 'bout my yellow, I ain't wild about my brown
You can't tell the difference when the sun goes down
Hey, hey, hey, daddy, let me shave 'em dry

When you see two women running hand to hand
Bet your life one's got the other's man
Hey, hey, hey, daddy, let me shave 'em dry

Come here, daddy, lay in my arms
When your wife comes, tell her I don't mean no harm
Hey, hey, hey, daddy, let me shave 'em dry.

SISSY BLUES (*Thomas Dorsey*)

I shimmied last night, the night before
I'm going home tonight, I won't shimmy no more

Ah, hello, Central, it's 'bout to run me wild
Can I get that number, or will I have to wait a while?

I dreamed last night I was far from harm
Woke up and found my man in a sissy's arms

Ah, hello, Central, it's 'bout to run me wild
Can I get that number, or will I have to wait a while?

Some are young, some are old
My man says sissies got good jelly roll

Ah, hello, Central, it's 'bout to run me wild
Can I get that number, or will I have to wait a while?

My man's got a sissy, his name is Miss Kate
He shook that thing like jelly on a plate

Ah, hello, Central, it's 'bout to run me wild
Can I get that number, or will I have to wait a while?

Now all the people ask me why I'm all alone
A sissy shook that thing and took my man from home

Ah, hello, Central, it's 'bout to run me wild
Can I get that number, or will I have to wait a while?

SLAVE TO THE BLUES (*Thomas Dorsey*)

Ain't robbed no bank, ain't done no hangin' crime
Ain't robbed no bank, ain't done no hangin' crime
Just been a slave to the blues, dreamin' 'bout that man of mine

Blues, please tell me do I have to die a slave?
Blues, please tell me do I have to die a slave?
Do you hear me pleadin', you going to take me to my grave

I could break these chains and let my worried heart go free
If I could break these chains and let my worried heart go free
But it's too late now, the blues have made a slave of me

You'll see me raving, you'll hear me cryin'
Oh, Lord, this lonely heart of mine
Whole time I'm grieving, from my hat to my shoes
I'm a good hearted woman, just am a slave to the blues.

SLEEP TALKING BLUES (*J. Sammy Randall*
   and Gertrude Rainey)

You got a bad habit, daddy, talkin' in your sleep
You got a bad habit, daddy, talkin' in your sleep
You talk so much some of these nights, it should be worth one dollar a peep

Do all your talkin', daddy, before you go to bed
Do all your talkin', daddy, before you go to bed
If you speak out of turn, your friends will hear of you being dead

When you talk in your sleep, be sure your mama's not awake
When you talk in your sleep, be sure your mama's not awake
You call another woman's name, you'll think you wake up in a earthquake

Do all your talkin', be careful as you can
Do all your talkin', be careful as you can
The insurance will bring in take for my man

I warned you, daddy, nice as a mama could do
I warned you, daddy, nice as mama could do
You hear me talkin' to you, undertaker will be visitin' you.

SLOW DRIVING MOAN (*Gertrude Rainey*)

I've rambled 'til I'm tired, I'm not satisfied
I've rambled 'til I'm tired, I'm not satisfied
Don't find my sweet man gon' ramble 'til I die

Ah, Lord, Lord, Lordy Lord
Ah, Lord, Lordy, Lordy Lord
Ah, Lord, Lord, Lordy Lord

Got the slow driving blues, blue as I can be
Got the slow driving blues, blue as I can be
Don't play that band, mister, just play the blues for me

Oh, you've been feeling the same, I know our love is just the same
And now you know mama'll be home some day, I'll hear you call my name
I'm a common old rollin' stone, just got the blues for home sweet home

[Spoken] Yes, sir!

[Sung] I'm a common old rollin' stone, just got the blues for home sweet home.

SOON THIS MORNING (*Gertrude Rainey and Bessie Smith*)

Longing for Chicago, ain't got no railroad fare
Longing for Chicago, ain't got no railroad fare
'Cause I got a easy rider, up the road somewhere

He ain't good looking, ain't got no Poro hair
He ain't good looking, ain't got no Poro hair
He's got a disposition to take him any ole where

Soon this morning, just about the break of day
Soon this morning, just about the break of day
I caught my good man making his getaway

[Spoken] Goodbye and farewell

Lord, I feel my trouble rising with the sun
Lord, I feel my trouble rising with the sun
'Cause I know my daddy is loving some other one.

SOUTH BOUND BLUES (*Tom Delaney*)

Yes I'm mad, my heart's sad
The man I love treat me so bad
He brought me out of my home town
Took me to New York and throwed me down

Without a cent to pay my rent
I'm left alone without a home
I told him I would leave him and my time ain't long
My folks done sent me money, and I'm Dixie bound

Oh, you done me wrong, you throwed me down
You caused me to weep and to moan
I told him I'd see him, honey, some of these days
And I'm going to tell him 'bout his low down dirty ways

Done bought my ticket, Lord, and my trunk is packed
Goin' back to Georgia, folks, I sure ain't comin' back
My train's at the station, I done sent my folks the news
You can tell the world I've got those South bound blues

Done bought my ticket, Lord, and my trunk is packed
Goin' back to Georgia, folks, mama sure ain't comin' back
My train's at the station, I done sent my folks the news
You can tell the world I've got those South bound blues.

SOUTHERN BLUES (*Gertrude Rainey*)

House catch on fire, and ain't no water 'round
If your house catch on fire, ain't no water 'round
Throw your trunk out the window, buildin' burn on down

I went to the gypsy, to have my fortune told
I went to the gypsy, to have my fortune told
He said, "Doggone you, girlie, doggone your bad luck soul."

I turned around, went to that gypsy next door
I turned around, went to that gypsy next door
He said, "You can get a man, anywhere you go."

Let me be your rag doll, until your Chinee come
Let me be your rag doll, 'til your Chinee come
If she beats me raggin', she's got to rag it some.

STACK O'LEE BLUES (*Jasper Taylor*)

Stack O'Lee was a bad man, everybody knows
And when they see Stack O'Lee comin', they give him the road
He was my man, but he done me wrong

Stack O'Lee, Stack O'Lee was so desperate and bad
He'd take everything his women would bring, and everything they had
He was my man, but he done me wrong

Stack O'Lee's on the warpath, and you'd better run
'Cause Stack O'Lee, oh he's a bad man and he'll kill you just for fun
He was my man, but he done you wrong

Stack O'Lee's in jail now, with his face turned to the wall
Dirty women and old corn whiskey was the cause of it all
He was my man, but he done you wrong

Eight-hundred-dollar coffin and a eighty-dollar hat
Carried him to the cemetery, but they did not bring him back
He was my man, but he done me wrong.

STORMY SEA BLUES *(Thomas Dorsey)*

Rainin' on the ocean, it's stormin' on the sea
Rainin' on the ocean, it's stormin' on the sea
The blues in that shower, stormin' down on me

I hear thunder, I'm caught out in the storm
I hear thunder, I'm caught out in the storm
Man I love done packed his grip and gone

I hear the wind blowin', I'm left here all alone
I hear the wind blowin', I'm left here all alone
That storm won't be over 'til my daddy come back home

I see the lightnin' flashin', I see the waves a-dashing, I'm tryin' to spread the news
I feel this boat a-crashin', I'm trying to spread the news
My man has done quit me, and left me with the stormy sea blues.

SWEET ROUGH MAN *(J. Sammy Randall and Gertrude Rainey)*

I woke up this mornin', my head was sore as a boil
I woke up this mornin', my head was sore as a boil
My man beat me last night with five feet of copper coil

He keeps my lips split, my eyes as black as jet
He keeps my lips split, my eyes as black as jet
But the way he love me makes me soon forget

Every night for five years, I've got a beatin' from my man
Every night for five years, I've got a beatin' from my man
People says I'm crazy, I'll explain and you'll understand

My man, my man, Lord, everybody knows he's mean
My man, my man, Lord, everybody knows he's mean
But when he starts to lovin', I wring and twist and scream

Lord, it ain't no maybe 'bout my man bein' rough
Lord, it ain't no maybe 'bout my man bein' rough
But when it comes to lovin', he sure can strut his stuff.

THOSE ALL NIGHT LONG BLUES (*J. Guy Suddoth*)

I haven't slept for maybe a week
'Cause my man and I don't speak
There's no reason why he should treat me this way
'Cause the way I worry, I will soon be old and gray

Don't want to do nothing that's wrong
But can't stand this treatment long
I just lay and suffer, cry and cry all night long
'Cause the way I'm worried, Lordy, it sure is wrong

All night long, all night long, there's just one man on my mind
Can't sleep a wink at night for cryin'
All night long, Lord, my worries just renews
And I suffer with those all night blues

All night long, all night long, there's just one man on my mind
Can't sleep a wink at night for cryin'
All night long, Lord, my worries just renews
And I suffer with those all night blues.

THOSE DOGS OF MINE (*Gertrude Rainey*)

Looka here, people, listen to me
Believe me, I'm telling the truth
If your corns hurt you, just like mine
You'd say these same words too

Out for a walk, I stopped to talk
Oh, how my corns did burn

I had to keep on the shady side of the street
To keep out the light of the sun

Oh, Lord, these dogs of mine
They sure do worry me all the time
The reason why, I don't know
Sometimes I soak 'em in Sapolio

Lord, I beg to be excused
I can't wear me no sharp-toed shoes
Oh, Lordy, how the sun do shine
Down on these hounds of mine

Oh, Lordy, these dogs of mine
They sure do worry me all the time
The reason why, I don't know
Sometimes I soak 'em in Sapolio

Lord, I beg to be excused
I can't wear me no sharp-toed shoes
Oh, Lordy, how the sun do shine
Down on these hounds of mine.

TITANIC MAN BLUES (*Gertrude Rainey and J. Mayo Williams*)

Everybody fall in line, going to tell you 'bout that man of mine
It's the last time, Titanic, fare thee well

Now you've always had a good time, drinking your high-priced wine
But it's the last time, Titanic, fare thee well

Feel you're like a ship at sea, but you certainly made a fool of me
It's the last time, Titanic, fare thee well

It's a hard and bitter pill, but I've got somebody else that will
It's the last time, Titanic, fare thee well

Now I won't worry when you're gone, another brown's got your water on
It's the last time, Titanic, fare thee well

Now I'm leavin' you, there's no doubt, yes, your mama's gonna put you out
It's the last time, Titanic, fare thee well.

TOAD FROG BLUES (*J. Guy Suddoth*)

Lord, hear me prayin', my man treats me like a hound
Lord, hear me prayin', my man treats me like a hound
I got the toad low blues and I can't get no lower down

When you hear a frog croaking, you'll know they're cryin' for more rain
When you hear a frog croaking, you'll know they're cryin' for more rain
But when you hear me cryin', I'm cryin' because I can't ride a train

You gonna look for me some morning, but baby, I will be long gone
You gonna look for me some morning, but baby, I will be long gone
Then your low down ways will bring those mean blues on

If I don't lose these blues, I'll be in some undertaker's morgue
If I don't lose these blues, I'll be in some undertaker's morgue
I'm tired of eating one meal, hopping, too, just like a frog

I can't get no higher, sure can't get no lower down
I can't get no higher, sure can't get no lower down
I got the toad frog blues and I'm sure Lordy Dixie bound.

TOUGH LUCK BLUES (*J. Sammy Randall*
   and Gertrude Rainey)

When a black cat crosses you, bad luck I heard it said
When a black cat crosses you, bad luck I heard it said
One must've started 'cross me, got halfway and then fell dead

Things sure breakin' hard, worse than ever before
Things sure breakin' hard, worse than ever before
My sugar told me, speak to him no more

Yeah, my right hand's raised to the good Lord above
Yeah, my right hand's raised to the good Lord above
If they was throwin' away money, I'd have on boxing gloves

If it was rainin' down soup, thick as number one sand
If it was rainin' down soup, thick as number one sand
I'd have a fork in my pocket and a sifter in my hand

My friend committed suicide, while I was away at sea
My friend committed suicide, while I was away at sea
They want to lock me up for murder in the first degree.

TRAVELING BLUES (*Composer unknown*)

Train's at the station, I heard the whistle blow
The train's at the station, I heard the whistle blow
I done bought my ticket and I don't know where I'll go

I went to the depot, looked up and down the board
I went to the depot, looked up and down the board
I asked the ticket agent, "Is my town on this road?"

The ticket agent said, "Woman, don't sit and cry."
The ticket agent said, "Woman, don't you sit and cry
The train blows at this station, but she keeps on passing by."

I hear my daddy calling some other woman's name
I hear my daddy calling some other woman's name
I know he don't need me, but I'm gonna answer just the same

I'm dangerous and blue, can't stay here no more
I'm dangerous and blue, can't stay here no more
Here come my train, folks, and I've got to go.

TRUST NO MAN (*Lillian Hardaway Henderson*)

I want all you women to listen to me
Don't trust your man no further'n your eyes can see
I trusted mine with my best friend
But that was the bad part in the end

Trust no man, trust no man, no further than your eyes can see
I said, trust no man, no further than your eyes can see
He'll tell you that he loves you and swear it is true
The very next minute he'll turn his back on you
Ah, trust no man, no further than your eyes can see

Just feed your daddy with a long-handled spoon
Be sure to love him, morning, night, and noon
Sometimes your heart will ache and almost bust
That's why there's no daddy good enough to trust

Trust no man

[SPOKEN]
Say! Take Ma Rainey's advice! Don't trust *no* man.
I mean, not even your own man!
All right now! You're goin' with me, but just don't trust nobody!
You see where it got me, don't you?
He sure will leave you.

[SUNG]
Ah, trust no man, trust no man, no further than your eyes can see
Ah, trust no man, no further than your eyes can see
He'll stay with you in the winter, like the money you loan
Look out in the summer, you'll find your cheater gone
I said, trust no man, no further than your eyes can see.

VICTIM TO THE BLUES (*Thomas Dorsey*)

My man left this morning just about half past four
My man left this morning just about half past four
He left a note on his pillow, said he couldn't use me no more

Then I grasped my pillow, turned over in my bed
I grasped my pillow, turned over in my bed
I cried about my daddy 'til my cheeks turned cherry red

It's awful hard to take it, it's such a bitter pill
It's awful hard to take it, it's such a bitter pill
If the blues don't kill me, that man and mean treatment will

Too sad to worry, too mean to fight
Too slow to hurry, too good to lie
That man he left me, never said goodbye
Too well to stay and too sick to die
Folks they think I'm crazy, I'm just a victim to the blues.

WALKING BLUES (*Gertrude Rainey and Lovie Austin*)

Woke up this morning, up this morning, with my head bowed down, hey, hey,
    hey
Woke up this morning, with my head bowed down
I had that mean old feelin', I was in the wrong man's town

Mailman's been here, mailman's been here, but didn't leave no news, hey, hey,
    hey
Mailman's been here, but didn't leave no news
That's the reason why mama's got the walkin' blues

Walked and walked 'til I, walked and walked 'til I almost lost my mind, hey, hey,
    hey
Walked and walked 'til I almost lost my mind
I'm afraid to stop walking, 'cause I might lose some time

Got a short time to make it, short time to make it, and a long ways to go, Lord,
    Lord, Lord
Short time to make it, and a long ways to go
Tryin' to find the town they call San Antonio

Thought I'd rest me, thought I'd rest me, I couldn't hear no news, Lord, Lord,
    Lord
Thought I'd rest me, I couldn't hear no news
I'll soon be there, 'cause I got the walkin' blues.

WEEPING WOMAN BLUES (*Bessie Smith and Gertrude Rainey*)

Lord, you see me weepin', and you hear me cryin'
Lord, you see me weepin', and you hear me cryin'
I ain't weepin' 'bout no money, just that man of mine

Lord, this mean old engineer, cruel as he could be
This mean old engineer, cruel as he could be
Took my man away and blowed the smoke back at me

I'm going down South, won't be back 'til fall
I'm going down South, won't be back 'til fall
If I don't find my easy rider, ain't comin' back at all

I'd rather be in the river, drifting like a log
I'd rather be in the river, drifting like a log
Than to be in this town, treated like a dog.

WRINGING AND TWISTING BLUES (*Paul Carter*)

I had my fortune told, and the gypsy took my hand
And she made me understand, that I had lost my man
She said I had the wringin' and the twistin' blues

I twisted my nervous hands and then I shook my head
Went home and jumped in bed, and when I heard what she said
And now I've got the wringin' and the twistin' blues

He told me that he loved me, I found it wasn't true
'Cause he's done gone and left me, I've nothing else to do

But if I know that woman that caused my heart to moan
I'd cook a special dinner, invite her to my home

I had some green cucumbers, some half-done tripe and greens
Some buttermilk and codfish, some sour kidney beans

If she eats what's on my table, she will be graveyard bound
I'll be right there to tell her, when they put her in the ground
"You're the cause of me having those wringin' and a-twistin' blues."

Get a paper in the morn, and you will read the news
Where a poor gal's dead and gone, with the wringin' and twistin' blues
Now I've got the wringin' and the twistin' blues.

YA DA DO (*Lovie Austin*)

Every evenin' 'bout half past four
Sweet piano playin' near my door
And turn to raggin', you never heard such blues before

There's a pretty little thing they play
It's very short, but folks all say
"Oh, it's a-pickin'," when they start to want to cry for more

I don't know the name, but it's a pretty little thing, goes

Ya da da do, ya da da do
Fill you with harmonizing, minor refrain
It's a no-name blues, but'll take away your pains

Ya da da do, ya da da do
Everybody loves it, ya da do do do

Ya da da do, ya da da do
Fill you with harmonizing, minor refrain
It's a no-name blues, but'll take away your pains

Ya da da do, ya da da do
Everybody loves it, ya da do do do.

YONDER COME THE BLUES (*Gertrude Rainey*)

I worry all day, I worry all night
Every time my man comes home he wants to fuss and fight
When I pick up the paper to read the news
Just when I'm satisfied, yonder come the blues

I went down to the river each and every day
Tryin' to keep from cryin' and do myself away
I walked and walked 'til I wore out my shoes
I can't walk no further, yonder come the blues

Some folks never worry, things all come out right
Poor me, lie down and suffer, weep and cry all night
When I get a letter, it never bring good news
Every time I see the mailman, yonder come the blues

Go back blues, don't come this way
Lordy, give me something else besides the blues all day
Every man I've loved, I've been misused
And when I want some lovin', yonder come the blues

People have different blues and think they're mighty bad
But blues about a man the worst I've ever had
I been disgusted and all confused
Every time I look around, yonder come the blues.

Lyrics to Songs

Recorded by

BESSIE SMITH

AFTER YOU'VE GONE (*T. Layton and H. Creamer*)

Now, listen, honey, while I say
How can you tell me that you're going away?
Don't say that we must part
Don't break my achin' heart

You know I love you true for many years
Love you night and day
How can you leave me, can't you see my tears?
So listen while I say

After you've gone and left me cryin'
After you've gone, there's no denyin'
You'll feel blue, you'll feel sad
You'll miss the dearest pal you ever had

There'll come a time, now, don't forget it
There'll come a time when you'll regret it
Some day when you grow lonely
Your heart will break like mine and you'll want me only
After you've gone, after you've gone away

After you've gone, left me cryin',
After you've gone, there's no denyin'
You'll feel blue, you'll feel sad
You'll miss the best pal you ever had, Lord

There'll come a time, now, don't forget it
There'll come a time when you'll regret it
Some day when you grow lonely
Your heart'll break like mine and you'll want me only
After you've gone, after you've gone away.

AGGRAVATIN' PAPA (*R. Turk, J. R. Robinson, and A. Britt*)

I know a triflin' man, they call him Triflin' Sam
He lives in Birmingham way down in Alabam'

Now the other night he had a fight with a gal named Mandy Brown
She plainly stated she was aggravated as she shouted out to him

Aggravatin' papa, don't you try to two-time me
I said don't two-time me

Aggravatin' papa, treat me kind or let me be
I mean just let me be

It's been a while, I'll get you told
Stop messin' 'round sweet jelly roll

If you stay out with a high brown baby
I'll smack you down and I don't mean maybe

Aggravatin' papa, I'll do anything you say, anything you say
But when you go strutting, do your strut around my way

So papa, just treat me pretty, be nice and kind
The way you treatin' me will make me lose my mind

Aggravatin' papa, don't you try to two-time me

Just treat me pretty, be nice and sweet
I've got a darn forty-four that don't repeat

Aggravatin' papa, don't you try to two-time me.

ALEXANDER'S RAGTIME BAND (*Irving Berlin*)

Oh, my honey, oh, my honey, you better hurry and let's go down there
Ain't you goin', ain't you goin' to that leaderman, ragged meter man
Oh, honey, oh, honey, let me take you to Alexander's grandstand brass band
Ain't you coming along?

Come on and hear, come on and hear Alexander's ragtime band
Come on and hear, come on and hear, it's the best band in the land
They can play the bugle call like you never heard before
Sounds so natural that you'll wanna go to war
That's just the best band in the land, oh honey lamb

Come on along, come on along, let me take you by the hand
Up to the man, up to the man, who is the leader of the band
And if you care to hear the Swanee River played in ragtime
Come on and hear, come on and hear Alexander's ragtime band

Come on and hear, come on and hear Alexander's ragtime band
Come on and hear, come on and hear, it's the best band in the land

Listen to the bugle call
Yeah, it's the best band in the land, oh, honey lamb

Come on along, come on along, let me take you by the hand
Up to the man, up to the man, who is the leader of the band
And if you care to hear the Swanee River played in ragtime
Come on and hear, come on and hear Alexander's ragtime band.

ANY WOMAN'S BLUES (*Lovie Austin*)

My man ain't actin' right
He stays out late at night
And still he says he loves no one but me

But if I find that gal
That tried to steal my pal
I'll get her told, just you wait and see

I feel blue, I don't know what to do
Every woman in my fix is bound to feel blue, too

Lord, I love my man better than I love myself
Lord, I love my man better than I love myself
And if he don't have me, he won't have nobody else

My man got teeth that light up on the street
My man got teeth that light up on the street
And every time he smiles he throws them lights on me

His voice sound like chimes, I mean the organ kind
His voice sound like chimes, I mean the organ kind
And every time he speak, his music ease my troublin' mind.

AT THE CHRISTMAS BALL (*Fred Longshaw*)

[SPOKEN]
Unknown man: Hey, Bessie, Christmas here.
Smith: Hear, hear! Hooray for Christmas!

[SUNG]
Christmas comes but once a year, and to me it brings good cheer
And to everyone who likes wine and beer

Happy New Year is after that, happy I'll be, that is a fact
That is why I like to hear, folks, I say, that Christmas is here

Christmas bells will ring real soon, even in the afternoon
There'll be no chimes shall ring
At the Christmas ball

Everyone must watch their step, or they will lose their rep
Everybody's full of pep
At the Christmas ball

Grab your partner, one and all, keep on dancin' round the hall
And there's no one to fall, don't you dare to stall
If your partner don't act fair, don't worry, there's some more over there
Takin' a chance everywhere
At the Christmas ball.

BABY DOLL (*Bessie Smith*)

Honey, there's a funny feelin' 'round my heart and it's 'bout to drive your mama
     wild
It must be somethin' they call the Cuban doll, it weren't your mama's angel
     child
I went to see the doctor the other day, he said I's well as well could be
But I says, "Doctor, you don't know really what's worryin' me."
I wanna be somebody's baby doll so I can get my lovin' all the time
I wanna be somebody's baby doll to ease my mind
He can be ugly, he can be black, so long as he can eagle rock and ball the jack
I want to be somebody's baby doll so I can get my lovin' all the time,
     I mean, to get my lovin' all the time
Lord, I went to the gypsy to get my fortune told
She said, "You in hard luck, Bessie, doggone your bad luck soul."
I wanna be somebody's baby doll so I can get my lovin' all the time,
     I mean, to get my lovin' all the time.

BABY, HAVE PITY ON ME (*B. Moll and Clarence Williams*)

You show your sympathy to every bird and bee
But when it comes to me, dear, you laugh at every plea
Sweetheart, I need the bliss, the bliss of your sweet kiss
What can the answer be, dear, I can't go on like this

Like a beggar, what can I do?
Hungry for kisses and starvin' for you
Press your lips to my lips, Lord, have pity on me

Cravin' for affection, my cravin' is strong
Put your arms around me where they belong
Press me, caress me, oh, have pity on me

One kiss and I'll know, I'll go riding on a rainbow
Straight up to heaven, I will fly right to the sky
Can't you hear me cryin' for sweet sympathy?
No love like your love can answer my plea
Press your lips to my lips, Lord, have pity on me

One kiss and I'll know, I'll go riding on a rainbow
Straight up to heaven, Lord, I'll fly right to the sky
Can't you hear me cryin' for sweet sympathy?
No love like your love can answer my plea
Press your lips to my lips, have pity on me.

BABY, WON'T YOU PLEASE COME HOME
(*Clarence Williams*)

I've got the blues, I feel so lonely
I'd give the world if I could only
Make you understand
It surely would be grand

I'm gonna telephone my baby
Ask him won't you please come home
'Cause when you gone
I'm worried all day long

Baby, won't you please come home
Baby, won't you please come home

I have tried in vain
Never more to call your name
When you left you broke my heart
That will never make us part
Every hour in the day
You will hear me say

Baby, won't you please come home, I mean
Baby, won't you please come home

Baby, won't you please come home
'Cause your mama's all alone
I have tried in vain
Never more to call your name

When you left you broke my heart
That will never make us part
Landlord's gettin' worse
I got to move May first

Baby, won't you please come home, I need money
Baby, won't you please come home.

BACKWATER BLUES (*Bessie Smith*)

When it rains five days and the skies turn dark as night
When it rains five days and the skies turn dark as night
Then trouble's takin' place in the lowlands at night

I woke up this mornin', can't even get out of my door
I woke up this mornin', can't even get out of my door
That's enough trouble to make a poor girl wonder where she wanna go

Then they rowed a little boat about five miles 'cross the pond
Then they rowed a little boat about five miles 'cross the pond
I packed all my clothes, throwed 'em in and they rowed me along

When it thunders and lightnin', and the wind begins to blow
When it thunders and lightnin', and the wind begins to blow
There's thousands of people ain't got no place to go

Then I went and stood upon some high old lonesome hill
Then I went and stood upon some high old lonesome hill
Then looked down on the house where I used to live

Backwater blues done caused me to pack my things and go
Backwater blues done caused me to pack my things and go
'Cause my house fell down and I can't live there no mo'

Mmmmmmmmm, I can't move no mo'
Mmmmmmmmm, I can't move no mo'
There ain't no place for a poor old girl to go.

BEALE STREET PAPA (*R. Turk and J. R. Robinson*)

Jennie Neal down in Beale killed her papa there
Left him cold, got him told that she didn't care

Oh Joe, her beau, looked just like he would die
If you were near him you would hear him start his mournsome cry

Beale Street papa, why don't you come back home?
It isn't proper to leave your mama all alone

Sometimes I was cruel, that was true
But papa, you know mama never two-timed you
Mmmm-hmmmm, I'm blue, so how come you do me like you do?

I'm cryin', Beale Street papa, don't mess around with me
There's plenty pettin' that I can get in Tennessee

I'll still get my sweet cookin' constantly
But not the kind you serve to me

So Beale Street papa, come back home
So how come you do me like you do?

I'm cryin', Beale Street papa, don't mess around with me
There's plenty pettin' that I can get in Tennessee

I bought a rifle, razor, and a knife
A poster card can't save my life

So, Beale Street papa, come back home.

BLACK MOUNTAIN BLUES (*H. Cole*)

Back in Black Mountain, a child will smack your face
Back in Black Mountain, a child will smack your face
Babies cryin' for liquor, and all the birds sing bass

Black Mountain people are bad as they can be
Black Mountain people are bad as they can be
They uses gunpowder just to sweeten their tea

On this Black Mountain, can't keep a man in jail
On this Black Mountain, can't keep a man in jail
If the jury finds them guilty, the judge'll go they bail

Had a man in Black Mountain, sweetest man in town
Had a man in Black Mountain, the sweetest man in town
He met a city gal, and he throwed me down

I'm bound for Black Mountain, me and my razor and my gun
Lord, I'm bound for Black Mountain, me and my razor and my gun
I'm gonna shoot him if he stands still, and cut him if he run

Down in Black Mountain, they all shoots quick and straight
Down in Black Mountain, they all shoots quick and straight
The bullet'll get you if you starts a-dodgin' too late

Got the Devil in my soul, and I'm full of bad booze
Got the Devil in my soul, and I'm full of bad booze
I'm out here for trouble, I've got the Black Mountain blues.

BLEEDING HEARTED BLUES (*Lovie Austin*)

When you sad and lonely
Thinkin' about you only
Feelin' destructive and blue

Ah, your heart is achin'
Yes, it's almost breakin'
No one to tell your troubles to

That's the time you hang you head and begin to cry

All your friends forsake you
Trouble overtakes you
And your good man turns you down

People talk about you
Everybody doubts you
And your friends can't be found

Not a soul to ease your pain
You will plead in vain
You've got those bleeding hearted blues

Yeah, baby, tell me what's on your mind
Pretty papa, tell me what's on your mind
You keep my poor heart achin', I'm worried all the time

I'd give up every friend that I have
Yes, I'd give up every friend that I have
I'd give up my mother, I'd even give up dear old Dad.

BLUE, BLUE (*Bessie Smith*)

Blue, blue, I got a tale to tell you, I'm blue
Something comes over me, daddy, and I'm blue about you

Listen to my story and everything'll come out true
When your man is gone, your rent is all due
He's not comin' back, you know he's all through

You weep and cry, feel like you could die
If you was a bird, you'd take wings and fly

Here is one thing'll make you blue, blue
When you ain't got a daddy to tell your troubles to

Step right out and think, start right in to wink
Keep feeling in your heart, you'll start right in to drink

If you've ever been blue, you know how a woman feels
If you've ever been blue, you know how a good woman feels
You are worried, child, honey, yes indeed

Blue, blue, I had a tale to tell you, I was blue
Something fell on me, daddy, and I was blue over you
You done listened to my story, and everything come out true.

BLUE SPIRIT BLUES (*Spencer Williams*)

Had a dream last night that I was dead
Had a dream last night that I was dead
Evil spirits all around my bed

The Devil came and grabbed my hand
The Devil came and grabbed my hand
Took me way down to that red hot land

Mean blue spirits stuck they forks in me
Mean blue spirits stuck they forks in me
Made me moan and groan in misery

Fairies and dragons spittin' out blue flames
Fairies and dragons spittin' out blue flames
Showin' their teeth, for they was glad I came

Demons with their eyelids drippin' blood
Demons with their eyelids drippin' blood
Draggin' sinners through that brimstone flood

"This is hell," I cried, cried with all my might
"This is hell," I cried, cried with all my might
Oh, my soul, I can't bear the sight

Started runnin' 'cause it is my cup
Started runnin' 'cause it is my cup
Run so fast 'til someone woke me up.

BO-WEEVIL BLUES (*Gertrude Rainey and Lovie Austin*)

Hey, bo-weevil, don't sing them blues no more
Hey, bo-weevil, don't sing them blues no more
Bo-weevils here, bo-weevils everywhere you go

I'm a lone bo-weevil, been out a great long time
I'm a lone bo-weevil, been out a great long time
Gonna sing this song to ease bo-weevil's troublin' mind

I don't want no sugar put into my tea
I don't want no sugar put into my tea
Some mens are so evil, I'm scared they might poison me

I went downtown, I bought myself a hat, I brought it back home, I laid it on the
    shelf
I looked at my bed, I'm tired sleepin' by myself
I'm tired sleepin' by myself.

BYE BYE BLUES (*P. Carter*)

I feel blue, I'm going to do something that may look wrong
When my man comes, he'll be surprised to find that I'm gone

I done found out we can't agree, no matter how I try
I wrote a note will get his goat when he reads this last goodbye

I've got those bye bye blues, I mean those long gone blues
I'm goin' to where you off my mind
I've got those low down blues, I mean those graveyard blues
They keep me worried all the time

[SUNG TWICE]
So I'm makin' a change I think will do me good
Because everybody told me in my neighborhood
As long as I stay I'm gonna be confused
I'm sorry, sweet papa, I've got those bye bye blues, I mean those bye bye blues.

CAKE WALKING BABIES (FROM HOME)
(*Chris Smith, H. Troy, and Clarence Williams*)

Cake walkers may come, cake walkers may go
But I wanna tell you 'bout a couple I know
High steppin' pair, they'll be there
When it comes for bizness, not a soul can compare

Here they come, look at 'em demonstratin'
Goin' some, and they syncopatin'
Talk of the town, easin' 'round
Pickin' 'em up and layin' 'em down

Dancin' fools, ain't they demonstratin'
They in a class of they own
Now, the only way to win is to cheat 'em
You may tie 'em, but you'll never beat 'em
Strut your stuff, they're cake walkin' babies from home

Here they come, look at 'em syncopatin'
Goin' some, ain't they demonstratin'
Talk of the town, easin' 'round
They pickin' 'em up and layin' 'em down

Dancin' fools, ain't they syncopatin'
They in a class of they own

Oh, the only way to win is to cheat 'em
You may tie 'em, but you'll never beat 'em
Strut your stuff, strut your stuff, cake walkin' babies from home.

CARELESS LOVE BLUES (*W. C. Handy*)

Love, oh love, oh careless love
You fly through my head like wine
You wrecked the life of a many poor gal
And you let me spoil this life of mine

Love, oh love, oh careless love
In your clutches of desire
You made me break a many true vow
Then you set my very soul on fire

Love, oh love, oh careless love
All my happiness I've left
You fill my heart with them worried ole blues
Now I'm walkin', talkin' to myself

Love, oh love, oh careless love
Trusted you now it's too late
You made me throw my only friend down
That's why I sing this song of hate

Love, oh love, oh careless love
Night and day I weep and moan
You brought the wrong man into this life of mine
For my sin 'til judgment I'll atone.

CEMETERY BLUES (*S. Laney and Spencer Williams*)

Folks, I know a gal named Cemetery 'Lize down in Tennessee
She has got a pair of mean old graveyard eyes full of misery
Every night and day, you can hear her sing the blues away

I'm goin' down to the cemetery, 'cause the world is all wrong
I'm goin' down to the cemetery, 'cause the world is all wrong
Out there with the spooks to hear 'em sing my sorrow song

Got a date to see a ghost by the name of Jones
Got a date to see a ghost by the name of Jones
Makes me feel happy to hear him rattle his bones

He's one man I always know just where to find
He's one man I always know just where to find
When you want true lovin', go and get the cemetery kind

He ain't no fine dresser, he don't wear nothin' but a sack
Say, he ain't no fine dresser, he don't wear nothin' but a sack
Every time he kisses me, that funny feelin' creeps up my back.

CHICAGO BOUND BLUES (*Lovie Austin*)

Late last night I stole away and cried
Late last night I stole away and cried
That's a blues for Chicago, and I just can't be satisfied

Blues on my brain, my tongue refused to talk
Blues on my brain, my tongue refused to talk
I was followin' my daddy, but my feet refused to walk

Mean old fireman, cruel old engineer
Lord, mean old fireman, cruel old engineer
You took my man away and left his mama standin' here

Big red headline, tomorrow *Defender* news
Big red headline, tomorrow *Defender* news
Woman dead down home with old Chicago blues, I said blues.

COLD IN HAND BLUES (*Jack Gee* and Fred Longshaw*)

I've got a hard workin' man
The way he treats me, I can't understand

He works hard every day
And on Thursday throws away his pay

Now I don't want that man
Because he's done gone cold in hand

Now I've tried hard to treat him kind
I've tried hard to treat him kind
But it seems to me his love is gone blind

The man I've got must have lost his mind
The man I've got must have lost his mind
The way he quit me, I can't understand

I'm gonna find myself another man
I'm gonna find myself another man
Because the one I've got has done gone cold in hand.

Edward Brooks, in The Bessie Smith Companion, *suggests that Smith, rather than Gee, co-authored this song with Longshaw.*

DEVIL'S GONNA GET YOU (*Porter Grainger*)

It's a long, long lane that has no turnin'
There's a fire that always keeps on burnin'

Mr. Devil down below, pitchfork in his hand
And that's where you are goin' to go, do you understand?

Devil's gonna get you, Devil's gonna get you
Ah, the Devil's gonna get you, man, just as sure as you born

Devil's gonna get you, Devil's gonna get you
Ah, the Devil's gonna get you, the way you carryin' on

You'll go away, stay for weeks, on your doggone freak
Come back home, get in my bed and turn your back on me

Oh, the Devil's gonna get you, I mean, the Devil's gonna get you
Man, the Devil's gonna get you, sure as you born

Dirty two-timer, dirty two-timer, dirty two-timer, you ain't comin' clean
Oh, the Devil's gonna get you, I mean, the Devil's gonna get you
Oh, the Devil's gonna get you, you know what I mean

I don't want no two-time stuff from my regular man
Don't want nothin' that's been used, 'cause it's second hand

The Devil's gonna get you, oh, the Devil's gonna get you
Man, the Devil's gonna get you, sure as you born to die.

DIRTY NO-GOODERS BLUES (*Bessie Smith*)

Did you ever fall in love with a man that was no good?
Did you ever fall in love with a man that is no good?
No matter what you did for him, he never understood

The meanest things he could say would thrill you through and through
The meanest things he could say would thrill you through and through
And there wasn't nothin' too dirty for that man to do

He'd treat you nice and kind 'til he win your heart and hand
He'd treat you nice and kind 'til he win your heart and hand
Then he get so cruel, that man you just could not stand

Lawd, I really don't think no man's love can last
Lawd, I don't think no man's love can last
They'll love you to death, then treat you like a thing of the past

There's nineteen men livin' in my neighborhood
There's nineteen men livin' in my neighborhood
Eighteen of them are fools and the one ain't no doggone good

Lawd, Lawd, Lawd, Lawd, Lawd, Lawd, oh Lawd
Lawd, Lawd, Lawd, Lawd
That dirty no-good man treats me just like I'm a dog.

DIXIE FLYER BLUES (*Bessie Smith*)

[SPOKEN]
Unknown man: Hold that train!

[SUNG]
Hold that engine, let sweet mama get on board
Hold that engine, let sweet mama get on board
'Cause my home ain't here, it's a long way down the road

Come back, choo-choo, mama's gonna find a berth
Come back, choo-choo, mama's gonna find a berth
Goin' to Dixieland, it's the grandest place on earth

Dixie Flyer, come on and let your drivers roll
Dixie Flyer, come on and let your drivers roll
Wouldn't stay up North to save nobody's doggone soul

Blow your whistle, tell 'em mama's comin' through
Blow your whistle, tell 'em mama's comin' through
Pick it up a little bit, 'cause I'm feelin' mighty blue

Here's my ticket, take it, please, conductorman
Here's my ticket, take it, please, conductorman
Goin' to my mammy way down in Dixieland.

DON'T CRY BABY (*S. Unger and S. Bernie*)

Honey, please don't cry, listen to me
There's no reason why we shouldn't agree
If I hurt your feelin's, I apologize
You the only one that I idolize

[SUNG TWICE]
Don't cry baby, don't cry baby, dry your eyes and let's be sweethearts again
I didn't mean to make you feel blue
Honest, I'll never do it again
Won't you forgive, won't you forget
Do as I ask you to
I'll never let you regret, just start anew
You know I'm sorry, oh, so sorry
Don't cry baby, there's no one but you.

DOWN HEARTED BLUES (*Alberta Hunter and Lovie Austin*)

Gee, but it's hard to love someone
When that someone don't love you
I'm so disgusted, heartbroken too
I've got those down hearted blues

Once I was crazy 'bout a man
He mistreated me all the time
The next man I get has got to promise me
To be mine, all mine

Trouble, trouble, I've had it all my days
Trouble, trouble, I've had it all my days
It seem like trouble going to follow me to my grave

I ain't never loved but three mens in my life
I ain't never loved but three men in my life
My father, my brother, the man that wrecked my life

It may be a week, it may be a month or two
It may be a week, it may be a month or two
But the day you quit me, honey, it's comin' home to you

I got the world in a jug, the stopper's in my hand
I got the world in a jug, the stopper's in my hand
I'm gonna hold it until you men come under my command.

DO YOUR DUTY (*Wesley Wilson*)

If I call three times a day, baby
Come and drive my blues away
When you come, be ready to play
Do your duty

If you want to have some luck
Give your baby your last buck
Don't come quackin' like a duck
Do your duty

I heard you say you didn't love me, baby, yesterday at Mrs. Brown's
I don't believe a word she said, she's the lyin'est woman in town

Oh, babe, when I need attention at home
I'll just call you on the telephone
Come yourself, don't send your friend Jones
Do your duty

If my radiator gets too hot
Cool it off in lots of spots
Give me all the service you've got
Do your duty

If you don't know what it's all about
Don't sit around my house and pout
Do, you'll catch your mama tippin' out
Do your duty

If you make your own bed hard, that's the way it lies
If I'm tired of sleepin' by myself, you're too dumb to realize

Oh, babe, I'm not tryin' to make you feel blue
I'm not satisfied with the way that you do
I've got to help you find somebody to
Do your duty.

DYIN' BY THE HOUR (*G. Brooks*)

It's an old story, everytime it's a doggone man
It's an old story, everytime it's a doggone man
But when that thing is on you, you just drift from hand to hand

I'd drink up all that acid if it wouldn't burn me so
I'd drink up all that acid if it wouldn't burn me so
And telephone the Devil, that's the only place I'd go

Once I weighed two hundred, I'm nothin' but skin and bones
Once I weighed two hundred, I'm nothin' but skin and bones
I would always laugh, but it's nothin' but a moan and a groan

Lord, I'm dyin' by the hour about that doggone man of mine
I'm dyin' by the hour 'bout that doggone man of mine
He said he didn't love me, that is why I'm dyin' and losin' my mind.

DYING GAMBLER'S BLUES (*Jack Gee*)*

Listen here, all you nice men
Listen here, all you nice men
My best friend is dyin' today
This morning I left at half past nine
All the gamblers on the line
One kneeled down and tried to pray
My best friend passed away
Last night I hear my man cryin'
Everybody says he was dyin'
Hold me, hold me, they cried
All the women, they cried
Little children, they cried
Nobody wants to see a good gambler die

My man said before he died
Place a deck of cards at his side
Lay a pair of dice on his chest
He's one more good gambler and he's gone to rest
Oh me, oh me, have mercy, have mercy on me
I ain't got nobody to pity poor old me
I fell down on my knees, I raised my hands, and I wanted to scream
Because there's nobody wants to see a good gambler die.

Edward Brooks, in The Bessie Smith Companion, *suggests that Smith, rather than Gee, probably wrote this song.*

EASY COME, EASY GO BLUES (W. *Jackson and E. Brown*)

Some folks they always cryin', cryin' them mean old blues
Not me, you never even see me frown
Some folks just walk around tryin', tryin' hard love to lose
But I said let it come, good, bad, or bum
I'm the happiest gal in the town

Easy come, easy go, nothin' ever worries me
Shuffle on like this song, don't know old misery

If my sweet man trifles, or if he don't
I'll get someone to love me anytime he won't
Easy come, easy go, right from my head to shoes

Don't want to be no skinny vamp or nothin' like that
Daddy always knows just where his sweet mama's at
I'm overflowing with those easy come, easy go blues

This world owes me a plenty lovin', hear what I say
Believe me, I go out collectin' 'most every day
I'm overflowing with those easy come, easy go blues.

EAVESDROPPER'S BLUES (J. *C. Johnson*)

I heard the folks a talkin' here yesterday
As I listened by the door
But eavesdroppers they never hear no good, they say,
And I heard things that hurt me so

They said I had a man I give my money to
They said I had a man I give my money to
And if I was broke he would turn my eyes all blue

They talked about my pa who was blind in one eye
They talked about my pa who was blind in one eye
They said he was a sinner and was too mean to cry

I never knocked nobody, wonder why they pick on me
I never knocked nobody, wonder why they pick on me
There's going to be a funeral if they don't let me be

I never stop to listen to try and hear no good news
I never stop to listen to try and hear no good news
I hear things about me give me those eavesdropper's blues.

EMPTY BED BLUES, PART I (*J. C. Johnson*)

I woke up this mornin' with an awful achin' head
I woke up this mornin' with a awful achin' head
My new man had left me just a room and a empty bed

Bought me a coffee grinder, got the best one I could find
Bought me a coffee grinder, got the best one I could find
So he could grind my coffee, 'cause he had a brand new grind

He's a deep sea diver with a stroke that can't go wrong
He's a deep sea diver with a stroke that can't go wrong
He can touch the bottom and his wind holds out so long

He knows how to thrill me and he thrills me night and day
Lord, he knows how to thrill me, he thrills me night and day
He's got a new way of lovin' almost takes my breath away

Lord, he's got that sweet somethin', and I told my gal friend Lou
He's got that sweet somethin', and I told my gal friend Lou
From the way she's ravin', she must have gone and tried it too.

EMPTY BED BLUES, PART II (*J. C. Johnson*)

When my bed get empty, make me feel awful mean and blue
When my bed get empty, make me feel awful mean and blue
My springs are gettin' rusty, sleepin' single like I do

Bought him a blanket, pillow for his head at night
Bought him a blanket, pillow for his head at night
Then I bought him a mattress so he could lay just right

He came home one evening with his spirit way up high
He came home one evening with his spirit way up high
What he had to give me made me wring my hands and cry

He give me a lesson that I never had before
He give me a lesson that I never had before
When he got through teachin' me, from my elbow down was sore

He boiled my first cabbage and he made it awful hot
He boiled my first cabbage and he made it awful hot
Then he put in the bacon, it overflowed the pot

When you get good lovin', never go and spread the news
Yeah, it will double cross you and leave you with them empty bed blues.

FAR AWAY BLUES (*G. Brooks*)
(*Duet sung with Clara Smith*)

We left our southern home and wandered north to roam
Like birds, went seekin' a brand new field of corn
We don't know why we are here
But we're up here just the same
And we are just the lonesomest girls that's ever born

Some of these days we are going far away
Some of these days we are going far away
Where we have got a lots of friends and don't have no roof rent to pay

Oh, there'll come a day when from us you'll hear no news
Oh, there'll come a day when from us you'll hear no news
Then you will know that we have died from those lonesome far away blues.

FLORIDA BOUND BLUES (*Clarence Williams*)

Goodbye North, hello South
Goodbye North, hello South
It's so cold up here that the words freeze in your mouth

I'm goin' to Florida where I can have my fun
I'm goin' to Florida where I can have my fun
Where I can lay out in the green grass and look up at the sun

Hey, hey, redcap, help me with this load
Redcap porter, help me with this load
Step aside, hold that steamboat, Mr. Captain, let me get on board

I got a letter from my daddy, he bought me a sweet piece of land
I got a letter from my daddy, he bought me a small piece of ground
You can't blame me for leavin', Lord, I mean I'm Florida bound

My papa told me, my mama told me too
My papa told me, my mama told me too
Don't let them bell-bottomed britches make a fool outa you.

FOLLOW THE DEAL ON DOWN (*T. Delaney*)

[*SPOKEN*]
Stop rollin' them bones and listen to me!

[*SUNG*]
I had a gamblin' man, he's hard to understand
He just kept me worried and goin' around
He would skin and shoot his dice, couldn't give him no advice
He followed the deal on down

He was a gambler, I mean, he was a gambler
And he'd always lay his money down
If he win or if he lose, he would never sing the blues
He followed the deal on down

He took sick the other day, and his bills I had to pay
None of his good friends could be found
Not a penny to his name, of course he's not to blame
Lord, he followed the deal on down

He was a gambler, yes, he was a gambler
And he would always go from town to town
The gamblin' life he craved, it laid the poor boy in his grave
He followed the deal on down.

FOOLISH MAN BLUES (*Bessie Smith*)

Men sure deceitful, they getting worse every day
Lord, men sure deceitful, they getting worse every day
Actin' like a bunch of women, they just gabbin', gabbin', gabbin' away

There's two things got me puzzled, there's two things I can't understand
There's two things got me puzzled, there's two things I can't understand
That's a mannish actin' woman and skippin', twistin', woman actin' man

Lord, I used to love that man, he always made my poor heart ache
Yes, I love that man, he makes my poor heart ache
He's crooked as a corkscrew, and evil as a copperheaded snake

I knew a certain man who spent years runnin' a poor gal down
I knew a certain man who spent a year runnin' a poor gal down
And when she let him kiss her, the fool blabbed it all over town.

FRANKIE BLUES (*E. Johnson*)

Frankie was a good fellow
To everyone he knew
I had some trouble with Frankie
That made me feel so blue

He packed his grip for a trip
And said, "I'm leaving here, honey dear."
He called to see me next day
I was mad and this is what I said

"I'm worried now, I won't be worried long."
I miss sweet Frankie since he's been gone, yes I do
He went away, he knows he's done me wrong

I'll tell you, now I'm weepin' like a willow tree
Since sweet Frankie's went away from me
Where he's gone I do not know
He will see some place near Baltimo'

Yes, I will pay 'most any fair reward
If you will find Frankie, Lord
I been to Frisco, Hackensack
Tryin' to find Frankie and bring him back

Somebody find that sweet Frankie of mine, ease my mind
Yes, I will pay 'most any fair reward
If you will find Frankie, Lord

I phoned my angels, they didn't hear
I phoned Saint Peter, "Send a brown down here."
Somebody find that sweet Frankie of mine
And ease my mind.

FROSTY MORNING BLUES (*E. Brown*)

How come I'm blue as can be, how come I need sympathy?
I know what's troublin' me, listen and you'll see, because
The good man that I love left me all alone
Woke up this morning at four, when I heard him slammin' my door

Did you ever wake up on a frosty morning and discover your good man gone?
Did you ever wake up on a frosty morning and discover your good man gone?
If you did you'll understand why I'm singin' this mournful song

Well, he didn't provide and he wasn't handsome, so he might not appeal to you
Well, he didn't provide and he wasn't handsome, so he might not appeal to you
But he give me plenty lovin' and I never had to beg him to

Now my damper is down and my fire ain't burnin' and a chill's all around my
    bed
My damper is down and my fire ain't burnin' and a chill's all around my bed
When you lose a man you love, then a gal is just as good as dead.

GIMME A PIGFOOT (*Wesley Wilson*)

[SPOKEN]
Twenty-five cents? Hah! No, no, I wouldn't pay twenty-five cents to go in
    nowhere, 'cause listen here . . .

[SUNG]
Up in Harlem every Saturday night
When the highbrows get together it's just too tight

They all congregates at an all night strut
And what they do is tut, tut, tut

Ole Hannah Brown from 'cross town
Gets full of corn and starts breakin' 'em down

Just at the break of day
You can hear old Hannah say

Gimme a pigfoot and a bottle of beer
Send me, gate, I don't care

I feel just like I wanna clown
Give the piano player a drink because he's bringin' me down

He's got rhythm, yeah, when he stomps his feet
He sends me right off to sleep

Check all your razors and your guns
We gonna be rasslin' when the wagon comes

I want a pigfoot and a bottle of beer
Send me, 'cause I don't care
Slay me, 'cause I don't care

Gimme a pigfoot and a bottle of beer
Send me, gate, I don't care

I feel just like I wanna clown
Give the piano player a drink because he's bringin' me down

He's got rhythm, yeah, when he stomps his feet
He sends me right off to sleep

Check all your razors and your guns
Do the shim sham shimmy 'til the risin' sun

Gimme a reefer and a gang o' gin
Slay me, 'cause I'm in my sin
Slay me, 'cause I'm full of gin.

GIN HOUSE BLUES (*H. Troy and Fletcher Henderson*)

I've got a sad sad story today
I've got a sad sad story today
I'm goin' to the gin house when the whistle blows
My troubles come like rain, that starts then pours and pours

My man keeps me cryin' all night
My man keeps me cryin' all night
I'm goin' to the gin house, set out by myself
I mean to drown my sorrows, my sweet somebody else

I've got those worse kind of gin house blues
I've got those worse kind of gin house blues
I'll make one trip there to see can I ease my mind
And if I do I'm gonna make it my last time

It takes a good smart woman these days
It takes a good smart woman these days
To hold her man when these gals have got so many different ways
I mean to watch my man, don't care what these other gals say

I've got to see the conjure man soon
I've got to see the conjure man soon
Because these gin house blues is campin' 'round my door
I want him to drive them off so they won't come back no more.

GOLDEN RULE BLUES (*Bessie Smith*)

I can't understand, I can't keep my man
Won't someone please find him if you can
Tell him this for me

Give me back my key I let him have five years ago
Bring me back my key I let him have five years ago
You don't know how to use it, you don't need it no more

Looked for you at home, you never can be found
Looked for you at home, you never can be found
That's the reason why you can't carry my key around

Pretty papa, you must learn the rule
Pretty papa, you must learn the rule
Go to work every morning like all the other men do

Bring me your pay after your work every day
Bring me your pay after your work every day
That's the only way you can make your pretty mama stay.

A GOOD MAN IS HARD TO FIND (*E. Green*)

My heart is sad and I'm all alone, my man treats me mean
I regret the day that I was born and that man I ever seen
My happiness has no space left today
My heart is broke, that's why I say

Lord, a good man is hard to find, you always get another kind
Yes, and when you think that he's your pal
You look and find him fooling 'round some old gal
Then you rave, you are crazed, you want to see him down in his grave

So if your man is nice, take my advice
Hug him in the morning, kiss him at night
Give him plenty lovin', treat your good man right
'Cause a good man nowadays sho' is hard to find

Lord, a good man is so hard to find, we always get that rough old kind
Yes, when you think that he's your pal
You look and find him hangin' 'round some old gal
Then you rave, child, you're crazed, you'll want to see him dead, layin' in his
    grave

So if your man is nice, take my advice
Hug him in the morning, kiss him at night
Give plenty smack, madam, treat your man right
'Cause a good man nowadays sho' is hard to find.

GRAVEYARD DREAM BLUES (*Ida Cox*)

Blues on my mind, blues all around my head
Blues on my mind, and blues all around my head
I dreamed last night that the man that I love was dead

I went to the graveyard, fell down on my knee
I went to the graveyard, fell down on my knee
And I asked the gravedigger to give me back my real good man, please

The gravedigger looked me in the eye
The gravedigger looked me in the eye
Said "I'm sorry, lady, but your man has said his last goodbye."

I wrung my hand and I wanted to scream
I wrung my hand and I wanted to scream
But when I woke up, I found it was only a dream.

GULF COAST BLUES (*Clarence Williams*)

I've been blue all day
My man's gone away

He has left his mama cold
For another gal, I'm told

I tried to treat him kind
I thought he would be mine

That man I hate to lose
That's why mama's got the blues

The man I love, he has done left this town
The man I love, he has done left this town
And if it keeps on snowing, I will be Gulf Coast bound

The mailman passed, but he didn't leave no news
The mailman passed, but he didn't leave no news
I'll tell the world he left me with those Gulf Coast blues

Some of you men sure do make me tired
Some of you men sure do make me tired
You've got a mouthful of "gimme," a handful of "much obliged."

HARD DRIVING PAPA (*G. Brooks*)

Lord, I wish I could die, 'cause my man treats me like a slave
Lord, I wish I could die, my man treats me like a slave
That's a why he drives me, I'm sinkin' low, low in my grave

He's a hard drivin' papa, drives me all the time
Drives me so hard, I'm 'fraid that I'll lose my mind
And when the sun starts sinkin', I start sinkin' into cryin'

Lord, I rise in the morning, dressed when the clock strikes four
Five o'clock, I'm washin' and scrubbin' somebody's floor
He takes all my money and starts to cry for more

I'm goin' to the river feelin' so sad and blue
I'm goin' to the river feelin' so sad and blue
Because I love him, 'cause there's no one can beat me like he do.

HARD TIME BLUES (*Bessie Smith*)

My man said he didn't want me, I'm getting tired of his dirty ways
I'm going to see another brown
I'm packin' my clothes, I'm leavin' town
Getting outdoors, lettin' him know
And he'll see a hard time
Now there's no need of cryin', just put me off your mind
And you'll see a hard time
When your good woman is gone, you will see a hard time

[Spoken] Don't say a word, just listen.

The risin' sun ain't gonna set in the east no more
The risin' sun ain't gonna set in the east no more
Lord, I'm a good woman, I can get a man any place I go

You can say what you please, you will miss me
There's a lots of things you are bound to see
When your friends forsake you and your money's gone
Then you'll look around, all your clothes in pawn
Down on your knees, you'll ask for me
There's no one else you will want to see
Then you'll pray a prayer that men pray everywhere, Lord
When your good woman is gone, when your good woman is gone.

HATEFUL BLUES (*E. Johnson*)

Woke up this mornin' hateful and blue 'cause my daddy treated me wrong
He's got his satchel, packed his clothes upon his back and gone, I say he's gone
Yes, I'm low down, nothin' ever worries me long, I said long

I cried last night and I cried all night before, cried the blues
And I said that I ain't gonna cry no more, no more
If he can stand to leave me, I can stand to see him go, I said go

Yes, I'm hateful 'cause he treats me so unkind
If I find that man while hurt is on my mind

If I see him I'm gon' beat him, gon' kick and bite him, too
Gonna take my weddin' butcher, gonna cut him two in two

The ambulance is waitin', the undertaker, too
A suit in doctor's office, all kinds of money for you

Ain't gonna sell him, gon' keep him for myself
Gonna cut on him until a piece this big is left

'Cause my love has been abused
Now I got the hateful blues.

HAUNTED HOUSE BLUES (*J. C. Johnson*)

[SPOKEN]
Don't bring no ghosts in the front, carry 'em 'round to the back door.

[SUNG]
This house is so haunted with dead men I can't lose
This house is so haunted with dead men I can't lose
And a sneaky old feelin' gives me those haunted house blues

I can't sleep no more, I done lost my appetite
I can't sleep no more, done lost my appetite
'Cause my mistreatin' daddy hangs around me day and night

He moans when I'm sleepin', he wakes me at two A.M.
He moans when I'm sleepin', he wakes me at two A.M.
And he makes me swear I'll have no other man but him

Now I'm so worried and I'm blue all the time
Now I'm so worried and I'm blue all the time
Go tell the undertaker to fix that old coffin of mine

[SPOKEN]
Lord, help us to get right!

[SUNG]
I'm scared to stay here, I'm scared to leave this town
I'm scared to stay here, I'm scared to leave this town
But a feelin' just tell me to burn this house on down, hainted* house on down.

*Haunted (haint = ghost).

HE'S GONE BLUES (*Bessie Smith*)

I feel blue, I want someone to cheer me
So confused, because my man's not near me
I'm getting tired of bein' alone
I want my good man to come on home
He's gone and left me
He's gone away to stay

I never had a man in my whole life
To treat me this-a-way
I work hard both the night and day
I even let him draw my pay
He packed his grip and left on Christmas Day
Oh well, I guess he's gone

Any fair-minded woman liable to go insane
When the best man she had has gone astray
Since my man has gone, he's gone away to roam
All I can say, he's gone, gone, gone
He's gone and left me
He's gone away to stay

I never had a man in my whole life
To treat me this-a-way
I work hard both the night and day
I even let him draw my pay
He packed his grip and left on Christmas Day
Oh well, I guess he's gone
Oh well, I guess he's gone.

HE'S GOT ME GOIN' (*Joe Davis*)

Don't know what's come over me, done lost my self-control
He's the sugar in my tea, the jelly in my roll
Got me goin', he's got me goin', but I don't know where I'm headed for

Gee, I've got a lovin' man, one of them handsome brutes
He's built according to that plan, too bad when it suits
Got me goin', he's got me goin', but I don't know where I'm headed for

I can't sleep a doggone wink, unless he's by my side
Mine's so different, I just can't think without my easy ride
Got me goin', he's got me goin', but I don't know where I'm headed for

Lay and listen to the clock, ticks loud as a drum
Hear the crowing of a cock, still my man ain't come
Got me goin', got me goin', but I don't know where I'm headed for

Wouldn't be no two-time gal, just one man's enough
I don't need no two men, 'cause my one man knows his stuff
Got me goin', got me goin', but I don't know where I'm headed for

Got a heart, but just one man knows how to get to it
For he's got the only key that's a perfect fit
Got me goin', he's got me goin', but I don't know where I'm headed for

'Fraid to advertise my man, simply scared to death
These gals'll hear about him and try him for they self
Got me goin', got me goin', but I don't know where I'm headed for.

HOMELESS BLUES *(Porter Grainger)*

Mississippi River, what a fix you left me in
Lord, Mississippi River, what a fix you left me in
Mudholes of water, clear up to my chin

House without a steeple, didn't even have a door
House without a steeple, didn't even have a door
Plain old two-room shanty, but it was my home sweet home

Ma and Pa got drowned, and Mississippi, you to blame
My Ma and Pa got drowned, and Mississippi, you to blame
Mississippi River, I can't stand to hear your name

Homeless, yes, I'm homeless, might as well be dead
Ah, you know I'm homeless, homeless, yes, might as well be dead
Hungry and disgusted, no place to lay my head

Wished I was an angel, but I'm a plain old black crow
Wished I was a nigger,* but I'm a plain old black crow
I'm gonna flap my wings and leave here and never come back no more.

*This is the lyric Smith sings here.

HONEY MAN BLUES (G. *Brooks*)

I've got the blues, and it's all about my honey man
I've got the blues, and it's all about my honey man
What makes me love him I sure don't understand

I'd rather be in the ocean floating like a log
I'd rather be in the ocean floating like a log
Than to stay with him and be mistreated like a dog

My heart's on fire, but my love is icy cold
My heart's on fire, but my love is icy cold
But I'm goin' right to his face and get him told

I'll fix him if it's twenty years from now
I'll fix him if it's twenty years from now
I'll have him belling just like a cow

I was born in Georgia, my ways are underground
I was born in Georgia, my ways are underground
If you mistreat me, I'll hunt you like a hound.

HOT SPRINGS BLUES (*Bessie Smith*)

If you ever get crippled, let me tell you what to do
Lord, if you ever get crippled, let me tell you what to do
Take a trip to Hot Springs, and let 'em wait on you

When they put you in the water and do the bathhouse rag
Lord, they'll put you in the water and do the bathhouse rag
And if you don't get well, you'll sure come back

With the steam and the sweat and the hot room too
With the steamin' sweat, and hot room too
If that don't cure you, tell me what will it do

Some come here crippled, some come here lame
Some come here crippled, some come here lame
If they don't go away well, we are not to blame

Hot spring water sure runs good and hot
Hot spring water sure runs boilin' hot
I want everybody know it sure comes from a rock.

HOUSE RENT BLUES (*T. Wallace*)

[SPOKEN]
Where's that coal man? I want a big lump of coal this morning.

[SUNG]
On a cold, dark and stormy night
On a cold, dark and stormy night
They want to put me out and it wasn't daylight

There on my door they nailed a sign
There on my door they nailed a sign
I got to move from here if the rent man don't change his mind

See me comin', put your woman outdoors
See me comin', put your woman outdoors
You know I ain't no stranger, and I been here before

Lordy, what a feelin', rent man comes a-creepin', in my bed a-sleepin'
He left me with those house rent blues.

HUSTLIN' DAN (*J. Crawford*)

Listen, sportin' fellas, all you brown and black gals, too
Tell you 'bout a black man, best that ever wore a shoe
Hustlin' Dan, he was my man

Talk about your lovers, he could more than satisfy me
Master of my weakness, everything a man could be
Hustlin' Dan, oh, he's my man

He was one good gambler, he would gamble anywhere
Knows the game and plays it, always plays it on the square
Hustlin' Dan, yes, he's my man

Yes, he was a hustler, ramblers called him Hustlin' Dan
Born down on the levee, was a rough and tumble man
Hustlin' Dan, mmmm, he's my man

He got sick one mornin' just about the break of day
T.B. was upon him, had to send my man away
Hustlin' Dan, he was my man

While he was in Denville, sent him money all the time
Prayed to the Lord above me, please don't take that man of mine
Hustlin' Dan, Lord, he's my man

Since he's gone and left me, bought myself a big forty-four
Gonna join my good man, I don't wanna live no more
Hustlin' Dan, Lord, he's my man.

I AIN'T GOIN' TO PLAY NO SECOND FIDDLE
(*Perry Bradford*)

Let me tell you, daddy, mama ain't gon' set and grieve
Pack up your duds and get ready to leave
I've stood your foolishness long enough
So now I'm gonna call your bluff

On certain things I'm gonna call your hand
So now, daddy, here's my plan
I ain't gonna play no second fiddle, I'm used to playin' lead

You must think that I am blind
You been cheatin' me all the time
Why did you still flirt?
And you know just how it hurt
To see you with my chum
Do you think that I am dumb?

You cause me to drink
When I set down and think
And see that you never take heed

I called to your house the other night
Caught you and your good gal havin' a fight
I ain't gonna play no second fiddle, 'cause I'm used to playin' lead

I caught you with your good time vamp
So now, papa, I'm gon' put out your lamp
Now, papa, I ain't sore
You ain't gon' mess up with me no more

I'm gonna flirt with another sheep
Then you gonna hang your head and weep
I ain't gonna play no second fiddle, 'cause I'm used to playin' lead.

I AIN'T GOT NOBODY (*R. Graham and Spencer Williams*)

They've been sayin' all around, and I begin to think it's true
It's hard to love some man when he don't care for you

Once I had a lovin' man, as good as any in this town
But now I'm sad and lonely, he's done throwed me down

I ain't got nobody, nobody, nobody cares for me
That's why I'm always sad and lonely
Won't some good man take a chance with me?

I sings good songs all the time
Want some brown to be a pal of mine
I ain't got nobody, nobody, ain't nobody cares for me

I sings good songs all the time
Won't some man be a pal of mine?
I ain't got nobody, nobody, ain't nobody cares for me.

I'D RATHER BE DEAD AND BURIED IN MY GRAVE (*P. Fuller*)

I'm like a fox without a hole, a ship without a sail
Like a dog who's got a dozen cans danglin' on his tail
I'd rather be dead and buried in my grave, mean old grave

Just soon to wallow in the mud as to be treated like a hog
I feel like I'm somebody's old sheep killin' dog
I'd rather be dead and buried in my grave, mean old grave

It's a man has got me sniffin', sniffin' dope and drinkin' gin
Yes, it's another one that put me in this old hole I'm in
He hurt me when he left, nobody but the Lord can tell
I asked him where's he goin', he said, "Go to hell."
I'd rather be dead and buried in my grave, mean old grave

Dug a hole for his picture, faced it to the ground
Sprinkled salt around to keep him from around
I'd rather be dead and buried in my grave, mean old grave

That man is my master and I'm nothin' but a slave
That's why I'd rather be dead and buried in my grave, mean old grave.

IF YOU DON'T, I KNOW WHO WILL (*Clarence Williams,* *S. Smith, and T. Brymn*)

Daddy, I want some furs and things
Daddy, I wants a diamond ring

Aeroplanes, motorcars, and such
If your little mama ain't askin' too much

From you, from you
Won't you give me what I want, daddy, do

If you don't, I know who will
If you don't, I know who will

You may think that I'm just bluffin'
But I'm one gal ain't s'posed to want for nothin'

I've got my wantin' habits on
I've had 'em on since this morn'

Man, you've got to help me 'long
If you don't, it's goodbye John

Squeeze me 'til I feel the thrill
Love me 'til I get my fill

'Cause if you don't and say you won't
I know who will, Mr. So-and-so, I know who will

If you don't, I know who will
If you don't, I know who will

You might think that I'm just bluffin'
But I'm one gal ain't s'posed to want for nothin'

I've got my wantin' habits on
I've had 'em on since this morn'

Man, you've got to help me 'long
If you don't, it's goodbye John

Squeeze me 'til I feel the thrill
Love me 'til I get my fill

'Cause if you don't and say you won't
I know who will, my other papa, I know who will.

I'M DOWN IN THE DUMPS (*L. Wilson and W. Wilson*)

My man's got something, he gives me such a thrill
Every time he smiles at me I can't keep my body still

I done cried so much, look like I've got the mumps
I can't keep from worryin' 'cause I'm down in the dumps

I had a nightmare last night when I laid down
When I woke up this morning my sweet man couldn't be found

I'm going down to the river, into it I'm gonna jump
Can't keep from worryin' 'cause I'm down in the dumps

Someone knocked on my do' last night when I was sleep
I thought it was that sweet man of mine makin' his 'fore day creep

'Twas nothing but my landlord, a great big chump
Stay 'way from my door, Mr. Landlord, 'cause I'm down in the dumps

When I woke up, my pillow was wet with tears
Just one day from that man of mine seem like a thousand years

But I'm gonna straighten up, straighter than Andy Gump
Ain't no use of me tellin' that lie 'cause I'm down in the dumps

I'm twenty-five years old, that ain't no old maid
I got plenty of feelin' and vitality, I'm sure that I can make the grade

I'm always like a tiger, I'm ready to jump
I need a whole lots of lovin' 'cause I'm down in the dumps.

I'M GOING BACK TO MY USED TO BE (*J. Cox*)
(*Duet sung with Clara Smith*)

I feel sad, you feel blue, I can hardly sleep at night
For your man was so unkind and I know I didn't treat him right
You goin' back to your first love, 'cause a good man is hard to find
I say you have got some grand good man, believe me, he is sure on my mind

I'm goin' back, yeah, you're turnin' back
I'm goin' back to my used to be
You goin' back, I'm goin' back 'cause my man was so good to me

Went out the window when times was rough
[Spoken] Look out there, Clara, you know your man was in the pool yard
    struttin' his stuff

Bessie, I'm goin' back, Clara, you say you're goin' back
I'm goin' back to my used to be, and it's this morning

Back to my used to be, what can you use him for
Crazy about my used to be, he ain't good lookin'
I love my used to be.

I'M WILD ABOUT THAT THING (*Spencer Williams*)

Honey, baby, won't you cuddle near
Let sweet mama whisper in your ear
I'm wild about that thing
It makes me laugh and sing
Give it to me, papa, I'm wild about that thing

Do it easy, honey, don't get rough
From you, papa, I can't get enough
I'm wild about that thing
Sweet joy it always brings
Everybody knows it, I'm wild about that thing

Please don't hold it, baby, when I cry
Gimme every bit of it, else I'll die
I'm wild about that thing
Sha-da-jing-jing-jing
All the time I'm cryin', I'm wild about that thing

What's the matter, papa, please don't stall
Don't you know I love it and I wants it all
I'm wild about that thing
Just give my bell a ring
You can press my button, I'm wild about that thing

If you want to satisfy my soul
Come on and rock me with a steady roll
I'm wild about that thing
Gee, I like your ting-a-ling
Kiss me like you mean it, I'm wild about that thing

Come on, turn the lights down low
When you say you're ready, just say let's go
I'm wild about that thing
Come on and make me feel it, I'm wild about that thing

All about it when you hold me tight
Let me linger in your arms all night
I'm wild about that thing
My passion's got the fling
Come on, hear me cryin', I'm wild about that thing.

IN THE HOUSE BLUES (*Bessie Smith*)

Settin' in the house with everything on my mind
Settin' in the house with everything on my mind
Lookin' at the clock and can't even tell the time

Walkin' to my window, and lookin' out of my door
Walkin' to my window, and lookin' out of my door
Wishin' that my man would come home once more

Can't eat, can't sleep, so weak I can't walk my floor
Can't eat, can't sleep, so weak I can't walk my floor
Feel like hollerin' murder, let the police squad get me once more

They woke me up before day with trouble on my mind
They woke me up before day with trouble on my mind
Wringin' my hands and screamin', walkin' the floor hollerin' and cryin'

Catch 'em, don't let them blues in here
Catch 'em, don't let them blues in here
They shakes me in my bed, can't set down in my chair

Oh, the blues has got me on the go
Oh, they've got me on the go
They runs around my house, in and out of my front door.

IT MAKES MY LOVE COME DOWN (*Bessie Smith*)

When I see two sweethearts spoon
Underneath the silvery moon
It makes my love come down

I wanna be around
Kiss me, honey, it makes my love come down

Cuddle close, turn out the light
Do just what you did last night
It makes my love come down, I wanna be in town
Sweet, sweet daddy, it makes my love come down

Wild about my toodle-oh
When I get my toodle-oh
It makes my love come down, want every pound
Hear me cryin', it makes my love come down

Likes my coffee, likes my tea
Daffy about my stingaree
It makes my love come down, I wanna be around
Oh, sweet papa, it makes my love come down

If you want to hear me rave
Honey, give me what I crave
It makes my love come down, actin' like a clown
Can't help from braggin', it makes my love come down

Come on and be my desert sheik
You so strong and I'm so weak
It makes my love come down, to be loveland bound
Red hot papa, it makes my love come down

If you want me for your own
Kiss me nice or leave me alone
It makes my love come down, it makes my love come down
Take me bye bye, it makes my love come down

When you take me for a ride
When I'm close up by your side
It makes my love come down, ridin' all around
Easy ridin' makes my love come down.

IT WON'T BE YOU (*Bessie Smith and L. Miller*)

You have really broke my heart
I wished I knew before we start

I thought you'd always be true
That's why I left my home for you

But everything has turned out wrong
And you have left me all alone
'Til I made up my mind
To get someone who always will be kind

[SUNG TWICE]
No matter how cruel he may be, it won't be you
If he beats me and breaks my heart, it won't be you
He may love me and treat me kind
Love me so hard I'll lose my mind
I'm satisfied to know it won't be you.

I USED TO BE YOUR SWEET MAMA (*L. Miller and Fred Longshaw*)

Yes, I'm mad and have a right to be
After what my daddy did to me
I lavished all my love on him
But I swear I'll never love again
All you women understand
What it is to be in love with a two-time man
The next time he calls me sweet mama in his lovin' way
This is what I'm going to say

"I used to be your sweet mama, sweet papa
But now I'm just as sour as can be
So don't come stallin' around my way expectin' any love from me
You had your chance and proved unfaithful
So now I'm gonna be real mean and hateful
I used to be your sweet mama, sweet papa
But now I'm just as sour as can be."

[SPOKEN]
I ain't gonna let no man worry me sick
Or turn this hair of mine gray
Soon as I catch him at his two-time tricks
I'm gonna tell him to be on his way

To the world I scream, "No man can treat me mean
And expect my love all the time."
When he roams away, he'd better stay
If he comes back he'll find

[SUNG]
"You've had your chance and proved unfaithful
So now I'm gonna be real mean and hateful
I used to be your sweet mama, sweet papa
But now I'm just as sour as can be."

I'VE BEEN MISTREATED AND I DON'T LIKE IT
   (*Fred Longshaw*)

Folks, there is somethin' I can't understand
Why a good woman gets a no-good man

I'm gonna leave here and the time ain't long
Because my man has done me wrong

I've been mistreated and I don't like it, there's no use to say I do
I've been mistreated and I don't like it, so I must tell to you

Once upon a time, I stood for all he did
Those days are gone, believe me, kid
I've been mistreated and I don't like it, there's no use to say I do

Once upon a time I stood for all he did
Those days are gone, man, believe me
I've been mistreated and I don't like it, Lord, no use to say I do
I mean, no use to say I do.

I'VE GOT WHAT IT TAKES (*Clarence Williams
     and H. Jenkins*)

Old stingy Jenny saved up all her pennies
Straight to the bank she would go
The sharks would hound her, hands around her
But none could get her dough

Jenny's fella was a slick high yella
Sent away to jail one day
He cried for bail and turned real pale
When I heard Jenny say

"I've got what it takes, but it breaks my heart to give it away
It's in demand, they wants it every day
I've been savin' it up for a long, long time
To give it away would be more than a crime

"Your eyes may roll, your teeth may grit
But none of my money will you get
You can look in my bankbook, but I'll never let you feel my purse
'Cause I'm one woman b'lieve in safety first, safety first

"Say, if you want my money, here's my plan
I'm savin' it up for a real good man
I've got what it takes, but it breaks my heart to give it away

"I've got what it takes, but it breaks my heart to give it away
It's in demand, folks cryin' for it every day
I've been savin' it up for a long, long time
To give it away would be more than a crime

"Your eyes may roll, your teeth may grit
But none of this small change will you get
You can look in my bankbook, but I'll never let you put your hands on my purse
Lord, I'm one woman b'lieve in safety first, safety first

"Say, if you want my money, here's my plan
I'm not savin' it up for no snake-hip man
I've got what it takes, but it breaks my heart to give it away."

I WANT EVERY BIT OF IT (*Clarence Williams and Spencer Williams*)

Listen to my plea this mornin', mama's gonna get you told
Pay attention to my warning, 'cause you been actin' quite too bold
Everything you give me must suit me to a tee

I want every bit of it or none at all, 'cause I don't like it secondhand
I want all your kisses or none at all, give me lots of candy, honey, love is grand

Mama likes lovin' both night and day, I don't like no two-time, that is why I say
I want every bit of it or none at all, 'cause I don't like it secondhand
No, I don't like it secondhand

I want every bit of it or none at all, 'cause I don't like it secondhand
I want all your kisses or none at all, love good aplenty, honey, that's my
   command
Mama likes foolin' when lights are low, when you start to makin' love, no one
   knows
I want every bit of it or none at all, 'cause I don't like it secondhand
No, I can't use it secondhand.

JAIL HOUSE BLUES (*Bessie Smith and Clarence Williams*)

Lord, this house is gonna get raided, yes sir!

Thirty days in jail with my back turned to the wall, turned to the wall
Thirty days in jail with my back turned to the wall
Look here, Mr. Jail Keeper, put another gal in my stall

I don't mind bein' in jail, but I got to stay there so long, so long
I don't mind bein' in jail, but I got to stay there so long, so long
When every friend I had is done shook hands and gone

You better stop your man from ticklin' me under my chin, under my chin
You better stop your man from ticklin' me under my chin
'Cause if he keeps on ticklin', I'm sure gonna take him on in

Good mornin', blues, blues, how do you do, how do you do
Good mornin', blues, blues, how do you do
Say, I just come here to have a few words with you.

JAZZBO BROWN FROM MEMPHIS TOWN (*G. Brooks*)

Don't you start no crowin', lay your money down
I've got mine on Jazzbo, that Memphis clarinet hound
He ain't got no equal nowhere in this land
So let me tell you people, 'bout this Memphis man

Jazzbo Brown from Memphis town, he's a clarinet hound
He can't dance, he can't sing, but lordy, how he can play that thing
He ain't seen no music school, he can't read a note
But he's the playinest fool on that Memphis boat

When he wraps his big fat lips 'round that doggone horn
Captain out on sea and ship, Lord, carryin' on
I could dance a month or so if that fool would only blow
Jazzbo Brown, that clarinet hound from Memphis town

Jazzbo Brown from Memphis town, he's a clarinet hound
When he blows and pats his feet, makes a butcher leave his meat
He don't play no classy stuff like them Hoffman Tales
What he plays is good enough for the Prince of Wales

He can moan and he can groan, I ain't foolin' you
There ain't nothin' on that horn that old Jazz can't do
Set your dime, mark your card, then I'll give you all the odds on
Jazzbo Brown, that clarinet hound from Memphis town.

J. C. HOLMES BLUES (*G. Horsley*)

Listen, people, if you want to hear a story told about a brave engineer
J. C. Holmes was the rider's name, a heavyweight wheelman with a mighty fame

J. C. said with a smile so fine, "Woman gets tired of one man all the time
Get two or three if you have to hide
If the train go and leave you got a mule to ride."

In the second cabin said Miss Alice Brown
"Born to ride with Mr. J. C. or die
I ain't good-lookin' and I don't dress fine
But I'm a ramblin' woman with a ramblin' mind."

Yes, the conductor hollered, "All aboard."
And the porter said "We gotta unload
Look-a here, son, we oughta been gone
I feel like ridin' if it's all night long."

J. C. said just before he died
Two more roads he wanted to ride
Everybody wondered what road it could be
He said the Southern Pacific and the K and the P*

*This line is very difficult to discern. While a number of railroad lines were designated by letters (e.g.,
M. & O. for Mobile & Ohio, or I.C. for Illinois Central) "the K and the P" may or may not be
accurate here.

J. C. said, "I don't feel right
I saw my gal with a man last night
Soon as I get enough steam just right
I been mistreated and I don't mind dyin'."

KEEP IT TO YOURSELF (*Clarence Williams*)

If your man is nice and sweet, servin' you lots of young pigmeat
Oh, yeah, keep it to yourself
If you know you are standin' fat, got him worried where you at
Oh, yeah, keep it to yourself

He don't fall for no one, he don't call for no one
He don't give nobody none of his L-O-V-E, 'cause it's yours
If your man is full of action, givin' you a lots of satisfaction
Oh, yeah, keep it to yourself

If he's gotta have a kiss and a squeeze, makes me weak way down in my knees
Oh, yeah, keep it to yourself
If he tries to treat you right, give you lovin' every night
Oh, yeah, keep it to yourself

He don't fall for no one, he don't call for no one
He don't give nobody none of his L-O-V-E, 'cause it's yours
With your man you've got the best go, don't broadcast it on nobody's radio
Oh, yeah, keep it to yourself.

KEEPS ON A-RAININ' (PAPA HE CAN'T MAKE NO TIME) (*Spencer Williams and M. Kortlander*)

One dark and stormy night Bill Jones was feelin' blue
Things didn't seem just right, so he didn't know just what to do

I said, "Bill, please tell me, ain't you satisfied?"
Bill looked around so pitiful and to me he replied

"Keeps on a-rainin', look how it's rainin', papa he can't make no time
Wind keep blowin', cold wind blowin', soon I'll find the seventh line."

In the wintertime when it's ice and snow, you know your pretty mama's got to
   have some dough
Keeps on a-rainin', look how it's raining, papa he can't make no time

"Ain't the snow just beautiful," some people say, but I'd rather see it in a movie
   picture play
Keeps on snowin', look how it's snowin', papa he can't make no time.

KITCHEN MAN (*Andy Razaf and A. Bellenda*)

Madame Bucks was quite deluxe
Servants by the score, Pullmans at each door
Butlers and maids galore
But one day Dan, her kitchen man
Gave in his notice he's through
She cried, "Oh, Dan, don't go
It'll grieve me if you do

"I love his cabbage, gravy, his hash
Daffy about his succotash
I can't do without my kitchen man
Wild about his turnip tops
Likes the way he warms my chops
I can't do without my kitchen man

"Anybody else can leave, and I would only laugh
But he means too much to me, and you ain't heard the half
Oh, his jelly roll is so nice and hot
Never fails to touch the spot
I can't do without my kitchen man

"His frankfurters are oh, so sweet
How I like his sausage meat
I can't do without my kitchen man
Oh, how that boy can open clams
No one else can touch my hams
I can't do without my kitchen man

"When I eat his donuts, all I leave is the hole
Anytime he wants to, why, he can use my sugar bowl
Oh, his baloney's really worth a try
Never fails to satisfy
I can't do without my kitchen man."

LADY LUCK BLUES (*W. Weber and Clarence Williams*)

Bad luck has come to stay, trouble never ends
My man has gone away with a girl I thought was my friend

I'm worried down with tears*
Lordy, can't you hear my prayer

Lady luck, lady luck, won't you please smile down on me
Now's the time, friend of mine, I need your sympathy

I've got a horseshoe on my door
I've knocked on wood 'til my hands are sore

Since my man done turned me loose
I've got those lady luck blues, I mean
I've got those lady luck blues

Lady luck, lady luck, won't you please smile down on me
Now's the time, friend of mine, I need your sympathy

I've got his picture turned upside down
I've sprinkled goofer dust all around

Since my man is gone, I'm all confused
I've got those lady luck blues, find my good man
I've got those lady luck blues.

The last word of this line is virtually inaudible.

LOCK AND KEY (*H. Creamer and J. Johnson*)

I can see that you and me will have a terrible fallin' out
No one at the barbers' ball will know what it's all about

They'll hear a shot and see you duck, and when the smoke is cleared away
Then the band will crawl from behind the stand, and then you'll hear me say

When I get home I'm gonna change my lock and key
When you get home you'll find an awful change in me

If I don't change my mind, another thing you will find
That your baby maybe has got another baby on the Pullman line

You did your stuff, so get yourself another home
I said it long enough, so pack your little trunk and roam

I used to love you once but you took and made a fool out of me
Oh, when I get home I'm gonna change this old lock and key

[SPOKEN]
Take off that suit I bought you, gimme that hat and that red vest, too
Take off my watch and gimme my ring, I want them shoes and everything
You just got to be the ladies' squeeze, well, let 'em squeeze you in your BVDs
If you say much, I'll shoot them off, I'll shoot them off if I hear you cough

[SUNG]
'Cause when I get home I'm gonna change my lock and key
When you get home you'll find a place where home used to be

And if I don't change my mind, another thing you will find
That your baby maybe has got another baby just as good and kind

You cheated on me, and that's the thing that made me sore
I'll change that key, or get myself another door

As far as my concern, you're a gypsy homeless as a flea
'Cause when I get home I'm gonna change my lock and key, believe me!

LONESOME DESERT BLUES (*Bessie Smith*)

A fly will stick to jelly, and wood will stick to glue
But a man won't stick to a woman, no matter what she do
The wrong way I'm bound to choose

That man of mine is triflin', and he don't mean me right
He's got another sweetie, he stays out late at night
That is why I've got those desert blues

I'm gonna travel to the desert, out in the western land
I'm gonna end my troubles in the burnin' sand

Temptation I can't refuse
For that man of mine I'm bound to lose

My mind is like a rowboat out on the stormy sea
He's with me right now, in the morning where will he be?

Lord, Lord, Lord, Lord, Lord, oh, Lord, Lord, Lord, Lord
I'm so nervous, I'm shakin' in my shoes
I'm burnin' up, I've got those lonesome desert blues.

LONG OLD ROAD (*Bessie Smith*)

It's a long old road, but I'm gonna find the end
It's a long old road, but I'm gonna find the end
And when I get there I'm gonna shake hands with a friend

On the side of the road, I sat underneath a tree
On the side of the road, I sat underneath a tree
Nobody knows the thought that came over me

Weepin' and cryin', tears fallin' on the ground
Weepin' and cryin', tears fallin' on the ground
When I got to the end I was so worried down

Picked up my bag, baby, and I tried it again
Picked up my bag, baby, and I tried it again
I got to make it, I've got to find the end

You can't trust nobody, you might as well be alone
You can't trust nobody, you might as well be alone
Found my long lost friend and I might as well stayed at home.

LOOKIN' FOR MY MAN BLUES (*Composer unknown*)

Lookin' for my man, he can strut his stuff
Lookin' for my man, he can strut his stuff
And when he starts a-struttin', I don't know when I've got enough

Hello, Central, give me long distance phone
Hello, Central, give me long distance phone
I'm lookin' for my man, 'cause he done left me all alone

He's a short black man, listen, people, that ain't all
He's a short black man, listen, people, that ain't all
He's got what it takes to make these monkey women fall

He's a red hot papa, melt hearts as cold as ice
He's a red hot papa, melt hearts as cold as ice
Girls, if he ever love you once, you bound to love him twice

I'm lookin' for that man, I'm gonna stop singin' these blues
I'm lookin' for that man, I'm gonna stop singin' the blues
I'll walk 'til I find him, if I wear out this last pair of shoes.

LOST YOUR HEAD BLUES (*Bessie Smith*)

I was with you, baby, when you didn't have a dime
I was with you, baby, when you didn't have a dime
Now that you got plenty money, you have thrown your good gal down

Once ain't for always, two ain't for twice
Once ain't for always, two ain't for twice
When you get a good gal, you better treat her nice

When you were lonesome, I tried to treat you kind
When you were lonesome, I tried to treat you kind
But since you've got money, it's done changed your mind

I'm gonna leave, baby, ain't gonna say goodbye
I'm gonna leave, baby, ain't gonna say goodbye
But I'll write you and tell you the reason why

Days are lonesome, nights are long
Days are lonesome, nights are so long
I'm a good old gal, but I've just been treated wrong.

LOUISIANA LOW DOWN BLUES (*Spencer Williams*)

Lou'siana, Lou'siana, mama's got the low down blues
Lou'siana, Lou'siana, mama's goin' on a cruise

Tonight when I start walkin', although the road is hard
I'm gonna keep on walkin' 'til I get in my own backyard

Mississippi River, Mississippi River, I know it's deep and wide
Mississippi River, I know it's deep and wide
Won't be satisfied 'til I get on the other side

Gon' to keep on trampin', gon' keep on trampin' 'til I get on solid ground
Gonna keep on trampin' 'til I get on solid ground
On my way to Dixie, Lord, I'm Lou'siana bound

Got a low down feelin', a low down feelin', I can't lose my heavy load
Got a low down feelin', I can't lose my heavy load
My home ain't up North, it's further down the road.

LOVE ME DADDY BLUES (*Fred Longshaw*)

I ain't got nobody, I want somebody
That's why I'm sad and blue
I feel mistreated, I don't know what to do
And if the blues don't kill me, they will thrill me through and through
Now I'm blue and lonesome too
I ain't got nobody to tell my troubles to
My man he left today and if he don't come back I'll go astray
I love him and try to treat him kind all the time

[SUNG TWICE]
Now I know that my man's no good
Because he knocked me down today with a six-foot rule
Now that he's gone away I can't help but go astray
He left me with them lovin' oh daddy blues.

MAMA'S GOT THE BLUES (*S. Martin and Clarence Williams*)

Some people say that the worried blues ain't bad
Some people say the worried blues ain't bad
But it's the worst old feeling that I've ever had

Woke up this morning with a jinx around my bed
I woke up this morning with a jinx around my bed
I didn't have no daddy to hold my achin' head

Brownskin's deceitful but a yella man is worse
Brownskin's deceitful but a yella man is worse
I'm gonna get myself a black man and play safety first

I got a man in Atlanta, two in Alabama, three in Chattanooga
Four in Cincinnati, five in Mississippi, and six in Memphis, Tennessee
If you don't like my peaches, please let my orchard be.

ME AND MY GIN (*H. Burke*)

Stay 'way from me 'cause I'm in my sin
Stay 'way from me 'cause I'm in my sin
If this place gets raided, it's me and my gin

Don't try me, nobody, 'cause you will never win
Don't try me, nobody, 'cause you will never win
I'll fight the Army, Navy, just me and my gin

Any bootlegger sho' is a pal of mine
Any bootlegger sho' is a pal of mine
'Cause a good ol' bottle of gin will get it all the time

When I'm feelin' high, ain't nothing I won't do
When I'm feelin' high, 'tain't nothing I won't do
Keep me full of liquor and I'll sho' be nice to you

I don't want no clothes and I don't need no bed
I don't want no clothes and I don't need no bed
I don't want no pork chops, just give me gin instead.

MEAN OLD BEDBUG BLUES (*Joe Davis*)

Well, bedbug sure is evil, they don't mean me no good
Yeah, those bedbugs sure is evil, they don't mean me no good
Thinks he's a woodpecker, and I'm a chunk of wood

When I lay down at night, I wonder how can a poor gal sleep
When I lay down at night, I wonder how can a poor gal sleep
When some is holding my hand, others eatin' my feet

Bedbugs as big as a jackass will bite you and stand and grin
Bedbugs as big as a jackass will bite you and stand and grin
Will drink all the bedbug poison, turn around and bite you again

Somethin' moaned in the corner, I tried my best to see
Somethin' moaned in the corner, and I went over and see
It was a bedbug was a-prayin', "Lord, give me some more to eat."

Got myself a wishbone, bedbugs done got my goat
Got myself a wishbone, with it cut they own doggone throat.

MIDNIGHT BLUES (*B. Thompson and Spencer Williams*)

Daddy, daddy, please come back to me
Daddy, daddy, please come back to me
Your mama's lonesome as she can be

You left me at midnight, clock was strikin' twelve
Left me at midnight, clock was strikin' twelve
To face this cruel world all by myself

Woke up at midnight sad and blue
Miss my daddy from my side

Left alone to be among my fate
That's why I'm sighin', cryin'

I just can't refuse
I feel so troubled, heartbroken too

Whoa, misery I can't hide
At twelve o'clock, I unlock my hate

I've got the meanest kind
Lonesome midnight blues.

MISTREATIN' DADDY (*Porter Grainger and B. Ricketts*)

Daddy, mama's got the blues, the kind of blues that's hard to lose
'Cause you mistreated me and drove me from your door

Daddy, you ain't heard the news, there's another papa in your shoes
You ain't even got a chance with me no more, so be on your p's and q's

Mistreatin' daddy, mistreatin' mama all the time
Just because she wouldn't let you
Mistreatin' daddy, mama's drawed the danger line
If you cross it I'll get you

If you see me setting on another daddy's knee
Don't bother me, I'm as mean as can be

I'm like the butcher right down the street
I can cut you all to pieces like I would a piece of meat

Mistreatin' daddy, you used to knock your mama down, when you knew I fell for
    you
Had me so nervous I would start jumping 'round, yes, every time I saw you

But I have got you off of my mind
And found another daddy who's just my kind
Mistreatin' daddy, I've got another papa now

I've got a tip of people talkin' about
I will grab my daddy and turn him wrongside out
Mistreatin' daddy, I've got a good papa now.

MOAN, YOU MOURNERS (*Spencer Williams*)

[SPOKEN]

Sisters and brothers, we met here on some serious business. It's been some
    backbitin' goin' on and the thing I want to know is, who's been doin' it. It's a
    shame, it's a shame, it's a shame. The thing I wants to know is what bit me on
    my—I mean *who* bit me on *my* back.

[SUNG]

Hey, you sinners, hear my call
Satan's waitin' for you all
Better get your souls washed white
Better see the light (Amen!)
Fiery furnace down below
If you ain't right, down you'll go
To original hot brimstone
Let you start right in to moan

[SUNG TWICE]

You better get down on your knee
And let the good Lord hear your plea
'Cause if you want to rest with ease
Moan, you mourners

Just bend your head way down and pray
To have the Devil chased away
Come, let your souls be saved today
Moan, you mourners

Singin' hallelujah, blood of the lamb, let your voices rise
Hear me talkin' to you, ain't got no time to sham if you want to get to paradise
You must repent without a doubt
And let the good Lord hear you shout
Religion turns you inside out
Moan, you mourners.

MONEY BLUES (*D. K. Leader and H. Eller*)

Samuel Brown from way down in Tennessee
Had a wife made his life full of misery

Now his gal sure could sing and how she'd moan the blues
And Sam said, "I sure like to hear, except this here bad news

" 'Daddy, I needs money,' gives it to you, honey
'Daddy, I need money now.'

"All day long I hear that song
'Papa, it's your fault if I go wrong.'

"Fast as I can lend it, how you like to spend it
It disappears somehow

"I've got beer money, you've got champagne
If you don't stop spendin', I will have to wait

" 'Daddy, I need money,' gives it to you, honey
'Daddy, I need money now, daddy, I need money now
Daddy, I need money,' gives it to you, honey
'Daddy, I need money now.'

"All day long I hear that song
'Papa, it's your fault if I go wrong.'

"Fast as I can lend it, how you like to spend it
It disappears somehow

"I've got beer money, you like champagne
If you don't stop spendin', I will have to wait

" 'Daddy, I need money,' gives it to you, honey
'I need a small piece of money now
I can use a piece of small change now.' "

MOONSHINE BLUES (*Gertrude Rainey*)

Drunk all night, babe, drunk the night before
But when I get sober, I ain't gon' drink no more
Because my friend has left me standin' in my door

My head goes 'round and around, babe, since my baby left town
I don't know if the river's runnin' up or down
But there's one thing certain, mama's gonna leave this town

You'll find me reelin' and rockin', howlin' like a hound
I'll catch the first train that's goin' South bound

Oh, stop, you'll hear me say stop, right through my brain
Oh, stop that train, oh, stop that train, so I can go back home again

Yeah, I'm upon my knees, play that again for me
'Cause I'm about to be a-losin' my mind

Can't stand up, can't sit down
The man I love has left this town

Girls, I feel like screamin', I feel like cryin'
I been mistreated, and I don't mind dyin'

I'm going home, going to settle down
Going to stop my runnin' around

Tell everybody that comes my way
I've got them moonshine blues, I say, I've got them moonshine blues.

MOUNTAIN TOP BLUES (*Spencer Williams*)

Feelin' sad and sorrowful, run over with the blues
Feelin' sad and sorrowful, run over with the blues
Someone buy me poison, that's the kind of death I'd use

Goin' up to the mountain top, throw myself down in the sea
Climb up to a mountain, throw myself down in the sea
Let the fishes and waves make a big fuss over me

Find a big high rock to jump from, stones all thick down on the ground
Big high rock to jump from, stones all thick down on the ground
When you find me you will see lots of pieces layin' around

Deep hole in the river, mama's gonna step right in
Deep hole in the river, mama's gonna step right in
I feel the hopeless cannot pause and laugh out loud at me*

*This line is very difficult to discern; it may or may not be accurate.

Got myself a brand new hammock, placed it underneath a tree
Got myself a hammock, placed it underneath a tree
I hope the wind will blow so hard, the tree will fall on me.

MUDDY WATER (*P. De Rose, H. Richman, and J. Trent*)

Dixie moonlight, Swanee shore
Headed homebound just once more
To my Mississippi Delta home

Southland has got grand garden spots
Whether you believe or not
I hear those trees a-whispering, "Come on back to me."

Muddy water 'round my feet
Muddy water in the street
Just God's own shelter
Down on the Delta
Muddy water in my shoes
Reelin' and rockin' to them low down blues

They live in ease and comfort down there, I do declare
Been away a year today to wander and roam
I don't care, it's muddy there
But, see, it's my home

Got my toes turned Dixie way
'Round the Delta let me lay
My heart cries out for muddy water.

MY MAN BLUES (*Bessie Smith*)
(*Duet sung with Clara Smith*)

Bessie: Clara, who was that man I saw you with the other day?
Clara: Bessie, that was my smooth black daddy that we call Charlie Gray.
Bessie: Don't you know that's my man? Yes, that's a fact.
Clara: I ain't seen your name printed up and down his back.
Bessie: You better let him be.
Clara: What, old gal? Because you ain't talkin' to me.
Bessie: That's my man, I want him for my own.

Clara: [Spoken] No! No! [Sung] He's my sweet daddy.
        You'd better leave that man alone.

Bessie: See that suit he got on? I bought it last week.

Clara: I been buyin' his clothes for five years, for that is my black sheik.

[CHARLIE WHISTLES]

[SPOKEN]

Bessie: Is that you, honey?

Charlie: 'Tain't nobody but—who's back there?

Clara: It sounds like Charlie.

Bessie: It 'tis my man, sweet papa Charlie Gray.

Clara: Your man? How do you git that way?

Bessie: Now, look here, honey. I been had that man for sumpteen years.

Clara: Child, don't you know I'll turn your damper down?

Bessie: Yes, Clara, and I'll cut you every way but loose!

Clara: Well, you might as well be get it fixed.

Bessie: Well, then.

[SUNG]

Bessie: I guess we got to have him on cooperation plan.
        I guess we got to have him on cooperation plan.

[SPOKEN]

Clara: Bessie!

Bessie: Clara!

[SUNG]

Both: Ain't nothin' different 'bout all those other two-time men.

[SPOKEN]

Bessie: How 'bout it?

Clara: Suits me.

Bessie: Suits me too.

Clara: Well, then.

MY SWEETIE WENT AWAY (*L. Handman and R. Turk*)

I've got a lovesick tale to tell to you, though it ain't no 'fair of mine
It's 'bout a gal named Sue and a boy named Lou, they were fighting all the time

Sue came home one afternoon, and found an empty dining room
Without a word, her turtle dove had flown
She began to moan

My sweetie went away, but he didn't say where, he didn't say when, he didn't say
    why
Or bid me goodbye, I'm blue as I can be

I know he loves another one, but he didn't say who, he didn't say when, he didn't
    say what
His mama has got that took my sweetie from me

I'm like a little lost sheep and I can't sleep
But I keep tryin' to forget my triflin' papa
Has left his mama all alone, I groan

My sweetie went away, but he didn't say where, he didn't say when, he didn't say
    why
I know I'll die
Why don't he hurry home?

I'm like a little lost sheep and I can't sleep
But I keep tryin' to forget my triflin' papa
Has left his mama all alone, I groan

My sweetie went away, but he didn't say where, he didn't say when, he didn't say
    why
I know I'll die
Why don't he hurry home?

NASHVILLE WOMAN'S BLUES (*Fred Longshaw*)

Folks, I know you all have heard the blues
But this is one you likely never knew

Down in Nashville, Tennessee
Every night about half past three
The women down there, they does the chivaree

Down in Nashville, Tennessee
Down in Nashville, Tennessee
Women down there, they does the chivaree

If you go down there you have no time to lose
Just go uptown and buy a new pair of shoes

Folks down there, they drinks a lots of booze
You can say just what you choose
I have got those Nashville woman's blues

Down there, they strut they stuff
Down there, they strut they stuff
The way they strut, it really ain't no bluff

You can say what you choose
I have got those Nashville woman's blues.

NEED A LITTLE SUGAR IN MY BOWL
(Clarence Williams, D. Small, and T. Brymn)

Tired of bein' lonely, tired of bein' blue
I wished I had some good man to tell my troubles to

Seem like the whole world's wrong since my man's been gone
I need a little sugar in my bowl
I need a little hot dog on my roll

I can stand a bit of lovin' oh so bad
I feel so funny, I feel so sad

I need a little steam heat on my floor
Maybe I can fix things up so they'll go

What's a matter, hard papa, come on and save your mama's soul
'Cause I need a little sugar in my bowl, doggone it
I need some sugar in my bowl

I need a little sugar in my bowl
I need a little hot dog between my rolls

You gettin' different I've been told
Move your finger, drop somethin' in my bowl

I need a little steam heat on my floor
Maybe I can fix things up so they'll go

Get off your knees, I can't see what you're drivin' at
It's dark down there, looks like a snake

Come on here and drop somethin' here in my bowl
Stop your foolin', and drop somethin' in my bowl.

NEW GULF COAST BLUES (*Clarence Williams*)

I done packed my clothes, gonna leave my woes
Goin' to a better place with a smile upon my face
When that steamboat blows, when that Gulf train goes
You'll hear me say goodbye, because here's the reason why

The Gulf of Mexico flows into the Mobile Bay
The Gulf of Mexico flows into the Mobile Bay
I'm gonna let that cold stream of water flow over my head some day

Tell me, Mr. Mailman, what is on your mind?
Tell me, Mr. Mailman, what is on your mind?
When you pass my door, look like you are blind

My eyes are brown, my teeth are pearly white
My eyes are brown, my teeth are pearly white
Because my skin is dark don't mean my heart ain't right.

NEW ORLEANS HOP SCOP BLUES (*G. W. Thomas*)

Old New Orleans is a great big old southern town
Where hospitality you will surely find
The population there is very, very fair
With everything they do, white folks do it too
They have a dance, surely it's something rare there

Glide, slide, prance, dance, hop, stop
Take it easy, honey, I can never get tired
Of dancin' those hop scop blues

Once more you glide, slide, prance, dance
The hop scop blues will make you do a lovely shake
They'll make you feel so grand when you join hand in hand
I'll never get tired of dancin' those hop scop blues

Once more, you glide, slide, prance, I said dance, oh, hop, now stop
Take it easy, honey, oh, I can never get tired
Of dancin' those hop scop blues

Look out now, you glide, slide, I said prance, dance
Hop scop blues will make you do a lovely shake
They'll make you feel so grand when you join hand in hand
I'll never get tired of dancin' those hop scop blues.

NOBODY IN TOWN CAN BAKE A SWEET JELLY ROLL
LIKE MINE (*Clarence Williams and Spencer Williams*)

In a bakery shop today
I heard Miz Mandy Jenkins say

She has the best cake, you see
And they were fresh as fresh could be

And as the people would pass by
You would hear Miz Mandy cry

"Nobody in town can bake a sweet jelly roll like mine, like mine
No oven in town can bake a sweet jelly roll so fine, so fine

"It's worth lots of dough
The boys tell me so

"It's fresh every day
You hear 'em all say

"Don't be no dunce
Just try it once
You'll be right in line

"Somebody told me I made the best jelly roll in town, I say in town
You must admit that I'm a jelly roll bakin' hound, bakin' hound

"Good jelly roll, jelly roll, it's so hard to find
We always get the other kind
Nobody in town can bake a sweet jelly roll like mine

"Somebody told me I made the best jelly roll in town, I say in town
You must admit that I'm a jelly roll bakin' hound, bakin' hound

"Good jelly roll, jelly roll, from the bakery shop
Will surely make a bullfrog hop
Nobody in town can bake a sweet jelly roll like mine, like mine."

NOBODY KNOWS YOU WHEN YOU'RE DOWN AND OUT (*Jimmy Cox*)

Once I lived the life of a millionaire
Spending my money, I didn't care
I carried my friends out for a good time
Buying bootleg liquor, champagne and wine

When I began to fall so low
I didn't have a friend and no place to go
So if I ever get my hands on a dollar again
I'm gonna hold on to it 'til them eagles grin

Nobody knows you when you're down and out
In my pocket, not one penny
And my friends, I haven't any
But if I ever get on my feet again
Then I'll meet my long lost friend
It's mighty strange, without a doubt
Nobody knows you when you're down and out
I mean, when you're down and out

Mmmm, when you're down and out
Mmmm, not one penny
And my friends, I haven't any
Mmmm, I done fell so low
Nobody wants me 'round their door
Mmmm, without a doubt
No man can use you when you're down and out
I mean, when you're down and out.

NOBODY'S BLUES BUT MINE (*Clarence Williams*)

Daddy, daddy, where did you stay last night?
Daddy, daddy, where did you stay last night?
Don't you realize you ain't treatin' me right?

Now that I'm grievin' and I may be sad
'Tain't nobody's blues but mine

When I was with you I never was glad
'Tain't nobody's blues but mine

When bad luck overtakes me and old time friends refuse
I wake up in the morning with them heart sickening blues

If I play the game and I lose this time
'Tain't nobody's blues but mine.

OH DADDY BLUES (*E. Herbert and W. Russell*)

Just like a flower I'm fading away
The doctor calls to see me most every day
But he don't do me no good
Why? Because I'm lonesome for you
And if you care for me, then you will listen to my plea

Oh, daddy, look what you doing, look what you doing
Oh, daddy, you with your fooling, think what you're losing
All the little love I gave you
Is going to make you feel so awfully blue
When you miss me, and long to kiss me
You'll curse the day that you ever quit me

Oh, daddy, think when you all alone
You'll get to want me, just wait and see
But there will be someone else making love to me
Then, daddy, daddy, you won't have no mama at all

Oh, daddy, look what you doing, look what you doing
Oh, daddy, you and your fooling, think what you're losing
All the little love I gave you
Is going to make me feel so awfully blue
When you miss me, and long to kiss me
You'll curse the day that you ever quit me

Oh, daddy, think when you all alone
You know that you are getting old
You'll miss the way I baked your jelly roll
Then, daddy, daddy, you won't have no mama at all.

ON REVIVAL DAY (*Andy Razaf and K. Macomber*)

Have you ever seen a church begin to rock
Heard a sundown deacon preachin' to his block

Have you ever seen old Satan on a run?
Then follow me, see just how it's done

And have you ever heard a sermon stir your soul
Make you crave the river Jordan as you go
Have you ever felt as though you'd like to shout?
Then come on and let them feelin's out

Oh, Lord, just hear those sisters groanin'
And hear those brothers moanin'
Repentin' and atonin' on Revival Day

They're talkin' to the spirit
Just like you see and hear it
They're sinful and they fear it on Revival Day

When that congregation starts to sing
Nothin' in this world don't mean a thing
Oh, glory hallelujah
Makes you feel so peculiar
The Devil cannot rule you on Revival Day

Glory, glory, hymns are purifyin'
Wash my sins away, Lordy, Lordy, feel just like a lion
Lordy, Lordy, I's reborn today
Oh, just hear those sisters groanin'
And hear them brothers moanin'
Repentin' and atonin' on Revival Day

Oh, they're talkin' to the spirit
Just like you see and hear it
They sinful and they fear it on Revival Day

When that congregation starts to sing
Nothin' in this world don't mean a thing
Oh, glory hallelujah
Makes you feel so peculiar
The Devil cannot rule you on Revival Day.

ONE AND TWO BLUES (G. Brooks)

Our love starts way down home below the Dixon line
You pick cotton down on the farm and everything were fine

But things have changed while you stayed still, you are in the rear
So you have to catch up soon or they'll be some changes made

I've got them one and two blues what I can't lose
They haunts me night and day
And if you can't bring more, daddy, there's the door
That small change won't pay

If you want me to love you heap a much
Let mama feel that money touch
From now on, small change I refuse
Mama's got them one and two blues

Quit messin' around, you hear what I say
Start in to bringin' eight hours a day
If you must be a rat, here's the fact
Be a long-tailed one, have plenty of jack
Small change I refuse, mama's got them one and two blues
I scream, mama's got them one and two blues.

OUTSIDE OF THAT (*Clarence Williams and J. H. Trent*)

I've got the meanest man in the land
But his love is that thick and grand
His kiss just lingers on my lips
And thrills me to my fingertips

People say I'm a fool
He's heartless and oh so cruel
But outside of that he's all right with me
Outside of that, he's as sweet as he can be

I love him as true as stars above
He beats me up but how he can love
I never loved like that since the day I was born

I said for fun I don't want you no more
And when I said that I made sweet papa sore
He blacked my eye, I couldn't see
Then he pawned the things he gave to me
But outside of that, he's all right with me

I said for fun I don't want you no more
And when I said that I made sweet papa sore

[SPOKEN]
When he pawned my things, I said you dirty old thief
Child, then he turned around and knocked out both of my teeth

[SUNG]
Outside of that, he's all right with me.

PICKPOCKET BLUES (*Bessie Smith*)

My best man, my best friend told me to stop peddlin' gin
They even told me to keep my hands out people's pocket where their money
    was in

But I wouldn't listen or have any shame
Long as someone else would take the blame

Now, I can see it all come home to me
I'm settin' in the jail house now, I mean, I'm in the jail house now
I done stop runnin' around with this one and these good lookin' browns

Any time you'd see me, I was good time bound
With this one, that one, most all in town

I'm in the jail house now, I'm settin' in the jail house now
I'm settin' in the jail house now, I mean, I'm in the jail house now
I done stop runnin' around with all of my good lookin' browns.

PINCHBACK BLUES (*Bessie Smith*
    and Irving Johns)

[SPOKEN]
Girls, I wanna tell you about these sweet men. These men goin' 'round here
    tryin' to play cute. I'm hard on ya, boys, yes sir.

[SUNG]
I fell in love with a sweet man once, he said he loved me too
He said if I'd run away with him what nice things he would do

I'd travel around from town to town, how happy I would feel
But don't you know, he would not work, girls, take this tip from me

Get a workin' man when you marry, and let all these sweet men be
Child, it takes money to run a business, and with me I know you girls will agree

There's one thing about this married life that these young girls have got to know
If a sweet man enter your front gate, turn out your lights and lock your door

Yes, get a working man when you marry, let all these pinchbacks be
Child, it takes money to run a business, and with me I know you girls will agree

And if this panic stay on much longer, I'll hear all these young girls say
That it's a long way to Oklahoma, but these little pinchbacks, take 'em away.

PLEASE HELP ME GET HIM OFF MY MIND (*Bessie Smith*)

I've cried and worried, all night I've laid and groaned
I've cried and worried, all night I've laid and groaned
I used to weigh two hundred, now I'm down to skin and bones

It's all about a man who always kicked and dogged me 'round
It's all about a man who always kicked and dogged me 'round
And when I try to kill him that's when my love for him comes down

I've come to see you, gypsy, beggin' on my bended knees
I've come to see you, gypsy, beggin' on my bended knees
That man put something on me, oh, take it off of me, please

It starts at my forehead and goes clean down to my toes
It starts at my forehead and goes clean down to my toes
Oh, how I'm sufferin', gypsy, nobody but the good Lord knows

Gypsy, don't hurt him, fix him for me one more time
Oh, don't hurt him, gypsy, fix him for me one more time
Just make him love me, but please, ma'am, take him off my mind.

POOR MAN'S BLUES (*Bessie Smith*)

Mister rich man, rich man, open up your heart and mind
Mister rich man, rich man, open up your heart and mind
Give the poor man a chance, help stop these hard, hard times

While you're livin' in your mansion, you don't know what hard times means
While you're livin' in your mansion, you don't know what hard times means
Poor working man's wife is starvin', your wife's livin' like a queen

Please, listen to my pleading, 'cause I can't stand these hard times long
Oh, listen to my pleading, can't stand these hard times long
They'll make an honest man do things that you know is wrong

Poor man fought all the battles, poor man would fight again today
Poor man fought all the battles, poor man would fight again today
He would do anything you ask him in the name of the U.S.A.

Now the war is over, poor man must live the same as you
Now the war is over, poor man must live the same as you
If it wasn't for the poor man, mister rich man, what would you do?

PREACHIN' THE BLUES *(Bessie Smith)*

Down in Atlanta GA under the viaduct every day
Drinkin' corn and hollerin' hooray, pianos playin' 'til the break of day
But as I turned my head I loudly said
Preach them blues, sing them blues, they certainly sound good to me
I been in love for the last six months and ain't done worryin' yet
Moan them blues, holler them blues, let me convert your soul
'Cause just a little spirit of the blues tonight
Let me tell you, girls, if your man ain't treatin' you right
Let me tell you, I don't mean no wrong
I will learn you something if you listen to this song
I ain't here to try to save your soul
Just want to teach you how to save your good jelly roll
Goin' on down the line a little further now, there's a many poor woman down
Read on down to chapter nine, women must learn how to take their time
Read on down to chapter ten, takin' other women men you are doin' a sin
Sing 'em, sing 'em, sing them blues, let me convert your soul
Lord, one old sister by the name of Sister Green
Jumped up and done a shimmy you ain't never seen
Sing 'em, sing 'em, sing them blues, let me convert your soul.

PUT IT RIGHT HERE (OR KEEP IT OUT THERE)
   (Porter Grainger)

I've had a man for fifteen year, give him his room and board
Once he was like a Cadillac, now he's like a old worn-out Ford

He never brought me a lousy dime, and put it in my hand
So there'll be some changes from now on, accordin' to my plan

He's got to get it, bring it, put it right here
Or else he's gonna keep it out there

If he must steal it, beg it, or borrow it somewhere
Long as he gets it, child, I don't care

I'm tired of buying porkchops to grease his fat lips
And he'd have to find another place for to park his old hips

He must get it and bring it and put it right here
Or else he's gonna keep it out there

The bee gets the honey and brings it to the comb
Else he's kicked out of his home sweet home

To show you that they brings it, watch the dog and the cat
Everything, even, brings it from the mule to the gnat

The rooster gets the worm and brings it to the hen
That ought to be a tip to all you no-good men

The groundhog even brings it and puts it in his hole
So my man has got to bring it, doggone his soul

He's got to get it, bring it, and put it right here
Or else he's gonna keep it out there

If he must steal it, beg it, borrow it somewhere
Long as he gets it, child, I don't care

I'm gonna tell him like the Chinaman, when you don't bringem check
You don't getem laundry if you breakem damn neck*

You've got to get it, bring it and put it right here
Or else you gonna keep it out there.

*This racist caricature of Chinese speech can be found in other songs as well. The last phrase here is
virtually inaudible.

RAINY WEATHER BLUES (G. *Brooks*)

The rain sure am fallin', pourin' down from the sky
The rain sure am fallin', pourin' down from the sky
Feelin' wet all over, I could lay right down and die

Ain't got no jug or stopper, so I don't need no water now
Ain't got no jug or stopper, so I don't need no water now
Seem like the sun oughta shine and dry things right now

Yes, I'll find myself a raincoat and a man to tote it 'round
Yes, I'll find myself a raincoat and a man to tote it around
'Cause I got to keep on walking in the rain in this man's town

Got myself a red hot iron, gonna keep it in my bed
Got myself a red hot iron, gonna keep it in my bed
Fill myself with good old moonshine, and lay there, let the rain fall 'til I'm dead.

RECKLESS BLUES (*Fred Longshaw*)

When I was nothing but a child
When I was nothing but a child
All you men tried to drive me wild

Now I am growing old
Now I am growing old
And I got what it takes to get all of you men told

My mama says I'm reckless, my daddy says I'm wild
My mama says I'm reckless, my daddy says I'm wild
I ain't good looking, but I'm somebody's angel child

Daddy, mama want some loving
Daddy, mama want some huggin'
Darn it, pretty papa, mama want some loving, I vow
Darn it, pretty papa, mama want some loving right now.

RED MOUNTAIN BLUES (*H. Troy*)

Goin' around Red Mountain in the morning
Goin' around Red Mountain sure as you born
And if you never never no more see me again
Remember me when I'm gone

Now set down and write a letter for me
And send it straight to the man I love
Just tell him when you find him I'll be gone
A-roamin' the roads above

Down in the valley, my head was hangin' low
My poor heart was achin', gee, it hurt me so
Fortune-teller told me what I had to do
Get myself some snakeroot, start right in to chew

Got myself some snakeroot, John the Conqueror, too
Chewed them both together, I know what they will do
Took some in my pocket, put some in my boot
That don't make him love me, I'll start right in to shoot

Goin' around Red Mountain in a hurry
I'm going where I can't change my mind
And if I can't get rid of all my worries
Then I'll be gone for a long, long time.

ROCKING CHAIR BLUES (*Bessie Smith and Irving Johns*)

Did you ever wake up with Charlie all on your mind?
Did you ever wake up with Charlie all on your mind?
He plays the blues to his congregation, yeah, hear his trombone whine

He'll make you laugh, he'll make you cry
He'll sit right down and moan
He'll weep and moan, then I'll hear you say
Lord, I wonder where my lovin' man has gone

See, see, rider, you see, I'm goin' away
I won't be back until you change your way
I won't be back until you change your way

I'm goin' to the river, carry a brand-new rocking chair
I'm goin' to the river, carry a brand-new rocking chair
I'm gonna ask Mr. Tadpole did the blues ever stop by here

Blues jumped a rabbit, runnin' for a solid mile
Blues jumped a rabbit, runnin' for a solid mile
The rabbit turned over and cried like a natural child.

SAFETY MAMA (*Bessie Smith*)

Let me tell you how and what one no-good man done to me
He called me pretty, young, and wild, after that he let me be

He'd taken advantage of my youth, and that you understand
So wait awhile, I'll show you, child, just how to treat a no-good man

Make him stay at home, wash and iron
Tell all the neighbors he done lost his mind

Give your house rent shake on Saturday night
Monday morning you'll hold collectors good and tight

You see a man you really like
Let him bite that monkey brother in his back

When his cruel heart turn, his love breaks down
Hold him where you got him, make him stay in town

'Cause I'm a safety woman lookin' for a safety man

I made him stay at home, help me wash and iron
The neighbors knows he done lost his mind

I give a house rent shake one Saturday night
Monday morning I held collectors good and tight

I've seen a man I really like
I let him bite the monkey brother smack in his back

When his cruel heart turn, his love breaks down
I hold it where I had it and he stayed in town

I'm a safety woman, and I had to have a safety man

Say, I ain't good looking, I'm built for speed
I got everything a pigmeat need

'Cause I'm a safety woman lookin' for a safety man.

SALT WATER BLUES (G. *Brooks*)

I've got a man, he lives down by the sea
I've got a man, he lives down by the sea
But that doggone salty water sure ain't got 'em for me

He sent me a letter, nothin' in it but a note
He sent me a letter, nothin' in it but a note
I sat right down and wrote him, man, I ain't no billy goat

I may be crazy, but mama ain't nobody's fool
I may be crazy, but mama ain't nobody's fool
Before I stand your doggin', I'll eat grass like a Georgia mule

Settin' on a church stone, worried in both heart and soul
Settin' on a church stone, worried in both heart and soul
Feelin' lower than a possum hidin' in a groundhog's hole

I'm crazy 'bout my sugar, my sugar and my ol' long sheik
I'm crazy 'bout my sugar, my sugar and my ol' long sheik
But that doggone salty water taste too doggone bad for me.

SAM JONES BLUES (A. Bernard, R. Turk, and J. R. Robinson)

[SPOKEN]
Who is that knockin' on that door? Jones? You better get away from there, Joe. I
    don't know nobody named Jones. You in the right church, brother, but the
    wrong pew.

[SUNG]
Sam Jones left his lovely wife just to step around
Came back home 'bout a year, lookin' for his high brown

Went to his accustomed door and he knocked his knuckles sore
His wife she came, but to his shame, she knew his face no more

Sam said, "I'm your husband, dear."
But she said, "Dear, that's strange to hear
You ain't talkin' to Mrs. Jones, you speakin' to Miss Wilson now

"I used to be your lofty mate
But the judge done changed my fate

"Was a time you could have walked right in and called this place your home
    sweet home
But now it's all mine for all time, I'm free and livin' all alone

[SPOKEN]
"Don't need your clothes, don't need your rent, don't need your ones and twos
Though I ain't rich, I know my stitch, I earns my struttin' shoes

"Say, hand me the key that unlocks my front door
Because that bell don't read 'Sam Jones' no more, no
You ain't talkin' to Mrs. Jones, you speakin' to Miss Wilson now."

SEE IF I'LL CARE (*Clarence Williams and A. Hill*)

You say that you leavin' and that you're going away
But before you leave, dear, please let me have my say

I know that you feel good now with nothin' on your mind
But just mark my words, dear, there'll come a time

I know you're gonna pay
You'll want me back some day
To drive the blues away
Then see if I care

And when you feelin' blue
No one to talk to you
And you don't know what to do
Then see if I care

Though you think nothing of me and say that you don't love me
The time is comin' when you won't feel like you do now

You're gonna call my name
You know that you to blame
And you won't be the same
Then see if I'll care

Oh, you're gonna pay
Lord, you'll want me back some day
To drive your blues away
Then see if I care

And when you feelin' blue
No one to talk to you
And you don't know what to do
Then see if I care

Though you think nothin' of me and you don't love me
The time is comin' when you won't feel like you do now

You're gonna call my name
You know that you to blame
Lord, you won't be the same
Then see if I care.

SEND ME TO THE 'LECTRIC CHAIR (*G. Brooks*)

Judge, your honor, hear my plea before you open up your court
But I don't want no sympathy, 'cause I done cut my good man's throat
I caught him with a triflin' Jane I warned him 'bout before
I had my knife and went insane, and the rest you ought to know

Judge, judge, please, mister judge, send me to the 'lectric chair
Judge, judge, good mister judge, let me go away from here
I want to take a journey to the Devil down below
I done killed my man, I want to reap just what I sow
Oh, judge, judge, Lordy, Lordy, judge, send me to the 'lectric chair

Judge, judge, hear me, judge, send me to the 'lectric chair
Judge, judge, send me there, judge, I love him so dear
I cut him with my barlow, I kicked him in the side
I stood there laughing over him while he wallowed 'round and died
Oh, judge, judge, Lordy, judge, send me to the 'lectric chair

Judge, judge, sweet mister judge, send me to the 'lectric chair
Judge, judge, good, kind judge, burn me 'cause I don't care
I don't want no bondsman to go my bail
I don't want to spend no ninety-nine years in jail
So, judge, judge, good, kind judge, send me to the 'lectric chair.

SHIPWRECK BLUES (*Bessie Smith*)

Captain, tell your men to get on board
Heist your sail, just pull into another shore

I'm dreary in mind, and I'm so worried in heart
Oh, the best of friends sure have got to part

Blow your whistle, captain, so your men'll know what to do
Blow your whistle, captain, so your men'll know what to do
When a woman gets dreary, t'ain't no tellin' what she won't do

It's cloudy outdoors, as can be, oh it's cloudy as can be
That's the time I need my good man with me

It's rainin' and it's stormin' on the sea
It's rainin', it's stormin' on the sea
I feel like somebody has shipwrecked poor me.

SINFUL BLUES (*Perry Bradford*)

I got my opinion and my man won't act right
So I'm gonna get hard on him right from this very night
Gonna get me a gun long as my right arm
Shoot that man because he done me wrong
Lord, now I've got them sinful blues

Look here, folks, don't think I'm rough
'Cause I'm a good woman and I knows my stuff
That's why I'm sinful as can be

My man may look slow, but I can't kick
'Cause he knows a lots of little dirty tricks
That's why I'm sinful as can be

Goin' down to the river, take a rope and a rock
Tie it around my neck, jump over the dock
That's why I'm sinful as can be

I want all you girls to let my man be
Everything he got belongs to me
That's why I'm sinful as can be

Get your pistol, I got mine
Been mistreated, don't mind dyin'
That's why I'm sinful as can be

I told all you girls to leave my man alone
There's nothin' in the streets he can't get at home
That's why I'm sinful as can be.

SING SING PRISON BLUES (*Porter Grainger and F. Johnson*)

Gonna journey up the Hudson, goin' on a lonesome trail
Gonna journey up the Hudson, goin' on a lonesome trail
They can put me in the death house, or keep me in the Sing Sing Jail

I wrote and asked the warden why they call the jail the Sing Sing
I wrote and asked the warden why they call the jail the Sing Sing
He said stand here by this rock pile and listen to them hammers ring

Big doin' in the courthouse, paper sellin' for fifty cents
Big doin's in the courthouse, papers sellin' for fifty cents
All the judge tryin' to tell me, my lawyer pleadin' self-defense

The judge said, "Listen, Bessie, tell me why you killed your man."
The judge said, "Listen, Bessie, tell me why you killed your man."
I said, "Judge, you ain't no woman, and you can't understand."

You can send me up the river or send me to that mean old jail
You can send me up the river or send me to that mean old jail
I killed my man and I don't need no bail.

SLOW AND EASY MAN (*S. Red*)

Don't care where he is, don't care what he does
All my love is his, he's my only one
Find my slow and easy man

Folks call him a rat, I don't care about that
He's the one that knows where he's stayin' at
Find my slow and easy man

Met them here and there, met them everywhere
He's the only man that can make me care
Find my slow and easy man

Don't care if he's up, don't care if he's down
Kisses is my cup, sweetest man in town
Find my slow and easy man

Though he curse and fight, wouldn't treat me right
Love him just the same, so sweet and nice
Find my slow and easy man

Hear my lonesome wail, if he's back in jail
I would sell my soul just to raise his bail
Find my slow and easy man.

SOBBIN' HEARTED BLUES (*P. Bradford*)

You treated me wrong, I treated you right
I worked for you both day and night

You bragged to women that I was your fool
So now I've got them sobbin' hearted blues

The sun's gon' shine in my back door some day
The sun's gon' shine in my back door some day
It's true I love you, but I won't take mean treatments anymore

All I want is your picture, it must be in a frame
All I want is your picture, and it must be in a frame
When you're gone, I can see you just the same

I'm gon' start walkin' 'cause I got a wooden pair of shoes
I'm gon' start walkin', I got a wooden pair of shoes
Gon' keep on walkin' 'til I lose these sobbin' hearted blues.

SOFT PEDAL BLUES (*Bessie Smith*)

There's a lady in our neighborhood who runs a buffet flat
And when she gives a party, she knows just where she's at

She give a dance last Friday night that was to last 'til one
But when the time was almost up, the fun had just begun

But she walked into the room and yelled to the crowd
"Have all the fun, ladies and gentlemen, but don't make it too loud.

"Oh, please, Mr. Leaderman, play it all night long
I like the words and music to this little song
How it moans away, it's nearly break of day

"Early in the morn, so put that soft pedal on
I'm drunk and full of fun—YAHOO!
Go and spread the news, I've got them soft pedalin' blues

"Early in the morn, so put that soft pedal on
I'm drunk and full of fun—YAHOO!
Go and spread the news, 'cause I've got them soft pedalin' blues
Early in the mornin'—YAHOO!—I've got them soft pedalin' blues."

SORROWFUL BLUES (*Bessie Smith and Irving Johns*)

If you catch me stealin', I don't mean no harm
If you catch me stealin', I don't mean no harm
It's a mark in my family and it must be carried on

I got nineteen men and I want one mo'
I got nineteen men and I want one mo'
If I get that one more, I'll let that nineteen go

I'm gonna tell you, daddy, like the Chinaman told the Jew
I'm gonna tell you, daddy, like the Chinaman told the Jew
If you don't likey me, me sho' don't likey you

It's hard to love another woman's man
It's hard to love another woman's man
You can't get him when you want him, you got to catch him when you can

Have you ever seen peaches grow on sweet potato vine?
Have you ever seen peaches grow on sweet potato vine?
Just step in my backyard and take a peep at mine.

SPIDER MAN BLUES (*Bessie Smith and H. Gray*)

Early in the mornin' when it's dark and dreary outdoors
Early in the mornin' when it's dark and dreary outdoors
Spider man makes a web and hides while you sleeps and snores

Never try to sleep, mean eyes watch me day and night
Never try to sleep, mean eyes watchin' day and night
Catch every fly as fast as she can light

That black man of mine sure has his spider ways
That black man of mine sure has his spider ways
Been crawlin' after me all of my natural days

I'm like a poor fly, spider man, please let me go
I'm like a poor fly, spider man, please let me go
You've got me locked up in your house and I can't break down your door

Somebody please kill me and throw me in the sea
Somebody please kill me and throw me in the sea
This spider man of mine is going to be the death of poor me.

SQUEEZE ME (*Clarence Williams and Thomas "Fats" Waller*)

Daddy, you've been doggone sweet on me
Daddy, you the only one I see
You know I need but you, 'cause you my man
You can love me like no one can

Somethin' 'bout you I can't resist
And when you kiss me, daddy, I stay kissed

Now, daddy, squeeze me, squeeze me again
Oh, daddy, don't stop 'til I tell you when
Now, daddy, squeeze me, kiss me some more
Oh, Lord, like you did before

Your papa Cupid is standing close by
Now, daddy, don't let sweet baby cry
Pick me up on your knee
I just get so, you know, when you squeeze me

Squeeze me, squeeze me again
Now, daddy, don't stop 'til I tell you when
Now, daddy, squeeze me, kiss me some more
Oh, Lord, like you did before

Your papa Cupid is standing close by
Daddy, don't let sweet mama cry
Pick me up on your knee
I just get so, you know, daddy, when you squeeze me.

STANDIN' IN THE RAIN BLUES (*Bessie Smith*)

Standin' in the rain and ain't a drop fell on me
Standin' in the rain and ain't a drop fell on me
My clothes is all wet, but my flesh is as dry as can be

It can rain all day, I ain't got no place to go
It can rain all day, I ain't got no place to go
Because it's cold outside in that ice and snow

If it rain five days, that won't give me no blues
If it rain five days, that won't give me no blues
I've got my raincoat and hat, umbrella, boots and shoes

Rain, rain, rain, don't rain on me all day
Rain, rain, rain, don't rain on me all day
'Cause if I get too wet, I've got to go into the house and stay.

ST. LOUIS BLUES (*W. C. Handy*)

I hate to see the evening sun go down
I hate to see the evening sun go down
It makes me think I'm on my last go 'round

Feelin' tomorrow like I feel today
Feelin' tomorrow like I feel today
I'll pack my grip and make my getaway

St. Louis woman wears her diamond ring
Pulls a man around by her apron string

Wasn't for powder and this store-bought hair
The man I love wouldn't go nowhere, nowhere

I got them St. Louis blues, just as blue as I can be
He's got a heart like a rock cast in the sea
Or else he would not go so far from me.

ST. LOUIS GAL (*J. R. Robinson*)

Worried in the nighttime, worried in the day
'Cause another sweetie took my man away

Down in St. Louis, there I lost my pride and joy
St. Louis woman stole the heart of my big boy

I'm cryin', St. Louis gal, just look what you done done, I said what you done
    done
St. Louis gal, you gonna have some fun, I mean a lots of fun

I'm always cryin' the blues, both night and day
Now that he's gone

But you will shake in your shoes, hear what I say
'Cause some fine morn without any warning

St. Louis gal, I'm gonna handle you, I said manhandle you
You'll find yourself in a jam, as sure as anything what am

Down in Missouri there'll come a time
Your life won't be worth a dime
You stole my pal, St. Louis gal

I'm going a huntin', root-dooti-doot
You know just what I'm gonna shoot
You stole my pal, St. Louis gal.

SWEET MISTREATER (*H. Creamer and J. Johnson*)

He was a Jack from Jacksonville, she was a Lou from Louisville
Oh, this high brown daddy fell like old pussy in the well
She used to vamp him now and then, then run around with other men
So on the telephone every night, he'd call and moan

"Oh, you mistreater, oh, you lowdown cheater, no one can be so sweet when
    you're lovin' you
But when you strut your Lizzy and you knock them dizzy
When you mess around and cheat the way you do
When you out, there's no doubt, you as smart as can be
But how come you so dumb when you easin' home to me?
Oh, you lowdown cheater, oh, you red hot mistreater
Oh, sweet mistreater, don't mistreat me so

"Oh, you mistreater, oh, you dirty mistreater, no one can be so sweeter when you
    are lovin' you
Oh, you look so willin', but this wait is killin'
Tell me, how come you save it the way you do?
Yeah, you wring and you twist and you can't leave soon enough
Unless someone insists they will let you do your stuff
Oh, tell Saint Peter, you a no-good cheater
Oh, sweet mistreater, don't mistreat me so."

'TAIN'T NOBODY'S BIZNESS IF I DO (*Porter Grainger and E. Robbins*)

There ain't nothin' I can do or nothin' I can say
That folks don't criticize me
But I'm going to do just as I want to anyway
And don't care if they all despise me

If I should take a notion to jump into the ocean
'Tain't nobody's bizness if I do, do, do, do

If I go to church on Sunday, then just shimmy down on Monday
'Tain't nobody's bizness if I do, if I do

If my friend ain't got no money and I say take all mine, honey
'Tain't nobody's bizness if I do, do, do, do
If I give him my last nickel and it leaves me in a pickle
'Tain't nobody's bizness if I do, if I do

Well, I'd rather my man would hit me than to jump right up and quit me
'Tain't nobody's bizness if I do, do, do, do
I swear I won't call no copper if I'm beat up by my papa
'Tain't nobody's bizness if I do, if I do.

TAKE IT RIGHT BACK ('CAUSE I DON'T WANT IT HERE) (*H. Gray*)

You came home about half past three
Wakin' me up, papa, you was botherin' me
Take it right back to the place where you got it
I don't want a bit of it left here

You just leapin' and rollin' drunk
Smellin' just like you been with any old skunk
Take it right back to the place where you got it
Mama don't want a bit of it left here

Please, let me understand
I don't want nothin' that is secondhand
Take it right back to the place where you got it
You can't leave a bit of it in here

When I tell you that I'm good and through
There ain't nothin' that your mama wouldn't do
Take it right back to the place where you got it
You can't leave a bit of it in here

Been your cook but I'm gettin' you told
You got the last of my jelly roll
Take it right back to the place where you got it, child
You shan't leave a bit of it in here

You just like one of these old tomcats
Always chasin' these no-good rats

Take it right back to the place where you got it
You can't leave a bit of it in here

Don't come shootin' your no-good sass
You ain't got nothin' that I must have
Take it right back to the place where you got it
You can't leave a bit of it in here

I ain't worried, I'm doin' very fine
You keep yours and I'll hold on to mine
Take it right back to the place where you got it
You can't leave a bit of it in here

If you think that I miss you, sir
That's simply your D.B.A.
Take it right back to the place where you got it
I'm gonna pick up the broom and sweep it outta here.

TAKE ME FOR A BUGGY RIDE (*S. Wilson*)

You my man, you so nice and brown
Sweetest man in this town

I heard you say you was goin' away
And leavin' here to stay

I feel like I could cry
And here's the reason why

Daddy, you really knows your stuff when you take me for a buggy ride
I like you when you got your habits on, you can shift your gear with so much
    pride

I gets a funny feelin' when you gaze into my eyes
You give me such a thrill you make my thermometer rise

I'm happy when you by my side
When you take me for a buggy ride

Daddy, you as sweet as you can be when you take me for a buggy ride
When you set me down upon your knee and ask me to be your bride

When you hug and kiss me, it makes me feel fine
I gets this funny feelin' up and down my spine

You don't need no teachin', you don't need no guide
When you take me for a buggy ride

Your lovin' ain't so forte in the park
But you a lovin' poor creature in the dark

You ain't so hot, what can it be
That makes me say, "Daddy, take all of me."

You always ready every time that I call
What I like about you, you never stall

You ain't no preacher, you a good old soul
You done sent salvation to my sorry soul

I can't kick, but I'm satisfied
When you take me for a buggy ride.

THEM "HAS BEEN" BLUES (*W. E. Skidmore and M. Walker*)

Maybe you'd like to know, know why I'm blue, know why I'm blue, know why
    I'm blue
Maybe some day, it might happen to you, yes, it might happen to you
When I tell my story, listen, please do
It's sad but true, please hear it through
Now, if you've got a papa, then you will know just why the blues affect me so

Did you ever wake up with the sun's early rise
And feel around the place where your sweet sweet papa lies
And when you find that he's gone, and his pillow ain't even warm
Prepare yourself for the news, child, you've got them has been blues

You reach out for your stockings, you reach out for your skirt
You don't know what you're doing, your feelings sho' is hurt
You try to find your wrapper, can't even find your hat
You stumble over the rocker, then you start to curse the cat

Rush to the front door and pull it open wide
Then you find the message stickin' right outside
It reads, "Goodbye, sweet mama, now don't you feel so blue
I've got another woman that's a better gal than you."

Did you ever wake up with the sun's early rise
And you feel around the place where your man used to lay
And then you rush to hang your head, and climb right back in bed
Be satisfied with the news, Lord, you got them has been blues.

THEM'S GRAVEYARD WORDS (G. *Brooks*)

I've got a man I had for a year, but he just won't treat me right
He knocked me silly with a rocking chair 'cause I stayed out one night

But he done got my goat, 'cause he told me to my face
That he done bought some gal a new fur coat, and she's done taken my place

Won't somebody open up his eyes, 'cause that is graveyard words
And I'll show him before he dies that them is graveyard words

I can see the undertaker puttin' flowers on doors
And a traveler goin' where he never come back no mo'

Tell him that I'll fix him sure as two and two is four, 'cause them is graveyard
    words
Go and tell him that he is slowly dyin', 'cause them is graveyard words
Please don't let me lose my rightful mind, 'cause them is graveyard words

I done polished up my pistol, my razor's sharpened too
He'll think the world done fell on him when my dirty work is through
Tell him that I'll do just what I said I'll do, 'cause them is graveyard words.

THERE'LL BE A HOT TIME IN THE OLD TOWN
TONIGHT (T. *Metz*)

Come along, get ready, wear your brand brand new gown
For there's going to be a meeting in this good good old town
When you know everybody and they all know you
And you get a rabbit foot to keep away them hoodoo

When you hear that the preachin' has began
Bend down low for to drive away your sin
When you get religion you'll want to shout and sing
There'll be a hot time in old town tonight, my baby

When you hear them bells go ding-a-ling
All join around and sweetly you must sing
When the birds ensue and the chorus will all join in
There'll be a hot time in old town tonight

There'll be girls for everybody in this good good old town
There's Miss Gonzola Davis and Miss Gondula Brown
There's Miss Henrietta Beezer and she's all dressed in red
I just hugged and kissed her, and to me then she said

"Please, oh, please, oh, do not let me fall
You are mine and I love you best of all
You'll be my man, or I'll have no man at all."
There'll be a hot time in old town tonight, my baby

When you hear them bells go ding-a-ling
All join around and sweetly you must sing
When the birds ensue and the chorus will all join in
There'll be a hot time in old town tonight.

THINKING BLUES (*Bessie Smith*)

Did you ever set thinkin' with a thousand things on your mind?
Did you ever set thinkin' with a thousand things on your mind?
Thinking about someone who has treated you so nice and kind

Then you get an old letter and you begin to read
You'll get an old letter and you'll begin to read
Got the blues so bad 'til that man of mine I want to see

Don't you hear me, baby, knockin' on your door?
Don't you hear me, baby, knockin' on your door?
Have you got the nerve to drive me from your door?

Have you got the nerve to say that you don't want me no more?
Have you got the nerve to say that you don't want me no more?
The good book says you've got to reap what you sow

Take me back, baby, try me one more time
Take me back, baby, try me one more time
That's the only way I can get these thinkin' blues off my mind.

TICKET AGENT, EASE YOUR WINDOW DOWN
(*Spencer Williams*)

Tell me what's wrong with me
My man we can't agree
Now he's tried to steal away
That is why you hear me say
Now, I've got the blues, yes, I've got the blues
Gonna sing 'em night and day

Ticket agent, ease your window down
Ticket agent, ease your window down
'Cause my man's done quit me and tried to leave this town

I'd rather see this whole world sloppy drunk
I'd rather see this whole world sloppy drunk
Than to see my man startin' in to pack his trunk

If he don't want me, he had no right to stall
If he didn't want me, he had no right to stall
I can get more men than a passenger train can haul

He stole my money and he pawned my clothes
He stole my money, he pawned my clothes
And which way my daddy went, a gypsy only knows

I hate a man that don't play fair and square
I hate a man that don't play fair and square
'Cause you can get a crooked daddy 'most anywhere.

TROMBONE CHOLLY (*G. Brooks*)

I know a fool that blows a horn, he came from way down South
I ain't heard such blowin' since I was born
When that trombone's in his mouth, he wails and moans, he grunts and groans
He moans just like a cow
Nobody else can do his stuff 'cause he won't teach 'em how
Oh, Cholly, blow that thing, that slide trombone
Make it talk, make it sing, Lordy, where did you get that tone?
If Gabriel knowed how you could blow, he'd let you lead his band, I know
Oh, Cholly, blow that thing, play that slide trombone
Oh, Cholly, do you know you blows a horn
Yes, I swing to and fro when you carryin' on

You ain't seen such shakin' hips like when that horn is to your lips
Oh, Cholly, blow that thing, that slide trombone
Oh, Cholly, make it sing, that slide trombone
You'll even make a king get down off his throne
And he would break a leg, I know, by doin' the Charleston while you blow
Oh, Cholly Green, play that thing, I mean that slide trombone.

WASHWOMAN'S BLUES (*Spencer Williams*)

All day long I'm slavin', all day long I'm bustin' suds
All day long I'm slavin', all day long I'm bustin' suds
Gee, my hands are tired, washin' out these dirty duds

Lord, I do more work than forty-'leven Gold Dust Twins
Lord, I do more work than forty-'leven Gold Dust Twins
Got myself a achin' from my head down to my shins

Sorry I do washin' just to make my livelihood
Sorry I do washin' just to make my livelihood
Oh, the washwoman's life, it ain't a bit of good

Rather be a scullion cookin' in some white folks' yard
Rather be a scullion cookin' in some white folks' yard
I could eat aplenty, wouldn't have to work so hard

Me and my ole washboard sho' do have some cares and woes
Me and my ole washboard sho' do have some cares and woes
In the muddy water, wringin' out these dirty clothes.

WASTED LIFE BLUES (*Bessie Smith*)

I've lived a life but nothin' I've gained
Each day I'm full of sorrow and pain
No one seems to care enough for poor me
To give me a word of sympathy

Oh, me! Oh, my! Wonder what will the end be?
Oh, me! Oh, my! Wonder what will become of poor me?

No father to guide me, no mother to care
Must bear my troubles all alone
Not even a brother to help me share
This burden I must bear alone

Oh, me! Oh, my! Wonder what will my end be?
Oh, me! Oh, my! Wonder what will become of poor me?

I'm settin' and thinkin' of the days gone by
They fills my heart with pain
I'm too weak to stand and too strong to cry
But I'm forgettin' it all in vain

Oh, me! Oh, my! Wonder what will my end be?
Oh, me! Oh, my! Wonder what will become of poor me?

I've traveled and wandered almost everywhere
To get a little joy from life
Still I've gained nothin' but wars and despair
Still strugglin' in this world of strife

Oh, me! Oh, my! Wonder what will my end be?
Oh, me! Oh, my! Wonder what will become of poor me?

WEEPING WILLOW BLUES (*P. Carter*)

I went down to the river, sat beneath the willow tree
The dew dropped on those willow leaves, and it rolled right down on me
And that's the reason I've got those weepin' willow blues

I went up on the mountain, high as any gal could stand
And looked out on the engine that took away my lovin' man
And that's the reason I've got those weepin' willow blues

I heard the whistle blowin', the fireman rang the bell
They're takin' away that willow tree that give me this weepin' spell
And that's the reason I've got those weepin' willow blues

When you're broken hearted and your man is out of town
Go to the river, take the chair and then set down

And if he don't come back to you I'll tell you what to do
Just jump right overboard, 'cause he ain't no more to you

Folks, I love my man, I kiss him mornin', noon, and night
I wash his clothes and keep him clean and try to treat him right

Now he's gone and left me after all I've tried to do
The way he treats me, girls, he'll do the same thing to you
That's the reason I've got those weepin' willow blues.

WHAT'S THE MATTER NOW? (*Clarence Williams and Spencer Williams*)

Papa, papa, Tree Top Tall, hear your lovin' mama call
You ain't doin' so good, you ain't treatin' me like you should
Papa, papa, hear my plea, stop mistreatin' me
You stay, stay away, that's why you hear me say

What's the matter now, what's the matter now?
Haven't seen you, honey, since way last spring
Tell me, pretty papa, have you broke that thing?
What's the matter now, say we can't get along somehow
I ain't had no sugar in a long time
Tell me, what's the matter now, daddy, tell me what's the matter now?

What's the matter now, what's the matter now?
You never give me lovin' like a daddy should
Tell me, do you really think I'm made of wood?
What's the matter now, cruel daddy, we can't get along somehow
Mama wants some honey from that honeycomb
Tell me, what's the matter now, daddy, tell me what's the matter now?

WHOA, TILLIE, TAKE YOUR TIME (*T. Layton and H. Creamer*)

Tillie Brown was a dancin' fool
Spent her time in a dancin' school
When the band would play
Tillie would start ready to sway
First one out on the ballroom floor
She never got enough, she just craved for more
When she start to sway, all the girls and boys would say

"Whoa, Tillie, take your time, whoa, Tillie, take your time
There ain't no use to hurryin' 'cause you want to prance

You got all night to do that dance
Whoa, Tillie, lay 'em down, whoa, Tillie Brown
You don't know what to shake, when you shake, what you break
Whoa, Tillie, take your time

"Whoa, Tillie, take your time, whoa, Tillie, take your time
There ain't no use to hurryin' 'cause you want to prance
Look out there, Tillie, you got all night to do that dance
Whoa, Tillie, lay 'em down, whoa, Tillie, Tillie Brown
You don't know what to shake, when you shake, what you break
Whoa, Tillie, take your time."

WOMAN'S TROUBLE BLUES (*Jack Gee**)

When a woman gets in trouble, everybody throws her down
When a woman gets in trouble, everybody throws her down
She'll look for her friends, and none can be found

I got to go to jail innocent, I got to do my time
I got to go to jail innocent, I got to do my time
Because the judge is so cruel, he won't take no fine

When I get out I'm gonna leave this town
When I get out I'm gonna leave this town
Everybody'll miss me when they don't see me around

There ain't but one thing worries my troublin' mind
There ain't but one thing worries my troublin' mind
The man I love left me behind

My man left me, that's why I'm all confused
My man left me, that's why I'm all confused
He left me with them troublin' blues.

*Edward Brooks, in The Bessie Smith Companion, suggests that Smith, rather than Gee, probably composed this song.

WORK HOUSE BLUES (*T. Wallace*)

Everybody's cryin' the work house blues all day, oh Lord, oh Lord
The work is so hard, thirty days is so long, oh Lord, oh Lord
I can't plow, I can't cook, if I'd ran away, wouldn't that be good

'Cause I'm goin' to the Nation, goin' to the territor'
Say I'm bound for the Nation, bound for the territor'
I got to leave here, I got to get the next train home

Work house sets way out on a long old lonesome road
Work house sets way out on a long old lonesome road
I'm a hard luck gal, catch the devil everywhere I go

Say, I wished I had me a heaven of my own
Say, I wished I had a heaven of my own
I'd give all those poor girls a long old happy home

Say, he used to be mine, but look who's got him now
Say, he used to be mine, but look who's got him now
Say, she sure can keep him, he don't mean her no good nohow.

WORN OUT PAPA (*Spencer Williams*)

Papa, papa, you in a good man's way
Papa, papa, you in a good man's way
I can find one better than you any time of day

You ain't no good so you better haul your freight
You ain't no good, you better haul your freight
Mama wants a live wire, papa, you can take the gate

I'm a red hot woman, just full of flamin' youth
I'm a red hot woman, just full of flamin' youth
You can't call me, daddy, you no good, that's the truth

All my time I wasted havin' you to bother me
All my time I wasted havin' you to bother me
You give me the willies, now I'm glad I'm free

I'm one woman don't want no no-good man
Yes, I'm one woman don't want no no-good man
You just like a worn out, badly bent electric fan

Your youth done failed, all your pep's done gone
Your youth done failed, all your pep's done gone
Pick up that suitcase, man, and travel on.

YELLOW DOG BLUES (*W. C. Handy*)

Ever since Miz Suzy Johnson lost her jockey Lee
There's been much excitement and more to be

You can hear moanin', moanin' night and morn
She's wonderin' where her easy rider's gone

Cablegram goes off in inquiry
Telegram goes off in sympathy

Letters came from down in 'Bam
Everywhere that Uncle Sam
Is the ruler of delivery*

All day the phone rings, it's not for me
At last good tidings fill my heart with glee
This message came from Tennessee

"Dear Sue, your easy rider struck this burg today
On a southbound rattler beside the Pullman car
I seen him there, and he was on the hog."

All you easy riders got to stay away
They had to vamp it but the hike ain't far
He's gone to where the Southern cross the Yellow Dog.

Handy's words are: "Everywhere that Uncle Sam/Has the Rural Free Delivery."

YES, INDEED HE DO (*Porter Grainger*)

I don't know what makes it rain, can't tell what makes it snow
Well, I don't claim to know it all, but there's some things I do know

There's one thing in particular that I never have to guess
I ask myself this question, and I have to tell me yes

Oh, do my sweet, sweet daddy love me? Yes, indeed he do
Is he true as stars above me? What kind of fool is you?

He don't stay from home all night more than six times a week
No, I know that I'm his Sheba, and I know that he's my sheik

And when I ask him where he's been, he grabs a rocking chair
Then he knocks me down and says, "It's just a little love lick, dear."

But if some woman looks at him, I'll tear her half in two
Oh, do my sweet, sweet daddy love me? Yes, indeed he do

Of course my sweet daddy loves me, yes, indeed he do
If he beats me or mistreats me, what is that to you?

I don't have to do no work except to wash his clothes
And darn his socks and press his pants and scrub the kitchen floor

I wouldn't take a million for my sweet, sweet daddy Jim
And I wouldn't give a quarter for another man like him

Gee, ain't it great to have a man that's crazy over you?
Oh, do my sweet, sweet daddy love me? Yes, indeed he do.

YODELING BLUES (*Clarence Williams*)

The blues, the blues, the yodeling blues
They seem to haunt me all the time
Because I ain't got no one that will console my mind

It seems to me no happiness will I ever find, no happiness will I find

Lord, Lord, Lord, Lord, Lord, Lord, Lord, Lord
My man went out without a cause

I wonder who put them jinx on me, I said them jinx on me
I wonder who put them jinx on me, low down jinx on me
My man gone back to his used to be

I'm gonna yodel, yodel my blues away, I said my blues away
I'm gonna yodel, yodel my blues away (YEE HOO!)
I'm gonna yodel 'til things come back my way

I've got the blues, oh spread the news
I've got those doggone yodelin' blues.

YOU DON'T UNDERSTAND (*Clarence Williams,*
  Spencer Williams, and J. Johnson)

Here I am, girls of mine, pleading but it's all in vain
Gee, I am out of line, can't we make it up again
You know, baby, there's no maybe, I love only you
You the only one and no one else will do

It makes me forgive when you turn me away
But I know, dear, that you don't understand
Won't you believe anything I say
But I know, dear, that you don't understand

Open up your heart, let me in your heart, I'm pleadin'
No one else will do 'cause it's only you I'm needin'
My faith you hold, my love in your hands
But I know, dear, that you don't understand

I'm so blue, in despair, 'cause you have turned me down
I don't know if you care I don't come around
You know, honey, it's so funny when you treat me bad
Won't you hear me pleadin', 'cause I'm goin' mad

It makes me cry when you laugh in my face
But I know, dear, that you don't understand
Now I see why I can't hold first place
'Cause I know, dear, that you don't understand

For your love I've strived, sure as I'm alive, I'll bet you
Then you'll forgive, soon you'll forgive, I'll get you
Then you'll see all the things that I've planned
But I know, dear, that you don't understand.

YOUNG WOMAN'S BLUES (*Bessie Smith*)

Woke up this mornin' when chickens were crowin' for day
Felt on the right side of my pillow, my man had gone away

By his pillow he left a note
Readin' "I'm sorry, Jane, you got my goat."

No time to marry, no time to settle down
I'm a young woman and ain't done runnin' 'round
I'm a young woman and ain't done runnin' 'round

Some people call me a hobo, some call me a bum
Nobody knows my name, nobody knows what I've done

I'm as good as any woman in your town
I ain't no high yella, I'm a deep killer brown

I ain't gonna marry, ain't gon' settle down
I'm gon' drink good moonshine and run these browns down

See that long lonesome road, Lord, you know it's gotta end
And I'm a good woman and I can get plenty men.

YOU OUGHT TO BE ASHAMED (*Porter Grainger*)

You'll be sorry, daddy, you just wait and see, daddy, wait and see
Wouldn't treat a dog the way you treatin' me, like you treatin' me
I'm a total nervous wreck with a millstone 'round my neck, I'm as through as any
    gal can be
Don't be surprised if you see me hangin' from a tree, hangin' from a tree
You ought to be ashamed, shame, ashamed, shame of what you done to me

But daddy, I'm to blame, I'm to blame for lettin' you have my company
I'm a poor weak vessel and I just can't help myself
And daddy, when you quit me I can't crawl up on no shelf
But you ought to be ashamed, shame, ashamed, shame of how you treatin' me
You ought to be ashamed, shame, ashamed, shame of what you done to me

But daddy, I'm the same, just the same, you will find that I will always be
You can dodge me and neglect me, treat me like a hound
I'll be here waitin' for you when you tired a-runnin' 'round
But you ought to be ashamed, shame, ashamed, shame of how you treatin' me.

YOU'VE BEEN A GOOD OLE WAGON (*J. Henry*)

Look-a here, daddy, I want to tell you, please get out of my sight
I'm playin' quits now, right from this very night
You've had your day, don't set around and frown
You've been a good ole wagon, daddy, but you done broke down

Now, you better go to the blacksmith shop, and get yourself overhauled
There's nothing about you to make a good woman fall
Nobody wants a baby when a real man can be found
You've been a good old wagon, daddy, but you done broke down .

When the sun is shining, it's time to make hay
Automobiles are the rage, you can't make that wagon pay

When you were in your prime, you loved to run around
You've been a good old wagon, honey, but you done broke down

There's no need to cry, and make a big show
This man has taught me more about lovin' than you will ever know
He is the king of lovin', this man deserve a crown
He's a good ole wagon, daddy, and he ain't broke down.

YOU'VE GOT TO GIVE ME SOME (*Spencer Williams*)

Lovin' is the thing I crave, for your love I'd be your slave
You gotta gimme some, yes, gimme some
Can't you hear me pleading, you gotta gimme some

Said Miss Jones to old Butcher Pete, "I want a piece of your good old meat
You gotta gimme some, oh, gimme some
I crave your round steak, you gotta gimme some."

Sweet as candy in a candy shop, it's just your sweet, sweet lollipop
You gotta gimme some, please gimme some
I love all-day suckers, you gotta gimme some

To the milkman I heard Mary scream, said she wanted a lots of cream
You gotta gimme some, oh, gimme some
Fetch it when you come, sir, you gotta gimme some

Hear my cryin' on my bended knee, if you wanna put my soul at ease
You gotta gimme some, please gimme some
Can't stand it any longer, you gotta gimme some

Zebra called up camel's sugar lump, said, "I'm goin' crazy about your hump
You gotta gimme some, please gimme some
I can't wait a day, you gotta gimme some."

Jaybird said to the peckerwood, "I'll let you peck like a pecker should
But gimme some, yes, gimme some
I'm crazy 'bout them worms, you gotta gimme some."

NOTES

INTRODUCTION

1. Patricia Hill Collins's *Black Feminist Thought* (Boston: Unwin Hyman, 1990) argues that black feminist knowledges, particularly those that have not been produced in written form, are "subjugated knowledges" in the Foucaultian sense. She draws from oral accounts of everyday practices, as well as from written texts, in her own attempt to constitute a black feminist tradition. It should also be pointed out that Beverly Guy-Sheftall's recently published anthology *Words of Fire: An Anthology of African-American Feminist Thought* (New York: New Press, 1995) includes in the chapter spanning 1920–1957 an article by Communist leader Claudia Jones, which explicitly addresses class issues.

2. Robert Dixon and John Godrich, *Recording the Blues* (New York: Stein & Day, 1970), pp. 33–34. Jackson recorded, on Paramount, Rainey's label. "Papa Charlie had eight records in the 1200 series in 1925—only Ida Cox and Ma Rainey had more—and was one of Paramount's most successful artists for a further five years" (p. 34).

3. Cheryl Wall, "Whose Sweet Angel Child? Blues Women, Langston Hughes, and Writing During the Harlem Renaissance," in Arnold Rampersad, *Langston Hughes: The Man, His Art, and His Continuing Influence*, ed. C. James Trotman (New York: Garland, 1995), p. 39.

4. I borrow this term from Aida Hurtado's work, *The Color of Privilege: Three Blasphemies on Race and Feminism* (Ann Arbor: University of Michigan Press, 1996).

5. See Sandra Lieb's discussion of Ethel Waters's recording of "Oh Daddy Blues." Waters recorded this song in 1921. In 1923 Bessie Smith, Edna Hicks, Mattie Hite and Eva Taylor recorded covers, and in 1927, Gertrude Rainey recorded it as "Oh Papa Blues." *Mother of the Blues: A Study of Ma Rainey* (Amherst: University of Massachusetts Press, 1981), pp. 69–73.

6. Gertrude "Ma" Rainey, "Oh Papa Blues," Paramount 12566, Aug. 1927. Reissued on *Ma Rainey*, Milestone M-47021, 1974.

7. Bessie Smith, "Oh Daddy Blues," Columbia A-3888, Apr. 11, 1923. Reissued on *Bessie Smith: The World's Greatest Blues Singer*, Columbia CG 33, 1972.

8. *The Complete Gertrude "Ma" Rainey Collection 1923/28*, vols. 1–4: King

Jazz KJ 181 FS, KJ 182 FS, KJ 183 FS, and KJ 184 FS, 1994; *Bessie Smith: The Complete Recordings*, vols. 1–5: Columbia C2K 47091 (1991), C2K 47471 (1991), C2K 47474 (1992), C2K 52838 (1993), and C2K 57546 (1996).

9. Daphne Duval Harrison, *Black Pearls: Blues Queens of the 1920s* (New Brunswick: Rutgers University Press, 1988), p. 10.

10. Sherrie Tucker, a graduate student in the History of Consciousness Department at the University of California, Santa Cruz, is writing a book and dissertation on all-women's jazz and swing bands of the 1940s.

11. María Herrera-Sobek, *The Mexican Corrido: A Feminist Analysis* (Bloomington: Indiana University Press, 1990).

12. Based on an oral history with the Hijas de Cuauhtémoc, a 1970s Chicana feminist collective, Maylei Blackwell (like Tucker a graduate student in the History of Consciousness Department at the University of California, Santa Cruz) wrote a qualifying essay entitled "Contested Histories and Retrofitted Memory: Chicana Feminist Subjectivities Between and Beyond Nationalist Imaginaries."

13. Stuart Hall, "What Is This 'Black' in Black Popular Culture?" in Gina Dent, ed., *Black Popular Culture* (Seattle: Bay Press, 1992), p. 27.

I USED TO BE YOUR SWEET MAMA

1. Bessie Smith, "I Used to Be Your Sweet Mama," Columbia 14292-D, Feb. 9, 1928. Reissued on *Empty Bed Blues*, Columbia CG 30450, 1972.

2. According to Hazel Carby, "[w]hat has been called the 'Classic Blues,' the women's blues of the twenties and early thirties, is a discourse that articulates a cultural and political struggle over sexual relations: a struggle that is directed against the objectification of female sexuality within a patriarchal order but which also tries to reclaim women's bodies as the sexual and sensuous objects of song." "It Just Be's Dat Way Sometime: The Sexual Politics of Women's Blues," *Radical America* 20, no. 4 (June–July 1986), p. 12.

3. See Henry Pleasants, *The Great American Popular Singers* (New York: Simon & Schuster, 1974). According to Lawrence Levine, "the physical side of love which, aside from some tepid hand holding and lip pecking, was largely missing from popular music, was strongly felt in the blues." *Black Culture and Black Consciousness: Afro-American Thought from Slavery to Freedom* (New York: Oxford University Press, 1975), p. 279.

4. Bessie Smith's first recording, a cover of Alberta Hunter's "Down Hearted Blues," sold 780,000 copies in less than six months. Chris Albertson, *Bessie* (New York: Stein & Day, 1972), p. 46.

5. The central place of the blues in the elaboration of a postslavery black cultural consciousness has been examined widely in works like LeRoi Jones's pioneering *Blues People* and Lawrence Levine's engaging study *Black Culture and Black Consciousness*. While both suggest important approaches to the understanding of racial dimensions of African-American culture, scant attention is accorded gender consciousness. Daphne Duval Harrison's trailblazing study *Black Pearls* reveals, in fact, how rich women's blues can be as a terrain for explorations of the place gender occupies in black cultural consciousness.

6. See W. E. B. Du Bois, *Black Reconstruction in America* (New York: Harcourt, Brace, 1935).

7. See Herbert Gutman, *The Black Family in Slavery and Freedom, 1750–1925* (New York: Pantheon, 1976), chap. 9.

8. Lawrence Levine cites a rowing song heard by Frances Kemble in the late 1830s and characterized by her as nonsensical, but interpreted by Chadwick Hansen as containing hidden sexual meanings.

> *Jenny shake her toe at me,*
> > *Jenny gone away;*
> *Jenny shake her toe at me,*
> > *Jenny gone away.*
> *Hurrah! Miss Susy, oh!*
> > *Jenny gone away;*
> *Hurrah! Miss Susy, oh!*
> > *Jenny gone away.*

Black Culture and Black Consciousness, p. 11. (Frances Anne Kemble, *Journal of a Residence on a Georgian Plantation in 1838–1839* [1863; reprint, New York: Knopf, 1961], pp. 163–164.) "Chadwick Hansen [in "Jenny's Toe: Negro Shaking Dances in America," *American Quarterly* 19 (1967), pp. 554–63] has shown that in all probability what Miss Kemble heard was not the English word 'toe' but an African-derived word referring to the buttocks." The Jenny of whom the slaves were singing with such obvious pleasure was shaking something more interesting and provocative than her foot.

9. According to James Cone, "The spiritual . . . is the spirit of the people struggling to be free . . . [it] is the people's response to the societal contra-

dictions. It is the people facing trouble and affirming, 'I ain't tired yet.' But the spiritual is more than dealing with trouble. It is a joyful experience, a vibrant affirmation of life and its possibilities in an appropriate esthetic form. The spiritual is the community in rhythm, swinging to the movement of life." *The Spirituals and the Blues: An Interpretation* (New York: Seabury, 1972), pp. 32–33.

10. Popular musical culture in the African-American tradition continues to actively involve the audience in the performance of the music. The distinction, therefore, is not between the relatively active and relatively passive stances of the audience. Rather it is between a mode of musical presentation in which everyone involved is considered a "performer"—or perhaps in which no one, the song leader included, is considered a "performer"—and one in which the producer of the music plays a privileged role in calling forth the responses of the audience.

11. See James Cone's discussion of the liberation content of the spirituals. John Lovell, Jr. (*Black Song: The Forge and the Flame* [New York: Macmillan, 1972]) also emphasizes the relationship between the slave community's yearning for liberation and the music it produced in the religious tradition of Christianity.

12. Levine, p. 175.

13. Religious themes are to be found in some of the prison work songs recorded by folklorists such as Alan Lomax during the thirties, forties, and fifties.

14. See Giles Oakley, *The Devil's Music: A History of the Blues* (New York and London: Harcourt Brace Jovanovich, 1976), pp. 97–99.

15. See Henry Louis Gates, Jr., *The Signifying Monkey: A Theory of African-American Literary Criticism* (New York: Oxford University Press, 1988), chap. 1.

16. See Zora Neale Hurston, *Mules and Men* (Bloomington: Indiana University Press, 1978), stories on Jack and the Devil, p. 164, and about "unh hunh" as a word the Devil made up, p. 169.

17. *Wild Women Don't Have the Blues*, dir. Christine Dall, Calliope Film Resources, 1989, videocassette.

18. When applied to the religious contours and content of slave-initiated cultural community, the infamous observation by the young Karl Marx that religion is the "opium of the people" elucidates the utopian potential of slave religion; but, in this context, Marx's observation simultaneously goes too far and not far enough.

> Religious *suffering is at the same time an* expression *of real suffering and a protest against real suffering. Religion is the sigh of the oppressed creature, the sentiment of a heartless world, and the soul of soulless conditions. It is the* opium *of the people*. . . . *Religion is only the illusory sun around which man revolves so long as he does not revolve around himself.*

Karl Marx, "The Critique of Hegel's Philosophy of Right" in Karl Marx, *Early Writings*, ed. T. B. Bottomore (New York: McGraw-Hill, 1963), pp. 43–44.

Marx goes too far in the sense that he assumes a necessarily and exclusively ideological relationship between religious consciousness and material conditions, i.e., that religion is fundamentally false consciousness and that the "self" or community it articulates is necessarily an illusion. Such an all-embracing conception of religion cannot account for its extrareligious dimensions. On the other hand, he does not go far enough when he dismisses the revolutionary potential of religious consciousness.

19. See Lovell, chaps. 17 and 18.

20. Marx, p. 44.

21. See Houston A. Baker, Jr., *Blues, Ideology, and Afro-American Literature* (Chicago: University of Chicago Press, 1984).

22. Cone, p. 112. C. Eric Lincoln originated the term "secular spirituals."

23. Levine, p. 237.

24. Julio Finn argues that "the jook joint is to the blues what the church is to the spiritual, and the bluesman on stage is in his pulpit. Contrary to the 'holy' atmosphere which reigns in the church, the jook joint is characterized by its rowdiness—the noise and smoke and drinking are necessities without which its character would be fatally altered, for that would alter the music, which is in no small way shaped by it." Julio Finn, *The Bluesman* (London: Quartet, 1986), p. 202. Unfortunately, Finn confines his discussion to blues men and does not consider the role of women.

25. See Joan Landes, "The Public and the Private Sphere: A Feminist Reconsideration," in Johanna Meehan, ed., *Feminists Read Habermas* (London: Routledge, 1995). According to Aida Hurtado in "Relating to Privilege: Seduction and Rejection in the Subordination of White Women and Women of Color" (*Signs: A Journal of Women and Culture in Society*, 14, no. 4, [Summer 1989]), "the public/private distinction is relevant only for the white middle and upper classes since historically the American state has intervened constantly in the private lives and domestic arrangements

of the working class. Women of Color have not had the benefit of the economic conditions that underlie the public/private distinction. Instead the political consciousness of women of Color stems from an awareness that the public is *personally* political."

26. Du Bois points out that in many border states, slave-breeding became a main industry: "The deliberate breeding of a strong, big field-hand stock could be carried out by selecting proper males, and giving them the run of the likeliest females. This in many Border States became a regular policy and fed the slave trade." *Black Reconstruction in America*, p. 44.

27. Gutman, pp. 80 and 388.

28. Slave narratives by Frederick Douglass, Solomon Northrup, and Harriet Jacobs contain poignant descriptions of family separations. See also Gutman, chap. 8.

29. Ralph Ellison, *Shadow and Act* (New York: Vintage, 1972), p. 245.

30. Oakley, p. 59.

31. Angela Y. Davis, *Women, Race, and Class* (New York: Random House, 1981).

32. Bessie Smith, "Sam Jones Blues," Columbia 13005-D, Sept. 24, 1923. Reissued on *Any Woman's Blues*, Columbia G 30126, 1972.

33. Harrison, *Black Pearls*, p. 287.

34. See Mary P. Ryan's discussion of the cult of motherhood in *Womanhood in America: From Colonial Times to the Present* (New York: Franklin Watts, 1975).

35. Bessie Smith, "Poor Man's Blues," Columbia 14399-D, Aug. 24, 1928. Reissued on *Empty Bed Blues*, Columbia CG 30450, 1972.

36. Bessie Smith, "Pinchback Blues," Columbia 14025-D, Apr. 4, 1924. Reissued on *Empty Bed Blues*, Columbia CG 30450, 1972.

37. Bessie Smith, "Take Me for a Buggy Ride," Okeh 8945, Nov. 24, 1933. Reissued on *The World's Greatest Blues Singer*, Columbia CG 33, 1972.

38. Albertson, p. 188. The four songs she recorded on November 24, 1933, were "Do Your Duty," "Gimme a Pigfoot," "Take Me for a Buggy Ride," and "I'm Down in the Dumps."

39. See Edward Brooks, *The Bessie Smith Companion* (New York: Da Capo, 1982), pp. 224–25.

40. Gertrude "Ma" Rainey, "Blame It on the Blues," Paramount 12760, Sept. 1928. Reissued on *Ma Rainey*, Milestone M-47021, 1974.

41. Gertrude "Ma" Rainey, "Shave 'Em Dry," Paramount 12222, 1924. Reissued on *Ma Rainey's Black Bottom*, Yazoo 1071, n.d.

42. Gertrude "Ma" Rainey, "Gone Daddy Blues," Paramount 12526, Aug. 1927. Reissued on *Ma Rainey*, Milestone M-47021, 1974.

43. Gertrude "Ma" Rainey, "Misery Blues," Paramount 12508, Aug. 1927. Reissued on *Blues the World Forgot*, Biograph BLP-12001, n.d.

44. Bessie Smith, "Money Blues," Columbia 14137-D, May 4, 1926. Reissued on *Nobody's Blues but Mine*, Columbia CG 31093, 1972.

45. Bessie Smith, "Young Woman's Blues," Columbia 14179-D, Oct. 1926. Reissued on *Nobody's Blues but Mine*, Columbia CG 31093, 1972.

46. Bessie Smith, "Hateful Blues," Columbia 14023-D, Apr. 9, 1924. Reissued on *Empty Bed Blues*, Columbia CG 30450, 1972.

47. Bessie Smith, "Weeping Willow Blues," Columbia 14042-D, Sept. 26, 1924. Reissued on *Empty Bed Blues*, Columbia CG 30450, 1972.

48. Bessie Smith, "Yes, Indeed He Do," Columbia 14354-D, Aug. 24, 1928. Reissued on *Empty Bed Blues*, Columbia CG 30450, 1972.

49. Bessie Smith, "Safety Mama," Columbia 14634-D, Nov. 20, 1931. Reissued on *The World's Greatest Blues Singer*, Columbia CG 33, 1972.

50. See chap. 3 herein for a more comprehensive discussion of the role of travel in the postslavery male experience and, consequently, in the shaping of the blues. According to Houston Baker, "Afro-Americans—at the bottom even of the vernacular ladder in America—responded to the railroad as a 'meaningful symbol offering both economic progress and the possibility of aesthetic expression.' [James Alan McPherson, *Railroad: Trains and Train People in American Culture* (New York: Random House, 1976), p. 9.] This possibility came from the locomotive's drive and thrust, its promise of unrestrained mobility and unlimited freedom. The blues musician at the crossing . . . became an expert at reproducing or translating these locomotive energies." Baker, *Blues, Ideology, and Afro-American Literature*, p. 11.

51. Robert Johnson, "Hellhound on My Trail." Reissued on Robert Johnson, *The Complete Recordings*, Columbia compact discs C2K 46222, CK 46234, 1990.

52. See Paul Oliver, *The Meaning of the Blues* (New York: Collier, 1960), p. 85.

53. Bessie Smith, "Chicago Bound Blues," Columbia 14000-D, Dec. 4, 1923. Reissued on *Any Woman's Blues*, Columbia G 30126, 1972.

54. Chap. 3 herein examines themes of travel in Gertrude Rainey's blues.

55. Sandra Lieb, *Mother of the Blues*, p. 83.

56. A total of 160 Bessie Smith recordings are available today. However, if

parts I and II of "Empty Bed Blues" are counted as one song—which they
are in some instances (Brooks, for example)—then the total may be given
as 159.

57. Alberta Hunter, "Down Hearted Blues"; Bessie Smith, "Down Hearted
Blues," Columbia A3844, Feb. 16, 1923. Reissued on *The World's Greatest
Blues Singer*, Columbia CG 33, 1972.

58. Paul Garon, *Blues and the Poetic Spirit* (New York: Da Capo, 1978), p. 33.

59. Bessie Smith, "Down Hearted Blues."

60. Gertrude "Ma" Rainey, "Barrel House Blues," Paramount 12082, Dec.
1923. Reissued on *Queen of the Blues*, Biograph BLP-12032, n.d.

61. Daphne Duval Harrison points out that women "employed the bragging,
signifying language of males to boast of fine physical attributes and high-
powered sexual ability. . . . The prurient nature of many of these blues led
to a spate of community activism seeking to ban them. Black newspapers
waged the battle against performers who included them in their repertoire
and accused them of using lewd lyrics as a substitute for talent. This was
clearly not the case because the best of the blues women sang sexual blues
sometimes. Admittedly, some were openly lascivious and left little to the
imagination." *Black Pearls*, p. 106.

62. Bessie Smith, "Mistreatin' Daddy." Columbia 14000-D, Dec. 4, 1923.
Reissued on *Any Woman's Blues*, Columbia G 30126, 1972.

63. Gertrude "Ma" Rainey, "Honey, Where You Been So Long?" Paramount
12200, Mar. 1924. Reissued on *Queen of the Blues*, Biograph BLP-
12032, n.d.

64. Gertrude "Ma" Rainey, "Lawd, Send Me a Man Blues," Paramount 12227,
May 1924. Reissued on *Queen of the Blues*, Biograph BLP-12032, n.d.

65. Bessie Smith, "Baby Doll," Columbia 14147-D, May 4, 1926. Reissued on
Nobody's Blues but Mine, Columbia CG 31093, 1972.

66. See Sara Evans's study, *Personal Politics: The Roots of Women's Liberation in the Civil Rights Movement and the New Left* (New York: Knopf,
1979).

67. See Michere Githae Mugo, *Orature and Human Rights* (Rome: Institute
of South African Development Studies, NUL, Lesotho, 1991).

68. See Oakley's discussion of work and song, pp. 36–46.

69. Bessie Smith, "Yes, Indeed He Do."

70. Brooks, p. 143.

71. Bessie Smith, "Outside of That," Columbia A 3900, Apr. 30, 1923. Reissued on *The World's Greatest Blues Singer*, Columbia CG 33, 1972.

72. See Susan Schechter, *Women and Male Violence: The Visions and Struggles of the Battered Women's Movement* (Boston: South End, 1982), for an examination of the early antiviolence movement. An excellent recent study, specifically focusing on black women and domestic violence, is Beth Richie's *Compelled to Crime: The Gender Entrapment of Battered Women* (New York: Routledge, 1996).

73. References to the Chinese women's revolutionary tactic "speak bitterness" or "speak pains to recall pains" can be found in many of the second-wave feminist writings on consciousness-raising. See, for example, Robin Morgan's *Sisterhood Is Powerful: An Anthology of Writings from the Women's Liberation Movement* (New York: Vintage, 1970), p. xxv. See also Irene Pesliki's widely circulated document, "Resistances to Consciousness." It can be found in Morgan's *Sisterhood Is Powerful* and Leslie B. Tanner's edited volume *Voices from Women's Liberation* (New York: Signet, 1971).

74. Gertrude "Ma" Rainey, "Black Eye Blues," Paramount, 12963, Sept. 1928. Reissued on *Ma Rainey*, Milestone M-47021, 1974.

75. Bessie Smith. "Please Help Me Get Him off My Mind," Columbia 14375, Aug. 24, 1928. Reissued on *Empty Bed Blues*, Columbia CG 30450, 1972.

76. Bessie Smith, "It Won't Be You," Columbia 14338-D, Feb. 21, 1928. Reissued on *Empty Bed Blues*, Columbia CG 30450, 1972.

77. Bessie Smith, "Slow and Easy Man," Columbia 14384-D, Aug. 24, 1928. Reissued on *Empty Bed Blues*, Columbia CG 30450, 1972.

78. Bessie Smith, "Eavesdropper's Blues," Columbia 14010-D, Jan. 9, 1924. Reissued on *Any Women's Blues*, Columbia G 30126, 1972.

79. Bessie Smith, "Love Me Daddy Blues," Columbia 14060-D, Dec. 12, 1924. Reissued on *The Empress*, Columbia CG 30818, 1972.

80. Bessie Smith. "Hard Driving Papa," Columbia 14137-D, May 4, 1926. Reissued on *Nobody's Blues but Mine*, Columbia CG 31093, 1972.

81. Bessie Smith, " 'Tain't Nobody's Bizness If I Do," Columbia A3898, Apr. 26, 1923. Reissued on *The World's Greatest Blues Singer*, Columbia CG 33, 1972.

82. Brooks, p. 109.

83. Bessie Smith, " 'Tain't Nobody's Bizness If I Do."

84. Ibid.

85. Gertrude "Ma" Rainey, "Sweet Rough Man," Paramount 12926, Sept. 1928. Reissued on *Ma Rainey*, Milestone M-47021, 1974.

86. Lieb, p. 120.

87. Carby, p. 18.

88. Rainey, "Sweet Rough Man."

89. "All magic is word magic, incantation and exorcism, blessing and curse. Through Nommo, the word, man establishes his mastery over things. 'In the beginning was the Word, and the Word was with God, and the Word was God,' so begins the gospel according to St. John, and it looks as if Nommo and the *logos* of St. John agreed. Yet the apostle continues: 'The same (i.e. the word) was in the beginning with God. All things were made by it and without it was not anything made that was made.' In the gospels the word remains with God, and man has to testify to it and proclaim it. Nommo, on the other hand, was also, admittedly, with Amma, or God, in the beginning, but beyond that everything comes into being only through the word, and as there is Muntu [human being], the word is with the muntu. Nommo does not stand above and beyond the earthly world. *Logos* becomes flesh only in Christ, but Nommo becomes 'flesh' everywhere. According to the apostle, *Logos* has made all things, once for all, to become as they are, and since then all generated things remain as they are, and undergo no further transformation. Nommo, on the other hand, goes on unceasingly creating and procreating, creating even gods." Janheinz Jahn, *Muntu: The New African Culture* (New York: Grove, 1961), p. 132.

90. Paula Giddings, *When and Where I Enter: The Impact of Black Women on Race and Sex in America* (New York: Morrow, 1984). See chaps. 5 and 6.

91. See Ida B. Wells, *Crusade for Justice: The Autobiography of Ida B. Wells,* ed. Alfreda M. Duster (Chicago and London: University of Chicago Press, 1970).

92. See Paula Giddings for historical account of the origins of the myth of the Black rapist as a political weapon (p. 27).

93. See Alice Walker's discussion of the attack on *The Color Purple* by prominent black men in *The Same River Twice: Honoring the Difficult: A Meditation on Life, Spirit, Art, and the Making of the Film "The Color Purple," Ten Years Later* (New York: Simon & Schuster, 1996).

94. Bessie Smith, "Black Mountain Blues," Columbia 14554-D, June 22, 1930. Reissued on *The World's Greatest Blues Singer,* Columbia CG 33, 1972.

95. Bessie Smith, "Sinful Blues," Columbia 114052-D, Dec. 11, 1924. Reissued on *The Empress,* Columbia CG 30818, 1972.

96. Gertrude "Ma" Rainey, "See See Rider Blues," Paramount 12252, Dec. 1925. Reissued on *Ma Rainey*, Milestone M-47021, 1974.

97. Gertrude "Ma" Rainey, "Rough and Tumble Blues," Paramount 12303, 1926. Reissued on *The Immortal Ma Rainey*, Milestone MLP-2001, 1966.

98. Bessie Smith, "Them's Graveyard Words," Columbia 14209-D, Mar. 3, 1927. Reissued on *The Empress*, Columbia CG 30818, 1972.

99. Gertrude "Ma" Rainey, "Cell Bound Blues," Paramount 12257, 1925. Reissued on *The Immortal Ma Rainey*, Milestone MLP-2001, 1966.

100. Bessie Smith, "Sing Sing Prison Blues," Columbia 14051-D, Dec. 6, 1924. Reissued on *The Empress*, Columbia CG 30818, 1972.

101. Bessie Smith, "Send Me to the 'Lectric Chair," Columbia 14209-D, Mar. 3, 1927. Reissued on *The Empress*, Columbia, CG 30818, 1972. A barlow is a large pocketknife with one blade.

102. Bessie Smith, "Hateful Blues."

103. Albertson, pp. 132–33.

104. Harrison, pp. 111, 64.

105. Ida Cox, "Wild Women Don't Have the Blues," Paramount 12228, 1924. Reissued on *Wild Women Don't Have the Blues*, Riverside RLP 9374, n.d.

106. Bessie Smith, "Easy Come, Easy Go Blues," Columbia 14005-D, Jan. 10, 1924. Reissued on *Any Woman's Blues*, Columbia G 30126, 1972.

107. Gertrude "Ma" Rainey, "Prove It on Me Blues," Paramount 12668, June 1928. Reissued on *Ma Rainey*, Milestone M-47021, 1974.

108. Lieb, p. 125.

109. *Lesbian Concentrate: A Lesbianthology of Songs and Poems*, Olivia Records MU 29729, 1977.

110. Carby, p. 18.

111. See text of Memphis Willie B. Borum's "Bad Girl Blues" in Eric Sackheim, ed., *The Blues Line* (New York: Schirmer, 1968), p. 288.

112. Gertrude "Ma" Rainey, "Sissy Blues," Paramount 12384, 1928. Reissued on *Oh My Babe Blues*, Biograph BLP-12011, n.d.

MAMA'S GOT THE BLUES

1. Gertrude "Ma" Rainey, "Trust No Man," Paramount 12395, Aug. 1926. Reissued on *Ma Rainey*, Milestone M-47021, 1974.

2. Paula Giddings, *When and Where I Enter*, p. 95.

3. Mary Church Terrell, "What Role Is the Educated Negro Woman to Play in the Uplifting of Her Race?" quoted in Giddings, p. 98.

4. This theme of the Black women's club movement was first formulated by Fannie Barrier Williams in an address she gave at a worldwide gathering of women during the 1893 World Columbian Exposition:

    I regret the necessity of speaking to the question of the moral progress of our women because the morality of our home life has been commented on so despairingly and meanly that we are placed in the unfortunate position of being defenders of our name. . . . While I duly appreciate the offensiveness of all references to American slavery, it is unavoidable to charge to that system every moral imperfection that mars the character of the colored American. The whole life and power of slavery depended upon an enforced degradation of everything human in the slaves. The slave code recognized only animal distinctions between the sexes and ruthlessly ignored those ordinary separations of the sexes that belong to the social state. It is a great wonder that two centuries of such demoralization did not work a complete extinction of all the moral instincts.

    The Present Status and Intellectual Progress of Colored Women (Chicago, 1893), quoted in Eleanor Flexner, *Century of Struggle: The Woman's Rights Movement in the United States* (New York: Atheneum, 1974), pp. 187–88.

5. Gertrude "Ma" Rainey. "Prove It on Me Blues," Paramount 12668, June 1928. Reissued on *Ma Rainey*, Milestone M-47021, 1974.

6. Bessie Smith, "A Good Man Is Hard to Find," Columbia 14250-D, Sept. 27, 1927. Reissued on *The Empress*, Columbia CG 30818, 1972.

7. W. E. B. Du Bois, *Darkwater: Voices from Within the Veil* (New York: Harcourt, Brace & Howe, 1920). See Patricia Hill Collins's account of the epistemological implications of this discourse in *Black Feminist Thought*.

8. See Angela Y. Davis, *Women, Race, and Class*, chap. 1.

9. Gertrude "Ma" Rainey, "Rough and Tumble Blues," Paramount 112311, 1926. Reissued on *The Immortal Ma Rainey*, Milestone MLP-2001, 1966.

10. Gertrude "Ma" Rainey, "Wringing and Twisting Blues," Paramount 12338, Dec. 1925. Reissued on *The Immortal Ma Rainey*, Milestone MLP-2001, 1966. In another verse, the means of poisoning the rival are detailed:

    I had some green cucumbers, some half done tripe and greens
    Some buttermilk and codfish, some sour kidney beans.

These images from black culinary culture reflect a number of myths—as well as realities—regarding dangerous foods: unripe cucumbers, uncooked pork, milk and fish (considered a deadly combination), and beans gone bad.

11. Bessie Smith, "Any Woman's Blues," Columbia 13001-D, Oct. 16, 1923. Reissued on *Any Woman's Blues*, Columbia G 30126, 1972.

12. Bessie Smith, "St. Louis Gal," Columbia 13005-D, Sept. 24, 1923. Reissued on *Any Woman's Blues*, Columbia G 30126, 1972.

13. Bessie Smith, "Empty Bed Blues," Columbia 14312-D, Mar. 20, 1928. Reissued on *Empty Bed Blues*, Columbia CG 30450, 1972.

14. Bessie Smith, "He's Got Me Goin'," Columbia 14464-D, Aug. 20, 1929. Reissued on *Any Woman's Blues*, Columbia G 30126, 1972.

15. As an aside, this makes for an interesting contribution to the debate on modernism and African-American culture, especially considering the similarities between the techniques associated with Cubism in the visual arts and the blues perspective. See Houston Baker's *Modernism and the Harlem Renaissance* (Chicago and London: University of Chicago Press, 1987).

16. Gertrude "Ma" Rainey, "Sleep Talking Blues," Paramount 12760, Sept. 1928. Reissued on *Ma Rainey*, Milestone M-47021, 1974.

17. Gertrude "Ma" Rainey, "Jealous Hearted Blues," Paramount 12252, Dec. 1925. Reissued on *Ma Rainey*, Milestone M-47021, 1974.

18. Gertrude "Ma" Rainey, "Jealousy Blues," Paramount 12364, March 1926. Reissued on *Oh My Babe Blues*, Biograph BLP-12011, n.d..

19. Bessie Smith, "My Man Blues," Columbia 14098-D, Sept. 1925. Reissued on *Nobody's Blues but Mine*, Columbia CG 31093, 1972.

20. Brooks, *The Bessie Smith Companion*, p. 95.

21. Bessie Smith, "Lookin' for My Man Blues," Columbia 14569-D, Sept. 28, 1927. Reissued on *The Empress*, Columbia CG 30818, 1972.

22. Rainey, "Trust No Man."

23. Bessie Smith. "Keep It to Yourself," Columbia 14516-D, Mar. 27, 1930. Reissued on *Any Woman's Blues*, Columbia G 30126, 1972.

24. Harrison, *Black Pearls*, p. 110.

25. Levine, *Black Culture and Black Consciousness*, p. 221.

26. Koko Taylor in *Wild Women Don't Have the Blues*, dir. Christine Dall, Calliope Film Resources, 1989, videocassette.

27. Collins, p. 213

28. Rainey, "Trust No Man."

29. Bessie Smith, "Safety Mama," Columbia 14634-D, Nov. 20, 1931. Reissued on *The World's Greatest Blues Singer*, Columbia CG 33, 1972.

30. Bessie Smith, "Pinchback Blues," Columbia 14025-D, Apr. 5, 1924. Reissued on *Empty Bed Blues*, Columbia CG 30450, 1972.

31. *St. Louis Blues*, dir. Dudley Murphy, Gramercy Studio of RCA Photophone, presented by Radio Pictures, 1929. W. C. Handy coauthored the script for this film, the release of which occasioned a protest by the NAACP.

32. Albertson, *Bessie*, p. 159.

33. Bessie Smith, "A Good Man Is Hard to Find."

34. Gertrude "Ma" Rainey, "Jelly Bean Blues," Paramount 12238, Feb. 1927. Reissued on *Ma Rainey*, Milestone M-47021, 1974.

35. Gertrude "Ma" Rainey, "Moonshine Blues," Paramount 12603, Dec. 1927. Reissued on *Ma Rainey*, Milestone M-47021, 1974.

36. Bessie Smith, "Moonshine Blues," Columbia 14018-D, Apr. 19, 1924. Reissued on *Empty Bed Blues*, Columbia CG 30450, 1972.

37. Bessie Smith, "You Don't Understand," Columbia 14487-D, Oct. 11, 1929. Reissued on *Any Woman's Blues*, Columbia G 30126, 1972.

38. Gertrude "Ma" Rainey, "Titanic Man Blues," Paramount 12374, Jan. 1926. Reissued on *Blues the World Forgot*, Biograph BLP-12001, n.d.

39. Bessie Smith, "I Used to Be Your Sweet Mama," Columbia 1492-D, Feb. 9, 1928. Reissued on *Empty Bed Blues*, Columbia CG 30450, 1972.

HERE COME MY TRAIN

1. Gertrude "Ma" Rainey, "Traveling Blues," Paramount 12706, June 1928. Reissued on *Blues the World Forgot*, Biograph BLP-12001, n.d.

2. William Craft, *Running a Thousand Miles for Freedom; or, The Escape of William and Ellen Craft from Slavery* (1860; reprint, Miami, Fla.: Mnemosyne, 1969).

3. Harriet Brent Jacobs, *Incidents in the Life of a Slave Girl, Written by Herself*, ed. Jean Fagan Yellin (Cambridge: Mass.: Harvard University Press, 1987)

4. Levine, *Black Culture and Black Consciousness*, p. 262.

5. Zora Neale Hurston. *Their Eyes Were Watching God* (New York: Harper & Row, 1990), p. 15.

6. Ben Sidran, *Black Talk* (New York: Da Capo, 1981), p. 24.
7. Finn, *The Bluesman*, p. 199.
8. Lovell, *Black Song*, p. 249.
9. "All God's Children Got Shoes (Wings)," ibid. p. 285.
10. Houston Baker, *Blues, Ideology, and Afro-American Literature*, p. 8.
11. Lieb, *Mother of the Blues*, p. 7.
12. Gertrude "Ma" Rainey, "Runaway Blues." Paramount 12902, Sept. 1928. Reissued on *Ma Rainey*, Milestone M-47021, 1974.
13. Gertrude "Ma" Rainey, "Leavin' This Morning," Paramount 12902, Sept. 1928. Reissued on *Ma Rainey*, Milestone M-47021, 1974.
14. Gertrude "Ma" Rainey, "Walking Blues," Paramount 12082, Dec. 1923. Reissued on *Queen of the Blues*, Biograph BLP-12032, n.d.
15. Sidran, p. 24.
16. Rainey, "Traveling Blues."
17. Quoted in Lieb, p. 46. No citation for original source.
18. Peetie Wheatstraw's "C. & A. Blues" includes the following verse: "When a woman gets the blues, she hangs her head and cries / When a man gets the blues, he flags a freight train and rides." Vocalion 04592, March 17, 1931.
19. Rainey, "Runaway Blues."
20. Gertrude "Ma" Rainey, "Weeping Woman Blues," Paramount 12455, Feb. 1927. Reissued on *Blues the World Forgot*, Biograph BLP-12001, n.d.
21. Bessie Smith, "Lookin' for My Man Blues," Columbia 14569-D, Sept. 28, 1927. Reissued on *The Empress*, Columbia CG 30818, 1972.
22. Bessie Smith, "Frankie Blues," Columbia 14023-D, Apr. 8, 1924. Reissued on *Empty Bed Blues*, Columbia CG 30450, 1972.
23. Bessie Smith, "Mama's Got the Blues," Columbia A 3900, Apr. 30, 1923. Reissued on *The World's Greatest Blues Singer*, Columbia CG 33, n.d.
24. Lieb, p. 100.
25. Rainey, "Walking Blues."
26. Lieb, p. 101.
27. Gertrude "Ma" Rainey, "Slow Driving Moan," Paramount 12526, Aug. 1927. Reissued on *Ma Rainey*, Milestone M-47021, 1974.
28. Rainey, "Lost Wandering Blues."
29. Finn, p. 199.
30. Blind Lemon Jefferson, "Matchbox Blues," Paramount Master 4424-2, Apr. 1927.
31. Huddie Ledbetter, "Packing Trunk Blues," Columbia 530035, 1935.

32. Lieb, p. 95

33. Bessie Smith, "Sobbin' Hearted Blues," Columbia 14056-D, Jan. 14, 1925. Reissued on *The Empress*, Columbia CG 30818, 1972.

34. Gertrude "Ma" Rainey, "South Bound Blues," Paramount 12227, Mar. 1924. Reissued on *Queen of the Blues*, Biograph BLP-12032, n.d.

35. Gertrude "Ma" Rainey, "Bessemer Bound Blues," Paramount 12374, Dec. 1925. Reissued on *Ma Rainey*, Milestone M-47021, 1974.

36. Gertrude "Ma" Rainey, "Toad Frog Blues," Paramount 12242, Oct. 15, 1924. Reissued on *Blues the World Forgot*, Biograph BLP-12001, n.d.

37. Gertrude "Ma" Rainey, "Moonshine Blues," Paramount 12603, Dec. 1927. Reissued on *Ma Rainey*, Milestone M-47021, 1974.

38. Bessie Smith recorded Rainey's "Moonshine Blues" in April 1924; Rainey herself did not record the song until December 1927.

39. Cow Cow Davenport, "Jim Crow Blues." Lyrics quoted from Paul Oliver, *The Meaning of the Blues* (New York: Collier, 1960), p. 71.

40. Ibid.

41. Bessie Smith and Clara Smith, "Far Away Blues," Columbia 13007-D, Oct. 4, 1923. Reissued on *Any Woman's Blues*, Columbia G 30126, 1972.

42. Bessie Smith, "Louisiana Low Down Blues," Columbia 14031-D, July 22, 1924. Reissued on *Empty Bed Blues*, CG 30450, 1972.

43. Bessie Smith, "Dixie Flyer Blues," Columbia 14079-D, May 15, 1925. Reissued on *The Empress*, Columbia CG 30818, 1972.

44. Clara Smith, "L. & N. Blues," Columbia 14073-D, Mar. 1925.

45. Brooks, *The Bessie Smith Companion*, p. 119.

46. Bessie Smith, "Muddy Water," Columbia 14197-D, Mar. 2, 1927. Reissued on *The Empress*, Columbia CG 30818, 1972.

47. Albertson, *Bessie*, pp. 128, 129.

48. Ibid.

49. Paul Oliver, *Bessie Smith* (London: Cassell, 1960), pp. 27–28.

BLAME IT ON THE BLUES

1. Gertrude "Ma" Rainey, "Blame It on the Blues," Paramount 12760, Sept. 1928. Reissued on *Ma Rainey*, Milestone M-47021, 1974.

2. Samuel Charters, *The Poetry of the Blues* (New York: Avon, 1963), p. 152.

3. Oliver, *The Meaning of the Blues*, pp. 322–23.

4. Paul Garon, *Blues and the Poetic Spirit*, p. 109.

5. Oliver, p. 322.

6. Carman Moore, *Somebody's Angel Child: The Story of Bessie Smith* (New York: Dell, 1969), p. 86.

7. Brooks, *The Bessie Smith Companion*, p. 146.

8. John Chilton writes that Holiday's initial "guarded acceptance of the song was soon followed by a spate of passionate fervour for every stanza in the song, she felt that everyone in the world should hear the words. The big drawback to this was that the [people at] Columbia Record Company, to whom she was contracted, weren't willing to issue a recording of the song. However, they were not against its message and gave their permission when Billie and Milt Gabler asked if they could record the song for Commodore. This decision surprised and delighted Gabler, he said 'Billie and I were grateful to Columbia for allowing her to record this important song for my label.' " *Billie's Blues* (New York: Stein & Day, 1978), p. 70.

9. Albertson, *Bessie*, pp. 148, 149.

10. Bessie Smith, "Poor Man's Blues," Columbia 14399-D, Aug. 24, 1928. Reissued on *Empty Bed Blues*, Columbia CG 30450, 1972.

11. Bessie Smith, "Washwoman's Blues," Columbia 14375-D, Aug. 24, 1928. Reissued on *Empty Bed Blues*, Columbia CG 30450, 1972.

12. Ibid.

13. Brooks, p. 144.

14. Ibid., p. 145. The third line in this verse should read "I could eat aplenty."

15. Ibid.

16. *Prison Worksongs*, Arhoolie 2012, n.d.

17. Dora Jones organized the New York Domestic Workers' Union in the 1930s. Five years after the union was founded, only 350 out of 100,000 domestics in the state had been recruited. Gerda Lerner, ed., *Black Women in White America: A Documentary History* (New York: Pantheon, 1972), p. 232. See also Jacqueline Jones, *Labor of Love, Labor of Sorrow: Black Women, Work, and the Family from Slavery to the Present* (New York: Basic Books, 1985); and Judith Rollins, *Between Women: Domestics and Their Employers* (Philadelphia: Temple University Press, 1985).

18. Smith, "Washwoman's Blues."

19. In 1960, one-third of all black women workers were still doing household jobs, and one-fifth were nondomestic service workers. Jacqueline Johnson Jackson, "Black Women in a Racist Society," in Charles Willie et al., eds., *Racism and Mental Health* (Pittsburgh: University of Pittsburgh Press, 1973), p. 236.

20. Bessie Smith, "Jail House Blues," Columbia A 4001, Sept. 21, 1923. Reissued on *Any Woman's Blues*, Columbia G 30126, 1972.

21. Bessie Smith, "Work House Blues," Columbia 14032-D, July 23, 1924. Reissued on *Empty Bed Blues*, Columbia CG 30450, 1972.

22. Bessie Smith, "Sing Sing Prison Blues," Columbia 14951-D, Dec. 6, 1934. Reissued on *The Empress*, Columbia CG 30818, 1972.

23. Bessie Smith, "Send Me to the 'Lectric Chair," Columbia 14209-D, Mar. 3, 1927. Reissued on *The Empress*, Columbia CG 30818, 1972.

24. Gertrude "Ma" Rainey, "Chain Gang Blues," Paramount 12338, Dec. 1925. Reissued on *Ma Rainey*, Milestone M-47021, 1974.

25. Lieb, *Mother of the Blues*, p. 153.

26. Fletcher M. Green, "Some Aspects of the Convict Lease System in the Southern States," in *Essays in Southern History*, vol. 31 (Chapel Hill: University of North Carolina Press, 1949), p. 112. Quoted by Julie Browne in "The Labor of Doing Time," in Elihu Rosenblatt, ed. *Criminal Injustice: Confronting the Prison Crisis* (Boston: South End, 1996), p. 61.

27. Herbert Aptheker, ed., *A Documentary History of the Negro People in the United States, 1910–1932* (Secaucus, N.J.: Citadel, 1973), pp. 323–24. Mary Church Terrell wrote in a 1907 article entitled "Peonage in the U.S.: The Convict Lease System and the Chain Gang":

> It is no exaggeration to say that in some respects the convict lease system, as it is operated in certain southern States, is less humane than was the bondage endured by slaves fifty years ago. For, under the old régime, it was to the master's interest to clothe and shelter and feed his slaves properly, even if he were not moved to do so by considerations of mercy and humanity, because the death of a slave meant an actual loss in dollars and cents, whereas the death of a convict to-day involves no loss whatsoever either to the lessee or to the State.

The Nineteenth Century and After, Aug. 1907.

28. See Angela Y. Davis, *Women, Race, and Class*, chap. 1.

29. Aptheker, p. 324.

30. Gertrude "Ma" Rainey, "Ma and Pa Poorhouse Blues," Paramount 12718, 1929. Reissued on *Oh My Babe Blues*, Biograph BLP-12011, n.d.

31. Bessie Smith, "House Rent Blues," Columbia 14032-D, July 23, 1924. Reissued on *Empty Bed Blues*, Columbia CG 30450, 1972.

32. Ibid.

33. Bessie Smith, "I'm Down in the Dumps," Okeh 8945, Nov. 24, 1933. Reissued on *The World's Greatest Blues Singer*, Columbia CG 33, 1972.

34. Bessie Smith, "Baby, Won't You Please Come Home," Columbia A3888, Apr. 11, 1923. Reissued on *The World's Greatest Blues Singer*, Columbia CG 33, 1972.

35. Gertrude "Ma" Rainey, "Hustlin' Blues," Paramount 12804, June 1928. Reissued on *Oh My Babe Blues*, Biograph BLP-12011, n.d.

36. Carby, "It Just Be's Dat Way Sometime," p. 18.

37. Albertson, p. 127

38. According to the official report by the Red Cross, over 26,000 square miles were devastated and 637,476 people—of whom 53.8 percent were black—were directly assisted by the relief operations. *The Mississippi Valley Flood Disaster of 1927: Official Report of the Relief Operations* (Washington, D.C.: American National Red Cross), 1928, pp. 5, 32, 45.

39. Bessie Smith, "Backwater Blues," Columbia 14195-D, Feb. 17, 1927. Reissued on *Nobody's Blues but Mine*, Columbia CG 31093, 1972.

40. See the *18th Annual Report, for 1927, of the NAACP* in Aptheker, pp. 551–52.

41. John M. Barry. *Rising Tide: The Great Mississippi Flood of 1927 and How It Changed America.* (New York: Simon & Schuster, 1997), pp. 316–17.

42. Ibid., p. 320.

43. Ibid., p. 330.

44. Blind Lemon Jefferson, "Rising High Water Blues," Paramount 12487, 1927.

45. Barbecue Bob, "Mississippi Heavy Water Blues," Columbia 14222-D; June 15, 1927; lyrics quoted in Oliver, *The Meaning of the Blues.*

46. Sippie Wallace, "Flood Blues"; lyrics quoted in Oliver, *The Meaning of the Blues*, pp. 263–64.

> I'm standing in this water, wishing that I had a boat
> I'm standing in this water, wishing that I had a boat
> The only way I see is—take my clothes and float.
>
> The water is rising, people fleeing for the hills
> The water is rising, people fleeing for the hills
> Lord, the water will obey, if you just say, "Be still!"
>
> They sent out alarm for everybody to leave town,
> They sent out alarm for everybody to leave town
> But when I got the news I was high-water bound.
>
> They dynamite the levee—thought it might give us ease

> *They dynamite the levee — thought it might give us ease*
> *But some water's still rising, do it as they please.*

47. Bessie Smith, "Homeless Blues," Columbia 14260-D, Sept. 28, 1927. Reissued on *The Empress*, Columbia CG 30818, 1972.
48. Charley Patton, "High Water Everywhere," Paramount 12909. Reissued on *Charley Patton — Founder of the Delta Blues*, Yazoo L-1020.

> *Backwater at Blythville, doctor weren't around*
> *Backwater at Blythville, done took Joiner Town*
> *It was fifty families and children, suffer to sink and drown*

> *The water was risin', up at my friend's door*
> *The water were risin', up in my friend's door*
> *The man said to his womenfolk: "Lord, we's better'd row."*

> *The water it was risin', got up in my bed*
> *Lord, the water it rollin', got up to my bed*
> *I thought I would take a trip, Lord, out on a big ice sled*

> *Oh I hear, Lord, Lord, water upon my door*
> *[Spoken] You know what I mean? Same here*
> *I hear the ice boat, Lord, went sinking down.*

49. Rainey, "Blame It on the Blues."
50. Charters, p. 152.
51. According to Albert Murray, "the chances were that blues-oriented Afro-Americans acquired both the word and its special connotation from their Euro-American ancestors. English usage of the term blue devils to designate baleful demons has been traced back as far as 1616. Its figurative use as a metaphor for depression of spirits has been traced as far back as 1787, and its plural use as a name for apparitions seen or experienced during delirium tremens has been in use since 1822." *Stomping the Blues* (New York: McGraw-Hill, 1976), p. 64.
52. Bessie Smith, "Jail House Blues," Columbia A-4001, Sept. 21, 1923. Reissued on *Any Woman's Blues*, Columbia G 30126, 1972.
53. Giles Oakley, *The Devil's Music*, p. 50.
54. Eric Sackheim, *The Blues Line*, p. 462.
55. Gertrude "Ma" Rainey, "Slave to the Blues," Paramount 12332, Aug. 1927. Reissued on *Ma Rainey*, Milestone M-47021, 1974.
56. Gertrude "Ma" Rainey, "Yonder Come the Blues," Paramount 12357, 1926. Reissued on *Ma Rainey's Black Bottom*, Yazoo 1071, n.d.
57. Charters, p. 46.

58. Lieb, p. 95.

59. Gertrude "Ma" Rainey, "Tough Luck Blues," Paramount 12735, Sept., 1928. Reissued on *Ma Rainey*, Milestone M-47021, 1974.

60. Lieb, p. 158.

61. Rainey, "Tough Luck Blues."

62. Levine, *Black Culture and Black Consciousness*, p. 269–70.

PREACHING THE BLUES

1. Gertrude "Ma" Rainey, "Countin' the Blues." Paramount 12237, Dec. 1925. Reissued on *Ma Rainey*, Milestone M-47021, 1974.

2. See Angela Y. Davis, "The Black Women's Role in the Community of Slaves," *Black Scholar* 3, no. 4 (December 1971).

3. *Wild Women Don't Have the Blues*, videocassette.

4. Daniel P. Moynihan, *The Negro Family: The Case for National Action* (Washington, D.C.: U.S. Department of Labor, 1965).

5. See Wahneema Lubiano, "Black Nationalism and Black Common Sense: Policing Ourselves and Others" in Wahneema Lubiano, ed. *The House That Race Built: Black Americans, U.S. Terrain* (New York: Pantheon, 1997).

6. See Dorothy Scarborough, *On the Trail of Negro Folk-Songs* (Cambridge, Mass.: Harvard University Press, 1925).

7. "The directors did not want the company to appear too colored, and Bessie Smith . . . auditioning in February, was rejected because of her unmistakable nitty-grittiness. William Grant Still, a member of the Harlem Symphony and future composer, was music director of Black Swan. Du Bois and John Nail, James Weldon Johnson's brother-in-law and Harlem's largest real estate broker, were on its board of directors." David Levering Lewis, *When Harlem Was in Vogue* (New York: Knopf, 1981), p. 174.

8. Of course, the vision of the Devil in African-American folk beliefs is quite different from the Christian vision. The Devil figure in many black folktales symbolically represents black people, while God is the symbol of white people. In numerous instances, the Devil is a trickster capable of outsmarting everyone, including God. One of the humorous tales in Zora Neale Hurston's *Mules and Men* proposes an explanation for black people's use of the word "unh hunh" with the following story about the Devil:

    Ole Devil looked around hell one day and seen his place was short of help so he thought he'd run up to Heben and kidnap some angels to keep things runnin' tell he got reinforcements from Miami.

> *Well, he slipped up on a great crowd of angels on de outskirts of Heben and stuffed a couple of thousand in his mouth, a few hundred under each arm and wrapped his tail 'round another thousand and darted off towards hell.*
>
> *When he was flyin' low over de earth lookin' for a place to land, a man looked up and seen de Devil and ast 'im, "Ole Devil, Ah see you got a load of angels. Is you goin' back for mo'?"*
>
> *Devil opened his mouth and tole 'im, "Yeah," and all de li'l angels flew out his mouf and went on back to Heben. While he was tryin' to ketch 'em he lost all de others. So he went back after another load.*
>
> *He was flyin' low agin and de same man seen him and says, "Ole Devil, Ah see you got another load uh angels,"*
>
> *Devil nodded his head and said "unh hunh," and dat's why we say it today.* (pp. 169–170)

9. *Wild Women Don't Have the Blues*, videocassette.

10. Alice Walker, *The Color Purple* (New York, Washington Square, 1982), p. 49.

11. In Alice Walker's book on the making of the film *The Color Purple*, she indicates in a letter to Quincy Jones, the composer of the score, that she felt uncomfortable with the church scene in the screenplay. "It's really important to me that we get God out of the church and back into nature. . . . I would hate the last scene with Shug to be inside a church." *The Same River Twice: Honoring the Difficult*, pp. 142–43. Among the documents Walker includes in her book is an article by Carl Dix in which the author seems to concur with Walker:

    > *To have this woman come back to the church and into the embrace of her father, the preacher who had done sermons about her lifestyle as sin incarnate, definitely undercuts the rebel image of Shug (which was a big part of what drew Celie toward her) and undercuts the movie's overall strong stand against patriarchy.* (p. 197)

12. Lieb, *Mother of the Blues*, p. 47. Ma Rainey's involvement in the church during the last years of her life did not, however, hamper her continued relation to show business. She purchased and operated two theaters in Rome, Georgia, until her death, in 1939.

13. Bruce Cook, *Listen to the Blues* (New York: Scribner, 1975), p. 201.

14. Ibid., pp. 202, 204.

15. *Wild Women Don't Have the Blues*, videocassette.

16. Gertrude "Ma" Rainey, "Down in the Basement," Paramount 12395,

1926. Reissued on *Down in the Basement: A Third Collection of Classic Performances by the Legendary "Mother of the Blues,"* Milestone MLP 2017, c. 1971.

17. Bessie Smith, "Trombone Cholly," Columbia 14232-D, Mar. 3, 1927. Reissued on *The Empress,* Columbia CG 30818, 1972.

18. Bessie Smith, "Jazzbo Brown from Memphis Town," Columbia 14133-D, Mar. 18, 1926. Reissued on *Nobody's Blues but Mine,* Columbia 31093, 1972.

19. See LeRoi Jones (Amiri Baraka), *Blues People* (New York: Morrow, 1963).

20. "If there were no word, all forces would be frozen, there would be no procreation, no change, no life. 'There is nothing that there is not; whatever we have a name for, that is'; so speaks the wisdom of the Yoruba priests. The proverb signifies that the naming, the enunciation produces what it names. Naming is an incantation, a creative act. What we cannot conceive of is unreal; it does not exist. But every human thought, once expressed, becomes reality. For the word holds the course of things in train and changes and transforms them. And since the word has this power, every word is an effective word, every word is binding. There is no 'harmless,' noncommittal word. Every word has consequences. Therefore the word binds the muntu. And the muntu is responsible for his word." Janheinz Jahn, *Muntu,* p. 133.

21. Ibid., p. 132.

22. Rainey, "Countin' the Blues."

23. Paul Oliver's *Screening the Blues* contains a chapter entitled "Preaching the Blues" in which he points out that Bessie Smith was the first to introduce "the relationship between 'preaching' and 'blues' . . . with her mock sermon 'Preachin' the Blues,' the first to use this title." Among others, Big Bill Broonzy also recorded a song called "Preaching the Blues":

> Men go to church just to hide their dirt
> And women go to church just to show their skirts
> But there's a date coming an' it may be for you
> When Gabriel blows his trumpet
> Brother, what you gonna do?
> Brother, you better get down on your knees
> Well, and pray both day and night
> Now, you may have a good time with married women
> But you may go to hell that way.

Oliver also refers to "Preachin' the Blues" by Son House, and Robert

Johnson's "Preachin' Blues." Paul Oliver, *Screening the Blues: Aspects of the Blues Tradition* (New York: Da Capo, 1968), pp. 66–67.

24. Bessie Smith, "Preachin' the Blues," Columbia 14195-D, Feb. 17, 1927. Reissued on *Nobody's Blues but Mine*, Columbia CG 31093, 1972.

25. Bessie Smith, "On Revival Day," Columbia 14538-D, June 9, 1930. Reissued on *The World's Greatest Blues Singer*, Columbia CG 33, 1972.

26. Bessie Smith, "Moan, You Mourners," Columbia 14538-D, June 9, 1930. Reissued on *The World's Greatest Blues Singer*, Columbia CG 33, 1972.

27. Lawrence Levine writes that Bessie Smith made her "process of sacralizing the secular overt" in "Preachin' the Blues" and quotes Zutty Singleton, who said that Bessie Smith's blues "seemed almost like hymns." *Black Culture and Black Consciousness*, p. 235.

28. Smith, "Preachin' the Blues."

29. Ralph Ellison, "Remembering Jimmy," in *Shadow and Act*, p. 243.

30. Ibid.

31. Bessie Smith, "Soft Pedal Blues," Columbia 14075-D, May 14, 1925. Reissued on *The Empress*, Columbia CG 30818, 1972.

32. Bessie Smith, "Nashville Women's Blues," Columbia 14090-D, May 26, 1925. Reissued on *The Empress*, Columbia CG 30818, 1972.

33. Gertrude "Ma" Rainey, "Ya Da Do," Paramount 12257, Mar. 1924. Reissued on *Queen of the Blues*, Biograph BLP-12032, n.d..

34. Bessie Smith, "Yodeling Blues," Columbia A3939, June 14, 1923. Reissued on *The World's Greatest Blues Singer*, Columbia CG 33, 1972.

35. Bessie Smith, "Jail House Blues," Columbia A 4001, Sept. 21, 1923. Reissued on *Any Woman's Blues*, Columbia G 30126, 1972.

36. Gertrude "Ma" Rainey, "Memphis Bound Blues," Paramount 12311, 1926. Reissued on *The Immortal Ma Rainey*, Milestone MLP-2001, 1966. Thomas Dorsey is best known as the composer of the gospel song "Precious Lord." During the decade of the twenties, as a blues composer and performer, he used the stage name "Georgia Tom." Under that pseudonym, he performed with Ma Rainey and her Wildcat Band in 1923, and can also be heard on the piano on songs such as "Leavin' This Morning," "Tough Luck Blues," and "Sweet Rough Man." He collaborated with Tampa Red on such sexually explicit songs as "It's Tight Like That." See Albert Murray, *Stomping the Blues*, pp. 46, 206. See also Lawrence Levine, *Black Culture and Black Consciousness*, pp. 181–82.

37. Murray, *Stomping the Blues*, pp. 60–61.

38. Gertrude "Ma" Rainey, "Last Minute Blues," Paramount 12080, Dec. 1923. Reissued on *Queen of the Blues*, Biograph BLP-12032, n.d.

39. *Brown Sugar*, produced by Matthew Pook, Ebony Productions, 1985, videocassette.

40. Narration from *Wild Women Don't Have the Blues*, videocassette.

41. Ibid.

UP IN HARLEM EVERY SATURDAY NIGHT

1. Bessie Smith, "Gimme a Pigfoot." Okeh 8949, Nov. 24, 1933. Reissued on *The World's Greatest Blues Singer*, Columbia CG 33, 1972.

2. *Wild Women Don't Have the Blues*, videocassette.

3. Lieb, *Mother of the Blues*, p. 3.

4. Ibid., pp. 31–32.

5. Sterling Brown, *Southern Road* (Boston: Beacon, 1974), pp. 62ff.

6. Bessie Smith, "Down Hearted Blues," Columbia A 3844-D, Feb. 16, 1923. Reissued on *The World's Greatest Blues Singer*, Columbia CG 33, 1972.

7. Carl Van Vechten, *"Keep A-Inchin' Along": Selected Writings of Carl Van Vechten About Black Art and Letters*, ed. Bruce Kellner (Westport, Conn.: Greenwood, 1979), pp. 162–63.

8. See Paul Oliver, *Savannah Syncopators: African Retentions in the Blues* (New York: Stein & Day, 1970).

9. Bessie Smith, "Washwoman's Blues," Columbia 14375-D, Aug. 24, 1928. Reissued on *Empty Bed Blues*, Columbia, CG 30450, 1972.

10. Bessie Smith, "House Rent Blues," Columbia 14032-D, July 23, 1924. Reissued on *Empty Bed Blues*, Columbia CG 30450, 1972.

11. Bessie Smith, "Jail House Blues," Columbia A-4001, Sept. 21, 1923. Reissued on *Any Woman's Blues*, Columbia, G 30126, 1972.

12. Bessie Smith, "Backwater Blues," Columbia 14195-D, Feb. 17, 1927. Reissued on *Nobody's Blues but Mine*, Columbia CG 31093, 1972.

13. Bessie Smith, "Poor Man's Blues," Columbia 14399-D, Aug. 24, 1928. Reissued on *Empty Bed Blues*, Columbia CG 30450, 1972.

14. Quotation extracted from a brief item entitled "Bessie Smith, In Memoriam" that appeared in the English journal *Jazz Music* in 1942. Obtained from the Schomburg Center for Research in Black Culture's Bessie Smith clippings file, on microfilm. Authorship attributed only to "A.A." Page number and exact date not indicated, although year is referenced indi-

rectly in text: "It is five years since we lost [Bessie Smith]." Smith died in 1937.

15. Dan Morgenstern, "Hall of Fame Winner Bessie Smith: Empress of the Blues," *Down Beat*, Aug. 24, 1967, pp. 22–23.

16. Whitney Balliett, "Jazz Records—Miss Bessie," *New Yorker*, Nov. 6, 1971, pp. 160–72.

17. Richard Hadlock, *Jazz Masters of the Twenties* (New York: Macmillan, 1965), p. 227.

18. Steven Tracy, *Langston Hughes and the Blues* (Urbana: University of Illinois Press, 1988).

19. Langston Hughes, *The Weary Blues* (New York: Knopf, 1926).

20. Langston Hughes, *The Big Sea: An Autobiography* (New York: Hill & Wang, 1940), p. 217.

21. Langston Hughes, "The Glory of Negro History, A Pageant," in *The Langston Hughes Reader* (New York: George Braziller, 1958), p. 477.

22. "Songs Called the Blues," in *The Langston Hughes Reader*, pp. 161, 160.

23. Langston Hughes, "Shadow of the Blues," in *The Best of Simple* (New York: Hill & Wang, 1961), p. 166:

> "Since I'm busting this dollar, I might as well put a quarter in the juke box. What would you like to hear?"
>
> "If they've got any old-time blues on it, play them."
>
> "Will do," said Simple. "But there ain't no Bessie these days. Do you remember Bessie Smith?"
>
> "I certainly do. And Clara?"
>
> "I bet you don't remember Mamie?"
>
> "Yes, I do—all three Smiths, Bessie, Clara, and Mamie."
>
> "Boy, you must be older than me, because I only heard tell of Mamie. I am glad I am not as ageable as you. You's an old Negro!"
>
> "Come now! Let's see what else you might remember, before we start comparing ages. Speaking of blues singers, how about Victoria Spivey?"
>
> "You've gone too far back now if you remember Victoria."
>
> "How do you know how far back she was if you can't recall her?"

After comparing a few more memories, Hughes and Simple return to their discussion of the blues.

24. Ibid., pp. 167–68.

25. Letter from Van Vechten to Mencken, May 29, 1925, H. L. Mencken Col-

lection, Manuscript Division, New York Public Library, quoted in David Levering Lewis, *When Harlem Was in Vogue*, p. 98.

26. Van Vechten, p. 161.
27. Ethel Waters (with Charles Samuels), *His Eye Is on the Sparrow* (1951; reprint, New York: Da Capo, 1992), p. 195.
28. Albertson, *Bessie*, p. 143.
29. Hughes, *The Big Sea*, p. 251.
30. Albertson, p. 142.
31. Van Vechten, pp. 162–163.
32. Ibid., p. 165.
33. Bruce Kellner, *Carl Van Vechten and the Irreverent Decades* (Norman: University of Oklahoma Press, 1968), p. 270.
34. Baker, *Modernism and the Harlem Renaissance*, p. xvii.
35. Ibid., pp. 91–92.
36. Ibid., p. 93.
37. Nathan Huggins, ed., *Voices from the Harlem Renaissance* (New York: Oxford University Press, 1976), p. 339.
38. Ibid., pp. 9–10.
39. Ibid., p. 10.
40. Alain Locke, *The Critical Temper of Alain Locke: A Selection of His Essays on Art and Culture*, ed. Jeffrey C. Stewart (New York: Garland, 1983), pp. 109–10.
41. Ibid., p. 7.
42. Alain Locke, ed., *The New Negro* (1925; reprint, New York: Atheneum, 1977), p. 209.
43. Langston Hughes, "The Negro Artist and the Racial Mountain," in Huggins, ed., *Voices from the Harlem Renaissance*, p. 309.
44. Ibid., p. 308.
45. Derrick Stewart-Baxter, *Ma Rainey and the Classic Blues Singers* (New York: Stein & Day, 1970), p. 12.
46. Robert Dixon and John Godrich, *Recording the Blues*, p. 13.
47. Lewis, p. 174.
48. Ibid.
49. Van Vechten, pp. 165–66.
50. Lewis, p. 174.
51. Ibid.
52. Elaine Feinstein, *Bessie Smith: Empress of the Blues* (New York: Penguin,

1985), pp. 30–31. Feinstein makes questionable observations in her popular biography of Bessie Smith. Consider, for example, her comments regarding relationships between black women and men:

> A woman who had a partner who stayed with her (and many left home) was often brutally abused. A black man was likely to be so abominably treated in all his other relationships that he found it impossible to react humanly. Black women fell into the habit of thinking of their men as lazy, shiftless and irresponsible. (pp. 17–18)

53. See Hurston's *Mules and Men*, and *Tell My Horse: Voodoo and Life in Haiti and Jamaica* (1938; reprint, New York: Harper & Row, 1990).

54. Bessie Smith, "Red Mountain Blues," Columbia 14115-D, Nov. 20, 1925. Reissued on *Nobody's Blues but Mine*, Columbia CG 31093, 1972.

55. Zora Neale Hurston, "High John de Conquer," in Langston Hughes and Arna Bontemps, eds., *The Book of Negro Folklore* (New York: Dodd, Mead, 1958), pp. 93–94.

56. Ibid., pp. 101–2.

57. Hurston, *Mules and Men*, pp. 197–99.

58. Bessie Smith, "I'd Rather Be Dead and Buried in My Grave," Columbia 14304-D, Feb. 16, 1928. Reissued on *Empty Bed Blues*, Columbia CG 30450, 1972.

59. Hurston, *Mules and Men*, p. 197.

60. Bessie Smith, "Mama's Got the Blues," Columbia A 3900, Apr. 30, 1923. Reissued on *The World's Greatest Blues Singer*, Columbia CG 33, 1972.

61. Bessie Smith, "Yodeling Blues," Columbia A 3939, June 14, 1923. Reissued on *The World's Greatest Blues Singer*, Columbia CG 33, 1972.

62. Bessie Smith, "Gin House Blues," Columbia 14158-D, Mar. 18, 1926. Reissued on *Nobody's Blues but Mine*, Columbia CG 31093, 1972.

63. Bessie Smith, "Lady Luck Blues," Columbia A 3939, June 14, 1923. Reissued on *The World's Greatest Blues Singer*, Columbia CG 33, 1972.

64. Hurston, *Mules and Men*, p. 236.

WHEN A WOMAN LOVES A MAN

1. Billie Holiday, "When a Woman Loves a Man," Columbia PG 32121, Jan. 12, 1938. Reissued on *Billie Holiday: The Golden Years*, Columbia C3L-21, 1962.

2. Billie Holiday, with William Dufty, *Lady Sings the Blues* (1956; reprint, New York: Penguin, 1984), p. 39.

3. Ralph Ellison, *Shadow and Act*, p. 245.

4. John Chilton, *Billie's Blues*, p. 69.

5. Ibid, p. 104.

6. Mark Naison, *Communists in Harlem During the Depression* (New York: Grove, 1983), p. 301.

7. Charles Edward Smith, "Billie Holiday," in Nat Shapiro and Nat Hentoff, eds., *The Jazz Makers* (New York: Da Capo, 1979), p. 276.

8. Herbert Marcuse, *Eros and Civilization* (Boston: Beacon, 1955).

9. Herbert Marcuse, *The Aesthetic Dimension* (Boston: Beacon, 1978).

10. Ibid., p. xii.

11. Ibid., p. 2.

12. Ibid., p. x.

13. Ibid., p. 6.

14. Ibid., p. 29.

15. See Valerie Smith, " 'Loopholes of Retreat': Architecture and Ideology in Harriet Jacobs' *Incidents in the Life of a Slave Girl*," in Henry Louis Gates, Jr., ed., *Reading Black, Reading Feminist* (New York: Meridian, 1990).

16. As a result of the controversy arising out of the 1997 debate on the role of "Ebonics"—a term that has very different implications for a study of black English than the ones I explore here—in the Oakland Public Schools, there has been a great deal of popular discussion on this subject. I agree with those linguists and pedagogians who have argued for an acknowledgment of black English—with its distinct grammatical and metaphorical structures—as a different rather than inferior version of English on the grounds that it can assist students who only speak in the vernacular to learn standard English. However, I find some of the Afrocentric arguments for Ebonics extremely problematic. In this discussion of Billie Holiday, I am primarily concerned with the way black English eschews literality and produces multiple, often veiled meanings that contradict the surface meanings of words.

17. See June Jordan, *On Call: Political Essays* (Boston: South End, 1985).

18. Holiday, p. 39.

19. See Levine, *Black Culture and Black Consciousness*, pp. 344–58. Also see Daryl Cumber Dance, *Shuckin' and Jivin': Folklore from Contemporary Black Americans* (Bloomington: Indiana University Press, 1978).

20. Sidney Finkelstein, *Jazz: A People's Music* (New York: Citadel, 1948), p. 28.

21. Benny Green, *The Reluctant Art: The Growth of Jazz* (New York: Horizon, 1963), p. 125.

22. Charles Hamm has pointed out that "[t]he 1920s and '30s were an era of specialization in popular song. There were composers, lyricists, performers and publishers. . . ." *Yesterdays: Popular Song in America* (New York: Norton, 1979), p. 376.

23. David Ewen, *All the Years of American Popular Music* (Englewood Cliffs, N.J.: Prentice-Hall, 1977), p. 153. Ewen further points out: "Should a song grow popular with a girl's name in the title; should a spelling song or a song on an American-Indian subject gain popularity, it was not long before competitive songwriters began producing similar songs."

24. Billie Holiday, "Your Mother's Son-in-Law," Columbia 2856D, Nov. 27, 1933. Reissued on *The Golden Years*, Columbia C3L-21, 1962.

25. Billie Holiday, "Riffing the Scotch," Columbia 2867D, Dec. 18, 1933. Reissued on *The Golden Years*, Columbia C3L-21, 1962.

26. See Martin Williams's discussion of this period in *Where's the Melody?* (New York: Pantheon, 1961), p. 163.

27. Billie Holiday, "Yankee Doodle Never Went to Town," Brunswick 7550, Oct. 25, 1935. Reissued on *The Quintessential Billie Holiday*, vol. 1, 1933–35, Columbia compact disc CK40646, 1987.

28. Billie Holiday, "Eeny Meeny Miney Mo," Brunswick 7554, Oct. 25, 1935. Reissued on *The Quintessential Billie Holiday*, vol. 1, 1933–35, Columbia compact disc CK 40646, 1987.

29. Burnett James, "Billie Holiday and the Art of Communication," in *Essays on Jazz* (London: Sidgwick & Jackson, 1961), p. 14.

30. Billie Holiday, "You Let Me Down," Brunswick 7581, Dec. 3, 1935. Reissued on *The Golden Years*, vol. 2, Columbia C3L-40, 1962.

31. James, p. 56.

32. Audre Lorde explores this notion in depth in her reflections on the erotic as a source of female power:

> *The erotic is a resource within each of us that lies in a deeply female and spiritual plane, firmly rooted in the power of our unexpressed or unrecognized feeling. In order to perpetuate itself, every oppression must corrupt or distort those various sources of power within the culture of the oppressed that can provide energy for change. For women, this has meant a suppression of the erotic as a considered source of power and information within our lives.*
>
> *We have been taught to suspect this resource, vilified, abused and*

> *devalued within western society. On the one hand, the superficially erotic has been encouraged as a sign of female inferiority; on the other hand, women have been made to suffer and to feel both contemptible and suspect by virtue of its existence.*

Audre Lorde, "Uses of the Erotic: The Erotic as Power," in *Sister Outsider* (Trumansburg, N.Y.: Crossing Press, 1984), p. 53.

33. Billie Holiday, "Some Other Spring," Okeh 5021, July 5, 1939. Reissued on *The Golden Years*, Columbia C3C-21, 1962.

34. Interview with Billie Holiday on Tex McCleary's *Peacock Alley* television show (WABD-TV), New York City, Nov. 8, 1956.

35. Billie Holiday, "Yesterdays," Commodore 527, Apr. 20, 1939. Reissued on *Fine and Mellow*, Commodore XFL-14428, 1979.

36. John Miller Chernoff, *African Rhythm and African Sensibility: Aesthetics and Social Action in African Musical Idioms* (Chicago: University of Chicago Press, 1979), pp. 80–81.

37. Billie Holiday, "You're My Thrill," Decca 24796, Oct. 19, 1949. Reissued on *The Billie Holiday Story*, Decca DX161.

38. Linda Dahl, *Stormy Weather* (New York: Pantheon, 1984), p. 139.

39. Billie Holiday, "Lover, Come Back to Me," Commodore 569, Apr. 8, 1944. Reissued on *Strange Fruit*, Atlantic SD1614, 1972.

40. Billie Holiday, "There Is No Greater Love," Decca 23863, Feb. 13, 1947. Reissued on *The Billie Holiday Story*, Decca DX161, n.d.

41. Billie Holiday, "My Man," Decca 24638, Dec. 10, 1948. Reissued on *The Billie Holiday Story*, Decca DX161, n.d.

42. *The Long Night of Lady Day*, dir. John Jeremy, TCB/BBC-TV, 1984, videocassette.

43. Billie Holiday, "When a Woman Loves a Man."

44. Holiday, *Lady Sings the Blues*.

"STRANGE FRUIT"

1. Billie Holiday, "Strange Fruit," Commodore 526, Apr. 20, 1939. Reissued on *Strange Fruit*, Atlantic SD1614, 1972.

2. Holiday, *Lady Sings the Blues*, p. 84.

3. In a 1973 BBC interview, Artie Shaw (with whose band she had performed before being booked at Café Society, where "Strange Fruit" was born) remarked that Holiday "had developed a sense of total resignation to the fact that the large audience was not going to recognise her abilities. She

had a certain amount of inner pride, she was a very strong person, but as a singer I think she was completely resigned, at that time, that she would never have a mass audience." Chilton, *Billie's Blues*, p. 62.

4.   Ibid., pp. 73–74.

5.   Holiday, p. 92.

6.   Chilton, p. 201.

7.   Holiday, p. 84.

8.   Martin Williams called "Strange Fruit" "moving propaganda perhaps, but not poetry and not art," in Williams, "Billie Holiday: Actress Without an Act," in *The Jazz Tradition* (New York: New American Library, 1971), p. 75.

9.   Marcuse, *The Aesthetic Dimension*, p. 47.

10.   *Lady Sings the Blues*, directed by Sidney J. Furie, Paramount Pictures Corporation and Berry Gordy, 1972, film. Martin Williams, in discussing the last years of Holiday's career, writes: ". . . the frayed edge of her sound in her later years seems to come from a deeply suppressed sob which, if she ever let go, would bring tears she might never be able to stop. Perhaps I mean that quite literally; perhaps I mean that she seemed so determined not to feel a deeper self-pity that she couldn't see the terrible sadness of her self-destruction. She may have done a great deal of sympathy-begging, feeling sorry for herself, but that is not the same thing. Her life was truly tragic in that no one could help her and she could not help herself." "Billie Holiday: Actress Without an Act," in *The Jazz Tradition*, p. 76.

11.   Lewis Allen was the nom de plume used by Abel Meerpol, who was politically active in a range of progressive causes during that period. He later adopted the children of Julius and Ethel Rosenberg, who were executed in 1953.

12.   Chilton, pp. 68–69.

13.   *The Long Night of Lady Day*, dir. John Jeremy, TCB/BBC-TV, 1984, videocassette.

14.   Stuart Nicholson, *Billie Holiday* (Boston: Northeastern University Press, 1995).

15.   Donald Clarke, *Wishing on the Moon: The Life and Times of Billie Holiday* (New York: Viking, 1994), p. 163.

16.   Ibid., p. 164.

17.   Ibid.

18.   Holiday, p. 84.

19.   Ibid., pp. 68–69; Chilton, p. 75.

20. Chilton, p. 160.

21. William Z. Foster, *The Negro People in American History* (New York: International Publishers, 1954), p. 480. According to official estimates, forty-six black people were lynched in the South during the decade of the thirties. Gerald David Jaynes and Robin Williams, Jr., eds., *A Common Destiny: Blacks and American Society* (Washington, D.C.: National Academy Press, 1989), p. 59.

22. Paula Giddings, *When and Where I Enter*, p. 206. See also Jacquelyn Dowd Hall, *Revolt Against Chivalry: Jessie Daniel Ames and the Women's Campaign Against Chivalry*, rev. ed. (New York: Columbia University Press, 1993).

23. Ralph Ginzburg, *One Hundred Years of Lynching* (New York: Lancer, 1969), p. 222.

24. John Hope Franklin, *Race and History* (Baton Rouge and London: Louisiana State University Press, 1989), p. 281.

25. Giddings, p. 208.

26. *The Long Night of Lady Day*, videocassette.

27. Chilton, p. 68.

28. Foster, *The Negro People in American History*, p. 479.

29. Ibid., p. 480.

30. Robin D. G. Kelley, *Hammer and Hoe: Alabama Communists During the Great Depression* (Chapel Hill: University of North Carolina Press, 1990), p. 221.

31. Phillip Bonosky, "The 'Thirties' in American Culture," *Political Affairs*, May 1959.

32. Holiday, p. 74.

33. Ibid.

34. Ibid.

35. Chilton, p. 69.

36. Ibid., p. 104.

37. Frantz Fanon, "Racism and Culture," in *Toward the African Revolution* (New York: Grove, 1964), p. 41.

38. William Dufty, liner notes, *The Billie Holiday Story*, Decca DX161, n.d.

39. John White, *Billie Holiday: Her Life and Times* (New York: Universe, 1987), p. 55.

40. Holiday, p. 84.

41. In the chapter "Eros and Thanatos," in *Eros and Civilization*, Herbert Marcuse develops his revision of Freud's theory of the instincts:

> *The death instinct operates under the Nirvana principle: it tends toward that state of 'constant gratification' where no tension is felt—a state without want. This trend of the instinct implies that its destructive manifestations would be minimized as it approached such a state. If the instinct's basic objective is not the termination of life but of pain—the absence of tension—then paradoxically, in terms of the instinct, the conflict between life and death is the more reduced, the closer life approximates the state of gratification. Pleasure principle and Nirvana principle then converge. At the same time, Eros, freed from surplus-repression, would be strengthened, and the strengthened Eros would, as it were, absorb the objective of the death instinct.* (p. 187)

42. Leonard Feather, liner notes, *Billie Holiday: Strange Fruit*, Atlantic Records SD 1614, 1972.

43. Ibid.

44. Joachim Berendt, *The Jazz Book: From New Orleans to Rock and Free Jazz*, trans. Dan Morgenstern (New York: Lawrence Hill, 1975), p. 310.

45. In 1963, in the heat of the civil rights movement, as a response to the murder of Medgar Evers and to the bombing of the Sixteenth Street Baptist Church in Birmingham, Alabama, Nina Simone composed a song entitled "Mississippi God Damn," which became something of an anthem among activists during the Black Power era. Arnold Shaw, *Black Popular Music in America* (New York: Schirmer, 1986), p. 213. See Nina Simone (with Stephen Cleary), *I Put a Spell on You: The Autobiography of Nina Simone* (New York: Pantheon, 1991), pp. 88ff.

WORKS CONSULTED

Ackerman, Paul. "Historic Bessie Smith Set Aimed at Youth Market." *Billboard*, July 30, 1970.

Albertson, Chris. *Bessie*. New York: Stein & Day, 1972.

Albertson, Chris, and Gunther Schuller, eds. *Bessie Smith: Empress of the Blues*. New York: Walter Kane & Son, 1975.

Aptheker, Bettina. *Woman's Legacy: Essays on Race, Sex, and Class in American History*. Amherst: University of Massachusetts Press, 1982.

Aptheker, Herbert, ed. *A Documentary History of the Negro People in the United States*. Vol. 1. Reprint. Secaucus, N.J.: Citadel, 1969.

——. *A Documentary History of the Negro People in the United States, 1910–1932*. Vol. 2. Reprint. Secaucus, N.J.: Citadel, 1973.

Backus, Rob. *Fire Music: A Political History of Jazz*. Chicago: Vanguard, 1976.

Baker, David. " 'Jazz' Versus Academia." *Black World*, Nov. 1973.

Baker, Houston A., Jr. *Blues, Ideology, and Afro-American Literature*. Chicago: University of Chicago Press, 1984.

——. *Modernism and the Harlem Renaissance*. Chicago and London: University of Chicago Press, 1987.

Balliett, Whitney. "Billie, Big Bill, and Jelly Roll." *Saturday Review*, July 14, 1956.

——. "Jazz Records—Miss Bessie." *New Yorker*, Nov. 6, 1971.

Baraka, Amiri (LeRoi Jones), and Amina Baraka. *The Music: Reflections on Jazz and Blues*. New York: Morrow, 1987.

Barlow, William. "Blues and the Music Industry." *Popular Music and Society* 14, no. 2 (Summer 1990).

Barry, John M. *Rising Tide: The Great Mississippi Flood of 1927 and How It Changed America*. New York: Simon & Schuster, 1997.

Bastin, Bruce. *Red River Blues: The Blues Tradition in the Southeast*. Urbana: University of Illinois Press, 1986.

Berendt, Joachim. *The Jazz Book: From New Orleans to Rock and Free Jazz*. Translated by Dan Morgenstern. New York: Lawrence Hill, 1975.

Berger, John. *About Looking*. New York: Pantheon, 1980.

"Bessie Smith Grave, Unmarked Since '37, Finally Gets a Stone." *New York Times*, Aug. 9, 1970.

"Bessie Smith Set Pattern for Today's Blues Singers." *Ebony*, Aug. 1950.

"The Bessie Smith Story: Singer's Favorite Musician, Reflecting Her Moods, Was Joe Smith." *Afro-American*, Dec. 22, 1951.

"The Bessie Smith Story: 'Back Water Blues' One of Singer's Best." *Afro-American*, Dec. 29, 1951.

Billie Holiday Remembered. Compiled by Linda Kuehl and Ellie Schocket, assisted by Dan Morgenstern. New York: New York Jazz Museum, 1973. A 20-page booklet on Holiday's life.

"Billie Holiday's Tragic Life." *Ebony,* Sept. 1956.

Blackwell, Maylei. "Contested Histories and Retrofitted Memory: Chicana Feminist Subjectivities Between and Beyond Nationalist Imaginaries." Qualifying essay, University of California, Santa Cruz, 1997.

Blesh, Rudi. *Shining Trumpets.* New York: Da Capo, 1946.

Boas, Gunter H. "Supreme Singer of Jazz." *Jazz Journal,* Sept. 1952.

Boeckman, Charles. *And the Beat Goes On.* Washington, D.C.: Luce, 1972.

Bogle, Donald. *Brown Sugar: Eighty Years of America's Black Female Superstars.* New York: Harmony Books, 1980.

Bonner, Patricia. "Analyzing the World of Langston Hughes' Living Blues: The Blues Experience Approach." *Popular Music and Society* 14, no. 2 (Summer 1990).

Bonosky, Phillip. "The 'Thirties' in American Culture." *Political Affairs,* May 1959.

Bricktop, with James Haskins. *Bricktop.* New York: Atheneum, 1983.

Brooks, Edward. *The Bessie Smith Companion.* New York: Da Capo, 1982.

Brown, Ken, and Albert McCarthy. "Mother of the Blues." *Jazz Music,* Aug. 1943.

Brown, Marion. "Improvisation and the Aural Tradition in Afro-American Music." *Black World,* Nov. 1973.

Brown, Sterling. *Southern Road.* Boston: Beacon, 1974.

Brown Sugar (based on book *Brown Sugar* by Donald Bogle). Produced by Matthew Pook. Ebony Productions, 1985. Videocassette.

Browne, Julie. "The Labor of Doing Time." In Elihu Rosenblatt, ed., *Criminal Injustice: Confronting the Prison Crisis.* Boston: South End, 1996.

Brunt, Rosalind, and Caroline Rowan, eds. *Feminism, Culture, and Politics.* London: Lawrence & Wishart, 1982.

Bufwack, Mary A., and Robert K. Oermann. *Songs of Self-Assertion: Women in Country Music.* Somerville, Mass.: New England Free Press, 1977.

Cade, Toni. *The Black Woman: An Anthology.* New York: Signet, 1970.

Caravan, Guy, and Candie Caravan, eds. *We Shall Overcome: Songs of the Southern Freedom Movement.* New York: Oak, 1963.

Carby, Hazel. "It Just Be's Dat Way Sometime: The Sexual Politics of Women's Blues." *Radical America* 20, no. 4 (June–July 1986).

Carruth, Hayden. *Sitting In.* Iowa City: University of Iowa Press, 1986.

Cary, Michael D. "Political Dimensions of the Blues." *Popular Music and Society* 14, no. 2 (Summer 1990).

Caudwell, Christopher. *Illusion and Reality.* New York: International, 1937.

———. *Studies and Further Studies in a Dying Culture.* New York: Monthly Review, 1979.

Charters, Samuel. *The Bluesmakers.* New York: Da Capo, 1991.

———. *The Poetry of the Blues.* New York: Avon, 1963.

Chernoff, John Miller. *African Rhythm and African Sensibility: Aesthetics and Social Action in African Musical Idioms.* Chicago: University of Chicago Press, 1979.

Chilton, John. *Billie's Blues: The Billie Holiday Story.* New York: Stein & Day, 1978.

———. *Who's Who of Jazz: Storyville to Swing Street.* Philadelphia: Chilton, 1970.

Christian, Barbara T. *Black Feminist Criticism: Perspectives on Black Women Writers.* New York: Pergamon, 1985.

———. *Black Women Novelists.* Westport, Conn.: Greenwood, 1984.

———. "The Race for Theory." *Cultural Critique* 6 (Spring 1987).

Clarke, Donald. *Wishing on the Moon: The Life and Times of Billie Holiday.* New York: Viking, 1994.

Clarke, John Henrik, ed. *Harlem: A Community in Transition.* New York: Citadel, 1964.

Clifford, James. *The Predicament of Culture: Twentieth-Century Ethnography, Literature, and Art.* Cambridge, Mass.: Harvard University Press, 1988.

Collier, James Lincoln. *The Great Jazz Artists.* New York: Four Winds, 1977.

Collins, Patricia Hill. *Black Feminist Thought: Knowledge, Consciousness, and the Politics of Empowerment.* Boston: Unwin Hyman, 1990.

Coltrane, John. *John Coltrane Speaks.* San Francisco: Sunship, 1981.

Cone, James H. *The Spirituals and the Blues: An Interpretation.* New York: Seabury, 1972.

Cook, Bruce. *Listen to the Blues.* New York: Scribner, 1975.

Cooper, Anna Julia. *A Voice from the South: By a Black Woman of the South.* New York: Oxford University Press, 1988.

Courlander, Harold. *Negro Folk Music U.S.A.* New York: Columbia University Press, 1963.

Craft, William. *Running a Thousand Miles for Freedom; or, The Escape of William and Ellen Craft from Slavery.* 1860. Reprint. Miami, Fla.: Mnemosyne, 1969.

Dahl, Linda. *Stormy Weather: The Music and Lives of a Century of Jazz Women.* New York: Pantheon, 1984.

Dalton, David. *Piece of My Heart: The Life, Times, and Legend of Janis Joplin.* New York: St. Martin's, 1971.

Dance, Daryl Cumber. *Shuckin' and Jivin': Folklore from Contemporary Black Americans.* Bloomington: Indiana University Press, 1978.

Dance, Stanley. *The World of Earl Hines.* New York: Scribner, 1977.

Dance, Stanley, and J. Dance. "Lovelorn Lady." *Saturday Review,* Jan. 12, 1963.

Davis, Angela. *Women, Race, and Class.* New York: Random House, 1981.

"Death of Bessie Smith: Ballad for Twelve-Strings." *Voices,* Winter 1950.

de Lauretis, Teresa. *Technologies of Gender: Essays on Theory, Film, and Fiction.* Bloomington: University of Indiana Press, 1987.

Dent, Gina, ed. *Black Popular Culture.* Seattle: Bay Press, 1992.

De Veaux, Alexis. *Don't Explain: A Song of Billie Holiday.* New York: Harper & Row, 1980.

Dexter, Dave, Jr. *The Jazz Story from the 90's to the 60's.* Englewood Cliffs, N.J.: Prentice-Hall, 1964.

Dill, Bonnie. "Race, Class, and Gender: Prospects for an All-Inclusive Sisterhood." *Feminist Studies* 9 (Spring 1983).

Dixon, Robert, and John Godrich. *Recording the Blues.* New York: Stein & Day, 1970.

Douglas, Bibian Collier. "Music as a Cultural Force in the Development of the Negro Race." *Negro History Bulletin,* Feb. 1952.

" 'Down Hearted Blues' Was Bessie's First Hit Record." *Afro-American,* Dec. 15, 1951.

Du Bois, W. E. B. *Black Reconstruction in America.* New York: Harcourt, Brace, 1935.

———. *Darkwater: Voices from Within the Veil.* New York: Harcourt, Brace & Howe, 1920.

Dugan, James, and John Hammond. "An Early Black-Music Concert from Spirituals to Swing." *Black Perspective in Music* 2, no. 2 (Fall 1974).

Ecker, Gisela, ed. *Feminist Aesthetics.* Boston: Beacon, 1985.

Eisler, Hanns. *A Rebel in Music.* New York: International, 1976.

Ellison, Mary. *Extensions of the Blues.* London: John Calder, 1989.

Ellison, Ralph. *Shadow and Act.* New York: Vintage, 1972.

Elwood, Philip. "A Re-creation of Bessie Smith." *San Francisco Examiner,* Apr. 15, 1985.

" 'Empress of the Blues' Died 21 Years Ago Beside Dark Highway, North of Clarksdale." *Second Line,* July–Aug. 1959.

Enzensberger, Hans Magnus. *The Consciousness Industry.* New York: Seabury, 1974.

Epstein, Dena. *Sinful Tunes and Spirituals: Black Folk Music to the Civil War.* Urbana: University of Illinois Press, 1977.

Evans, Sara. *Personal Politics: The Roots of Women's Liberation in the Civil Rights Movement and the New Left.* New York: Knopf, 1979.

Ewen, David. *All the Years of American Popular Music.* Englewood Cliffs, N.J.: Prentice-Hall, 1977.

Fanon, Frantz. *Toward the African Revolution.* New York: Grove, 1964.

Feinstein, Elaine. *Bessie Smith: Empress of the Blues.* New York: Penguin, 1985.

Ferris, William. "Blues Roots and Development." *Black Perspective in Music* 2, no. 2 (Fall 1974).

Ferris, William, and Mary L. Hart. *Folk Music and Modern Sound.* Jackson: University Press of Mississippi, 1982.

Finkelstein, Sidney. *Art and Society.* New York: International, 1947.

———. *How Music Expresses Ideas.* New York: International, 1952.

———. *Jazz: A People's Music.* New York: Citadel, 1948.

Finn, Julio. *The Bluesman.* London: Quartet, 1986.

Fisher, Miles Mark. *Negro Slave Songs in the United States.* New York: Citadel, 1953.

Flexner, Eleanor. *Century of Struggle: The Woman's Rights Movement in the United States.* New York: Atheneum, 1974.

Flowers, Charlie. "Empty Bed Blues." *American Way,* Aug. 1974.

Floyd, Samuel A., Jr. "Black American Music and Aesthetic Communication." *Black Music Research Journal.* Fisk University, 1980.

———. "Toward a Philosophy of Black Music Scholarship." *Black Music Research Journal.* Fisk University, 1981–82.

Foster, William Z. *The Negro People in American History.* New York: International Publishers, 1954.

Franklin, John Hope. *From Slavery to Freedom: A History of Negro Americans.* New York: Vintage, 1969.

———. *Race and History.* Baton Rouge and London: Louisiana State University Press, 1989.

Freedman, Samuel G. "The Blues: Hidden Cola for Black Writers." *San Francisco Chronicle,* Dec. 2, 1984.

Frith, Simon. *Sound Effects: Youth, Leisure, and the Politics of Rock 'n' Roll.* New York: Pantheon, 1981.

Fulbright, Thomas. "Ma Rainey and I." *Jazz Journal,* Mar. 1956.

Gabler, Milt. "A Lady Named Billie—and I." *Down Beat,* Mar. 29, 1973.

Garber, Eric S. "Gladys Bently: A Forgotten Pioneer." Paper for Women's Studies 560, San Francisco State University, May 22, 1986.

———. "Tain't Nobody's Business—Homosexuality in Harlem in the 1920s." *Advocate,* May 13, 1982.

Garon, Paul. *Blues and the Poetic Spirit.* New York: Da Capo, 1978.

Gates, Henry Louis, Jr. *The Signifying Monkey: A Theory of African-American Literary Criticism.* New York: Oxford University Press, 1988.

———, ed. *Reading Black, Reading Feminist: A Critical Anthology.* New York: Meridian, 1990.

Giddings, Paula. *When and Where I Enter: The Impact of Black Women on Race and Sex in America.* New York: Morrow, 1984.

Ginzburg, Ralph. *One Hundred Years of Lynching.* New York: Lancer, 1969.

Giovanni, Nikki. "Only Bessie Could Equal Bessie Smith." *Encore,* June 1973.

Gleason, Ralph. *Celebrating the Duke and Louis, Bessie, Billie, Bird, Carmen, Miles, Dizzy, and Other Heroes.* New York: Delta, 1975.

Goines, Leonard. "The Blues as Black Therapy." *Black World,* Nov. 1973.

"Going Out Guide—Smith Town." *New York Times,* Nov. 3, 1974.

Goldberg, David Theo. *Racist Culture: Philosophy and the Politics of Meaning.* Oxford: Blackwell, 1993.

Gourse, Leslie, ed. *The Billie Holiday Companion: Seven Decades of Commentary.* New York: Schirmer, 1997.

Gray, Herman. *Producing Jazz: The Experience of an Independent Record Company.* Philadelphia: Temple University Press, 1988.

Green, Benny. *The Reluctant Art: The Growth of Jazz.* New York: Horizon, 1963.

Guerrero, Ed. "Bessie Smith in 'The St. Louis Blues' a Mixed Bag: Talent, Creativity, and Devaluation." *Critical Perspectives of the Third World America* 2, no. 1 (1984).

Gutman, Herbert. *The Black Family in Slavery and Freedom, 1750–1925.* New York: Pantheon, 1976.

Guy-Sheftall, Beverly. *Daughters of Sorrow: Attitudes Toward Black Women, 1880–1920.* Brooklyn, N.Y.: Carlson, 1990.

————. *Words of Fire: An Anthology of African-American Feminist Thought.* New York: New Press, 1995.

Hadlock, Richard. *Jazz Masters of the Twenties.* New York: Macmillan, 1965.

Hall, Jacquelyn Dowd. *Revolt Against Chivalry: Jessie Daniel Ames and the Women's Campaign Against Chivalry.* Rev. ed. New York: Columbia University Press, 1993.

Hall, Stuart. "What Is This 'Black' in Black Popular Culture?" In Gina Dent, ed., *Black Popular Culture.* Seattle: Bay Press, 1992.

Hamm, Charles. *Yesterdays: Popular Song in America.* New York: Norton, 1979.

Handy, W. C., ed. *A Treasury of the Blues.* New York: Charles Boni, 1926.

Haraway, Donna. *Simians, Cyborgs, and Women: The Reinvention of Nature.* New York: Routledge, 1991.

Harris, Sheldon. *Blues Who's Who.* New York: Arlington House, 1979.

Harrison, Daphne Duval. *Black Pearls: Blues Queens of the 1920s.* New Brunswick: Rutgers University Press, 1988.

Haskins, James. *Black Music in America.* New York: Crowell, 1987.

————. *The Cotton Club.* New York: Random House, 1977.

Hebdige, Dick. *Cut 'n' Mix: Culture, Identity, and Caribbean Music.* London: Routledge, 1990.

Hentoff, Nat. "Indigenous Music; Billie Holiday/Songs and Conversations." *Nation,* June 19, 1976.

————. "Indigenous Music; Billie Holiday/Songs and Conversations." *Nation,* July 17, 1976.

————. *The Jazz Life.* New York: Da Capo, 1961.

————. "The Soft Mythology of Jazz." *Show,* Nov. 1961.

Hentoff, Nat, and Albert J. McCarthy. *Jazz: New Perspectives on the History of Jazz.* 1959. Reprint. New York: Da Capo, 1974.

Herrera-Sobek, María. *The Mexican Corrido: A Feminist Analysis.* Bloomington: Indiana University Press, 1990.

Hill, Abram. "Bessie Smith." Manuscript from Writers Workshop. Aug. 24, 1939.

Hine, Darlene Clark, ed. *Black Women in America: An Historical Encyclopedia.* Brooklyn, N.Y.: Carlson, 1993.

Hodeir, André. *Jazz: Its Evolution and Essence.* Translated by David Noakes. New York: Grove, 1956.

————. *Toward Jazz.* Translated by Noel Burch. New York: Da Capo, 1976.

————. *The World's Jazz*. Translated by Noel Burch. New York: Grove, 1972.

Hoefer, George. "The Hot Box." *Down Beat*, Oct. 17, 1957.

Holiday, Billie, with William Dufty. *Lady Sings the Blues*. 1956. Reprint. New York: Penguin, 1984.

hooks, bell. *Ain't I a Woman: Black Women and Feminism*. Boston: South End, 1981.

————. *Black Looks: Race and Representation*. Boston: South End, 1992.

Horkheimer, Max, and Theodor W. Adorno. *Dialectic of Enlightenment*. Translated by John Cumming. New York: Continuum, 1944.

Huggins, Nathan Irvin. *Harlem Renaissance*. London: Oxford University Press, 1971.

————, ed. *Voices from the Harlem Renaissance*. New York: Oxford University Press, 1976.

Hughes, Langston. "Bessie Smith, 'The Empress of the Blues.' " In *Famous Negro Music Makers*. New York: Dodd, Mead, 1955.

————. *The Best of Simple*. New York: Hill & Wang, 1961.

————. *The Big Sea: An Autobiography*. New York: Hill & Wang, 1940.

————. *The Langston Hughes Reader*. New York: George Braziller, 1958.

————. *The Weary Blues*. New York: Knopf, 1926.

Hughes, Langston, and Arna Bontemps, eds. *The Book of Negro Folklore*. New York: Dodd, Mead, 1958.

Hurston, Zora Neale. *Mules and Men*. Bloomington: Indiana University Press, 1978.

————. *Tell My Horse: Voodoo and Life in Haiti and Jamaica*. 1938. Reprint. New York: Harper & Row, 1990.

————. *Their Eyes Were Watching God*. New York: Harper & Row, 1990.

Hurtado, Aida. *The Color of Privilege: Three Blasphemies on Race and Feminism*. Ann Arbor: University of Michigan Press, 1996.

————. "Relating to Privilege: Seduction and Rejection in the Subordination of White Women and Women of Color." *Signs: A Journal of Women and Culture in Society* 14, no. 4 (Summer 1989).

Industrial Workers of the World. *Songs of the Workers*. 34th ed. Chicago: Industrial Workers of the World, 1973.

Jackson, Jacqueline Johnson. "Black Women in a Racist Society." In Charles Willie et al., eds., *Racism and Mental Health*. Pittsburgh: University of Pittsburgh Press, 1973.

Jacobs, Harriet Brent. *Incidents in the Life of a Slave Girl, Written by Herself*. Edited by Jean Fagan Yellin. Cambridge, Mass: Harvard University Press, 1987.

Jahn, Janheinz. *Muntu: The New African Culture*. New York: Grove, 1961.

James, Burnett. *Billie Holiday*. New York: Hippocrene, 1984.

————. *Essays on Jazz*. London: Sidgwick & Jackson, 1961.

James, Joy. *Transcending the Talented Tenth: Black Leaders and American Intellectuals*. New York: Routledge, 1997.

Jaynes, Gerald David, and Robin Williams, Jr., eds. *A Common Destiny: Blacks and American Society*. Washington, D.C.: National Academy Press, 1989.

Johnson, Howard, and Jim Pines. *Reggae: Deep Roots Music.* New York: Proteus, 1982.

Johnson, James Weldon, and J. Rosemond Johnson. *The Book of American Negro Spirituals.* New York: Da Capo, 1991.

Jones, Bessie. *For the Ancestors: Autobiographical Memories.* Edited by John Stewart. Urbana: University of Illinois Press, 1983.

Jones, Hettie. *Big Star Fallin', Mama: Five Women in Black Music.* New York: Viking, 1974.

Jones, Jacqueline. *Labor of Love, Labor of Sorrow: Black Women, Work, and the Family from Slavery to the Present.* New York: Basic Books, 1985.

Jones, LeRoi (Amiri Baraka). *Black Music.* New York: Morrow, 1968.

———. *Blues People.* New York: Morrow, 1963.

Jones, Max. " 'I'm Settling in London,' Says Billie Holiday." *Melody Maker,* Feb. 28, 1959.

———. "She Was Original, Honest—Unique." *Melody Maker,* Aug. 8, 1959.

Jordan, June. *On Call: Political Essays.* Boston: South End, 1985.

Jost, Ekkehard. *Jazzmusiker: Materialien zur Soziologie der Afro-americanischen Musik.* Berlin: Ullstein Materialien, 1982.

———. *Sozialgeschichte des Jazz in den USA.* Frankfurt: Fischer, 1982.

Kahn, H. " 'They Call Me an Artist in Britain,' Says Billie Holiday." *Melody Maker,* Nov. 22, 1958.

Katz, Bernard. *The Social Implications of Early Negro Music in the United States.* New York: Arno, 1969.

Keil, Charles. *Urban Blues.* Chicago: University of Chicago Press, 1966.

Kelley, Robin D. G. *Hammer and Hoe: Alabama Communists During the Great Depression.* Chapel Hill: University of North Carolina Press, 1990.

Kellner, Bruce. *Carl Van Vechten and the Irreverent Decades.* Norman: University of Oklahoma Press, 1968.

Kemble, Frances Anne. *Journal of a Residence on a Georgian Plantation in 1838–1839.* 1863. Reprint. New York: Knopf, 1961.

Kennedy, Emmet R. *Mellows: A Chronicle of Unknown Singers.* New York: Albert & Charles Boni, 1925.

Kofsky, Frank. *Black Nationalism and the Revolution in Music.* New York: Pathfinder, 1970.

Kravetz, Sallie. *Ethel Ennis: The Reluctant Jazz Star.* Baltimore: Gateway, 1984.

Lady Sings the Blues. Directed by Sidney J. Furie. Paramount Pictures Corporation and Berry Gordy, 1972. Film.

Landes, Joan. "The Public and the Private Sphere: A Feminist Reconsideration." In Johanna Meehan, ed., *Feminists Read Habermas.* London: Routledge, 1995.

Lang, Ian. *Background of the Blues.* London: Workers Music Association, 1943.

Larkin, Philip. *All What Jazz.* New York: St. Martin's, 1970.

Lear, Len. "A Lawsuit for What's Owed Bessie Smith." *Sepia*, Sept. 1977.

Leonard, Neil. *Jazz: Myth and Religion*. New York: Oxford University Press, 1987.

Lerner, Gerda, ed. *Black Women in White America: A Documentary History*. New York: Pantheon, 1972.

Levin, Floyd. "The American Jazz Scene." *Jazz Journal*, Jan. 1952.

Levine, Lawrence. *Black Culture and Black Consciousness: Afro-American Thought from Slavery to Freedom*. New York: Oxford University Press, 1975.

Lewis, David Levering. *When Harlem Was in Vogue*. New York: Knopf, 1981.

Lewis, Lisa A. *Gender Politics and MTV*. Philadelphia: Temple University Press, 1990.

Lieb, Sandra. *Mother of the Blues: A Study of Ma Rainey*. Amherst: University of Massachusetts Press, 1981.

Locke, Alain. *The Critical Temper of Alain Locke: A Selection of His Essays on Art and Culture*. Edited by Jeffrey C. Stewart. New York: Garland, 1983.

———, ed. *The New Negro*. 1925. Reprint. New York: Atheneum, 1977.

The Long Night of Lady Day. Directed by John Jeremy. TCB/BBC-TV, 1984. Videocassette.

Lorde, Audre. *Sister Outsider*. Trumansburg, N.Y.: Crossing Press, 1984.

Lovell, John, Jr. *Black Song: The Forge and the Flame*. New York: Macmillan, 1972.

Lowe, Janet. "Bessie Smith, Blues Singers Go Down in Women's History." *News World*, July 5, 1980.

Lubiano, Wahneema, ed. *The House That Race Built: Black Americans, U.S. Terrain*. New York: Pantheon, 1997.

Lyons, Mary E. *Sorrow's Kitchen: The Life and Folklore of Zora Neale Hurston*. New York: Scribner, 1990.

Marcuse, Herbert. *The Aesthetic Dimension: Toward a Critique of Marxist Aesthetics*. Boston: Beacon, 1978.

———. *Eros and Civilization: A Philosophical Inquiry into Freud*. Boston: Beacon, 1955.

Marx, Karl. *Early Writings*. Edited by T. B. Bottomore. New York: McGraw-Hill, 1964.

Marx, Karl, and Friedrich Engels. *On Literature and Art*. Moscow: Progress, 1976.

McClary, Susan. *Feminine Endings: Music, Gender, and Sexuality*. Minneapolis: University of Minnesota Press, 1991.

McGuire, Philip. "Black Music Critics and the Classic Blues Singers." *Black Perspective in Music* 14, no. 2 (Spring 1986).

McMillan, Allan. "New York Sees Bessie Smith; Wonders Where She's Been." *Chicago Defender*, Mar. 28, 1936.

McPherson, James Alan. *Railroad: Trains and Train People in American Culture*. New York: Random House, 1976.

McRae, Barry. "The Ma Rainey and Bessie Smith Accompaniments." *Jazz Journal*, Mar. 1961.

Meehan, Johanna, ed. *Feminists Read Habermas*. London: Routledge, 1995.

Mercer, Kobena. *Welcome to the Jungle: New Positions in Black Cultural Studies*. New York: Routledge, 1994.

Meyer, Leonard B. *Emotion and Meaning in Music*. Chicago: University of Chicago Press, 1956.

Mingus, Charles. *Beneath the Underdog*. New York: Penguin, 1971.

The Mississippi Valley Flood Disaster of 1927: Official Report of the Relief Operations. Washington, D.C.: American National Red Cross, 1928.

Moore, Carman. "Blues and Bessie Smith." *New York Times*, Mar. 9, 1968.

———. *Somebody's Angel Child: The Story of Bessie Smith*. New York: Dell, 1969.

Mordden, Ethan. *That Jazz! An Idiosyncratic Social History of the American Twenties*. New York: Putnam, 1978.

Morgan, Robin, ed. *Sisterhood Is Powerful: An Anthology of Writings from the Women's Liberation Movement*. New York: Vintage, 1970.

Morgenstern, Dan. "Hall of Fame Winner Bessie Smith: Empress of the Blues." *Down Beat*, Aug. 24, 1967.

Morrison, Toni. *Jazz*. New York: Knopf, 1992.

Moynihan, Daniel P. *The Negro Family: The Case for National Action*. Washington, D.C.: U.S. Department of Labor, 1965.

Mugo, Michere Githae. *Orature and Human Rights*. Rome: Institute of South African Development Studies, NUL, Lesotho, 1991.

Muñoz, José, and Carlos Sampayo. *Billie Holiday: The Story of America's Greatest and Most Tragic Jazz Singer*. Seattle: Fantagraphic Books, 1993.

Murray, Albert. *Stomping the Blues*. New York: McGraw-Hill, 1976.

"Murrow Album Nominated for Recording Fame." *Courier News*, Feb. 8, 1977.

Naison, Mark. *Communists in Harlem During the Depression*. New York: Grove, 1983.

National Museum of American History. *Black American Popular Music: Rhythm and Blues, 1945–1955*. Washington, D.C.: Smithsonian Institution, 1986.

———. *Music of the Black American Composer*. Washington, D.C.: Smithsonian Institution, 1986.

Near, Holly. *Fire in the Rain—Singer in the Storm*. New York: Morrow, 1990.

Nemy, Enid. "A Ma Rainey Quartet Plays Its Own Special Music." *New York Times*, Oct. 28, 1984.

Neuls-Bates, Carol, ed. *Women in Music: An Anthology of Source Readings from the Middle Ages to the Present*. New York: Harper & Row, 1982.

"New York Sees Bessie Smith; Wonders Where She's Been." *Chicago Defender*, Mar. 28, 1936.

Nicholson, Stuart. *Billie Holiday*. Boston: Northeastern University Press, 1995.

Oakley, Giles. *The Devil's Music: A History of the Blues*. New York and London: Harcourt Brace Jovanovich, 1976.

Oliver, Paul. *Bessie Smith*. London: Cassell, 1960.

———. *Blues off the Record*. New York: Baton, 1984.

———. *Conversation with the Blues*. New York: Horizon, 1965.

———. *The Meaning of the Blues*. New York: Collier, 1960.

———. *Savannah Syncopators: African Retentions in the Blues*. New York: Stein & Day, 1970.

———. *Screening the Blues: Aspects of the Blues Tradition*. New York: Da Capo, 1968.

O'Meally, Robert. *Lady Day: The Many Faces of Billy Holiday*. New York: Arcade Publishing, 1991.

Outloud! A Collection of New Songs by Women. Oakland, Calif.: Inkworks, 1978.

Palmer, Robert. "The Real Ma Rainey Had a Certain Way with the Blues." *New York Times*, Oct. 28, 1984.

Panassié, Hugues. *Douze Années de Jazz*. Paris: Coprea, 1946.

———. *Hot Jazz: The Guide to Swing Music*. Translated by Lyle and Eleanor Dowling. 1936. Reprint. Westport, Conn.: Negro Universities Press, 1970.

———. *The Real Jazz*. 1942. Reprint. Westport, Conn.: Greenwood, 1973.

Parrish, Lydia. *Slave Songs of the Georgia Sea Islands*. Athens: University of Georgia Press, 1992.

Partington, Les. "Your Record Library." *Jazzology*, Sept. 1946.

Placksin, Sally. *American Women in Jazz*. New York: Wideview Books, 1982.

Pleasants, Henry. *The Great American Popular Singers*. New York: Simon & Schuster, 1974.

Polillo, Arrigo. "Bessie the Great." Translated by Fred Bouchard. *Jazz Journal*, Apr. 1969.

Reagon, Bernice Johnson, ed. *Black American Culture and Scholarship: Contemporary Issues*. Washington, D.C.: Smithsonian Institution, 1985.

Reasons, George. "She Had a Dream—Bessie Smith." *Newark Sunday News*, Mar. 28, 1971.

Richie, Beth. *Compelled to Crime: The Gender Entrapment of Battered Women*. New York: Routledge, 1996.

Rollins, Judith. *Between Women: Domestics and Their Employers*. Philadelphia: Temple University Press, 1985.

Rose, Tricia. *Black Noise: Rap Music and Black Culture in Contemporary America*. Hanover, N.H.: Wesleyan University Press, 1994.

Russell, Tony. *Blacks, Whites, and Blues*. New York: Stein & Day, 1970.

Ryan, Mary P. *Womanhood in America: From Colonial Times to the Present*. New York: Franklin Watts, 1975.

Sackheim, Eric, ed. *The Blues Line*. New York: Schirmer, 1968.

Scarborough, Dorothy. *On the Trail of Negro Folksongs*. Cambridge, Mass.: Harvard University Press, 1925.

Schechter, Susan. *Women and Male Violence: The Visions and Struggles of the Battered Women's Movement*. Boston: South End, 1982.

Schiffman, Jack. *Uptown: The Story of Harlem's Apollo Theatre.* New York: Cowles, 1971.

Schuler, Vic. "The Mystery of the Two Ma Raineys." *Melody Maker,* Oct. 13, 1951.

Schuller, Gunther. *Early Jazz: Its Roots and Musical Development.* New York: Oxford University Press, 1968.

———. *The Swing Era.* New York: Oxford University Press, 1989.

Shapiro, Nat, and Nat Hentoff. *Hear Me Talkin' to Ya.* New York: Dover, 1955.

———, eds. *The Jazz Makers: Essays on the Greats of Jazz.* New York: Da Capo, 1979.

Shaw, Arnold. *Black Popular Music in America.* New York: Schirmer, 1986.

Sidran, Ben. *Black Talk.* New York: Da Capo, 1981.

Simone, Nina, with Stephen Cleary. *I Put a Spell on You: The Autobiography of Nina Simone.* New York: Pantheon, 1991.

Skowronski, JoAnn. *Women in American Music: A Bibliography.* Metuchen, N.J.: Scarecrow Press, 1978.

Smith, Charles Edward. "Ma Rainey." In *Notable American Women, 1807–1950.* Cambridge, Mass.: Radcliffe College, 1963.

———. "Ma Rainey and the Minstrels." *Record Changer,* June 1955.

Smith, Valerie. " 'Loopholes of Retreat': Architecture and Ideology in Harriet Jacobs' *Incidents in the Life of a Slave Girl.*" In Henry Louis Gates, Jr., ed., *Reading Black, Reading Feminist.* New York: Meridian, 1990.

Southern, Eileen. "Music Research and the Black Aesthetic." *Black World,* Nov. 1973.

Spaeth, Sigmund. *The Facts of Life in Popular Song.* New York: Whittlesey House, 1934.

Spellman, A. B. *Four Lives in the Bebop Business.* New York: Pantheon, 1966.

Spelman, Elizabeth V. *Inessential Woman: Problems of Exclusion in Feminist Thought.* Boston: Beacon, 1988.

St. Louis Blues. Directed by Dudley Murphy. Gramercy Studio of RCA Photophone, presented by Radio Pictures. Film.

Stearns, Marshall W. *The Story of Jazz.* New York: Oxford University Press, 1956.

Stewart-Baxter, Derrick. "Billie Holiday To-day." *Jazz Journal,* Apr. 1956.

———. "Blues Digest." *Jazz Journal,* July 1973.

———. *Ma Rainey and the Classic Blues Singers.* New York: Stein & Day, 1970.

Tanner, Leslie B., ed. *Voices from Women's Liberation.* New York: Signet, 1971.

Tawa, Nicholas. *A Music for the Millions.* New York: Pendragon Press, 1984.

Taylor, Arthur. *Notes and Tones.* New York: Perigee Books, 1977.

Taylor, Frank C., with Gerald Cook. *Alberta Hunter: A Celebration in Blues.* New York: McGraw-Hill, 1987.

Terkel, Studs. "Bessie Smith—Empress of the Blues." In *Giants of Jazz.* New York: Crowell, 1975.

Terrell, Mary Church. *Colored Woman in a White World.* Washington, D.C.: Rans-dell Publishing, 1940.

Titon, Jeff Todd. *Early Downhome Blues.* Urbana: University of Illinois Press, 1977.

Tracy, Steven C. *Langston Hughes and the Blues.* Urbana: University of Illinois Press, 1988.

"The True Story of Bessie Smith's Death." *Second Line,* Sept.–Oct. 1959.

Turner-Rowles, Norman. "The Paramount Wildcat." *Jazz Journal,* Mar. 1954.

Vail, Ken. *Lady Day's Diary: The Life of Billie Holiday, 1937–1959.* Chessington, Surrey, U.K.: Castle Communications, 1996.

Van Vechten, Carl. *"Keep A-Inchin' Along": Selected Writings of Carl Van Vechten About Black Art and Letters.* Edited by Bruce Kellner. Westport, Conn.: Greenwood, 1979.

Vazquez, Adolfo Sanchez. *Art and Society.* New York: Monthly Review, 1973.

Walker, Alice. *The Color Purple.* New York: Washington Square, 1982.

———. *The Same River Twice: Honoring the Difficult: A Meditation on Life, Art, and the Making of the Film "The Color Purple," Ten Years Later.* New York: Simon & Schuster, 1996.

Wall, Cheryl. "Whose Sweet Angel Child? Blues Women, Langston Hughes, and Writing During the Harlem Renaissance." In Arnold Rampersad, *Langston Hughes: The Man, His Art, and His Continuing Influence.* Edited by C. James Trotman. New York: Garland, 1995.

Wallace, Michelle. *Invisibility Blues: From Pop to Theory.* London and New York: Verso, 1990.

Walton, Ortiz M. *Music: Black, White, and Blue.* New York: Morrow, 1972.

Waters, Ethel, with Charles Samuels. *His Eye Is on the Sparrow.* New York: Da Capo, 1992.

Weiler, A. H. "Welcome Back, Vincente." *Courier News,* Dec. 10, 1972.

Wells, Ida B. *Crusade for Justice: The Autobiography of Ida B. Wells.* Edited by Alfreda M. Duster. Chicago: University of Chicago Press, 1970.

"What Black Writers Owe to Music." *New York Times,* Oct. 14, 1984.

White, Deborah Gray. *Ar'n't I a Woman: Female Slaves in the Plantation South.* New York: Norton, 1985.

White, John. *Billie Holiday: Her Life and Times.* New York: Universe, 1987.

Whitney, Malika Lee, and Dermott Hussey. *Bob Marley: Reggae King of the World.* Jamaica: Kingston Publishers, 1982.

Wild Women Don't Have the Blues. Directed by Christine Dall. Calliope Film Resources, 1989. Videocassette.

Williams, Martin. *The Jazz Tradition.* New York: New American Library, 1971.

———. *Where's the Melody?* New York: Pantheon, 1961.

Williams, Patricia J. *The Alchemy of Race and Rights: Diary of a Law Professor.* Cambridge, Mass.: Harvard University Press, 1991.

Wilson, August. *Ma Rainey's Black Bottom: A Play in Two Acts.* New York: New American Library, 1985.

Wilson, John S. "All Bessie Smith's '78's Due in LP Series." *New York Times,* June 4, 1970.

———. "Bessie Smith's Successors." *New York Times,* Apr. 20, 1958.

Wilson, Mary. *Dream Girl: My Life as a Supreme.* New York: St. Martin's, 1986.

Winter, Nina. *Interview with the Muse.* Berkeley, Calif.: Moon Books, 1978.

Wintz, Cary D. *Black Culture and the Harlem Renaissance.* Houston, Texas: Rice University Press, 1988.

Worsfold, Sally Ann. "Empress of the Blues." *Storyville,* no. 25 (Oct.–Nov. 1969).

Young, Al. *Bodies and Soul.* Berkeley, Calif.: Creative Arts, 1981.

Young, Irene. *For the Record.* Oakland, Calif.: Olivia Records, 1982.

INDEX

AAA blues form, 79
abolitionists, 7
advice songs, 13–14, 16–17, 45, 53–54,
    57–62
Aesthetic Dimension, The (Marcuse),
    163–64
African cultures, xix, 7, 45, 49, 54, 122,
    155, 166, 167, 174
    religion in, 6, 33, 123, 158, 159
Afrocentric feminist epistemology, 57
"After You've Gone," 258
"Aggravatin' Papa," 258–59
AIDS, 131
Albertson, Chris, 60–61, 88–89, 96
alcohol, 22, 83
"Alexander's Ragtime Band," 88,
    259–60
Allen, Lewis, 184–85, 186, 194, 196
"All God's Children Got Shoes
    (Wings)," 71
American Civil Liberties Union
    (ACLU), 103
American Youth Congress, 191
Anderson, Ernie, 186
"Any Woman's Blues," 260
Any Woman's Blues (Washington, ed.),
    xiv
Apollo Theatre, 195
Armstrong, Louis, 144, 166
"Army Camp Harmony Blues," 200
Arrant, Lena, 224
Associated Communist Clubs of
    Harlem, 162
Association of Southern Women for the
    Prevention of Lynching (ASWPL),
    190
"At the Christmas Ball," 260–61

Austin, Lovie, 50, 200–201, 223, 229,
    253, 254–55, 260, 265–66, 267,
    270, 273–74
Autobiography of an Ex-Colored Man
    (Johnson), 150

"Baby, Have Pity on Me," 261–62
"Baby, Won't You Please Come Home,"
    106–7, 262–63
"Baby Doll," 24, 261
"Backwater Blues," 108–10, 143, 263–64
"Bad Girl Blues," 40
"Bad Luck Blues," 200
Badu, Erykah, 197
Baker, Houston, 71, 148–49
Bambara, Toni Cade, xiii
Barbecue Bob, 110
Barker, Danny, 121–22, 124, 137
"Barrel House Blues," 22, 200
barrelhouses, 133
Barry, John, 110
"Beale Street Papa," 264
Bellenda, A., 305
Berendt, Joachim, 196
Berlin, Irving, 88, 259–60
Bernard, A., 333
Bernie, S., 273
Berry, Chu, 15
"Bessemer Bound Blues," 81–82, 201
"Bessie Smith and Her Yellow Girl
    Revue," 88
Bessie Smith Companion, The (Brooks),
    26–27, 30, 52, 87–88, 95, 99–100,
    271, 276, 352
Bible, 7, 129
"Big Boy Blues," 201–2
"Big Feeling Blues," 202

Big Sea, The (Hughes), 145
Billie Holiday (Nicholson), 186
"Billie Holiday and the Art of Commu-
  nication" (James), 170–71
"Black Cat Hoot Owl Blues," 203
Black Codes, 103
"Black Dust Blues," 203
black English, 12, 13, 24, 165–68
"Black Eye Blues," 29, 204
black liberation movement, 113
"Black Mountain Blues," 34, 264–65
Black Pearls (Harrison), xvii–xviii, 13,
  37–38, 54
Black Swan Records, xii, 123, 152–54
Blake, Eubie, 149
"Blame It on the Blues," 15, 91, 111–12,
  204–5
"Bleeding Hearted Blues," 265–66
"Blue, Blue," 266
"blue devils," 113
"blue notes," 33
blues:
  AAA form of, 79
  African and European elements in,
    122–23
  black aesthetic and, 138–60
  black historical experience and,
    113–19, 141
  black women's self-understanding
    and, 37–38, 41, 142
  call-and-response patterns in, 20,
    54–57
  classic era of, xii–xiii, xvii–xviii, 5
  as collective property, 136
  country era of, 11, 69, 111
  critics and historians on, xiv, 44,
    92–95, 99–101, 113, 118
  derivation and meaning of term, 33,
    112, 113
  as "Devil's music," 6–7, 8, 123–24, 137
  emotional power of, 134–36

  female community evoked in, 59,
    62–65, 92
  feminism prefigured in, xv, xviii–ix,
    xx, 18, 28–30, 64, 128, 143, 155
  first recordings of, xii
  Harlem Renaissance and, xiii, 123,
    144–52
  Holiday and, 161, 168, 170–71
  improvisation of lyrics in, xvi
  integrated bands and, 15
  irony in, 12, 18, 25–28, 100, 143
  layers of meaning in, 24, 25–28, 100,
    143
  as live vs. recorded medium, 94–95,
    111
  male singers of, xii–xiii, 11
  marginalization of women's
    contributions to, xiv, 9, 44–45, 94,
    124–25
  models of black womanhood in, 45–46
  multiple perspectives in, 49
  naming process in, 33, 128–29
  personification of, 113–16
  political analysis and, 33
  as pornographic, 14–15
  religion and, 120–37
  sacred and secular blurred in, 8–9
  sales figures for recordings of, xii, 4,
    141, 152
  self-consciousness in, 127–28, 134–35
  sexuality in, xiii, xv–xvi, xvii, 3–41,
    42–65, 91, 118, 120, 131
  social protest and, 91–119
  spirituals and work songs compared
    with, 4–7
  taboos absent in, 107, 133–34
  thematic range of, 13
  travel and, 8, 19–20, 66–90, 120
  twelve-bar structure and, 17
  white listeners and, 141–42, 146–48,
    153

women's advice songs in, 13–14, 16–17, 45, 53–54, 57–62
"Blues, Oh Blues," 205
Blues and the Poetic Spirit (Garon), 94
"Blue Spirit Blues," 266–67
"Blues the World Forgot, Parts 1 and 2," 205–8
Bonosky, Phillip, 192
"Booze and Blues," 208
Borum, Memphis Willie B., 40
"Bo-Weevil Blues," 208–9, 267
Bradford, Perry, xii, 292, 336, 337–38
Britt, A., 258–59
"Broken Hearted Blues," 209
"Broken Soul Blues," 209–10
Brooks, Edward, 26–27, 30, 52, 87–88, 95, 99–100, 101, 271, 276, 352
Brooks, G., 275, 278, 285–86, 290, 302–3, 324–25, 329–30, 332–33, 335, 346, 348–49
Brown, E., 276, 281
Brown, Sterling, 139–41, 148–49
Brymn, T., 294, 319–20
buffet flats, 133, 137
Burke, H., 310–11
"Bye Bye Blues," 267–68

Café Society, 182, 184, 186, 190, 195
"Cake Walking Babies (From Home)," 268–69
call-and-response, 20, 54–57
"C. & A. Blues," 19
Carby, Hazel, 31–32, 40, 46, 107–8
"Careless Love Blues," 269
Carter, Paul, 47, 254, 267–68, 350–51
"Cell Bound Blues," 35, 210
"Cemetery Blues," 269–70
"Chain Gang Blues," 102–3, 210–11
Chapman, Tracy, 197
Charters, Samuel, 92, 93–94, 101, 113, 118

Cheek, Cordie, 189
"Chicago Bound Blues," 19, 270
Chilton, John, 162, 181–82, 184–85, 190
church, black, 9, 121, 123–26, 133, 137
    see also religions
circuses, 72
civil rights movement, 93, 191
Clarke, Donald, 186
class, 11
    "Poor Man's Blues" and, 95–98
    sexuality and, 42–44, 65
club movement, 43–44, 65
"Cold in Hand Blues," 270–71
Cole, H., 264–65
Collins, Patricia Hill, 56–57
Colored Advisory Commission, 110
Color Purple, The (film), 124
Color Purple, The (Walker), 124
Columbia Records, xii, 95, 141, 195
Commodore Records, 95, 195
Communist Party, 190
Communists in Harlem During the Depression (Naison), 162
compact discs, blues reissues on, xiii, xvi, xviii
Cone, James, 8, 9
consciousness-raising, 28–29, 42, 54–55, 64
convict lease system, 103–4
Cook, Bruce, 125–26
Coolidge, Calvin, 110
Cooper, Anna Julia, xiv
corridos, xviii
Costigan-Wagner bill, 191–92
"Countin' the Blues," 120, 128–29, 134, 211
country blues, 11, 69, 111
Cox, Ida, xii, xiii, 38, 94, 171, 284–85
Cox, Jimmy, 295–96, 322
Craft, Ellen, 67

Crawford, J., 291–92
"Crazy Blues," xii, 152
Creamer, H., 258, 306–7, 342, 351–52
Crenshaw, Kimberlé, xix

"Daddy Goodbye Blues," 211–12
D'Alvarez, Marguerite, 147
"Damper Down Blues," 212
Darkwater (Du Bois), 46
Davenport, Cow Cow, 84
Davis, Joe, 288–89, 311
Davis, Selma, 202, 203, 226, 230–31
"Dead Drunk Blues," 213
"Deep Moaning Blues," 213–14
Delaney, Tom, 245–46, 279
Dent, Gina, xix
De Rose, P., 316
De Veaux, Alexis, xiv
"Devil's Gonna Get You," 271
"Devil's music," blues viewed as, 6–7, 8,
    123–24, 137
Dexter, Dave, 182
"Dirty No-Gooders Blues," 272
"Dixie Flyer Blues," 86, 272–73
Dogon culture, 33
domesticity, blues women and, 9–10,
    11, 17–18, 22, 72
domestic service, 72, 98–102, 143
domestic violence, 3, 17, 25–33
    male vs. female responses to, 32
"Don't Cry Baby," 273
"Don't Fish in My Sea," 214
Dorsey, Thomas, 107, 135, 136, 203,
    204–5, 210–11, 216, 222–23,
    224–25, 227–28, 232, 233, 236,
    242–43, 247, 252, 382 n. 36
"Down Hearted Blues," 21, 141, 273–74
"Down in the Basement," 126–27, 215
"Do Your Duty," 274–75
"dozens, playing the," 166
"Dream Blues," 215
drum music, banning of, 167

Du Bois, W. E. B., 46, 152
Dufty, William, 186
"Dyin' by the Hour," 275
"Dying Gambler's Blues," 275–76

Early, Guy, 232
"Easy Come, Easy Go Blues," 38–39,
    276
"Eavesdropper's Blues," 30, 276–77
"Eeny Meeny Miney Mo," 169
Elegua, 6, 123
Eller, H., 314
Ellison, Ralph, 10, 132–33, 161–62
emancipation, 4, 7–10, 19, 22, 45, 67,
    68, 112, 131
"Empty Bed Blues, Parts I and II," 49,
    277–78
English, black, 12, 13, 24, 165–68
Eros and Civilization (Marcuse), 163
erotic, Lord's theory of, 172–73
Ewen, David, 168
"Explaining the Blues," 216
extramarital relationships, 3, 15–16, 17

families:
    blues women and, 13
    matriarchy and, 122
    slavery and, 10, 81
Fanon, Frantz, 193–94
"Far Away Blues," 84–85, 278
"Farewell Daddy Blues," 216–17
Feather, Leonard, 196
Federal Bureau of Investigation (FBI),
    162
Feinstein, Elaine, 154
feminism, 178
    blues as base for, 128
    blues women as precursors of, xv,
        xviii–xix, xx, 18, 28–30, 64, 143, 155
    consciousness-raising strategies in,
        28–29, 42, 54–55, 64
    race and, xix, 42, 55

field hollers, 167
Finkelstein, Sidney, 167
Finn, Julio, 69–70
Fisher, Fred, 222
"Flood Blues," 111
"Florida Bound Blues," 278–79
Florida Cotton Blossoms, 72
"Follow the Deal on Down," 279
"Foolish Man Blues," 280
" 'Fore Day Honry Scat," 217
fortune tellers, 156–57
Foster, William Z., 191
"Frankie Blues," 75, 280–81
Franklin, Aretha, 57
Franklin, John Hope, 189
"Freedom Now Suite," 196
Friendship Baptist Church, 125
"Frosty Morning Blues," 281
Fuller, P., 293

Gabler, Milt, 195
gangsta rap, 48
Garon, Paul, 21, 94
Gates, Henry Louis, Jr., 6
Gee, Jack, 270–71, 275–76, 352
"Georgia Cake Walk," 218
Georgia Smart Set, 72
Giddings, Paula, xix, 43, 188
Gillespie, Marcia, xix
"Gimme a Pigfoot," 138, 281–82
"Gin House Blues," 282–83
Glasco and Glasco, 224
"Glory of Negro History, The"
    (Hughes), 145
God, 117–18, 126, 128–29
"God Bless the Child," 162
"God's music," 6
"Gold Dust Twins," 98
"Golden Rule Blues," 283
"Gone Daddy Blues," 16, 219
"Goodbye Daddy Blues," 220
"Goodbye Mama Forever Blues," 220

Goodman, Benny, 15, 168
"Good Man Is Hard to Find, A," 45,
    61–62, 284
Goodson, Ida, 6–7, 126
"goofer dust," 159
gospel music, 5, 8, 130
Graham, R., 293
Grainger, Porter, 30, 271, 289, 312–13,
    328–29, 336–37, 342–43, 354,
    357
"Graveyard Dream Blues," 284–85
Gray, H., 339, 343–44
Great Depression, 96–97, 162, 168, 187,
    190–91
Green, Benny, 168
Green, E., 284
"Grievin' Hearted Blues," 221
"Gulf Coast Blues," 285

Hadlock, Richard, 144
Hagedorn, Jessica, xiv
Hall, Stuart, xix–xx
Hammond, John, 14, 15, 143–44
Handman, L., 317–18
Handy, W. C., 60, 136, 269, 341, 354
"Hard Driving Papa," 30, 285–86
"Hard Times Blues," 286
Harlem, 88, 139, 141, 162, 190
Harlem Renaissance, 133, 153, 189
    Baker on, 148–49
    blues and intellectuals of, xiii, 123,
        144–52
    goals of, 144, 159
    Hurston and, 155, 160
    literature vs. music as basis of, 149
Harris, Luke, xix
Harris, Sid, 235–36
Harrison, Daphne Duval, xvii–xviii, 13,
    37–38, 54
"Hateful Blues," 17, 36, 286–87
"Haunted House Blues," 287
Hawkins, Coleman, 88

Hayes-Rutherford Compromise (1877), 103
"Hear Me Talkin' to You," 221–22
Hegamin, Lucille, xii
"Hellhound on My Trail," 19
Henderson, Fletcher, 88, 282–83
Henderson, Lillian Hardaway, 57, 251–52
Henderson, Rosa, xii
Henry, J., 357–58
Herbert, E., xv, 237–38, 323
Herrera-Sobek, María, xviii
Herzog, Arthur, 186
"He's Gone Blues," 288
"He's Got Me Goin'," 49, 288–89
"high" culture, 120–21
High John the Conqueror, 156–57
"High Water Everywhere," 111
Hill, A., 334
Hill, Anita, xix
hip-hop culture, 122
Holiday, Billie, xviii, xx, 30, 57, 72, 161–97
    "aesthetic dimension" of, 164–65
    autobiography of, see *Lady Sings the Blues*
    biographies of, xiv, 186
    in blues tradition, 161, 168, 170–71
    critical opinion on, 172, 183
    father's death and, 187, 194
    favorite songs of, 172–74
    film biography of, 184, 193
    first recording session of, 168
    masochism ascribed to, 177–79
    mass audience sought by, 181–82
    racism experienced by, 192–93
    selection of songs recorded by, 168–69
    sexuality in songs of, 162, 165, 171, 172–73, 175–80, 195
    Smith's influence on, 144, 166, 197
    social awareness of, 162–63, 192

    social implications of love songs of, 161–80
    "Strange Fruit" and, see "Strange Fruit"
    stylistic abilities and importance of, xvii, 89, 161–62, 165, 168, 169–80, 183–84, 194, 196–97
Holiday, Clarence, 187, 194
"Homeless Blues," 111, 289
homosexuality, 3, 39–41, 45, 131, 133, 171
"Honey, Where You Been So Long?," 23, 222
"Honey Man Blues," 290
hoodoo (voodoo), 154–55, 156–59
Hoover, Herbert, 110, 191
Horsley, G., 303–4
"Hot Springs Blues," 290
"House Rent Blues," 105–6, 143, 291
"house rent shakes," 59
Huggins, Nathan, 149–50
Hughes, Langston, xiii, 123, 144–45, 149–50, 151–52
hunger marches, 190
Hunter, Alberta, xii, 21, 61, 137, 165, 171, 273–74
Hurston, Zora Neale, 6, 68
    blues and folk culture and, 123, 155, 156–60
"Hustlin' Blues," 222–23
"Hustlin' Dan," 291–92
hypersexualization, racial, 44, 108

"I Ain't Goin' to Play No Second Fiddle," 292
"I Ain't Got Nobody," 293
"I'd Rather Be Dead and Buried in My Grave," 158, 293
"If You Don't, I Know Who Will," 294
"I'm Down in the Dumps," 106, 295

"I'm Going Back to My Used to Be," 295–96

"I'm Wild About That Thing," 296–97

Incidents in the Life of a Slave Girl (Jacobs), 165

integration:
jazz audiences and, 190
jazz musicians and, 15

"In the House Blues," 297

irony, 12, 18, 25–28, 100, 143

"It Makes My Love Come Down," 297–98

"It Won't Be You," 30, 298–99

"I Used to Be Your Sweet Mama," 3, 63–65, 299–300

"I've Been Mistreated and I Don't Like It," 300

"I've Got What It Takes," 300–301

"I Want Every Bit of It," 301–2

Jackson, Lil' Son, 114

Jackson, Papa Charlie, xii, 104–5

Jackson, William, 241–42, 276

Jacobs, Harriet Brent, 67–68, 165

"Jail House Blues," 102, 113, 135, 143, 302

James, Burnett, 169, 170–71

jazz, 15, 151, 167, 190

"Jazzbo Brown From Memphis Town," 302–3

"J. C. Holmes Blues," 303

"Jealous Hearted Blues," 223

jealousy, as blues subject, 49–53

"Jealousy Blues," 50, 224

Jefferson, Blind Lemon, 78, 110

"Jelly Bean Blues," 62, 224

Jenkins, H., 300–301

"Jim Crow Blues," 84

Jim Crow segregation, 83–84, 86, 138, 141, 192–93

Johns, Irving, 326–27, 331, 338–39

Johnson, Bobby, 15

Johnson, E., 280–81, 286–87

Johnson, F., 336–37

Johnson, J., 306–7, 342, 355–56

Johnson, James Weldon, 150, 152

Johnson, J. C., 276–78, 287

Johnson, Robert, xiii, 19, 123

Jones, Gayl, xiii

jook joints, 133

Jordan, June, 166

Josephson, Barney, 184, 185–86, 190

jukeboxes, 168

"Keep It to Yourself," 53–54, 304

"Keeps on a-Rainin' (Papa He Can't Make No Time)," 304–5

Kelley, Robin D. G., 191

Kern, Jerome, 168, 173

"Kitchen Man," 305

Korall, Burt, 194

Kortlander, M., 304–5

Ku Klux Klan, 37

"Lady Luck Blues," 158–59, 306

Lady Sings the Blues (film), 184, 193

Lady Sings the Blues (Holiday), 161, 179, 182, 184, 186, 187

landlords, 105–6

"L. & N. Blues," 86

Laney, S., 269–70

Langston Hughes and the Blues (Tracy), 144

"Last Minute Blues," 136–37, 224–25

"Lawd, Send Me a Man Blues," 24, 225

Layton, T., 258, 351–52

Leadbelly, 79

Leader, D. K., 314

"Leaving This Morning," 73, 226

Legba, 6, 123

Lesbian Concentrate, 40

lesbianism, 13, 39, 45, 171

"Levee Camp Moan," 226–27
Levine, Lawrence, 5, 8–9, 55, 68, 119
Levy, John, 179
Lewis, David Levering, 154
Lieb, Sandra, 20, 31, 40, 75–76, 79,
    103, 116, 118, 138
"Lifting as We Climb" motto, 43
Lincoln, Abbey, 196
Lincoln, C. Eric, 8
Lincoln Theater, 88, 139
"Little Low Mama Blues," 227
"Lock and Key," 306–7
Locke, Alain, 150–51
"Log Camp Blues," 227–28
"Lonesome Desert Blues," 307
"Long Old Road," 308
Longshaw, Fred, 260–61, 270–71,
    299–300, 310, 318–19, 330
"Lookin' for My Man Blues," 53, 75,
    308
Lord, Audre, 172
"Lost Wandering Blues," 77–78, 79,
    228
"Lost Your Head Blues," 309
"Louisiana Hoodoo Blues," 229
"Louisiana Low Down Blues," 85, 86,
    309
love, romantic, 9–10, 11, 23
Lovell, John, Jr., 70
"Love Me Daddy Blues," 30, 310
"Lover, Come Back to Me," 175–76
"low" culture, blues viewed as, xiii,
    120–21, 123, 126–27
"Lucky Rock Blues," 229
lynchings, 34, 44, 84
    descriptions of, 188–89
    legislation against, 191–92
    "Strange Fruit" and, 95, 183–84,
        187–88, 193–94

"Ma and Pa Poorhouse Blues," 104–5,
    230–31

McCabe, Jewel Jackson, xix
McCallister, L., 241
McCleary, Tex, 173, 174
McKay, Louis, 179
Macomber, K., 323–24
McOwens, Billie, 217
McRae, Carmen, 174–75
"Mama's Got the Blues," 75, 158, 310
"Ma Rainey" (Brown), 139–41, 148–49
"Ma Rainey's Black Bottom," 231–32
"Ma Rainey's Mystery Record," 232
Marcuse, Herbert, 163–64, 165, 183
Marinoff, Fania, 147
marriage, 11–19
    in advice songs, 13–14, 16–17
    cultural perceptions of, 12
    extramarital relationships and, 3,
        15–16, 17
    language and, 12–13
    scarcity of blues women's references
        to, 11, 12–13, 18–19
Martin, Sara, 94, 310
Marx, Karl, 7
masochism, 25, 28, 30–31, 177–79
"Matchbox Blues," 78–79
matriarchy, black, 122
medicine shows, 72
"Memphis Bound Blues," 135–36, 233
Memphis Minnie, 94
"Me and My Gin," 310–11
"Mean Old Bedbug Blues," 311
men, black:
    as archetypal blues singers, 11
    black church dominated by, 9, 125,
        133, 137
    feminism and, xix
    popularity of blues recordings of,
        xii–xiii
    sexual stereotypes of, 34, 44
    travel and, 8, 19–20, 68, 69–70, 71–72
Metz, T., 346–47
Mexican folk ballads, xviii

middle class, black, 43–44, 45, 65, 122, 154, 171–72
middle class, white, 11
Middle Passage, 81
"Midnight Blues," 311–12
Miller, L., 298, 299–300
Million Man March, xix
"Misery Blues," 16–17, 233–34
Mississippi floods, 87–88, 108–10, 143
"Mississippi Heavy Water Blues," 110
"Mistreatin' Daddy," 22–23, 312–13
"Moan, You Mourners," 130, 313
Moll, B., 261–62
"Money Blues," 17, 314
Monroe, Jimmy, 179
"Moonshine Blues," 63, 83, 234, 314–15
Moore, Carman, 95
Mordecai, Jimmy, 60
"Morning Hour Blues," 235
Morrison, Toni, xiv
motherhood, 12–13, 72
Mother of the Blues (Lieb), 20, 31, 40, 75–76, 79, 103, 116, 118, 138
"Mountain Jack Blues," 235–36
"Mountain Top Blues," 315–16
movie industry, xiii, 61
Moynihan, Daniel Patrick, 122
"Muddy Water," 87–89, 316
Murphy, Dudley, 60
"My Man," 177–79
"My Man Blues," 51–53, 316–17
"My Sweetie Went Away," 317–18

Nail, John, 152
Naison, Mark, 162
naming process (nommo), 33, 128–29
"Nashville Woman's Blues," 134, 318–19
National Association for the Advancement of Colored People (NAACP), 113, 189, 191
National Association of Colored Women (NACW), 43, 191

National Council of Negro Women, 43
National Unemployed Councils, 190
Neal, Claude, 188–89
"Need a Little Sugar in My Bowl," 15, 319–20
"Negro Artist and the Racial Mountain, The" (Hughes), 151
Negro Family, The (Moynihan), 122
"Negro Spirituals, The" (Locke), 151
New Deal, 191
"New Gulf Coast Blues," 320
New Negro, The, 151
"New Negro, The" (Locke), 150–51
"New Orleans Hop Scop Blues," 320–21
Newton, Frankie, 15
Nicholson, Stuart, 186
"Night Time Blues," 236
Nix, Malissa, 222–23
"Nobody in Town Can Bake a Sweet Jelly Roll Like Mine," 321
"Nobody Knows You When You're Down and Out," 322
"Nobody's Blues But Mine," 322–23
nommo, 33, 128–29
North, 137
    black migration to, 44, 80, 171
    blues' function in, 155
    "house rent shakes" in, 59
    Smith as emblematic of, 83, 92
    travel songs and, 83–86, 89–90
Not Without Laughter (Hughes), xiii

Oakley, Giles, 11
"Oh Daddy Blues," xv–xvi, 323
"Oh My Babe Blues," 236–37
"Oh Papa Blues," xv, 237–38
Okeh Records, xii, 152
Oliver, Paul, 89, 93–95, 101, 118
"One and Two Blues," 324–25
"On Revival Day," 130, 323–24
oral tradition, xix, 25
"Outside of That," 27–28, 325–26

Pace, Harry, 152
Paramount Records, xii
Parham, H. Strathedene, 209–10
Parker, Charles J., 210–11
"Packing Trunk Blues," 79
Patton, Charley, 111
Pavageau, Annie, 125–26
Percy, Will, 110
"personal is political," 25, 42, 101
Pickens, William, 103
"Pickpocket Blues," 326
"Pinchback Blues," 13–14, 59–60, 61,
    326–27
"Please Help Me Get Him off My
    Mind," 30, 327
Poetry of the Blues, The (Charters), 92
poorhouses, 104–5
"Poor Man's Blues," 13, 95–98, 100,
    101, 102, 327–28
popular musical culture:
    patriarchy supported by, 10
    sexuality as treated in, 3, 23
pornography, 14–15
preachers, as professional caste, 9
"Preachin' the Blues," 129–30, 131,
    133, 328–29
Pridgett, Thomas, Jr., 125
prison, social protest and, 102–4, 143
prostitution, 91, 107–8
Proust, Marcel, 174
"Prove It on Me Blues," 39–40, 45, 238
"Put It Right Here (Or Keep It Out
    There)," 328–29

Rabbit Foot Minstrels, 72
race, 96, 97
    feminism and, xix, 42, 55
    hypersexualization and, 44, 108
"race records," xii, 15, 95, 141
racism, 120
    flood relief and, 108–10
    Holiday's experiences with, 192–93

"Strange Fruit" and, 181, 182–83,
    194–95
as subject of social protest in blues,
    108–10, 112–13, 117–19
in white response to blues, 92–95,
    141–42, 147–48
Radical Reconstruction, 103, 189
Rainey, Gertrude "Ma":
    advice songs by, 16–17, 45, 53, 57–58
    biography of, see *Mother of the Blues*
    birth of, 138
    black women addressed as
        community by, 62–63, 65, 92
    blues' emotional power expressed by,
        134–35
    blues' "lowness" celebrated by,
        126–27
    blues personified in songs of, 113–16
    Brown's poem about, 139–41, 148–49
    contemporary celebration of, 125
    description of, 121–22
    domestic violence in songs of, 29,
        31–33
    early career of, 72
    favorite song of, 73
    female rivalry and jealousy in songs
        of, 47–48, 50
    first recording made by, xii
    as lyricist, 63, 76, 77–78, 107–8, 128,
        200, 201–2, 203, 205, 208–9, 210,
        211–12, 213–14, 215, 216–17, 218,
        220, 221–22, 225, 226, 227–28,
        229, 230–32, 233–34, 235, 236–37,
        238, 239, 240–41, 241–42, 244–45,
        246, 247–49, 250–51, 253–54, 255,
        267, 314–15
    lyrics to songs recorded by, xvi–xvii,
        199–255
    marriage in songs of, 15–17
    as "Mother of the Blues," 15
    number of songs recorded by, 20, 138
    religion and, 125

as role model, 41, 138
sexuality of, 22, 39–40
in "Shadow of the Blues," 145–46
slavery in songs of, 114–15
social protest in songs of, 93–94,
  102–5, 107–8, 111–19
touring by, 139
travel in songs of, 66–67, 73–83
women's independence in songs of,
  20–21, 22, 24
"Rainy Weather Blues," 329–30
Randall, J. Sammy, 240, 244, 247–48,
  250–51
rape, 25, 33–34
Razaf, Andy, 323–24
"Reckless Blues," 330
Reconstruction, 103, 189
recording industry:
  black ownership in, *see* Black Swan
    Records
  blues material controlled by, 94–95
  exploitation of performers by, xiii
  marketing strategies of, xii–xiii, 141–42
  1929 stock market crash and, 14
  sales figures for blues in, xii, 4, 141,
    152
  see also "race records"
Red, S., 337
Redman, Don, 187
"Red Mountain Blues," 156, 330–31
religions, 120–37
  African, 6, 33, 123, 158
  blues as counterpart to, 129–30,
    133–34, 137
  "Devil's music" and, 6–7, 8, 123–24
  male domination in, 9, 133, 137
  Marx on, 7
  naming process and, 33, 128–29
  Rainey and, 125
  Smith's songs and, 129–31
religious music, *see* gospel music;
  spirituals

Richman, H., 316
Ricketts, B., 312–13
"Riffing the Scotch," 168
"Rising High Water Blues," 110
Rising Tide (Barry), 110
Roach, Max, 196
Robbins, E., 342–43
Robinson, J. R., 258–59, 264, 333,
  341–42
"Rocking Chair Blues," 331
Roosevelt, Franklin D., 189, 191, 192
Ross, Diana, 184
"Rough and Tumble Blues," 35, 47, 239
"Runaway Blues," 73, 74, 239
Rushing, Jimmy, 132, 161–62
Russell, W., xv, 237–38, 323

"Safety Mama," 18, 58, 331–32
St. Louis Blues (film), 60–61
"St. Louis Blues," 60–61, 341
"St. Louis Gal," 341–42
"Salt Water Blues," 332–33
"Sam Jones Blues," 11–12, 24, 333
Schiffman, Frank, 195
Schiffman, Jack, 195
Scottsboro Nine, 189
"Screech Owl Blues," 240
"secular spirituals," 8
"See If I'll Care," 334
"Seeking Blues," 241
"See See Rider Blues," 35, 240–41
segregation, 83–84, 86, 138, 141, 192–93
"Send Me to the 'Lectric Chair," 35–36,
  102, 335
sexuality, xiii, xv–xvi, xvii, 3–41, 42–65,
  70, 91, 118, 120
  blues women's realistic treatment of,
    23–24
  boasting and, 75
  class attitudes toward, 42–44, 65
  emancipation and, 4, 8, 9, 10, 45, 67,
    131

sexuality (*cont.*):
  female rivalry and, 45, 47–53
  gender role reversal and, 58
  in Holiday's songs, 162, 165, 171,
    172–73, 175–80, 195
  images and stereotypes of, 34, 44
  in men's vs. women's blues, 11
  in popular musical culture, 3, 23
  pornography and, 14–15
  of Rainey, 22, 39–40
  women's autonomy and, 131–32
"Shadow of the Blues" (Hughes),
    145–46
Shakur, Tupac, 48
"Shave 'Em Dry," 15–16, 241–42
Shaw, Artie, 192
"Shipwreck Blues," 335
Shufflin' Sam from Alabam', 72
Sidran, Ben, 69
Simone, Nina, 196
"Sinful Blues," 35, 336
"Sing Sing Prison Blues," 35–36, 102,
    336–37
"Sissy Blues," 40–41, 242–43
Skidmore, W. E., 345–46
slavery, 47, 102, 112, 120, 141
  abolition of, 4, 7–10, 19, 22, 45, 67,
    68, 131
  families and, 10, 81
  gender equality under, 121
  music in, *see* spirituals; work songs
  in Rainey's songs, 114–15
slaves:
  narratives by, 165
  runaway, 67–68
"Slave to the Blues," 114, 243
"Sleep Talking Blues," 35, 50, 244
"Slow and Easy Man," 30, 337
"Slow Driving Moan," 76, 244–45
Small, D., 319–20
Smalls, Biggie, 48

Smith, Bessie:
  advice songs by, 13–14, 49, 53–54,
    58–62
  alcohol and, 22, 83, 146
  Black Swan's rejection of, 123,
    152–54
  black women addressed as
    community by, 62, 63–65
  blues musicians celebrated by, 127
  blues titles of, 4, 141
  costumes of, 137
  decline in career of, xiii
  domestic violence in songs of, 26–28,
    30–31, 33
  earnings of, 141
  female rivalry and jealousy in songs
    of, 48, 49, 51–53
  film appearance of, 60–61
  final recording session of, 14
  first record made by, xii, 21, 141
  gospel-related songs recorded by, 130
  Hammond on, 143–44
  Holiday influenced by, 144, 166, 197
  hoodoo in songs of, 154–55, 156–59
  irony used by, 12, 18, 26–28, 100, 143
  Klan incident and, 37
  as lyricist, 17, 18, 51–53, 96, 129–30,
    133, 214, 235, 245, 253–54, 261,
    263–64, 266, 271, 272–73, 276,
    280, 283, 286, 288, 290, 297–99,
    302, 307, 308, 309, 316–17,
    326–28, 331–32, 335, 338–39, 340,
    347, 349–50, 356–57
  lyrics to songs recorded by, xvi–xvii,
    257–358
  marriage in songs of, 11–12, 13–14,
    17–18
  new consciousness of black identity
    and, 89–90
  North and, 80, 83, 84–85, 89–90,
    91–92

number of songs recorded by, 21, 95, 141
personality of, 37, 95
popular crossover hopes of, 14, 15, 61
popularity of, 141
record sales of, 4, 141
as role model, 41
social protest in songs of, 91–92, 94–102, 105–6, 108–10, 119
stylistic importance of, 143–44, 153
travel in songs of, 19–20, 80, 87–88
Van Vechten and, 142, 146–48
women's emotional stances in songs of, 21, 22–23, 24
Smith, Chris, 268–69
Smith, Clara, xii, 51–52, 84, 86, 145, 295, 316–17
Smith, Joe, 88
Smith, Lillian, 189–90
Smith, Mamie, xii, 9, 145, 152
Smith, Maud, 108
Smith, S., 294
Smith, Trixie, xii
"Sobbin' Hearted Blues," 80, 337–38
social protest, 91–119
in "Backwater Blues," 108–10
in "Blame It on the Blues," 111–12
blues' interpretive audience and, 92–93
blues viewed as lacking in, 92–95, 99–101, 113, 118
in "House Rent Blues," 105–6
in "Hustlin' Blues," 107–8
in "Ma and Pa Poorhouse Blues," 104–5
in "Poor Man's Blues," 95–98, 100, 101, 102
prison and, 102–4
in "Strange Fruit," 95
in "Washwoman's Blues," 98–102
"Soft Pedal Blues," 133, 338

"Some Other Spring," 172–73
"Sometimes You Look Like Lady Day" (Hagedorn), xiv
"Songs Called the Blues" (Hughes), 145
"Soon This Morning," 245
"Sorrowful Blues," 338–39
South, 137
convict lease system in, 103–4
folk roots in culture of, 155
post-World War I black migration and, 44
Radical Reconstruction era in, 103, 189
segregation in, 83–84, 86, 138, 141, 192–93
symbolic geography of, 83–84
travel songs and, 80–83, 87–88
"South Bound Blues," 80–81, 245–46
"Southern Blues," 246
Southern Negro Youth Congress, 191
"speak bitterness," 29
"Spider Man Blues," 339
Spielberg, Steven, 124
spirituals, xiii, 4–7, 85, 122, 145
collective nature of, 4, 7
freedom and, 5, 7, 70–71, 86
Locke on, 150–51
subversive potential of, 167–68
Spivey, Victoria, xii, 94
"Squeeze Me," 339–40
Stackhouse, Houston, 114
"Stack O'Lee Blues," 246–47
"Standin' in the Rain Blues," 340
Still, William Grant, 152–53
stock market crash (1929), xiii, 14, 96, 188
"Stormy Sea Blues," 247
"Strange Fruit," 181–97
Commodore and Columbia labels and, 95, 195
critics on, 162

"Strange Fruit" (*cont.*):
  genesis of, 189
  Holiday's introduction to, 184–87
  Holiday's premiere of, 182–83, 187
  listeners' responses to, 195–96
  lynchings and, 95, 183–84, 187–88,
    193–94
  as racial protest, 181, 182–83, 194–95
  social importance of, 196–97
Strange Fruit (Smith), 190
Suddoth, J. Guy, 208, 248, 250
"Sweet Mistreater," 342
"Sweet Rough Man," 31–33, 247–48

" 'Tain't Nobody's Bizness If I Do,"
    30–31, 342–43
"Take It Right Back ('Cause I Don't
    Want It Here)," 343–44
"Take Me for a Buggy Ride," 14, 15,
    344–45
Tan, 162–63
Taylor, Billy, 15
Taylor, Jasper, 246–47
Taylor, Koko, 56, 138
Teagarden, Jack, 15, 168
tent shows, 37, 137, 138
Terrell, Mary Church, xiv, 34, 43, 44,
    46
theater, xiii, 61, 88
Their Eyes Were Watching God
    (Hurston), 68–69
"Them 'Has Been' Blues," 345–46
"Them's Graveyard Words," 35, 346
"There Is No Greater Love," 176–77
"There'll Be a Hot Time in the Old
    Town Tonight" (Metz), 346–47
"Thinking Blues," 347
Thomas, George W., 213, 320–21
Thompson, B., 311–12
"Those All Night Long Blues," 248
"Those Dogs of Mine," 248–49

"Ticket Agent, Ease Your Window
    Down," 348
Tilford, Hooks, 200
Tin Pan Alley, 61, 88, 89, 165, 166, 168,
    181
"Titanic Man Blues," 63, 249
"Toad Frog Blues," 82, 250
Tolliver's Circus and Musical
    Extravaganza, 72
"Tough Luck Blues," 116–19, 250–51
"Toward a Critique of Negro Music"
    (Locke), 150
Tracy, Steven, 144
Trade Union Unity League, 190
trains, 70, 82, 86
travel, 19–20, 66–90, 120
  after emancipation, 8, 19, 67–68
  for men vs. women, 8, 19–20, 68–69,
    71
  North and, 44, 80, 83–86, 89–90, 171
  psychological meaning of, 69–70
  South and, 80–83, 87–88
  in spirituals, 5, 7, 70–71, 86
  urban migration, 44, 80
  vicarious enjoyment of, 66–67
"Traveling Blues," 66, 73, 74, 251
Trent, J., 316, 325–26
tricksters, 6, 156
"Trombone Cholly," 127, 348–49
Troy, H., 268–69, 282–83, 330–31
Trull, Teresa, 40
"Trust No Man," 42, 53, 57–58, 65,
    251–52
Truth, Sojourner, 7
Tubman, Harriet, 7, 37, 68
Turk, R., 258–59, 264, 317–18, 333
Turner, Nat, 7
twelve-bar blues form, 17

Underground Railroad, 7, 37, 68
unemployment, 190

Unger, S., 273
urban migration, 44, 80, 171

Vanity Fair, 146, 147
Van Vechten, Carl, 142, 146–48, 153
Vesey, Denmark, 7
"Victim to the Blues," 252
violence, image vs. reality of, 48
voodoo (hoodoo), 154–55, 156–59

"Wade in the Water," 70–71
Walker, Alice, xiii, 124
Walker, Frank, 95
Walker, M., 345–46
"Walking Blues," 73, 75–76, 253
Wall, Cheryl, xiii
Wallace, Michele, 178, 179
Wallace, Sippie, xii, 110–11
Wallace, T., 291, 352–53
Waller, Thomas "Fats," 339–40
Washington, Booker T., 148
Washington, Buck, 15
Washington, Isabel, 60
Washington, Mary Helen, xiii–xiv
"Washwoman's Blues," 98–102, 143, 349
"Wasted Life Blues," 349–50
Waters, Ethel, xii, 61, 146
   Black Swan's choosing of, 153
   religion and, 125
   style of, 148, 153
Weary Blues, The (Hughes), 144
Weber, W., 306
"Weeping Willow Blues," 17–18, 350–51
"Weeping Woman Blues," 74–75, 253–54
Wells, Ida B., xiv, 34, 44, 189
"What a Little Moonlight Can Do," 170
"What's the Matter Now?", 350
Wheatstraw, Peetie, 19

"When a Woman Loves a Man," 161, 179–80
White, Josh, 193
whites:
   blues and, 141–42, 146–48, 153
   lynchings protested by, 189–90, 194
"Whoa, Tillie, Take Your Time," 351–52
"wild woman," 38–39
"Wild Women Don't Have the Blues," 38
Williams, Clarence, 261–63, 268–69, 278–79, 285, 294, 300–302, 304, 305, 306, 310, 319–20, 320, 321, 322–23, 325–26, 334, 339–40, 350, 355–56
Williams, Fannie Barrier, 44
Williams, J. Mayo, 249
Williams, Sherley Anne, xiii
Williams, Spencer, 99, 266–67, 269–70, 293, 296–97, 301–2, 304–5, 309, 311–12, 313, 315–16, 321, 348, 349, 350, 353, 355–56, 358
Wilson, Edith, xii
Wilson, Leola B., 14, 295
Wilson, Wesley "Socks," 14, 274–75, 281–82, 295, 344–45
Wilson, Teddy, 168
Winters, Katie, 229
"Woman's Trouble Blues," 352
women, black:
   advice songs and, 13–14, 16–17, 45, 53–54, 57–62
   blues as evoking community of, 59, 62–65, 92
   and blues models of womanhood, 45–46
   club movement of, 43–44, 65
   domestic service and, 72, 98–102, 143
   domestic violence and, 25

women, black (*cont.*):
  economic independence and, 11–12,
    58–59
  as first blues recording artists, xii–xiii,
    5, 9
  in hip-hop culture, 122
  hypersexualization and, 108
  independent stance of, 20–22, 34–37
  light-skinned, 88
  in literature, xiii–xiv
  marginalization of contributions to
    blues, xiv, 9, 44–45, 94, 124–25
  matriarchy and, 122
  self-understanding of, 37–38, 41, 142
  sexual autonomy of, 131–32
  as writers, xiii–xiv
Women, Race, and Class (Davis), 121
women, white:
  in anti-lynching movement, 189–90
  rape and, 33–34
  travel and, 8, 19–20, 66–90
"Work House Blues," 102, 147, 352–53
working class, black, 42, 44, 45, 65,
    98–102, 112, 120–21, 122, 137,
    142, 143, 162–63
work songs, 4, 122, 167
Works Progress Administration (WPA),
    192

World War I, 97, 187
World War II, 191
"Worn Out Papa," 353
"Wringing and Twisting Blues," 47–48,
    254

"Ya Da Do," 134–35, 254–55
"Yankee Doodle Never Went to Town,"
    169
"Yellow Dog Blues," 354
"Yes, Indeed He Do," 18, 26–27, 28,
    354
"Yesterdays," 173–74
"Yodeling Blues," 135, 158, 355
"Yonder Come the Blues," 115–16,
    255
Yoruba religion, 6, 33, 123, 159
"You Don't Understand," 63, 355–56
"You Let Me Down," 169–70
Young, Lester, 165
Young Communist League, 190
"Young Woman's Blues," 17, 356–57
"You Ought to Be Ashamed," 357
"You're My Thrill," 174–75
"Your Mother's Son-in-Law," 168
"You've Been a Good Ole Wagon,"
    357–58
"You've Got to Give Me Some," 358

PERMISSIONS ACKNOWLEDGMENTS

Grateful acknowledgment is made to the following for permission to reprint previously published material:

Bambalina Music Publishing: "Lover, Come Back to Me" by Oscar Hammerstein II and Sigmund Romberg. Copyright 1928 (Renewed) by Warner Bros. Inc. Reprinted by permission of Bambalina Music Publishing.

Irving Berlin Music Company: "Alexander's Ragtime Band" by Irving Berlin. Copyright 1911 by Irving Berlin. Copyright renewed. International copyright secured. All rights reserved. Reprinted by permission of Irving Berlin Music Company, administered by Williamson Music Company, a division of The Rodgers and Hammerstein Organization.

Black Classic Press: Excerpt from *100 Years of Lynching* by Ralph Ginzburg (Baltimore: Black Classic Press, 1997). Reprinted by permission of Black Classic Press.

CR Publishing House: "Cold in Hand Blues" by Jack Gee. "House Rent Blues" by T. Wallace. "Reckless Blues" by F. Longshaw. "Weeping Willow Blues" by P. Carter. Reprinted by permission of CR Publishing House.

Christine Dall: Excerpts from *Wild Women Don't Have the Blues*, directed by Christine Dall (Calliope Film Resources, Inc., 1989). Reprinted by permission of Christine Dall.

Joe Davis Music: "He's Got Me Goin' " by Joe Davis. Reprinted by permission of Lucille Davis Bell, Joe Davis Music.

Doubleday: Excerpts from *Lady Sings the Blues* by Billie Holiday and William F. Dufty. Copyright © 1956 by Eleanora Fagan and William F. Dufty. Reprinted by permission of Doubleday, a division of Bantam Doubleday Dell Publishing Group, Inc.

Down Beat Magazine: Excerpt from "Hall of Fame Winner Bessie Smith: Empress of the Blues" by Dan Morgenstern (*Down Beat*, August 24, 1967). Reprinted by permission of *Down Beat Magazine*.

Garland Publications: Excerpt from *The Critical Temper of Alain Locke* by Alain Locke. Reprinted by permission of Garland Publications.

Greenwood Press: Excerpts from *Keep A-Inchin' Along: Selected Writings of Carl Van Vechten About Black Art and Letters*, edited by Bruce Kellner (Contributions in Afro-American and African Studies, no. 45, Greenwood Press, Westport, CT, 1979). Copyright © 1979 by Bruce Kellner and the Estate of Carl Van Vechten. All rights reserved. Reprinted by permission of Greenwood Press, a division of Greenwood Publishing Group, Inc.

Grove/Atlantic, Inc., and Faber and Faber Ltd.: Excerpts from *Muntu: The New African Culture* by Janheinz Jahn. Copyright © 1961 by Faber and Faber. Reprinted by permission of Grove/Atlantic, Inc., and Faber and Faber Ltd., London.

Handy Brothers Music Co., Inc.: "Careless Love" by W. C. Handy, Spencer Williams, and Martha E. Koenig. Copyright renewed. "I'm Goin Back to My Used to Be" by Jimmy Cox. Copyright renewed. "St. Louis Blues" and "The Yellow Dog Blues" by W. C. Handy. Published by Handy Brothers Music Co., Inc. International copyright secured. Reprinted by permission of Handy Brothers Music Co., Inc.

HarperCollins Publishers, Inc.: "Ma Rainey" from *The Collected Poems of Sterling A. Brown* edited by Michael S. Harper. Copyright 1932 by Harcourt Brace & Co. Copyright renewed 1960 by Sterling A. Brown. Excerpts from *Mules and Men* by Zora Neale Hurston (New York: HarperCollins, 1990). Reprinted by permission of HarperCollins Publishers, Inc.

Hill and Wang: Excerpt from "Poetry is Practical" from *The Big Sea* by Langston Hughes. Copyright 1940 by Langston Hughes. Copyright renewed 1968 by Arna Bontemps and George Houston Bass. Reprinted by permission of Hill and Wang, a division of Farrar, Straus & Giroux, Inc.

Hill and Wang and Harold Ober Associates: Excerpts from "Shadow of the Blues" from *The Best of Simple* by Langston Hughes. Copyright © 1961 by Langston Hughes. Copyright renewed 1989 by George Houston Bass. Reprinted by permission of Hill and Wang, a division of Farrar, Straus & Giroux, Inc., and Harold Ober Associates.

Henry Holt and Company, Inc.: Excerpt from *The Jazz Makers* by Nat Shapiro and Nat Hentoff. Copyright © 1957 by Nat Shapiro and Nat Hentoff. Reprinted by permission of Henry Holt and Company, Inc.

MCA Music Publishing: "Need a Little Sugar in My Bowl" by Clarence Williams, Tim Brymn, Dally Small. Copyright 1932 by MCA Music Publishing, a division of Universal Studios, Inc. "I Want Every Bit of It" by Clarence Williams and Spencer Williams. Copyright 1926 by MCA Music Publishing, a division of Universal Studios, Inc. " 'Tain't Nobody's Business (If I Do)" by Porter Grainger and Everett Robbins. Copyright 1922 by MCA Music Publishing, a division of Universal Studios, Inc. "I've Got What It Takes, But It Breaks My Heart to Give It Away" by Clarence Williams and Hezekiah Jenkins. Copyright 1929 by MCA Music Publishing, a division of Universal Studios, Inc. "Keeps on a-Rainin' " by Spencer Williams and Max Kortlander. Copyright 1923 by MCA Music Publishing, a division of Universal Studios, Inc. "Ma Rainey's Black Bottom" by Gertrude "Ma" Rainey. Copyright 1928 by MCA Music Publishing, a division of Universal Studios, Inc. "Mama's Got the Blues" by Sarah Martin and Clarence Williams. Copyright 1923 by MCA Music Publishing, a division of Universal Studios, Inc. "Money Blues" by Dave K. Leader and Harry Eller. Copyright © 1961 by MCA Music Publishing, a division of Universal Studios, Inc. "New Gulf Coast Blues" by Clarence Williams. Copyright 1923 by MCA Music Publishing, a division of Universal Studios, Inc. "Nobody in Town Can Bake a Jelly Roll Like Mine" by Clarence Williams and Spencer Williams. Copyright 1924 by MCA Music Publishing, a division of Universal Studios, Inc. "See If I'll Care" by Clarence Williams and Alex Hill. Copyright 1930 by MCA Music Publishing, a division of Universal Studios, Inc. "See See Rider" by Gertrude "Ma" Rainey. Copyright 1943, 1944 by MCA Music Publishing, a division of Universal Studios, Inc. "Squeeze Me" by

DeRose Music. "Strange Fruit" by Lewis Allen. Copyright 1939 (Renewed) by Music Sales Corporation (ASCAP). "(There Is) No Greater Love" by Marty Symes and Isham Jones. Copyright 1936 (Renewed) by Music Sales Corporation (ASCAP) and Isham Jones Music. International copyright secured. All rights reserved. Reprinted by permission of Music Sales Corporation.

Gloria Parker Music Company: "Soft Pedal Blues" by Bessie Smith. Reprinted by permission of Gloria Parker Music Company.

Political Affairs: Excerpt from "The 'Thirties' in American Culture" by Phillip Bonosky (*Political Affairs,* May 1959). Reprinted by permission of *Political Affairs.*

Polygram International Publishing, Inc.: "Yesterdays" by Jerome Kern and Otto Harbach. Copyright 1933 by Polygram International Publishing, Inc. All rights reserved. Reprinted by permission of Polygram International Publishing, Inc.

Radical America: Excerpt from "It Just Be's Dat Way Sometime" by Hazel Carby (*Radical America,* vol. 20, no. 4, June–July, 1986). Reprinted by permission of *Radical America.*

Random House, Inc.: Excerpts from "Remembering Jimmy" from *Shadow and Act* by Ralph Ellison. Copyright 1953, © 1964, renewed 1981, 1992 by Ralph Ellison. Reprinted by permission of Random House, Inc.

Scarborough House: Excerpts from *Billie's Blues* by John Chilton (New York: Stein and Day, 1975). Reprinted by permission of Scarborough House.

The Songwriters' Guild: "Empty Bed Blues" by J. C. Johnson (Record Music). "Muddy Water" by P. DeRose, H. Tischman, and J. Trent (DeRose Music). "On Revival Day" by Andy Razaf and K. Macomber (Razaf Music). "Mama's Got the Blues" by C. Williams and S. Martin. "Florida Bound Blues" by C. Williams. "New Gulf Coast Blues" by C. Williams. "Squeeze Me" by C. Williams, Fats Waller, B. Smith (Great Standards Music). Reprinted by permission of The Songwriters' Guild.

Sony/ATV Music Publishing: "Aggravatin' Papa" by J. Russel Robinson, Roy Turk, and Addy Britt. Copyright 1922 by Sony/ATV Tunes LLC and EMI Mills Music Inc. (Renewed). "Honey, Where You Been So Long" by Fred Fisher. Copyright 1923 by Sony/ATV Tunes LLC. "Muddy Water" by Harry Richman, Peter DeRose, and Jo Trent. Copyright 1926 by Sony/ATV Tunes LLC/Music Sales Corp./Broadway Music Corp. "Sam Jones Blues" by Roy Turk, J. Robinson, and Al Bernard. Copyright 1923 by Sony/ATV Tunes LLC/EMI Mills Music, Inc. and J. Russel Robinson, Inc. (Renewed). All rights on behalf of Sony/ATV Tunes LLC administered by Sony/ATV Music Publishing, 8 Music Square West, Nashville, TN 37203. All rights reserved. Reprinted by permission of Sony/ATV Music Publishing.

John Steiner: "Black Dust Blues," "Broken Hearted Blues (Broken Soul Blues)," "Daddy Goodbye Blues," "Deep Moaning Blues," " 'Fore Day Honry Scat," "Goodbye Mama Forever Blues," "Hear Me Talkin' to You," "Leavin' This Morning," "Run Away Blues," "Screech Owl Blues," "Sissy Blues," "Sleep Talking Blues," "South Bound Blues," "Sweet Rough Man," "Tough Luck Blues," "Trust No Man," "Weeping Woman Blues," as